MARICOPA'S COMMUNITY COLLEGES:

The TURBULENT EVOLUTION of an EDUCATION GIANT

RICHARD FELNAGLE

ELTON-WOLF PUBLISHING

Seattle • Vancouver • Los Angeles • Milwaukee • Denver • Portland

Library of Congress Catalog Number: 00-100528
ISBN: 1-58619-014-8

10 9 8 7 6 5 4 3 2 1

First Printing: March 2000
Printed in the United States of America

Designed and typeset
by Outline Graphic Design, Inc.

Published by Elton-Wolf Publishing
2505 Second Avenue, Suite 515
Seattle, WA 98121
206-748-0345
E-mail: info@elton-wolf.com
Internet: http://www.elton-wolf.com
Seattle • Vancouver • Los Angeles
Milwaukee • Denver • Portland

This history is dedicated to the faculty, staff, and students of the Maricopa County Community College District (MCCCD). Each person has helped shape this district and lived the history. A special thank you to the community leaders who have supported the evolution of the MCCCD. The publically elected, non-paid Governing Board Members, who exemplify this leadership, have shown the interest, wisdom, dedication and have taken the risks to turn a vision of a community college into a reality.

MARICOPA'S COMMUNITY COLLEGES:

The TURBULENT EVOLUTION of an EDUCATION GIANT

RICHARD FELNAGLE

ELTON-WOLF PUBLISHING

Contents

Contents

The first day I went poking around in the district's archives, I found this picture.

It had been abandoned upside down in a box of miscellany, and the colors were fading. As I wiped the dust off the glass, I recognized the figure standing in the middle as Dr. Paul Elsner, the chancellor of the Maricopa County Community College District for the past twenty-two years, but I hadn't a clue who the other three men were.

I showed the picture to other people in the office. The younger staff members couldn't identify the three mystery men either, but a couple of older staff people finally solved the problem. The seated man is Bob Hannelly, the Maricopa district's first president. The man standing on the left is John Prince, the district's second president, and the man standing on the right is Al Flowers, who was the district's acting president and then, after they changed the name of the job, acting chancellor between Prince and Elsner. Together, these four men ran the Maricopa County Community College District from its birth in December, 1962, through June, 1999.

The Maricopa County Community College District's first four leaders. Photograph taken as a part of Community College Week in Arizona, April, 1984.

And very few people I talked to that day could identify all four. That's when I really began to understand the need for this book . . . .

About four years ago, Paul Elsner became concerned about what he called "the loss of institutional memory." A lot of the district's old-timers had retired or died or drifted away, and no official record of the district's history existed anywhere. To try to arrest further memory loss, Elsner launched the History Project. A steering committee was formed, and they advertised for a faculty member who would like to write the district's official history.

When I saw their notice in my email at Mesa Community College (one of the district's ten affiliated colleges), I responded immediately. Forgive me if I gush, but I have been a Maricopa employee for over ten years, and Maricopa is without a doubt the best place for teaching and learning I have ever seen. (I mean it, too—nobody paid me to write that.) From time to time, some of my more reserved colleagues on the faculty disagree with my feelings about Maricopa, but I figure they are just being fashionably cynical or they have never taught anywhere else. I have, and I know good when I see it. So when the opportunity appeared to tell the Maricopa story, I jumped at the chance.

But after receiving the news that the History Project steering committee had given me the appointment I wanted so badly, I bounced out of my office and excitedly grabbed the first colleague I saw. "Isn't it wonderful?" I exclaimed. "I've just been commissioned to write the official history of the Maricopa County Community College District!" His jaw dropped, and his eyes bulged. "But who will read it?" he replied with the sort of distaste usually reserved for sour milk.

I stood there dripping with the cold water he had just splashed all over me and made a mental note not to mention his name anywhere in the book—so there!—but after I dried off and calmed down, I realized he had actually done me a real favor.

He was right. Institutional histories are not most people's idea of a must-read. Just because I was excited about writing Maricopa's history didn't mean anyone else would be excited about reading it. So, I made some executive decisions, and I need to explain them here. I realized that if the book were to have any hope of finding a readership, it must not look anything like conventional academic history. The book had to be entertaining, and it had to be shockingly honest. As I mentioned, many of my fellow Maricopans are rather cynical because (as I learned) the district has been through some hairy times. My colleagues would never willingly read anything good about the district if I didn't include the bad and the ugly as well.

Fortunately, the district gave me a completely free hand to include the tragedies along with the triumphs, and I have done so. However, some people may be offended that I have not adopted a more reverential tone and glossed over the more difficult events in Maricopa's history. I would remind those people that if we have learned nothing else in the second half of the twentieth century, we should have learned that trying to cover up truth is the most dangerous thing anyone can do. And in this case, the truth is that the Maricopa County Community College District is one of the largest and most successful institutions of higher learning in the United States, if not on earth. The institution is great precisely because it has been tested in the fire. The story of the bad times only makes the story of the good times all the more remarkable.

That much having been decided, I began to forge ahead. My charge was to write the history of the district, not the history of the ten individual colleges, but the history of the district *is* the history of those colleges. To resolve that dilemma, I decided to focus pri- marily on the founding of each of the dis- trict's ten colleges because starting new col- leges has been the district's most important (and most revealing) function. I would focus on other events from the history of individual colleges only when those events impacted on the district as a whole.

I also decided that the book should empha- size oral history. The district is still young enough that many of the people who made its history are still around, and I figured I could count on them to tell it like it was. To that end, my assistant and I interviewed nearly a hundred faculty, administrators, former stu- dents, and even a few outside observers over a three-year period. Among that group were as many current and former campus presi- dents and governing board members as we could locate. A few refused our requests for interviews, and we could not find a few oth- ers, but otherwise, we got quite an earful. The interviewees provided the real meat of this book, and we are forever grateful to them for allowing us to talk to them and use their words in this book.

The result was ten times the amount of origi- nal material than could be used in the book, so we decided to expand the scope beyond the printed page. We have created a companion web site, where we have posted edited tran- scripts of almost all the interviews. (They have been edited only to improve readability and to remove digressions and off-the-record com- ments.) In addition, the full texts of many important source documents have been made available, as well as some historic photographs that could not be included in the book. Audio and video excerpts from many of the inter- views are available online also. Throughout the text, reminders appear to call the reader's attention to the additional material.

The address for the History Project home page is http://www.mc.maricopa.edu/users/M3cdhistory/

Scholars and anyone else interested in learn- ing more about the history of the Maricopa County Community College District are wel- come to use the online material. The condi- tions for using the Internet material are explained online.

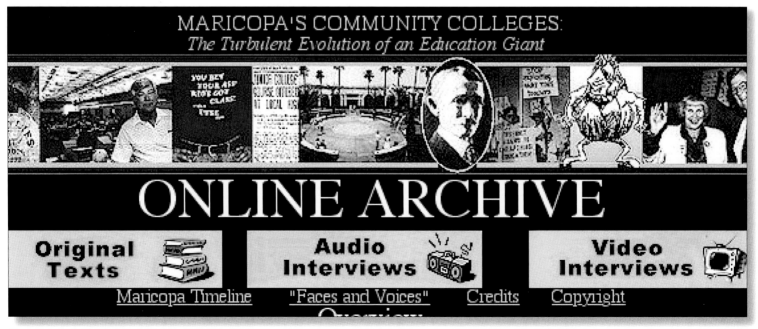

Home page for the Maricopa County Community College District History Project.

Acknowledgments

Many, many people have assisted me in the completion of this task, and I wish to express my gratitude to them here. In particular, I wish to acknowledge the special contributions of each of the following.

First, I acknowledge my debt to four unpublished Ph.D. dissertations that were of enormous help: John Prince's biography of E. W. Montgomery, Mabel Hughes Blue's early history of Phoenix College, Mildred Bulpitt's history of the evening college program at Phoenix College, and Rosejean Clifford Hinsdale's encyclopedic history of the Maricopa district's first ten years. I was also greatly helped by Phoenix College history professor John Goff's unpublished notes on the history of the district.

In addition to the interviews which we conducted specifically for this book, I also included excerpts from interviews conducted by others. I am especially grateful to Mildred Bulpitt for giving me access to the transcripts of her interviews from the 1960s and to Robert Wilcox for the interviews he did in the 1980s.

I also wish to thank:

• Bob Davies for allowing me access to his original materials.

• Scott Koczak for his help at Glendale.

• Linda Evans, Jan Bradshaw, and Doyle Burke for critiquing an earlier, much longer version of this manuscript.

• Frank Luna of the Phoenix College alumni office.

• Mesa's president Larry Christiansen for rescuing the project when it almost bottomed out, and Jamie Cavalier and Kaye McDonald for their support as well.

• GateWay's president Phil Randolph and William "Bill" Tse for helping to provide slides from Maricopa Tech's history.

• Steve Yturralde for the generous loan of his Glendale yearbooks.

• Zeno Johnston for his generous loan of his Phoenix Junior College yearbooks.

• Norb Bruemmer for the loan of his original copies of *The Prospector*.

• David and Kathy Schwarz for the loan of their original Scottsdale Artichoke T-shirt.

• Fay Freed, Arizona Room Librarian at the central branch of the Phoenix Public Library, for allowing us to borrow the Phoenix Union High School yearbooks.

• Steven L. Phalen, Library Specialist at ASU's Dept. of Archives & Manuscripts, for his time locating historic photographs from the McLaughlin collection.

• The *Arizona Republic*, the *Mesa Tribune*, and the *Scottsdale Daily Progress* for allowing us to use the photos and headlines as illustrations.

• All of the people we interviewed for giving us their time. And of that group, I particularly wish to thank the non-Maricopans: Polly Rosenbaum, Dick Richardson, Quentin Bogart, Lawrence Walkup, and Jonathan Marshall.

• In addition, I must express my sincere gratitude to all the folks in the various public information offices at the district's colleges. In particular, I with to thank Louise Gacioch and June Matthews at district for all their help and support. Louise in particular went over and above the call of duty to provide many of the illustrations used in this book and to help me find the others.

• I owe a huge debt of gratitude to Jean Born, the former head of the Mesa Library, for her help in setting up all the interviews we did, and—most important of all—to Maureen Douglas, my tireless and intrepid assistant for three years. Maureen schlepped around the video equipment, transcribed the interviews, spent countless hours in dusty archives in search of obscure facts, set up the early phases of the web site, and rigorously critiqued the first draft of the book. She listened patiently to my ideas and critiqued them ruthlessly. If not for Maureen, the book would not exist today.

• Finally, I must express my gratitude to my wife and family for their support through this whole four-year ordeal. You can use the computer now for a while, I promise.

— RICHARD FELNAGLE, Faculty
Department of English and Journalism
Mesa Community College

David R. Pierce

Preface

For anyone interested in the essential nature of community colleges, this is an important book. It is an informed and enlightening analysis of the dynamics of how they are led, how they are governed, and how complex organizations respond to change. It is also about greatness.

The prevailing perception of the Maricopa County Community College District today is a cutting-edge institution that is national in its vision and progressive in its thinking and programs. The district shines as an exceptional model, openly sharing its resources and intellectual assets. A related perception centers around Chancellor Paul Elsner, clearly one of the most talented and accomplished community college leaders in their almost 100-year history. I happen to share both of these perceptions.

However, Maricopa was not always held in such high esteem. The origin of then Phoenix Junior College in 1920 was decidedly typical of what most community colleges experience. The behavior of its board sometimes involved ethics that were marginal at best. Its CEOs, though competent, were not always viewed as visionary leaders. Its faculty was partisan and occasionally fractious, going so far as to threaten to strike during one particularly frustrating period. And the community seemed occasionally to question whether it needed the district at all. Chancellor Elsner was brought into the district in 1977 as a leader who would calm the "troubled waters." Fortunately for Maricopa and community colleges generally, the board's limited goal missed the target widely.

During the early eighties, Maricopa began a major metamorphosis that would transform it into one of this nation's most extraordinary and exemplary educational institutions. The transformation was not always even, or were the reasons for its momentum always clear-cut. It is Maricopa's complex and circuitous route from mediocrity to greatness that will most fascinate national audiences.

The understanding of how Maricopa evolved provides an important case study for all who care about community colleges. But it is particularly instructive for current and future graduate students, community college presidents, and trustees. This is an important lesson and a compelling story. Those who contributed to telling it are to be commended for their efforts.

Each reader will take away from this book a very individual impression. But none will be unaffected by the read. It is an intriguing journey, driven by an exceptional chancellor who eventually gains sufficient support and respect for his vision to translate it into reality. It chronicles the maturation of a board that comes to realize the wisdom of curtailing its own excessive tendencies and, instead, support its talented leader. It profiles a faculty that was able to overcome its narrow self-interest and embrace a broader, bolder vision. And it describes a community that gradually realizes that—by design or simple good fortune—it had been blessed with a tremendous asset that could immeasurably enrich its economy, its citizenry, and its quality of life.

At a key point in the book's narrative, the author states that an attempt was made to ". . . bring the community into the college before placing the college in the community." It is a pivotal concept that more than any other feature illuminates the exciting growth to greatness of Maricopa County Community College District.

— DAVID R. PIERCE, Ph.D.
President and CEO
American Association of Community Colleges

Preface

It is difficult to look back to 1962 when the district was established and see that by the end of 1998 it would become the largest community college district in our nation. What is evident though, is that the colleges have grown as Maricopa County has grown and thus each year colleges have served more and more students.

The growth of the district is a fact borne out by our enrollment data, but the impact of the district's colleges on the citizens is harder to determine. As the county grew, so did the need for new colleges to serve these areas. Thus, a single college, Phoenix College, has now grown to ten colleges, with additional sites being developed as satellites of some of the colleges. The areas of study have also changed as strictly lower division academic transfer subjects to a whole host of vocational and technical degrees and certificate programs which serve the workforce needs of our area. As more and more adults require retraining and upgrading of their skills, these functions have taken on an added importance. So has our need to serve all our citizens as we consider programs for high school students and senior citizens part of our role in serving the whole community.

Maricopa's growth and influence in its community I believe parallels what is occurring in all parts of our country. The fact that lifelong education has become an accepted ingredient in all of our lives puts the nation's community colleges on the forefront of the nation's higher education agenda. The fact that community colleges are to be found in so many of our large and small communities seems to testify to their importance. I find it interesting that other nations of the world are finding that our community college model would serve their citizen's needs as education becomes more and more necessary for a nation's success.

There are probably several events over the years that could be considered particularly significant but certainly none is more significant than the visionary leadership of our longtime chancellor, Dr. Paul Elsner, and the leadership team which he assembled to help manage the district. Part of the success I believe can be attributed to a stable governing board which for many years guided the chancellor in the right direction and then allowed him to function. Without the assistance of this kind of governing board many superb leaders have not been able to be successful.

Over the years Maricopa has been able to attract and retain outstanding faculty members whose reputation for quality teaching has become evident in the success of their students. Our faculty have proved to be innovative risk takers and have been encouraged to use whatever methods they wish to promote learning in their classrooms. Many have also enriched students' experiences by the use of technology, and many students are involved in distance learning which meets their needs.

I have often said that if community colleges did not exist they would need to be invented. The influence of the community colleges in their communities becomes quite evident by visiting a campus and observing the diversity of the student body and examining the college's schedules and catalogs to determine the various programs and services the campus provides. One has to ask where people would receive what they come to our colleges for if they did not exist. Where would the reentry person go to begin a new life and where would the senior citizen go for life enrichment? To my mind, community colleges provide a venue for all ages of people to come together to learn and grow and in the end enrich not only their own lives but the community itself.

— LINDA B. ROSENTHAL
President MCCCD Governing Board

1979

Chapter One

1979
The Little **INSURRECTION** That Failed

If any one moment in the history of the Maricopa County Community College District may be said to be the defining moment, it was the Great Faculty Insurrection of 1979. A very curious business, it looked like a strike—but it wasn't. The issue was supposed to be money—but it wasn't. And in the end, the whole affair accomplished nothing—but the district had been changed forever.

As 1979 began, faculty members were panicked about double-digit inflation eating holes in their paychecks. Negotiations for the next year's faculty contract (the so-called meet-and-confer process) had begun, and nationally, President Jimmy Carter had asked labor unions to limit demands for wage increases voluntarily to 7%. The faculty would have liked a larger increase but certainly was not going to accept less.

On January 30, the teachers opened their morning newspapers and received a nasty surprise. Dr. Paul Elsner, the district's new chancellor, had announced his intention to freeze the district's operating budget for the following year. Even though the district was projecting a 4% increase in enrollment, the chancellor was recommending the governing

Angry faculty at a strike meeting at Phoenix College.
Staff photo from the Phoenix Gazette, April 1, 1979.

board adopt the same size operating budget for the next fiscal year.

All over the district, faculty jaws dropped. Fists hit breakfast tables and rattled coffee cups. A budget freeze added to a 10% annual inflation rate was essentially a 10% salary cut!

The article went on to say that in lieu of a salary increase, all employees would receive "economic adjustments." Employees making less than $14,000 would receive $1,000, and everyone else would receive $950. Although the budget would be frozen, the portion of the budget allocated for faculty salaries would be increased by approximately 6% to pay for these adjustments.

Faculty members were dumbfounded. Why on earth did the chancellor want to freeze the budget? Enrollment was supposed to go up 4% next year—and more enrollment meant more money in the kitty. At the same time, the chancellor had just created one new college (Rio Salado) and was in the process of creating a second one (South Mountain)—all with existing district funds. Somehow, the district had found $3.5 million in loose change to bankroll those ventures, so obviously, the district was not hurting for funds. Why were faculty salaries being cut in this way?

Furthermore, the board had already promised $98,000 in salary increases and another $182,000 in additional fringe benefits for over a hundred district administrators. The board said those increases were necessary to bring administrative salaries into line with those of similar institutions. Were faculty salaries being cut to pay for the administrators' windfall?

All over the District, faculty jaws dropped. Fists hit breakfast tables and rattled coffee cups. A budget freeze added to a 10% annual inflation rate was essentially a 10% salary cut!

Worst of all, the chancellor's announcement summarily nullified the sacred meet-and-confer process. Did the new chancellor have absolutely no respect for faculty rights at all?

Faculty members were hurriedly summoned to emergency meetings. Press conferences were held. Accusations and counter-accusations were flung about: "The district has violated the faculty's rights!" "The faculty is distorting the facts!" "The district is squandering money on starting unnecessary colleges!" "The faculty is overpaid!" And so on and so forth.

The last hope for an orderly resolution of the conflict came at the governing board meeting on the night of March 24, 1979. More than 250 faculty members wearing red armbands and waving pasteboard signs stormed the district offices on East Washington. For more than four hours, the faculty demanded the board reject the chancellor's budget freeze and raise salaries by 10.5%, which was then the projected inflation rate for the following year. The shouting and fist-waving continued until well after midnight, but in the end, the board members turned their backs on the faculty and voted four to one to adopt the chancellor's budget freeze.

Faculty picketing at Scottsdale Community College. From the Scottsdale Daily Progress, April 5, 1979.

Then, the faculty began calling for a work slowdown or sick-out. Some even called for a full-blown teachers' strike, but in the end, the faculty opted for informational picketing to take its case to the general public.

Charles Evans, a longtime Mesa Community College faculty member, recalls what followed: *We didn't dismiss classes — we didn't do anything that would disrupt the operation of the school. I don't know whether that was true in all the schools across the district, but it certainly was at Mesa. Our attitude was we have a professional responsibility, and we shouldn't do anything that would disrupt the service to the students . . . Faculty, in their free hours in between classes, would go to various places in town — in some cases it was right out here on Southern and Dobson, and pass out leaflets to passing motorists. It became, actually, a hazard because it slowed traffic down. It really was not a very good thing to have happen.*

Mesa Community College faculty member Charles Evans picketing at the intersection of Dobson Road and Southern Avenue. Mesa Tribune, April 5, 1979.

100 teachers protest Rio Salado at MCC

By HAL DeKEYSER
Tribune staff writer

About 100 teachers from the Maricopa County Community College District conducted an "informational picket" Wednesday amid heavy traffic at the northwest corner of Mesa Community College.

Traffic at the normally congested intersection of Southern Avenue and Dobson Road was slowed further by the teachers, who handed fliers to passing motorists from 3 p.m. to 6 p.m.

The teachers protested what they called the district governing board's increase in part-time faculty, rapidly increasing costs of administration and the failure to finish MCC buildings.

Rio Salado College, the district's "college without walls" is central to the frustrations, said Ray Bruns, an MCC science instructor and president-elect of the District Faculty Association.

The school employs part-time instructors, and conducts classes at various Valley locations.

"Rio Salado is a financial failure, and the faculty is paying for it," he said.

Bruns said it costs twice as much to educate students at Rio Salado as in a traditional community college, and that establishment of the school has actually decreased enrollment.

"We're not striking," Bruns said. "This is an educational picket. We want to get the word out to the community about what's going on here."

A similar demonstration occurred

there are plans to conduct more such pickets next week at Scottsdale and Glendale community colleges.

Handbills passed out by the instructors also complained that the governing board has refused to meet with designated faculty representatives on the issues, and asked citizens to call their elected board representatives. "They're not negotiating with us; they're giving us mandates," Bruns said of the board. "They've failed to confer with us."

Bruns said administrators' ranks have swelled by 20 percent, while faculty numbers remained constant.

"There is one administrator to every six faculty members in the district," he said. "It costs as much to run the administration offices as it does to run each of the two community colleges (SCC and MCC)."

Mesa's governing board member, Dr. Merrill Christensen, said the board is trying to cut administrative costs and free more money for teacher salaries while holding down the overall operating budget of the district.

"I think Rio Salado is the basis of most of the problems," he said. "We're attempting to evaluate it and give some guidance based on a year's experience. To do away with it would be a mistake, but I think it needs some revisions."

Christensen said he favors returning some of the courses offered by Rio Salado to the jurisdiction of the local

These demonstrations continued at various times through the end of April. Eventually, the new chancellor wearied of the fist-shaking and name-calling. In a bold attempt to resolve the conflict, he sidestepped the governing board and went straight to the faculty with an offer

so well, but the cumulative effect was in line with President Carter's guidelines. True, Elsner had stepped on the faculty's collective bargaining toes, but even so, anyone could see that the response was out of proportion to the stimulus.

In the fall of 1977, the faculty discontent accelerated with the appointment of the new chancellor, Dr. Paul Elsner. Faculty at that time saw him as a ruthless outsider more interested in boosting enrollment than in maintaining quality education. Only five months on the job, Elsner stunned everyone by creating Rio Salado Community College, a school that would have no campus and no full-time faculty. A month later, the governing board surprised Elsner by announcing the creation of yet another college (South Mountain Community College), and Elsner endorsed the plan even though his own demographic experts tried to talk him out of it. The expansion, coupled with the incomprehensible budget freeze, convinced faculty that academic excellence was being compromised in the name of unbridled growth.

December 12, 1995, video interview with Charles Evans, Mesa Community College faculty. Transcript and audio excerpts available online.

http://www.mc.maricopa.edu/users/M3cdhistory/

of a 7% salary increase—the very amount they probably would have been willing to accept in the first place—but faculty negotiators stonily turned their thumbs down.

It didn't matter. In the end, the board passed the budget with the 7% increase anyway.

Then, the Great Faculty Insurrection just seemed to run out of gas. As the end of the semester approached, professors left the picket lines and returned to their offices to grade term papers and final exams. The annual graduation exercises were held, and many faculty dispersed for the summer—almost as if nothing at all had happened. Like a spring thunderstorm that blows through and shakes the leaves and rattles the shutters, the Great Insurrection had spent its fury and dissolved into the summer sunshine.

What Really Happened

Clearly, money was not the real issue. For anyone making $14,000 or less in 1979, an "economic adjustment" of $1,000 amounted to a pay increase of more than 7%. Faculty making more than $14,000 didn't fare quite

The real cause of the insurrection was a seething, roiling malaise that had been building up for nearly a decade. The problem went back to the founding of Scottsdale Community College in 1970 and the bloody war that had been fought—improbably—over whether the school athletes were to be called the Drovers or the Artichokes. Ill will from that struggle further inflamed a massive faculty protest over the appointment of an unqualified math professor at Phoenix College. Then came the reign of terror of Roger Brooks, a former student activist who was elected to the governing board and regularly threatened to fire any faculty or staff who got in his way. When the time came for the district's scheduled reaccreditation, the North Central Association of Colleges and Schools was so upset that it served notice the district had two years to clean up its act or have its accreditation yanked.

All these events had contributed to the district malaise. Something was fundamentally wrong with the district. It was changing—losing its focus—turning into something that the faculty didn't like.

Thus, the real purpose of the insurrection was to try to put the brakes on the new chancellor. To that end, the faculty created a curious wooden prop that was displayed wherever the faculty picketed. A four-foot-high plywood tombstone bore the legend:

Here Lies Quality Education,
1963-1977,
Upon the Arrival of
Paul Elsner, Chancellor.

Educational Evolution

The pain that faculty members in 1979 were feeling was real, but their diagnosis of the source was wrong. The district was not merely changing, it was evolving—and evolutionary change is always painful. That evolutionary process was the real source of the faculty malaise.

But evolving how? The answer lies in a fact that few people in the district today recall: Maricopa did not begin its life as a commu-

Teachers unite against district chief

By HAL DeKEYSER
Tribune staff writer

Teachers in the sprawling Maricopa County Community College District are angrier and more united than ever in the 16-year history of the system. The focus of their fury is Rio Salado College and its creator, Chancellor Paul A. Elsner.

The faculty leadership complains that since Elsner came to the district in November 1977 from Peralta, a community college district in Oakland, Calif., morale has plummeted and the quality of education in the district has been threatened.

A mock tombstone popped up at Glendale Community College. The epitaph read:

Here lies quality education
1963-1977
upon the arrival of Paul Elsner, Chancellor

The chancellor was supposed to give the district direction when he was hired to replace Al Flowers, acting chancellor and business

ministrator; a man who gets things done.

It was about four months after he arrived that Rio was formed, and it was the suddenness and secretness of the approval process that has cost Elsner the respect of teachers.

"When he was first hired, we heard good things about him," says Al Shipley, a Glendale Community College math teacher who headed the Faculty Executive Council Meet-and-Confer Committee this year. "The teachers had a good feeling about him.

"We also thought we would continue to be a part of the system, and we're not. We were ignored."

The faculty had nothing to say about Rio... say they showed up at sc... newspaper the ... going to the ... classes cost ... facilities we ...

Faculty m...

dying non-traditional education, and worked up recommendations in 1976.

"As far as I know and as far as I can determine from the rest of the committee, our report was probably filed under the wastebasket or something," said Maralee Murray, a GCC chemistry teacher on the committee. "It was not taken into consideration."

About two ... ...board had approved Rio, ...roughout the district that ...the college with teachers ...rocess too long. ...culty, through the Facul- ...e time was Carl Morris, ...r who now is the East ...ed in general discus- ...d out that the college

Mesa Tribune, May 6, 1979.

nity college district, but as a junior college district, and the two species are very different animals.[1]

Junior colleges began to appear in America toward the end of the nineteenth century. William Rainey Harper, the founding president of the University of Chicago, is usually considered the father of the junior college movement. Harper was a renowned classical and Biblical scholar—a real academic superstar and an educational snob. John D. Rockefeller handpicked Harper to be the University of Chicago's first president and then wrote him a check for $2 million to staff the place any way he wanted. Harper took that money and promptly went shopping for the best faculty money could buy—not unlike a modern-day George Steinbrenner buying baseball players.

Not coincidentally, Harper had a preference for eminent scholars like himself, men who preferred conducting research to dirtying their hands with the education of undergraduates, especially freshmen and sophomores. Harper's biographer Ratcliff explains Harper's point of view: "[Harper believed that] the last years of secondary school and the first years of college were periods of personal exploration

[1] As required by Arizona House Bill 126, the district renamed itself a community college district in June, 1971.

and citizen development. It was best not to confuse university studies (research, advanced studies in a specialized subject) with the general education which was prerequisite to it."

Ratcliff was trying to be tactful. Harper's real attitude may be reflected in a comment that Woodrow Wilson is supposed to have made: "Anyone who thinks two years of college is enough has never seen a sophomore. The sap has begun to rise, but it has not yet reached the brain."

Harper proposed the creation of junior colleges as separate institutions with separate faculties. Junior college faculty would devote themselves to the lesser occupation of teaching and allow the senior university faculty to devote themselves to the higher calling of research. In 1910, Joliet Junior College became the first modern junior college in the mold Harper had suggested. Soon, more than a dozen junior colleges (and their counterparts, 6-year high schools) were established

Picketing faculty walk past the plywood tombstone. Photo by Hal DeKeyser, Mesa Tribune, April 25, 1979.

to protect the University of Chicago faculty from first- and second-year students.

In California, the junior college concept became very popular, but for a different reason. Much of the state's population lived too far away from Palo Alto or Oakland to attend either of the state's great universities. In 1907, the California legislature passed a bill allowing high school districts to offer postgraduate classes. In the fall of 1910, Fresno High School became the first to do so. A report from 1910 explained:

There is no institution of higher education within two hundred miles of Fresno where students may continue their studies beyond the regular high school courses. Many of our high school graduates are but seventeen or eighteen years of age and parents are frequently loath to send these young people so far from home. Many who desire to continue their studies cannot afford the expense necessary to college attendance where the items of room and board mean so much.

Soon, junior colleges began to appear in other small towns all over America, wherever locals felt that the state university was too distant for their seventeen- and eighteen-year-old children. For precisely that reason, the Phoenix Union High School District launched its junior college program in 1920—the same junior college program that is the direct ancestor of today's Maricopa district. The students were the same age as traditional university freshmen and sophomores, and the curriculum paralleled that of the University of Arizona, where those students were expected to transfer.

Or rather, some of the students were expected to transfer. Implicit in Harper's concept of the junior college was the notion that junior colleges could also weed out those students who really weren't university material. Those students who were less academically inclined could get as much education as they could handle at a junior college and then part company with higher education. To that end, junior colleges usually prided themselves on being every bit as rigorous academically as their four-year counterparts.

Phoenix Union High School's junior college program was extremely rigorous, and within a few years, the North Central Association officially accredited Phoenix Junior College as a separate institution. In 1946, *Look* magazine placed Phoenix Junior College at the top of a list of the best junior colleges in America. (The list was alphabetical by state, but the honor was no less genuine.)

When the Maricopa County Junior College District was created in 1962, its first official act was to acquire Phoenix College (the school dropped the "junior" from its name in 1947). The governing board then set up Phoenix College extension campuses in the communities of Glendale and Mesa. These extensions retained Phoenix's primary emphasis on preparing students of traditional college age for transfer to one of Arizona's

three state universities. Thus, the Maricopa district began with deep and well-established junior college roots.

But even before the Maricopa County Junior College District acquired Phoenix College, a force for evolutionary change had begun to exert itself. The nature of that force can be illustrated effectively with the help of a document from 1929. That year, Harry Cross, the dean of Phoenix Junior College, produced his second annual dean's report. This document includes an astonishingly thorough demographic survey of the 384 students enrolled at Phoenix Junior College in the '28-'29 school year. The information includes such matters as the students' home states (14 were from states other than Arizona), students' church affiliation, students' income, the number of credit hours taken, and even the number of minutes per week the students spent (or claimed they spent) on their homework.

According to Cross, the median age for freshmen was 19 and for sophomores was 19.9. A close examination of Cross' figures reveals the average age of freshmen was 19.7, of sophomores was 20.8, and of the student body was 20.0.[2] Only 76 students—less than 20% of the total student body—were aged 25 or older, and the oldest student was 61.

The median age of students in the Maricopa district today is 27, but the average age of students in the Maricopa district is 30. More

than 5,000 students are over the age of 50—approximately 1,500 of those are over the age of 60! Nearly 90% of all the students hold down jobs while they take courses—roughly half of those jobs are full-time—and 78% of students attend school part-time.

Over a period of fifty years, the demographic makeup of the students changed dramatically. In 1929, the majority of the students at Phoenix Junior College had been traditional-age college freshmen and sophomores who attended school full-time. Those who had part-time jobs were working only a few hours a week to pay for school expenses while living at home. After World War II, an increasing number of adult students began to attend school part-time while holding down full-time jobs. By 1979, the majority of the students at the Maricopa Community Colleges were not even living with their parents—many were already parents themselves who supported their own families while attending school at the same time. In other words, these students just didn't fit the old junior college mold.

But the change was more than just a matter of age. Cross' 1929 report contains another essential fact. In it, he posed the question, "Does the Junior College function in providing higher education for students who would otherwise find such education an impossibility?" To find the answer, a questionnaire was handed out to Phoenix Junior College students at an assembly held on April 15, 1929. Students were asked, "If there were no Junior College present in this city, would you be in college?" Approximately half of the students enrolled for the 1928-29 term responded.

Report of the Dean for College Year 1928-1929, by H. A. Cross, Dean of the College, June 30, 1929.
Complete text available online.

http://www.mc.maricopa.edu/users/M3cdhistory/

[2] Cross's data seems to assume that each 18-year-old was exactly 18. If we assumed each 18-year-old was really 18.5, each 19-year-old was really 19.5, etc., the average ages of freshmen would be 20.2, sophomores would be 21.3, and the student body as a whole would be 20.5.

The answer was not what Cross had expected. Of those students responding, 64% answered yes. Only 12% answered no. The rest were not sure.

In other words, approximately two-thirds of the students enrolled in Phoenix Junior College in 1929 saw themselves as university material. Had the junior college not been there, those students believed they would have been in college somewhere else. In their minds, the only difference between the junior college and the university was that the junior college was in Phoenix and the university elsewhere.

By 1979, most of the students enrolled in the Maricopa colleges were not of tradi-tional college age. Most did not enter with the skills and the self-assurance of their pre-decessors. Many of these new students need-ed remedial course-work and help develop-ing study skills. Many would never have been allowed through the door at all back in 1929. Had the community college not been there, the majority of these students would not have been attending a university at all.

Thus, the Maricopa district in 1979 was no longer a junior college in name or in spirit. When the Maricopa faculty marched around their plywood tombstone and mourned the death of "quality education," they were really mourning the death of the junior college as they had known it. No wonder they thought the place was going to hell.

Maricopa Today

Fast-forward to 1998. William Rainey Harper wouldn't know what to think.

In 1998, Maricopa officially became the largest community college district in the United States. With an operating budget in excess of $600 million, the district enrolls in excess of 220,000 students annually. More than 165,000 are enrolled in classes that apply toward a conventional college degree, and the rest are in occupational or vocation-al programs. More than 5,000 are interna-tional students of refugee, visa, or immigrant status. Nearly 1,000 full-time faculty and more than twice that number of adjunct fac-ulty offer nearly 6,500 different courses at the ten independently administered colleges.

Profile: MARICOPA COUNTY

Roughly the same size as the state of Vermont, Mari-copa County covers a little over 9,200 square miles in the middle of Arizona. The county is home to about 2.8 million people, of whom approximately 1.3 mil-lion are older than twenty-five. Once upon a time, Maricopa was primarily an agricultural county, and although cotton and citrus and other crops are still grown year-round, only 12% of the total land area is now farmland. More than 96% of the county's popu-lation lives in one of the score of municipalities that cluster around Phoenix and share contiguous borders. The population is mostly white (85%); only 3.5% of the population is black, and only 1.8% is Native Amer-ican. People of Hispanic origin make up 16.3% of the population. The median age is 32 (slightly younger than the 32.9 nationally). More than half own their own homes.

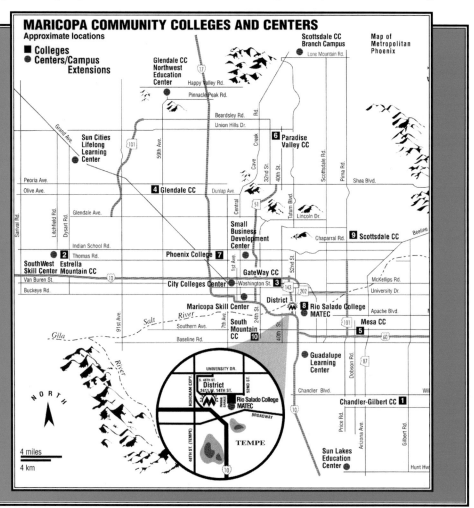

The Maricopa County Community College District, 1998.

Harper would also be astonished at the success of Maricopa's traditional transfer function. In the fall of 1996, more than half of Arizona State University's undergraduate students had attended one or more of the Maricopa Community Colleges. In the upper division, the percentage was even higher—fully two-thirds of the upper division students had MCCCD transfer credits. A whopping 80% of the University of Phoenix's students are Maricopa transfers, too. These statistics are even more remarkable in light of the fact that the majority of the community college students who transfer to ASU and the University of Phoenix were not what most people would consider traditional college students in the first place.

Maricopa is an absolutely magnificent community college system and is a model for the whole world of education."

One indicator of the status that the Maricopa district now enjoys is the district's rate of public participation. About one out of every ten adults in the county attends classes at one or more Maricopa colleges each semester. Approximately 40% of all adults now living in Maricopa County have taken at least one course at one of the ten colleges or received job training through a district program—almost one out of every two adults in the county! That rate of public participation grows even higher when all the people who annually attend various performances, athlet-

whelmingly approved a record-shattering $386-million capital improvement bond issue, the largest bond election ever passed by any community college district to that time.

The Turning Point

Looking backward to the origins of the Maricopa district, we can begin to see the real significance of the Great Faculty Insurrection of 1979. Had the forces that were clinging to the old junior college model been allowed to prevail, the natural process of evolution would have been arrested. The district today would probably consist of five or six small, perpetually underfunded junior colleges with annually declining enrollment. And everyone in Maricopa County would have been the poorer for that loss.

Fortunately, those forces did not prevail. The natural progress of institutional evolution was allowed to proceed unchecked, and the Maricopa district was allowed to pursue its destiny.

But what is that destiny? If a community college is not really the same thing as a junior college, then what exactly is a community college? Or more to the point, what exactly is the Maricopa County Community College District?

To answer both of those questions, we have to go back and start at the beginning . . .

A celebration held at the District Support Services Center in October, 1997, to honor Dr. Paul Elsner's twentieth anniversary as chancellor of the Maricopa district.

And what about Dr. Paul Elsner, in whose honor the faculty constructed their plywood tombstone? He remained at Maricopa's helm until he retired at the end of June 1999. He is nationally acclaimed as a visionary, one of the most honored and respected leaders in all of higher education. Robert Atwell, former president of the American Council on Education, once said, "Dr. Elsner is the superstar of college leaders in this country. What he has done for Maricopa and for all of American higher education has no equal.

ic events, public forums, and other events at the colleges are included. When all of the listeners for the district's two public radio stations and the radio reading service for the visually impaired are added in, almost everyone in Maricopa County benefits directly or indirectly from services offered by the MCCCD.

The ultimate testament to the high regard in which the citizens hold the district came in 1994 when Maricopa County voters over-

1910

1920
Benjamin McFall's **DREAM**

Admission Day Parade in Phoenix, Arizona, 1912. On the left is Phoenix's original City Hall. Arizona Collection, Arizona State University Libraries.

Education has always been a hard sell in Arizona. The problem goes back to the early years of the Arizona Territory when the residents were more concerned with subduing Indians than educating children. When the third territorial governor, A. P. Safford, persuaded the 1871 territorial legislature to pass a public school bill, the legislature did so, but only after stripping away all the funding. When Charles Trumbull Hayden managed to squeeze $5,000 out of the 1885 territorial legislature to found a Normal School in Tempe, he rushed to build the school before the legislature could meet again; he feared the parsimonious legislators might otherwise rescind his funding. When the citizens of Tucson learned that the same legislative session had awarded them $25,000 to start a state university, they pelted the messenger with ripe eggs, rotten vegetables, and possibly a dead cat. (They had wanted to hear that the legislature was moving the territorial capitol or the insane asylum to Tucson, and the university seemed like a poor consolation prize, at best.)

B. F. McFall (1858-1924)

Thus, Benjamin F. McFall must have seemed out of his mind to think he could convince anyone to start a junior college in Phoenix in 1910. But McFall knew what he was doing.

Born in Missouri in 1858, McFall was a strong believer in education. He attended Missouri State University, at Columbia, Missouri, for two years. In 1885, poor health caused him to move to Arizona, where he eventually bought a ranch six miles northeast of Phoenix and became one of Arizona's early pioneers in citrus farming. Local politics also attracted his attention, and at one time, he was elected recorder of Maricopa County. In 1903, he was elected to the Phoenix Union High School Board, on which he served for the next 22 years.

In 1910, McFall must have realized that conditions were right for a junior college in Phoenix. The population was approximately 11,000—quite impressive for what had started out as a sleepy little farm town in the middle of the Sonoran desert only 40 years before. The population had already doubled since the census of 1900, and the city was poised for another growth spurt because statehood for Arizona was imminent and Phoenix was about to

1910

become a new state capital. The Roosevelt Dam, under construction at the time, was expected to tame the unpredictable Salt River and bring inexpensive electricity to the city. Furthermore, Phoenix was becoming a vacation paradise for health-seekers from the East. Swanky resorts were opening up to accommodate the new industry of winter visitors. The city boosters saw dollar signs sprouting up everywhere they looked.

Even so, Phoenix was still Arizona's second-largest city. It lagged behind Tucson by several thousand people, and Phoenix's city fathers wanted their city to become the leading city in the state. As a result, they were eagerly seeking ways to attract new residents. McFall must have realized that a junior college in Phoenix could be just such an attraction.

But first, something had to be done about that old, dilapidated high school.

Phoenix Union High School

Actually, Phoenix in 1910 was lucky to have a high school at all. Since 1872, when Phoenix had opened its first elementary school in a back room of the county courthouse, the good burghers of Phoenix had been consistently reluctant to lavish money on school buildings.

About 25 pupils attended initially, and a single teacher taught all grades. Three years later, the city got tired of the kids in the courthouse and erected a one-room schoolhouse made from adobe—the least expensive type of building possible. In 1879, the territorial legislature authorized the bonding of school districts, and the Phoenix Elementary District No. 1 was born. The district promptly raised the money for a two-story, brick school building on North Central Avenue roughly where the Hotel San Carlos stands today.

In 1895, the city of Phoenix established a high school district to serve a union of the various elementary school districts that had evolved in the intervening years. Following the example of the legislature, Phoenix did not then appropriate any money for a high school building but simply designated two rooms on the second floor of the old Central School building for that purpose. Somehow, about ninety students managed to squeeze in.

The Central School Building circa 1890.
Arizona Collection, Arizona State University Libraries.

Profile: THE DEVELOPMENT OF PHOENIX

The phenomenal growth of Phoenix in its first forty years was not accidental. The first city fathers were boosters, entrepreneurs, and developers who understood that to sell land, they had to make it worth buying.

- *1867: Jack Swilling and his partners started a company to reopen canals that the Hohokam Indians had abandoned nearly four centuries previously. In 1868, irrigation water from the Salt River began to flow, and money from the sale of farmland began to flow into the pockets of Swilling and his partners.*
- *1871: Phoenicians lobbied territorial legislators to carve off a hunk of Yavapai County and create a new county, to be called Maricopa. Not coincidentally, Phoenix was named the new county seat—and the value of commercial property increased accordingly.*
- *1889: Armed with a war chest full of money, representatives from Phoenix persuaded the territorial legislators to move the capital to Phoenix. Developers made the deal irresistible by donating a parcel of land on the west side of town for the construction of the new capitol. Then, they subdivided the surrounding land and made a killing.*
- *1911: Roosevelt Dam was dedicated. The result was control over the flood-prone Salt River and an abundance of electrical power for new homes and businesses.*
- *1912: Arizona became a state on February 14. Phoenix property became more valuable again as overnight, the territorial capital became a state capital.*

Two years later, the school board convinced the voters to approve $15,000 to purchase the former residence of territorial secretary of state Clark Churchill. This multiroom, two-story structure (which faced west on Fifth Avenue just north of the intersection with Van Buren, roughly where the Phoenix

The old Churchill residence, the first home of the Phoenix Union High School. Arizona Collection, Arizona State University Libraries.

Channel Eleven studios now reside) became the new Phoenix Union High School.

Classes met in the Churchill house for the first time in 1898, but the structure proved inadequate almost immediately. The very next year, the school board needed another $10,000 to build an addition onto the north end of the building. (In this form, the building remained in use until it was torn down in 1949 to make way for a new cafeteria building.) In 1909, the voters authorized an additional $2,000 for a temporary building to try to ease the overcrowding, but by 1910, more than 300 students were attending

classes in what had previously been only a private home.

The city fathers recognized that something had to be done at once. Demographic projections warned that the population of Phoenix could triple in the next ten years. The old building had clearly outlived its usefulness, but trying to add another addition was not desirable. The structure was too old-fashioned—too Victorian—for an up-and-coming metropolis in the West. But at the same time, Phoenix's frugal city fathers couldn't say good-bye to the old structure entirely. The location was perfect, and building an entirely new building somewhere else was . . . well . . . too extravagant.

Looking for a solution to this dilemma, McFall and the other members of the school board turned their eyes toward California (where Arizonans were always looking for inspiration). They began to look at the way that new high schools were being built in Hollywood and Redlands. Instead of a single, all-encompassing building, each of these schools had been designed as a cluster of discrete buildings that resembled a small college campus. This approach made sense for Phoenix because the old Churchill building could be retained as one element of a larger high school campus, and as the city population continued to grow, more buildings could be added later. Still, though, the old Churchill building was an eyesore, and something had to be done about it.

California architect Norman Foote Marsh had designed the campus of Hollywood High School in 1909, so the Phoenix board hired

Marsh to design a similar campus for Phoenix. Marsh's design solved the aesthetic problem by placing the main entrance to the campus on East Van Buren, then one of Phoenix's busiest thoroughfares. The stodgy, old Churchill building was thus pushed to the back of the new campus, and the focus was redirected onto the three new buildings that Marsh designed in the trendy beaux-arts style, the preferred style for federal buildings in Washington, D.C., of that era. The centerpiece of Marsh's design was the auditorium, set back from the street and flanked by the domestic arts building and the science building. Framed in this way, the auditorium quickly became the central cultural facility for the city of Phoenix.

Phoenix embraced Marsh's design enthusiastically. Voters approved a $150,000 bond, and construction began. The high school moved into its new quarters in the fall of 1912. The old Churchill building was then remodeled (and some of the old gingerbread knocked off) and rechristened the Commercial Building in 1913.

The Domestic Arts and Sciences Building of the Phoenix Union High School campus after 1912. As designed by Norman Foote Marsh, the new campus faced onto East Van Buren Street and pushed the old Churchill residence to the back of the campus. Phoenix Public Library.

All these reasons must have led McFall to conclude that the Phoenix Union High School should follow Fresno's lead and establish a junior college program. The magnificent new high school that looked so very much like a small college campus could just as easily be one.

Neil Cook, PUHS Class of 1914 and Phoenix Junior College Professor of English 1922-1944. From the 1925 Phoenician.

One odd detail of Marsh's plan is that it included only limited athletic facilities. An article from the 1915 *Phoenician,* the Phoenix Union High School yearbook, complained: "One of our greatest needs is a suitable stadium in which to carry on our athletic activities. For several years we have been dependent on vacant lots for practice grounds. . . . This year we have been compelled to use the Indian School grounds and Riverside Park whenever we had games to play." That stadium was more than ten years away, and its advent would become one of the most celebrated events in PUHS history.

The Junior College Is Proposed

Although various documents confirm that B. F. McFall first suggested the idea of a junior college for Phoenix in 1910, none of those documents reveal how or why. Under the circumstances, though, the idea certainly should have occurred to somebody. The fact that the PUHS board turned to a California architect who had recently created an innovative high school campus suggests that the board was aware of trends in California education. Thus, McFall and the other board members must have have known about California's 1907 legislation permitting high schools to offer the first two years of college-level courses. McFall surely would have known that Fresno High School was preparing to launch a junior college program in 1910. The design of Marsh's campus for Phoenix may even have contributed. Not only did Marsh's design resemble a small college, but at the same time, Marsh was designing some of the first buildings for the new University of Redlands in California.

Furthermore, the situations in Fresno and Phoenix were very similar. In 1910, Fresno High School graduates desiring to continue

their studies had to travel to the University of California in Oakland or Stanford University in Palo Alto. Phoenix Union High School graduates desiring the same had to travel to the University of Arizona in Tucson or go out of state entirely. Of course, PUHS graduates could also continue their education at Tempe Normal School, but Tempe was too far away for Phoenix students to commute to classes in 1910. Students from Phoenix who enrolled at the Normal School had to live in a dormitory, so they might just as well have gone to the University of Arizona or the University of California. Also, the Normal School did not offer a Bachelor of Arts degree until 1929, when the school was reborn as Arizona State Teachers College at Tempe. Or, PUHS graduates could simply have abandoned the idea of a college degree and taken classes at the Lamson Inter-Collegiate and Business College (a fancy name for an ordinary business school), which had begun operation in Phoenix in 1889 (six years before the Phoenix Union High School District had been founded).

All these reasons must have led McFall to conclude that the Phoenix Union High School should follow Fresno's lead and establish a junior college program. The magnificent new high school that looked so very much like a small college campus could just as easily be one.

A junior college made sense for another reason, too. In 1910, the University of Arizona was apparently not attracting many students from outside of the Tucson area. An article from the March 14, 1923, issue of the *Arizona Wildcat* (the student newspaper for the U of A) quotes Dr. William V. Whitmore (a former member of the state board of regents) speaking at the annual Founders' Day celebration:

In 1911, twenty years after the University opened, there were twelve fully accredited high schools in Arizona. But not then, nor for four or five years later did the University get its proper percent of the graduates from these schools. This was the situation. Nearly all of the high school principals were from outside of Arizona. They knew very little about the University or the work being done here. When their students came to be graduated, it was quite natural that either the institution represented by that principal or some well-known institution east or west should be recommended to the students.

McFall realized that the University of Arizona's partisans in the legislature would never have allowed a rival four-year school to be established in Phoenix or anywhere else in the state. But U of A partisans would surely have welcomed a two-year junior college program in Phoenix to funnel students to Tucson.

Thus, McFall was clearly not out of his mind to suggest a junior college for Phoenix in 1910—but ten years would elapse before his dream would come to pass.

The Dream Delayed

Once the new high school was open, the board took its first tentative steps toward offering college-level courses. In 1913, PUHS enrolled its first two "post-graduate" students, a so-called "fifth-year class." The program continued for the next several years. In the 1915 PUHS yearbook, Neil Cook (class of 1914 and later one of Phoenix Junior College's founding faculty members) contributed an article about the post-graduates. Cook states that nearly twenty students had been enrolled that year in courses in short-

hand, typewriting, and bookkeeping, but Cook insists that these courses were a means and not an end: "The impression must not be given that we are fitting ourselves for our life's work as stenographers or bookkeepers. Such positions will serve, naturally, as a step on the way to the 'place higher up,' even tho [sic] this step is not taken inside of an office."

Cook then argues for the founding of a junior college program:

> *We post-graduates enrolled for the fifth time because we believed we could still learn something, therefore, why not a Junior College? . . . It would mean a university education for many who could work their way for two years but not four. It would mean two more years of home influence which the best authorities claim to be a very vital period, when the character of the young man or woman is still in the process of being moulded. It would mean the saving of money and many things that would fully compensate for the slight extra cost to the school district.*

Enthusiasm for a junior college began to build. Harry Cross' *Report of the Dean for College Year 1928-1929* states: "Shortly after the year 1915 the Junior College became a frequent informal topic of conversation among members of the 'board.' . . . They were united in their desire to create the unit." An article from the January 20, 1915, *Arizona Republican* confirms that, "The establishment of a two years' college course in high schools was initiated by the Arizona Central District Federation of Women's clubs at the meeting yesterday. While the council gathering of the general federation was in progress, the district organization met and endorsed college work in the public schools, and a committee was appointed . . . to advance the movement."

With all this interest, McFall might have hoped that the Phoenix Union High School would have started a junior college program in 1915, but tragedy suddenly intervened. Alvin K. Stabler, who had been the principal of the high school since 1908, fell ill and was no longer able to carry out his duties. As a result, the board had to set aside plans for a junior college program to find a replacement for Stabler.

In the fall of 1915, R. Thane Cook became Phoenix Union High School's new principal. Cook was ambitious but apparently not sympathetic to the idea of introducing college-level classes at the high school. According to news stories in the *Arizona Republican* for September 13, 1915, Cook chose instead to inaugurate a college preparatory program. Cook told the newspaper, "By installing the extra courses . . . we have made possible for a student in the course of his regular high school studies to select such classes as will fit him for any college. In other words, Phoenix High will now be a preparatory school as well as a high or intermediate school."

References to starting a junior college program in Phoenix then disappear from the newspapers for the next few years. McFall could not have been pleased. A college prep curriculum was fine, but once the students were graduated, they still needed opportunities for college-level work closer to home.

Then another problem delayed the creation of a junior college program still further. By 1916, the high school enrollment had swollen to over one thousand students. That fall, an article from the local newspaper, now called the *Arizona Republic*, reported, "Attending high school this year will not be unattended by discomfort for some. So popular has the institution become since it was enlarged four years ago, it is now impossible to make the original quarters do for the classes. . . . In fact some classes will have to be held off the campus in residences."

Even if the PUHS board had wanted to start a junior college program then, no space was available for it!

However, even that problem was forced to take a backseat to events that were taking place in Europe. Archduke Ferdinand had been assassinated in June of 1914, and the *Lusitania* had been sunk in May of the following year. On April 6, 1917, the United States declared war on Germany, and a military draft began one month later. By the time the Treaty of Versailles was signed on June 28, 1919, more than one-fourth of all American men between the ages of 18 and 45 were in uniform.

Back home, the leadership at the high school changed again. As of the fall of 1918, R. Thane Cook was gone, and the Phoenix Union High School had another new principal, Daniel F. Jantzen, who had previously been the head of the high school English department.

With the return of the young veterans, overcrowding at the high school was suddenly worse than ever. In May of 1919, the school board asked the voters for a $700,000 bond issue to expand the campus—but the voters said no. Overcrowding in the high school then became so bad in the fall of 1919 that, reportedly, approaches to the fire escapes had to be pressed into service for classroom space. In February of 1920, the school board appealed to the voters for a lesser amount, $376,000, and this time, the voters assented. The money was immediately put toward the construction of two new classroom buildings and the much-needed gymnasium.

Haste Almost Makes Waste

For ten years, McFall had waited to start a junior college program in Phoenix, and with the success of the $376,000 bond issue, he decided to wait no more. The postwar years had brought very uncertain times to Phoenix. According to a brief history published in the Phoenix Junior College Bulletin for 1925, "These were the days of readjustment after the World War. Money was scarce and prices were high. Parents were perplexed about their sons and their daughters who had finished high school. There was no work for them because the servicemen were placed in positions that young men could fill; they could not afford to go away to college." Furthermore—as Mabel Hughes Blue points out in her history of Phoenix College—young veterans returning from Europe did not find anything comparable to the GI Bill to assist them in continuing their education.

In 1920, McFall was president of the board. The other board members had long been in favor of the junior college, and principal Jantzen seemed to favor the idea, too. Seemingly on the spur of the moment, McFall and Jantzen approached Weston W. Carpenter, then head of PUHS's science department, about heading up a junior college program at the high school. In addition to his years of experience and leadership ability, Carpenter had taught some courses at Northern Arizona Normal School in the summer of 1919. In other words, he was practically college faculty already.

In the spring of 1920, Jantzen, McFall, and Carpenter hurriedly set to work to design the first-year junior college curriculum. Arizona had not yet passed any legislation empowering high schools to offer junior college programs, but the county superintendent of schools and the state attorney general assured McFall that the existing laws did not prohibit the PUHS from offering college-level courses.

The first public notice of the junior college program appears in the August 18, 1920, issue of the *Arizona Republic*. At the end of a lengthy article about the school year to come at PUHS, the following appears:

> *Launched as something of an experiment, which will be rapidly developed if it proves successful, will be the new classes in junior college work. These classes will be open to anyone who has been graduated from high school. The work will embrace a first year college course based upon the advice of several recognized universities. In order that definite arrangements can be made for this innovation in the educational curriculum of the school, all applicants for this work are urged to register as early as possible.*

On September 5, the *Republic* added, "The proposed course has been carefully worked out on the plan of the first year course in the University of Arizona, and the university authorities have been asked to approve it for full credit upon presentation of evidence that the work has been done creditably."

Not surprisingly, the first-year enrollment was very small. An article from the *Republic* on September 10 reveals that only ten students had yet enrolled. "There is still room for another 10 or 15, according to Principal Jantzen." The problem was that

Reproduction of the headline from the September 5, 1920, Arizona Republic.

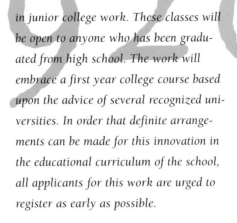

WESTON W. CARPENTER, *First Dean of Phoenix Junior College 1920-1923*

Born in 1889, Carpenter earned his BA from the University of Kansas in 1912. He started teaching at Phoenix Union High School in 1915, the same year as Jantzen, and two years later, Carpenter earned his MA from the University of Kansas. The 1917 PUHS yearbook shows that Carpenter taught biology and also coached the basketball team that year. The following year, he was in the Army. Following his honorable discharge on December 27, 1918, Carpenter (then twenty-eight years old) returned to his duties at PUHS.

Weston W. Carpenter, First Dean of Phoenix Junior College (1920-1923), from the 1923 Phoenician.

the junior college program had not been announced the previous spring when students were being graduated from the high school. Therefore, none of them could have planned to attend the new junior college program in the fall.

In fact, the program's entire first year seems to have been a complete improvisation. Absolutely no reference to the junior college program appears in any of the minutes of the PUHS governing board until the minutes of the meeting for April 8, 1921. At that meeting, Jantzen requested $90 to print five hundred copies of the Junior College bulletin for the second year of the program. The account of the episode in the minutes reveals some of the problems of acting in too much haste:

[Jantzen] also reported that he had conferred with County Superintendent Jones and State Superintendent Miss Toles and Governor Campbell with regard to the status of the Junior College, and had been advised by Superintendent Jones that there was nothing in the law to prevent the Phoenix Union High School from giving a course in Junior College, but money for same cannot be drawn from the State and County funds. Miss Toles and Governor Campbell expressed a similar opinion, but asked that action be deferred until the matter could be presented to the State Board of Education in session on the 18th day of April.

As required, Jantzen nervously went to the state board meeting on the 18th. The state

If you had decided to enroll in the junior college program in its inaugural year, your schedule would have been as follows:

Period I.
Girls: French, Miss McDaniel, or Spanish, Miss Green, four credits.
Boys: Military training, Capt. Jones, one credit.

Period II.
Boys and girls: English composition, Mr. Ayer, three credits.

Periods III and IV.
Boys and girls: Mathematics, Miss Whitfield or Mr. Elliott, five credits.

Periods V and VI.
Boys and girls: Chemistry, Mr. Carpenter, four credits.

Period VII.
Girls: Home economics, Miss Wingfield, two credits; physical training, Miss Hurley, one credit. Boys: French, Miss McDaniel, or Spanish, Miss Green, four credits.

Period VIII.
Girls: Home economics, as above. Boys: Mechanical arts, Mr. Turner, two credits.

The foregoing schedule gives a total of 19 units for university credit and covers every course in the curriculum of the university.

Arizona Republic September 5, 1920.

board considered the matter and then ruled that the PUHS was indeed within its legal jurisdiction to create the junior college program, but the state board reserved the right to approve the curriculum before permitting any state and county money to fund the program. Eventually, the curriculum and the funds were approved, but the program's ambiguous legal status remained a subject of concern until 1927.

The faculty were all high school teachers who offered the junior college courses in addition to their other teaching duties.

To distinguish themselves from the high school students, the dozen or so junior college students acted quickly to establish their own identity by assuming all the accoutrements of a college. As reported in the 1921 high school annual,

to worry about the program's survival, but enrollment for the second year picked up considerably. The junior college section of the 1922 PUHS yearbook includes the names of 89 students (an article in the same section says the enrollment was actually 93) and a faculty of 15 instructors.

With the expanded enrollment in the fall of 1921, the junior college managed to add the one thing it had been lacking: a football team.

Photos from left:
The faculty for the first year of the junior college program. All the teachers were from the high school faculty. From the 1921 Phoenician. Phoenix Public Library.

The students for the first year of the junior college program. From the 1921 Phoenician.

Phoenix Junior College's first football team, from Phoenix Union High School's Phoenician for 1922.

College Life in the Early '20s

Initially, the junior college was indistinguishable from the high school. For the first five years, the classes were held primarily in wooden cottages, or barracks, at the back of the high school campus. Lab science classes were held in the high school science labs.

The Junior College was almost barred from athletics during its first year due to the minuscule number of students. Its six boys and five girls were at a loss to know what branch of activities they should enter. The boys finally decided to organize a basketball team and the girls pledged themselves to support it 100 percent. Again, Carpenter was pressed into service as a coach. In the spring, the students wanted to field a baseball team, but they lacked sufficient players, so a student-faculty team was organized and reportedly won several games.

The small number of students in the junior college's first year must have caused McFall

Several games were played, but only one against another college. Phoenix beat Flagstaff Normal 28 to 0 in Phoenix. Basketball and baseball teams were also active.

By the end of its second year, the continuance of the junior college program was thus assured. His dream realized, McFall retired from the school board in 1924. Phoenix at last had a real junior college.

1922

1939
Chapter Three
The **Junior** College **GROWS UP**

In the third year of operation, the junior college took its first steps toward its eventual separation from the high school. In the fall of 1922, Neil Cook and John Laird became the first faculty hired specifically for the junior college. Cook (author of the article about the post-graduates) taught English, and Laird taught social studies.

The following year, Carpenter left to work on his doctorate, and John Laird became dean of the college.[1] Acquiring the nickname

John Laird, Second Dean of Phoenix College (1923-1926), from the 1926 Bear Tracks. Phoenix Public Library.

Cottonwood Court, the home of Phoenix Junior College from 1925-1929. Arizona Collection, Arizona State University Libraries.

"Daddy" Laird, he held that office for three years and then returned to the faculty when Harry A. Cross became Phoenix Junior College's third dean.

EARLY JUNIOR COLLEGE FACULTY

At the request of Robert Hannelly, dean of Phoenix College from 1947 to 1965 and the Maricopa district's first president, Millie Noble prepared a list of Phoenix College faculty with ten years or more of service. The following names appear on that list as faculty who were hired during the junior college's first decade:

Andres, Edward M. (1929-1953)
Campbell, Elizabeth (1927-1951)
Cook, Neil (1922-1944)
Hannelly, Robert J. (1927-1968)
Hoy, George D. (1927-1967)
Hubbard, Helen E. (1924-1957)
Laird, John (1922-1945)
Moseley, Elizabeth (1926-1940)
Myers, Clyde (1929-1947)
Phelps, Arthur L. (1926-1963)
Smelser, Joseph N. (1929-1966)
Smith, Euclid C. (1929-1945)
Stone, Donald F. (1929-1950)
Stone, Earle, L.(1929-1967)
Thayer, Elizabeth (1927-1940)
Trevillian, Bernice B. (1925-1957)

Harry A. Cross, Third Dean of Phoenix College (1926-1931), from the 1927 Bear Tracks. Phoenix Public Library.

By 1925, the high school was too pressed for space for the junior college program to continue on the high school campus any longer. The PUHS board then acquired four and a half acres of additional property at the corner of Seventh Street and Fillmore. The property included a large residence, which came to be known as Cottonwood Court. This property became the site of the junior college's first campus. Even so, the junior college continued to use the high school's laboratories for science classes.

Also in 1925, the high school board became disenchanted with Daniel Jantzen's leadership. According to John Prince's dissertation, the board was looking for a stronger admin-

---

1 From 1925-28, Carpenter also served as Professor of Educational Administration at George Peabody College for Teachers. In 1928, he joined the faculty at the University of Missouri in Columbia, Missouri as Professor of Education.

COTTONWOOD COURT

A description of the new facility appears in the first official junior college bulletin, published in the fall of 1925:

The Phoenix Junior College has a setting of many varieties of trees. . . . There is a large athletic field near the school buildings. . . . Trees border it on three sides. . . . All this makes a good background for the present building. In addition to the classrooms are the wide halls, the tastefully furnished office, the study hall and library, and a pleasant study and rest room for the girls.

This description adds, "Since the College has been moved to more dignified surroundings the attitude of the student body has undergone a decided change. There is an added dignity of bearing which makes of the already fine school spirit a really splendid thing."

YEAR	NUMBER
1920-1921	53
1921-1922	92
1922-1923	195
1923-1924	154
1924-1925	142
1925-1926	140
1926-1927	222
1927-1928	304
1928-1929	384
1929-1930	492 (estimate)

Phoenix Junior College enrollment in its first ten years. Numbers are from the 1929 dean's report.

istrator. In 1925, they found what they were looking for: E. W. Montgomery—a virtual dynamo, a veteran flesh-presser, and a gifted fund-raiser. Born in Indiana in 1882, Montgomery earned his BA (1909) and MA (1913) at Indiana University. Phoenix College faculty member John Goff recalls Montgomery as "an autocrat, an impressive speaker and great actor."

One of Montgomery's first tasks was to promote the construction of a much-needed stadium. By 1925, both the high school and the junior college teams were drawing large crowds, and the fact that the teams lacked their own facilities for games had become an embarrassment. Voters, however, were reluctant to spend tax money on a stadium; they felt increasing enrollments at the high school and the junior college dictated that new classroom buildings were needed more.

Montgomery then proposed a new stadium to be financed through the sale of $80,000 in revenue bonds, which could be paid off by ticket sales for stadium events instead of by the taxpayers. To address the issue of overcrowding, Montgomery proposed that the stadium seats would be supported by a three-story classroom building underneath. On December 28, 1925, the voters eagerly approved this scheme, but a taxpayer group filed a lawsuit alleging that the revenue bonds were illegal because a stadium is not used for educational purposes. The legal challenges went all the way to the Arizona Supreme Court, where the court ruled that physical education is still education. And so, the stadium was constructed, and the first football game was played there on October 27, 1927.

The stadium was built on the same side of Seventh Street as Cottonwood Court, and the majority of the new stadium's classrooms were assigned to the junior college program, thus effectively moving the remainder of the junior college classes out of the high school. According to author Mabel Hughes Blue,

PHOENIX COLLEGE'S FIRST PRESIDENT

Although E. W. Montgomery was initially hired as the new high school principal, the school board in 1926 changed his official title to Superintendent and Principal of the Phoenix Union High Schools (which then included the Phoenix Colored High School, which had been organized in 1922) and President of Phoenix Junior College. Thus, Montgomery was officially the first president of Phoenix Junior College although the dean of the college was the actual head administrator. This confusing distinction between "president" and "dean" would be continued for several years even after the Maricopa district was formed.

E. W. Montgomery, Superintendent of the Phoenix Union High School District and First President of Phoenix College (1925-1953).

"The college department was allowed one-half of the lower floor for physical training quarters, all of the second floor for laboratories and classrooms, and one-half of the third floor for the commercial department and library."

The new stadium proved so popular that the stadium bonds were retired in half the number of years originally planned, making E. W. Montgomery, Phoenix's first real football

THE 1927 JUNIOR COLLEGE LEGISLATION, SECTIONS 1-4

Section 1. That when a high school or a union high school district shall have an average daily attendance of 100 or more pupils in the high school of such district, as shown by the Principals' or Superintendents' reports of the preceding school year, and an assessed valuation of at least five million dollars, as shown by the last equalized assessment roll, and the Board of Education of such high school or union high school district shall deem it

Section 2. When a junior college has been formed in any high school or union high school district, the Board of Education of such district shall prescribe a junior college course of study, including not more than two years of work. The Board of Education of such district shall also adopt regulations governing

The classroom side of Montgomery Stadium, from the 1946 Phoenician.

Aerial view of PUHS from the 1946 Phoenician, Phoenix Union High School's yearbook. Montgomery Stadium is in the upper left corner of the picture. Just below is the area where Cottonwood Court formerly stood. The junior college building that was constructed in 1929 is also visible below and to the left of the stadium.

the organization of such courses of study and shall prescribe requirements for graduation from such courses.

Section 3. The Board of Education of the high school or union high school district shall have the power to include in its annual budget an amount necessary for the support of the junior college. Bonds for buildings and improvements of said junior colleges may be voted in the same manner that high school bonds are now voted.

Section 4. Whenever, in the opinion of the Board of Education of the high school or union high school district, the average daily attendance of the junior college is not sufficient to warrant the maintaining of such institution, the Board of Education of said district shall have the power to discontinue the junior college.

hero. In 1945, the stadium was renamed Montgomery Stadium in his honor.

The 1927 Junior College Legislation

The year 1927 was a very eventful one for Phoenix Junior College. Not only did the North Central Association accredit the college, but the state legislature also adopted SB 84, which legitimized the way in which the PUHS District had created the junior college.

advisable, said Board may establish a junior college in that district. When a junior college is established, the powers and duties of the Board of Education of the high school or union high school district in which the junior college is established, shall be such as are now provided by law for high school boards of trustees.

The 1929 Junior College Building, from the McLaughlin collection at Arizona State University.

Also in 1927, the evening college program at Phoenix Junior College began with twelve classes and nearly 300 students. The program quickly became very popular but was terminated in 1933 due to budget cuts brought on by the Depression. After World War II, however, the evening college returned and become a force of its own in the college's development.

The same year, Montgomery also went to the board to recommend another bond election. This time, he wanted $650,000, of which $175,000 would be used to finance a new building exclusively for the use of the junior college. In March of 1928, the voters approved this bond, and in the fall of 1929, the so-called Junior College Building was ready for use.

The new Junior College Building, Cottonwood Court, and the stadium firmly anchored the junior college at the corner of Fillmore and Seventh Street, and Seventh Street then became the dividing line between the junior college and the high school. Evelyn M. Shaw Munsil, Phoenix Junior College class of 1931, recalls the campus in those days:

> *The front entrance was right off Seventh Street, and you walked in, and as I remember the dean's office was right in there to the left—H. A. Cross was the dean; we called him "H. A."—and if you kept on going on through, you came to the combination gym-*

THE OTHER JUNIOR COLLEGE

Eastern Arizona College is in Thatcher, Arizona (a small town in southeastern Arizona). This school originated as St. Joseph Stake Academy, a private high school under the direction of the Church of Jesus Christ of Latter-day Saints. In 1921, the academy followed the example of Phoenix Union High School and added first-year college courses and, later, second-year courses as well. In 1926, the University of Arizona accredited the school, and the name was changed to Gila Junior College. In 1933, Graham County voters elected to assume support of the school as a county junior college, and in 1950, the name was changed to Eastern Arizona Junior College.

JACK WILLIAMS RECALLS PHOENIX JUNIOR COLLEGE

For *Phoenix Magazine's* October, 1970, issue (commemorating the city's 100th birthday), former Governor of Arizona Jack Williams contributed the following memories of his college years at Cottonwood Court:

Phoenix Junior College was a tall, three-story home . . . located on Seventh Street, adjacent to the Phoenix Union High School. There, a small class of junior college students absorbed learning in the old-fashioned rooms of the home. Not very formal surroundings and certainly not at all in keeping with what is expected today. From that improvised school building and in intimate contact with some very fine professors, a number of rather outstanding citizens were produced, including a former treasurer of Ford Motor Company, a full professor of transportation at Stanford, the late A. J. Bayless, 'Your Home Town Grocer,' and others too numerous to mention. . . Somehow that old junior college managed to instill a sense of patriotism, a sense of discipline and an interest in learning that is still a part of me.

Jack Williams, Phoenix Junior College Class of 1929 and Governor of Arizona 1967-75.

nasium/auditorium where you'd put on programs and that type of thing.

The old residence [Cottonwood Court] . . . We had our psychology class on the main floor, and I think there were at least two other rooms that were used for classes, and then I think the second floor is where they published their school paper.

Behind our building were the tennis courts, and then the stadium was over south of the tennis courts. . . . I had a biology class over there. Miss Hubbard had her biology classes in the second floor of the stadium.

. . . Daddy Laird was an older man, very kindly, and very staid. He wasn't provoked

to laughter very easily. He did object to the students going to sleep in his class, though. . . . I had Neil Cook in English. . . . He was a little bit reserved. Elizabeth Moseley [Dean of Women and Instructor in English] was also the sponsoring faculty member for the hoity-toity girls' sorority. She didn't have much to do with me, because I didn't sign up for sororities. . . .

We all enjoyed athletics, and I joined the hiking club. . . . Let me tell you about our hiking club. Well, I grew up in Phoenix, and we just never thought much about [the heat]. Open windows were the ventilation. . . . We would sleep in the back-yard. We would take cots out with blankets, and then if a sudden shower came, we'd grab them and run. Anyway, we'd come to school an hour or so early—the ones of us who belonged to the hiking

1. Every freshman is held responsible for the contents of this book. READ IT. During the first semester, freshmen must carry this book with them at all times. In case this book is lost, another may be secured from the college bookstore.

2. A list of freshmen who break any tradition or rule will be posted on the bulletin board each Friday morning.

3. Freshman boys shall wear the beanie from seven o'clock in the morning until six o'clock at night except on Saturdays, Sundays, and other holidays. The Beanie must be kept intact. The beanie shall not be worn in halls or classrooms.

4. Freshmen girls shall wear a small green ribbon on the left wrist in lieu of the beanie worn by

freshman boys.

5. When an upper classman calls "button," the freshman boy shall touch the button on his cap. When an upper-class girl calls "freshie," the freshman girl shall courtesy to the upper-class girl.

6. Freshmen shall not "queen" on the campus.

7. All freshmen shall be under the direction of the yell leader at athletic contests and shall take seats as he directs.

PENAL RULES FOR FRESHMEN FROM THE 1927-28 PHOENIX JUNIOR COLLEGE STUDENTS' HANDBOOK

8. Freshmen shall not be allowed to lounge on the steps, walk, or on the grass in front of the Junior College building.

9. Each freshman shall learn the school songs.

"PHOENIX JUNIOR COLLEGE" by J. Sumpter Shaw

In golden Arizona
Will Junior College stand,
As staunchly as the mountains
Of that enchanted land!
In wondrous Arizona
Are peaks that gleam with light,
And seem to beckon to us
To conquer every height!

In lovely Arizona
Are skies of ardent blue,
That smile o'er golden poppies,
Our colors bright and true!
In fairest Arizona
The cactus greets the rose,
And though we bow to beauty,
We're armed to meet our foes!

In the fields of sport and knowledge
We have laurels we must guard;
Stay right in there, Junior College,
Hit that line and hit it hard!

— From the 1927 student handbook.

PHOENIX JUNIOR COLLEGE, NORTH SEVENTH STREET, PHOENIX, ARIZONA

Reproduction of a full-page ad appearing in the 1927 PUHS yearbook.

Evelyn Shaw from the 1931 Bear Tracks.

club—and we'd hike around the vicinity of the college there. As we'd be walking along, sometimes we'd see a young man who'd been sleeping nude, evidently, on the front porch, because we'd see somebody jump up and grab a blanket when he heard all these ladies' voices coming down the sidewalk. We got a big kick out of that, of course.

Cross did not remain in the dean's office for long. The stock market crashed in 1929, the Depression began, and he and Superintendent Montgomery began to be at odds. According to Prince, "Hearsay has it that Cross was too independent, that he didn't take orders well. It is said the faculty liked him—because he

was independent." Prince further indicates that Cross' expenditures at the junior college may have exceeded his budget, a serious problem in hard times. Perhaps as a result, the PUHS board seriously considered discontinuing Phoenix Junior College as a cost-cutting measure. Montgomery, however, enthusiastically supported the program and kept the doors open.

In the summer of 1931, Cross resigned, and the board appointed his successor, Harry B. Wyman. Born in 1894 in Ohio, Wyman earned his BS, MA, and Ph.D. from Ohio State University. Before coming to Phoenix, Wyman had been a research chemist for the B. F. Goodrich Company, a high school principal at two schools in Ohio, and an instructor in principles of education at Ohio State, the latter for one year before coming to Phoenix.

Under Wyman's leadership, the junior college's fiscal problems apparently stabilized, and enrollments remained high. Phoenix historian, Brad Luckingham suggests a contributing factor may have been the ability of Arizona politicians to leverage a substantial amount of money from the New Deal and thus mitigate the effects of the Depression in Phoenix. The population continued to expand, and most people found their standard of living undiminished.

Increasing enrollments also meant that the little junior college campus was becoming inadequate. As the Depression began to wane in 1935, Montgomery began lobbying for building new facilities. The high school district needed an additional high school, a new junior college facility, and a gymnasium for Phoenix Union. To that end, Montgomery and the school board asked the voters to approve $786,000 in capital improvement bonds, which would be supplemented by WPA money and revenue bonds (for the gymnasium). Approval was given in September of 1938. A new junior college

Harry B. Wyman, Fourth Dean of Phoenix College (1931-1947). Photo from the Phoenix College Bear Tracks yearbook for 1947, Wyman's last year as dean of Phoenix College.

campus was then constructed at Thomas and Fifteenth Streets, and the junior college relocated there for the beginning of classes in the fall of 1939.

Wyman remained as dean until 1946, and Montgomery remained as Superintendent and President of Phoenix College until he retired in 1953.

June 12, 1997, video interview with Evelyn Shaw Munsil, PUHS Class of 1931. Transcript available online.

http://www.mc.maricopa.edu/users/M3cdhistory/

The Fate of the Junior College Building

After the college moved to its new campus, the old junior college building was soon recycled.

In 1935, the Phoenix Union High School District partnered with the State of Arizona and the Federal Vocational Department to open the Phoenix Vocational School in a rented garage at 601 West Adams. According to Homer Dukes' *Washington and Central, 1922-1979*, the school offered courses in sheet metal, body and fender repair, waitressing, auto mechanics, blacksmithing, and various office skills. The school was an immediate success and moved to larger quarters in 1937. With the departure of the junior college from

Firefighters decided to cut a hole in the roof to try to prevent the possibility of an explosion, but the hole caused an updraft that spread the fire rapidly throughout the rest of the building. At the height of the blaze, the smoke could be seen from all over the county.

Three hours later, the building was a total loss, estimated at approximately $750,000. All that remains of the building is the dedicatory plaque, which today graces the front façade of the Phoenix College auditorium.

YEAR	DAY DIVISION	EVENING DIVISION	TOTAL
1930-31	459	343	802
1931-32	13	170	683
1932-33	634	110	744
1933-34	600	26	626
1934-35	631		631
1935-36	572		572
1936-37	591		591
1937-38	565		565
1938-39	731		731
1939-40	780		780

Phoenix Junior College Enrollment 1930-1940 (Source: 1966 NCA Self-Study).

Arizona Republic June 8, 1961: "Aftermath of the Fire." From microfilm

Arizona Republic June 7, 1961: "Fire Destroys the Former Junior College Building." From microfilm.

Seventh and Fillmore in 1939, the building was remodeled and became the school's new home. In 1946, the school was renamed the Phoenix Technical School.

At about 11:00 AM, Tuesday morning, June 7, 1961, a fire broke out in the storage area under the stage, which was then used as part of the gym, and quickly spread to the rest of the building. Students in a cosmetology class and some office workers smelled the smoke and fled the building without injury.

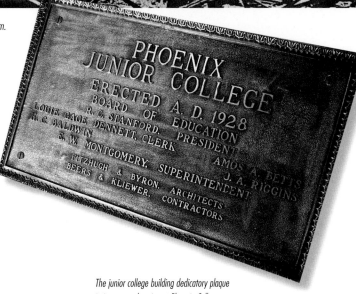

The junior college building dedicatory plaque in its present location at Phoenix College.

1 9 3 9

The move to the new campus in 1939 marked the end of Phoenix Junior College's adolescence. The school was nineteen years old, and the time was right to move away from home.

The venerable Phoenix architectural firm of Lescher and Mahoney designed the new campus. Following Norman Foote Marsh's example, the auditorium became the focal point of a campus quadrangle opening onto a major thoroughfare (Thomas Road). As had been the case at PUHS, two classroom buildings (the science building and the liberal arts building) flanked the auditorium. Linked to the auditorium by covered walkways, two smaller buildings housed the administration and the library, and the cafeteria was attached to the north end of the auditorium. The style was not old-fashioned Beaux Arts, but trendy Moderne, and the red brick in evidence today was plastered over and painted white to emphasize the streamlined details.

School officials worried about the location—Thomas Road between 11th and 15th Avenues—which many considered to be too far north and west of the center of town. The surrounding roads were not even paved yet! However, the campus was close to Encanto

An aerial view of Phoenix Junior College from the early 1940s.

Robert Hannelly, dean of Phoenix College at the time the Maricopa district was created, was a faculty member in the math department when the college moved to its new quarters in 1939. In 1967, he recalled his impressions of the new location to Mildred Bulpitt, dean of the evening division from 1961-78:

> It was right out in the middle of a lettuce field. In fact, I could hear the quail calling from my office over in the Liberal Arts Building. I've always been an avid hunter and wondered why I didn't bring my shotgun over and get some quail . . . Where Park Central [Mall] is now there was a dairy and this was all open country around the college . . . I used to talk to groups downtown and suggest they hold some of their meetings out on the campus, and they would say it was too far out. Cars weren't as good then and this was too far out in the country.

Park and the Encanto-Palmcroft subdivisions, were among the finest housing developments in the city at that time. Appropriately, the school gained in prestige what it lost in proximity. At the start of the school year, the school also enjoyed its largest enrollment to date, nearly 800 full-time students.

In 1939, Phoenix Junior College could easily have been mistaken for a small, elite, four-year liberal arts school with all the trimmings: fraternities, sororities, and varsity athletics. The school even had traditions, including green beanies for the freshies, a beloved school mascot (Bumstead the Bear), and the annual Bear Day, when students and faculty frolicked together at Riverside or Encanto Park. Furthermore, the school's reputation was growing; it was widely considered one of the finest junior colleges in the country.

Lescher and Mahoney's rendering of the proposed junior college campus, from the 1938 promotional pamphlet "Some Facts," ASU archives.

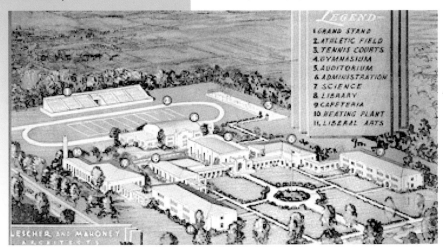

Robert Hannelly, president of Maricopa district 1963-68, interviewed by Mildred Bulpitt, July 12, 1967. Transcript and audio excerpts available online.

"We taught in the evening, on Saturdays and Sundays and during the summer . . ."

http://www.mc.maricopa.edu/users/M3cdhistory/

Unfortunately, this perfect little jewel of a junior college would not long remain in this idyllic state. The Second World War would soon be responsible for planting the seeds of change that would initiate the junior college's evolution into a community college.

The Junior College during the War

The most immediate effect of World War II on the junior college was a precipitous drop in enrollment, which bottomed out at 245 for the 1943-44 school year, the lowest since 1927. To prevent faculty layoffs, the college loaned out some staff to the local high schools to compensate for war-time teacher shortages. The school also retooled its academic program to address wartime needs. The October, 1944, issue of *Junior College Journal* featured Harry Wyman's article describing the effects of war on Phoenix Junior College:

YEAR	DAY DIVISION	EVENING DIVISION	TOTAL
1939-40	780		780
1940-41	732		732
1941-42	658		658
1942-43	379		379
1943-44	245		245
1944-45	339	190	529
1945-46	608	232	840
1946-47	1084	305	1389
1947-48	1246	192	1438
1948-49	1108	336	1444
1949-50	1190	485	1675

Phoenix Junior College Enrollment 1939-1950. Source: 1966 NCA Self-Study.

In all of the college courses in mathematics, reorganized to fit war needs, emphasis is placed upon the military implications of the work. The use of trigonometry, calculus and other mathematics courses in navigation, in the artillery, and in other branches of the armed forces, is stressed. The course in astronomy was revamped to direct the application of the science to navigation, both celestial and terrestrial. Problems were devised that gave the student experience in calculating distances, in charting courses, and in determining the most direct route from one point to another. . . . These problems were very real to young men whose lives were soon to depend upon their skill and precision in the use of instruments and on the accuracy of their calculations.

Wyman also described programs designed to deal with problems on the home front:

Working mothers mean that children must be cared for in a nursery or a preschool. People who are competent to take over the care of these children are not available in communities heavily affected by the war. To meet this need, a course is provided at Phoenix Junior College in play and nursery school, in which these students become acquainted with some of the problems that make these schools necessary, and with some of the simpler phases of child psychology, of play, and of child care.

Other special programs included courses in juvenile delinquency (which was apparently on the rise during the war years), training for nurses' aids ("In some instances entire sorority groups have enrolled in this work"), and crash courses in French and German.

Phoenix College also became a major center for training military pilots. Under the auspices of the War Service Training Program, the college expanded its Civilian Pilot Training Program, which had begun at PJC in 1939. Wyman's article states that the college gymnasium was converted into a dormitory for 150 men in this program. Between the start of the war and the close of this program in January of 1945, approximately 1,230 men were given their ground school training at PJC; the flying school itself was located at Sky Harbor Airport.

Describing this program to Mildred Bulpitt, Robert Hannelly commented:

We taught in the evening, on Saturdays and Sundays and during the summer . . . We used to have terrible experiences in room 112, the science lecture hall. I had a group in there and we had no air conditioning. One Sunday afternoon I had a four-hour session with these boys and every hour I would call for a ten-minute break so they could go out and take their shirts off and wring them out. We were fighting a war, so we worked through this. . . . We were really in the war and sometimes after the guys would complete our training they would go over to Germany. I remember one time reading the casualty list in the Battle of the Bulge and a lot of them were killed.

The Junior College after the War

In 1944, President Franklin Roosevelt signed the GI Bill of Rights, which enabled many returning veterans to attend college. As a result, full-time daytime enrollment at almost

THE FLYING SCHOOL
AFTER THE WAR

The civilian program resumed after the military training program for pilots ended in 1945. In 1947, the Civil Aeronautics Administration gave its seal of approval to the both the ground and flying school programs at Phoenix Junior College, only the second such certification to be granted in Arizona. (The other was at the University of Arizona.) The pro-gram was eventually discontinued in the 1960s for economic reasons.

the morale of participants in other athletics." But in the fall of 1946, eighty men showed up unannounced to try out for football, and the school was completely unprepared. No inter-collegiate games were played in '46, but a spring practice was held, and football was back with a vengeance in the fall of '47. Writing in *Bear Tracks* that fall, Betty Pagan observed, "With the return of people to the old Alma Mater, we find a revival of the school spirit. New students can't visualize how much lovelier college is with a band, football games, and students actually singing the school songs. I remember when the latter were merely interesting poems in the back of the bluebook."

The Phoenix Flying School, formerly the Southwest Airways Building, at Phoenix Sky Harbor Airport, 1948.

every college and university in America exploded. At Phoenix College, the day enrollment jumped from 339 students in the fall of 1944 to 1,084 students in the fall of 1946.

Yet the college was far from normal. The seeds of change had been planted, and the first signs of change began to emerge. Many of the students were older and more mature than the typical nineteen-year-olds that the junior col-lege had served previously. Furthermore, returning veter-ans were not entirely satisfied with Phoenix Junior College as they found it. Zeno Johnson, a

With many men enrolled again, the college seemed to return to its prewar state. Fraternities were revived, school clubs saw increased membership, and PJC was able to field basketball and baseball teams. The rebirth of football is particularly significant because a story in the September 27, 1946, issue of *Bear Tracks* indicates that the admin-istration had not been planning to resume football after the war: "In the past, the hang-overs from miserable football seasons put a damper on school spirit, thereby damaging

The Phoenix Junior College flying school receives the official approval of the Civilian Aeronautics Administration. Photo from the Arizona Republic, March 24, 1947. Left to right: Irvine D. Watts (director of the flying school), D. F. Stone (head of the Aeronautical Department), E. W. Montgomery (president of Phoenix College), Col. C. D. Doak (senior aeronautical inspector), and Bob Hannelly (dean of the college).

Phoenix College Flying School Certificate.

Mesa College faculty member who was a student at PJC then, recalls the veterans were "hell-raisers!" As he observed, "They'd been off, they had seen the world, fought the Japanese, the Germans, and so forth, and had come back to what essentially was a glorified high school."

First, the veterans demanded the school cancel its no-smoking policy. Then, in the fall of 1946, the veterans organized a boycott of the cafeteria to protest high food prices. The January 10, 1947, issue of *Bear Tracks* indicates that the GIs also had their backs up about the name of the college itself:

> *For instance, take the name Junior. It's a nice name—for an undernourished papa's boy. It more or less gives the impression that the lad is too small and too puny to make and to hold a name for himself . . . The connotations arising from that title give impetus to the impression that our college is inferior to other accredited*

THE ASSAULT ON ARIZONA STATE COLLEGE

Most veterans entered into all phases of college life with great enthusiasm—in a few cases, with a little too much enthusiasm. Robert Hannelly tells this story of how he narrowly aborted the veterans' Normandy-style assault on Arizona State College to liberate Bumstead, the college's kidnapped mascot. Bumstead was a 600-pound plaster-of-Paris bear that had originally been created as a promotion for Standard Oil. He had been acquired while the college was still at Cottonwood Court in 1929. When the college had moved to its present location, Bumstead had been installed in a prominent location in the quadrangle in front of the auditorium. From time to time, rival schools attempted to abduct Bumstead as a prank. One night, Bumstead was removed to the campus of Arizona State College, and the veterans overreacted. According to Hannelly:

> When the PC students, who at that time contained hundreds of World War II veterans,

heard of Bumstead's wherabouts, they prepared a caravan to Tempe to recover their beloved property. About 200 of them took off in every kind of vehicle, including a four-wheel drive truck equipped with lifting winches and chain pulleys. I heard about the excursion just as it left.

I headed for Tempe by a different route and I am sure that I exceeded the speed limit on the way. I was standing beside Bumstead when they arrived. The reason they were delayed was because they had stopped at a junkyard on Washington Street to buy some pieces of pipe. I hesitate to think of what use they expected to make of them. Suffice it to say, they were not even tempted to use them.

The PC students backed their powerful truck in toward Bumstead. The ground was wet. The tires made deep ruts. The Tempe students in the vicinity watched with mild interest. Probably none of them helped to place the bear there. Amid cheers, the truck and caravan left Tempe. After this episode, we had a top-level conference on how to avoid another episode. In time we dug out a truncated pyramid of space in the ground and filled it

Bear Tracks, December 6, 1946: "JC students rise in protest at high prices charged at the cafeteria."

December 19, 1995, video interview with Zeno Johnson, Mesa Community College faculty and PUHS Class of 1948. Transcript and audio excerpts available online.

http://www.mc.maricopa.edu/users/M3cdhistory/

> *institutions. This school is mature enough and scholastically high enough to deserve the title of at least "City College" if not big enough for a four-year institution.*

Apparently, that criticism hit home. During the summer of 1947, the school board dropped the word "Junior" from the name of the school. Beginning in the fall of 1947, the official name of the school became just Phoenix College.

with cement. We also filled the hollow plaster of Paris bear with [concrete] and installed reinforcing steel rods to hold the two blocks of [concrete] together.

Bumstead resisted further transportation, but he fell victim to malicious vandalism in the succeeding years. Eventually, his remains were buried with full honors, including a mock funeral oration which Hannelly delivered.

ONE DAY LAST WEEK SOME OF JC'S SMALL-TOWN "FANS" TOOK OLD BUMSTEAD AS A SOUVENIR AND "FORGOT" TO RETURN IT. SOO . . . OVER A HUNDRED LOYAL BEARS INDIGNANTLY ENTRAINED FOR ENEMY TERRITORY AND "LUGGED 'IM BACK."

BATTERED, BRUISED, AND FLAUNTING A BADLY APPLIED COAT OF PAINT, BUMSTEAD STANDS AGAIN—UNBOWED, UNBROKEN—ON THE JC CAMPUS.

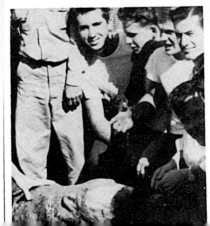

Then, the veterans started agitating for PJC to be made a four-year college. According to an article on the front page of the February 21, 1947, *Bear Tracks*, the student leaders approached Montgomery, the president of the college, and Hannelly, the dean, both of whom endorsed the concept. Subsequently, the PJC faculty met and approved the idea, and a committee headed by Montgomery presented the draft of a bill to State Representative Bob Hart. On February 17, he introduced HB 208 in the state legislature. In essence the bill would have permitted any Arizona junior college (of which only two were then in existence) to change itself into a four-year school.

The bill quickly died in committee and never resurfaced. One reason may have stemmed from the fact that two years earlier, the state legislature had been persuaded that the University of Arizona was not going to be able to handle all the returning veterans. On March 9, 1945, the legislature had officially upgraded the two state teachers colleges to full-fledged state colleges empowered to offer bachelor's degrees in arts and sciences. In

Below: Students moving Bumstead to new campus in 1939. PC Alumni scrapbook, courtesy of Joseph F. Heald.

Left: From Bear Tracks for November 1, 1946. The photos and text seem to describe the incident that Hannelly recalls.

1947, many students were beginning to have automobiles, and therefore, Phoenix students could live at home and commute to the state college in Tempe to complete a four-year degree. Thus, the present supply of four-year schools in the state seemed adequate.

Another reason the bill died may have been the way the bill's proponents underestimated Phoenix College's desire to remain a junior college. In 1946, *Look* magazine had honored Phoenix Junior College as one of the best in America. Many students and faculty agreed. Zeno Johnson, for instance, feels that Phoenix College was the highlight of his educational career:

> I still think, frankly, I got a better education by going my first two years [to Phoenix College]. I have five degrees now, and the one I am, frankly, most proud of is my AA degree from Phoenix College. And the other degrees include a Bachelor of Divinity from the Episcopal Theological School, and Harvard Divinity at Cambridge, you know, and all that sort of thing. My Ph.D. is from ASU, but I mean . . . I look back on it, and really, I am just almost moved to tears as I think about the joy that I felt when I graduated from Phoenix Junior College in the old Encanto Bowl.

In sum, the junior college was just fine the way it was. Why risk turning one of the country's best two-year colleges into a mediocre four-year college?

One other veterans' initiative did bring about a permanent change in the college. Previously, the school had only awarded a certificate of graduation, not an actual associate's degree. An editorial in the March 14, 1947 *Bear Tracks* asked why and noted that 71% of the public junior colleges were graduating students with the Associate of Arts degree. The article then went on to state:

Recent studies of the Commission on Junior College Terminal Education indicate that approximately three-fourths of the young people who enter junior colleges never go beyond the junior college with their formal education. Now, if that be true, then the terminal student does not achieve the degree of acknowledgment for his two-year studies that the transfer student is able to receive later on in his education. The associate's degree represents the only academic degree the terminal student will ever receive.

Ironically, the reason Phoenix College had not offered the associate's degree is clearly implied in this paragraph. In contrast to patterns at other junior colleges, Phoenix College still saw its mission primarily as serving transfer students, not so-called "terminal" students. That certificate of graduation from Phoenix Junior College had proven to be a valid ticket for entry to virtually any university that PJC graduates had wanted to attend. The idea of serving "terminal" students at Phoenix College was new.

The Phoenix College catalog for the 1947-48 school year does not contain any mention of the AA degree, but newspaper accounts confirm that Phoenix College began conferring the AA degree at the graduation exercises held in May of 1948. The Phoenix College Bulletin-Catalog for 1948-49 is the first one to include the words, "The Associate in Arts degree is conferred on all students who are graduated from Phoenix College."

The Evening College Returns

Other seeds of change were being planted at night. After the passage of the GI Bill in 1944, Wyman decided that the time had come to reinstate the evening college. No formal board action was required to reactivate the program, so Wyman simply proposed the idea to Montgomery, who supported the idea in principle but insisted that the program had to be self-supporting. He probably assumed that most of the night students would be veterans subsidized by the GI Bill, and therefore, tuition would not be a burden for them. So, the evening college was resurrected in the fall of 1944.

The revival of the evening college was the beginning of a significant evolutionary shift because the evening college challenged the way the institution saw itself. Previously, the mission of the junior college—not to mention the whole basis of its funding—had been to educate students who attended classes full-time during the day.

Part-time, adult students attending evening classes were welcome, but they fell outside the junior college's traditional mission. The high school was already offering night school classes for paying adults who wanted courses in office skills and self-improvement. With few exceptions, working adults past traditional college age were assumed to be people who didn't want to attend or weren't capable of attending college. Mildred Bulpitt concurs: "People did not think of older students coming back to school. They just didn't. Think of the way that a lot of people treated them when they came back in the '50s. They were not treated very nicely, a lot of them, to begin with. Faculty members didn't welcome them. It just wasn't done." No one had yet realized just how many adults might also want to enroll at a junior college to pursue the first two years of a four-year degree.

But the evening college soon made its presence felt. During the fall of 1944, eighteen classes in the evening college were offered to test the waters, and a total of 190 students enrolled. Evening enrollment then increased almost every year, and in the 1952-53 school year, for the first time, there were more students attending class at night than during the day.

Hannelly Becomes Dean

In the fall of 1946, Harry Wyman suddenly announced that he would retire at the end of that school year. His announced purpose was to devote more time to "writing on educational subjects." At age 52, he was really too young to retire. As the accompanying text box indicates, however, his career was far from over. The truth is that he was probably weary from all the upheaval of the postwar years.

In December, the board announced its intention to promote one of its most distinguished faculty members to become the next dean of the college: Dr. Robert Hannelly, then the head of the math department. He officially became the dean of Phoenix College in May of 1947.

Hannelly quickly expanded the offerings of the evening college. Previously, the schedule of course offerings had been determined by what courses faculty members wanted to teach in the evening to earn additional money. Hannelly encouraged the department chairs to schedule courses based on student need and interest and, if full-time faculty couldn't be found to cover the needed sections, to hire part-time faculty.

By 1950, almost all of the essential programs offered during the day were also taught at night. The rising significance of the evening college may be seen by comparing enrollment figures of the day and evening programs during the evening college's first ten years.

The evening students forever changed the focus and direction of Phoenix Junior College. When the evening college published its first bulletin in 1952, the slogan on the cover read, "A Community College for Community Needs." This bulletin marks the first time the phrase "community college" had been formally linked to Phoenix College.

Dr. Wyman Attains New Post, Leaves PJC After 16 Years

May 28, 1947

After sixteen years as dean of Phoenix Junior College, Dr. Harry B. Wyman, one of Arizona's foremost educators, retires this spring to take over the duties of assistant state superintendent of public instruction.

In the new post, which he will take over in September, he will serve as head of the division of education and director or secondary education. One of his chief responsibilities will be the certification of teachers, and the major part of his time will be spent working with the individual schools of the state.

Dr. Wyman received his doctor's degree from Ohio State University where he wrote his thesis under Dr. Boyd H. Bode, who is known in the field of education as a persistent advocate of newer and better things. He did his post-doctoral work at Columbia University.

Early in his career he worked as a chemist with the B. F. Goodrich Co. Each summer since 1933, Dr. Wyman has either taught or served as a consultant for some educational or industrial institution. Before coming to Phoenix in 1931 he supervised practice teaching for Ohio State.

Dr. Wyman has left Phoenix Junior College an inheritance of fine, progressive educational methods — methods which have put the school to the forefront of the nation's two year institutions. Students and faculty members alike deeply regret the loss of the "Dean" but at the same time feel that he is capable of proving a valuable asset to the public schools of Arizona and is deserving of the best wishes of all.

Good luck, Dean. We'll miss you.

Reproduction of Bear Tracks article from May 28, 1947.

YEAR	DAY DIVISION	EVENING DIVISION	TOTAL
1946-47	1084	305	1389
1947-48	1246	192	1438
1948-49	1108	336	1444
1949-50	1190	485	1675
1950-51	1084	566	1650
1951-52	984	667	1651
1952-53	906	929	1835
1953-54	1041	1072	2113
1954-55	1322	1159	2481
1955-56	1585	2010	3595

Phoenix College Fall Enrollment 1946-1956.

April 4, 1996, video interview with Mildred Bulpitt, dean of Phoenix College's evening division 1961-1978. Transcript and audio excerpts available online.

http://www.mc.maricopa.edu/users/M3cdhistory/

WYMAN AFTER PHOENIX COLLEGE

Wyman's career after his tenure at Phoenix College didn't go as he predicted. In the spring of 1947, Wyman abandoned the idea of writing and accepted an offer to become assistant state superintendent of public instruction and director of education and secondary education, effective in September of that year. According to an article in the Phoenix Gazette for March 18, 1966, things got interesting then. In October of 1947 — after barely a month as assistant superintendent — Wyman was given an indefinite leave of absence to accept the position of chief of public education in Berlin, Germany, under the Office of Military Government of the United States. His task there was to help rebuild the public school system in Germany after the Nazis had all but destroyed it.

When the Office of Military Government was disbanded in 1949, Wyman joined the US Foreign Service and continued to work with the German schools until 1952, when he moved to Washington to work for the Bureau of Education and Cultural Affairs. In 1957, he became the area director of cultural exchange with Europe; this job entailed working with the Fulbright program to bring foreign students and teachers to the United States. From 1959 to 1961, he was the area director of the African cultural exchange program, and from 1961 until he really retired in 1966, he was deputy chief of the foreign currency staff. Briefly, then, he returned to Phoenix College as a substitute teacher in sociology and psychology. He died in April, 1977.

45

1947

Dr. Robert Hannelly, *dean of Phoenix College 1947-1965.*

Millie Noble in 1955. Between 1947 and 1983, she served Phoenix College and the Maricopa district in many different capacities, including secretary to the dean, coordinator of professional personnel, and district manager of certificated personnel.

"She was the one [who] really ran that college. It was Millie Noble. You didn't go see Hannelly, you went to see Millie Noble."

— Gene Eastin

Chapter Five

1958

ENABLING *the* ENABLING *Legislation*

W hen Robert Hannelly was offered the position of dean of Phoenix College in 1946, he was probably as surprised as anyone. He was a scholar, not an administrator. Born in 1901 in Clinton, Iowa, he earned his bachelor's degree at Grinnell College in 1923 and his master's degree at Iowa State in 1926. The following year, he began teaching math at Phoenix Junior College while it was still housed in Cottonwood Court. In 1939, he received a Ph.D. in mathematics education from the University of Colorado. His administrative experience had been limited to chairing the math department and advising the Associated Students.

So, why was Hannelly offered the job? The reason is that Wyman's resignation had been completely unexpected, and with the student veterans causing all manner of upset, the board probably didn't want to bring in an outsider. Someone was needed who understood Phoenix College well and who had good people skills. At the same time, Hannelly appeared to have all the qualifications of a good college president. His academic credentials were impeccable. He was tall but soft-spoken, and he had a good sense of humor. The students liked him, the veterans liked him, and the faculty liked him.

Unfortunately, Hannelly's credentials were not matched by his administrative skills. Many people interviewed for this book recalled that while Hannelly was dean of Phoenix College, the person who took care of all the administrative details was his secretary, Millie Noble. She began working at Phoenix College in the fall of 1946 as the Veterans' Coordinator, and in the fall of 1955, she became the secretary to the dean. Gene Eastin, a longtime faculty member at Glendale Community College and later a member of the Maricopa governing board, stated flatly, "She was the one [who] really ran that college. It was Millie Noble. You didn't go see Hannelly, you went to see Millie Noble." Al Flowers, who became the finance director for the Phoenix Union High School District in 1958, recalls that where the budget was concerned, "We did everything for [Hannelly]. He was an academic head. I did their budgets. We did all their accounting. We did all their payroll. Did everything for them centrally. . . . He was in a different world."

In all fairness, though, Phoenix College really didn't need the dean to be a strong administrator. E. W. Montgomery was still president of the college, and Hannelly was always under his authority. If Hannelly didn't deal well with administrative matters, he did deal well with people. He avoided confrontation and preferred to try to build consensus

through good communication. To that end, one of Hannelly's first innovations when he took over in 1947 was to institute a weekly bulletin distributed to all faculty members. These bulletins continued throughout his tenure as dean at Phoenix College, and they represent a remarkable record of the day-to-day affairs of the college. Every event of any consequence to the school was included. Millie Noble, who typed the bulletins every week, recalls they were widely read:

For a while there, Hannelly didn't think so, and I said, "I'll make you a deal." He said, "What do you want to do?" I said, "In the middle of one of these little epistles, I'm going to put a little note: 'First one that reads this, bring it in and I'll give you a dollar.'" Head of the Chemistry Department brought it in, old Arthur Phelps. So, after that, you know, they would always read 'em because they didn't know if there was going to be something buried!

Many people in the district today have stories to tell about how well Hannelly communicated with others. Charles Evans recalls his job interview with Hannelly in 1963:

I sat outside his office for maybe two or three minutes—kind of getting a little more nervous all the time about what this great man was going to be like and how awed I would be by him. I was ushered into his office, and he rose from behind his

1947

elevator? You've requested both, and we have enough money for one." And I said, "You know, I wouldn't want you to think that I'm disrespectful, but," I said, "I have to laugh at this request. We need both of those things." And I said, "If I have to choose one of those things, I'll choose an elevator because there's nothing heavier than books. You've got to get 'em up and down." But you know, they didn't hurt me too much because later on, I brought in a request for the carpet, and they put that in the library at the same time.

Millie Noble in 1995. In that year, Phoenix College renamed the Science Building, which appears behind her, in her honor. Photo from the Phoenix Gazette, October 11, 1995.

April 18, 1996, audio interview with Millie Noble. Transcript available online.

http://www.mc.maricopa.edu/users/M3cdhistory/

"Sometimes things didn't go the way (Hannelly) wanted them to go, but I'll say one thing for him: he'd make a decision, and, whatever decision he made, he stuck by it."

desk and reached across and shook my hand. "Mr. Evans, so nice to meet you. Sit down right over there, please." And then he sat back down behind his desk, put his feet up on his desk, and said, "Mr. Evans, I hope you don't mind if I put my feet up on my desk." He said, "I find that it relaxes me after a day of golf." And you know, I didn't for a minute believe that he'd been playing golf. But it was such a nice way that he had of relaxing a person who might have been under some stress coming into his office. From that moment on, I just unbuttoned my coat and sat back and relaxed with him, and we just chatted. And that was my introduction to Robert Hannelly.

As Evans' anecdote suggests, Hannelly liked to put people at their ease. When faced with a difficult situation, Hannelly persuaded by indirection. An anecdote from Hannelly's years as president of the Maricopa district illustrates this tendency. At one point, the members of the Maricopa governing board demanded Hannelly justify his budget requests for the new Phoenix College library. When interviewed by Glendale Community College journalism professor Robert Wilcox, Hannelly recalled:

> The board said to me, "You made a pretty big request on this library at Phoenix College." I said, "Yeah, and we need it." And the president of the board said, "What would you rather have? Would you rather have carpets in the library or an

The story is quintessential Hannelly. He was a true man of reason. Rather than arguing with other people or throwing his weight around, he preferred simply to state the facts and let people come around to the right conclusion. If they didn't come around at first, then he would simply withdraw from the field and wait until they did.

Thompson and Prince

Hannelly's personality opposite at Phoenix College was J. Lee Thompson, whom Hannelly brought to Phoenix College to serve as the registrar in 1948. Thompson was Hannelly's enforcer. Born in Douglas, Arizona, in 1911, Thompson earned his BA

J. Lee Thompson, Registrar of Phoenix College 1945-60. From the Phoenix College yearbook Sandprints, 1955.

all over the county and the state. And I said, I believe that's a guy I'd like to have. So I hired him out of that department. And he was kind of rough, you know. He pushed people the wrong way, but I needed a little bit of that at the time. I needed someone with a firm hand because this was a pretty loose operation here. And Thompson was equal to the task.

In addition to serving as registrar, Thompson was also given the responsibility of overseeing the evening college. By 1954, the enrollment at the college exceeded 2,000 students for the first time—and more than half of those students were taking classes at night. Thompson protested that his dual responsi-

but his employment there was interrupted by a tour of duty with the United States Naval Reserve. In 1946, he was honorably discharged at the rank of Lieutenant Commander and returned to Phoenix Union. In 1948, Prince became a faculty member in the English department at Phoenix College.

Many people interviewed for this book have memories both pro and con of John Prince, but all agree that he projected an air of dignity and authority. Glenn Groenke, a former English faculty member at Mesa and Scottsdale Community Colleges, recalls that Prince was the epitome of a college English professor:

> Prince looked presidential and he spoke well. . . . And you know how people used to be with English teachers. They could quote Chaucer . . . or mention a little Shakespeare. All the people who were the number crunchers or the people who really couldn't read, they would say, "Oh, there's an English teacher! You better be careful of your language!" We were held in high esteem at that time.

Robert Wilcox's 1984 audio interview with Robert Hannelly. Transcript and audio excerpts available online.

"Once in a while, (the board) threw me a curve . . . But there's lots of ways of skinning the cat."

http://www.mc.maricopa.edu/users/M3cdhistory/

from the Arizona State Teachers College at Flagstaff in 1934 and his MA from the University of Arizona in 1940. Before coming to Phoenix College, Thompson had extensive experience as a school principal in several different Arizona schools. He was inducted into the Army in 1943, where he taught for about a year in the Ninth Service Command Special Training Center for Illiterates.

Speaking to Wilcox, Hannelly explained why he had chosen Thompson:

> [After the war], he was working in the state department of education and was the certification officer, and I heard he was being pretty tough on these teachers who did not meet the requirements of the state. . . . And they were bragging about it

bilities were too much for one person alone. He then asked for another Phoenix College faculty member, John Prince, to become the assistant director of the evening college program.

John Prince was born in Flint, Michigan, in 1911. A year later, his parents moved to Phoenix, where he attended St. Mary's grade school and Brophy Preparatory. In 1935, he was graduated from Phoenix College—he may even have been one of Hannelly's students. He transferred to the University of Arizona, where he earned his BA in 1937 and his MA in 1938. Returning to Phoenix, he taught English and coached tennis at Tolleson High School until 1941. In 1942, he transferred to Phoenix Union High School,

John Prince, Phoenix College English faculty 1948-55 and chair of the evening program 1955-60. From Phoenix College yearbook Sandprints, 1955.

At some point after joining the faculty at Phoenix College, John Prince apparently decided that he wanted to move up into administration.

Sept. 7, 1996, audio interview with Glenn Groenke, former Mesa and Scottsdale Community College faculty member. Transcript available online.

> "There were two colleges, really: there was the day college and the evening colleges, two separate identities vying with each other."

However, the Phoenix Union High School board would not consider Prince for an administrative position because Prince sent his children to Catholic schools instead of public schools. Al Flowers recalls:

Now, I worked with those board members there, so I'm telling you firsthand, not secondhand. And one of them said, "Anybody who wants to be an administrator in this district, especially a principal, and doesn't even send his own kids to the public schools is never going to be one." Made no bones about it. . . . Certain board members said, "We've got a good district here, one of the best in the country," which Phoenix Union was. "Send your kids to the public school, or forget about promotion in this district. You're not going to get it."

And the matter might have ended there, but J. Lee Thompson and Prince were friends, and Thompson—who apparently didn't bother asking the board's permission—simply announced Prince would be his assistant chair. Nobody wanted to argue with Thompson, so in the fall of 1954, Prince began to divide his time between his teaching and his administrative responsibilities.

The fact that Thompson first promoted Prince into administration and not Hannelly

may have caused Prince to be somewhat resentful toward Hannelly. Al Flowers recalls, "That was something that, I believe, was between Hannelly and Prince as a burr under the saddle." However, John Prince's daughter Mary Martha feels strongly that Hannelly never openly opposed Prince's career in any way: "I can only tell you that I never knew Bob Hannelly to be anything but supportive of my dad. I think he was a mentor; I think he enabled him in every way to continue in whatever his ambitions were."

Prince quickly warmed to being an administrator and was soon ready for more authority. In her dissertation on the history of the evening college program at Phoenix College, Mildred Bulpitt stated, "J. Lee Thompson recalls that the half-time Chairman [Prince] told him that he actually found himself teaching as a part-time activity since the evening college operation demanded so much of his time."

In 1955, Hannelly promoted Thompson to be the new dean of instruction for Phoenix College. The college got a new registrar, and John Prince then became the full-time chair of the evening college.

Around this time, Prince also began work on a Ph.D. at the University of Arizona. He had apparently decided that if he were going to rise much higher in administration, he would need a doctorate, which he earned in 1960. [1]

The Movement for More Junior Colleges

During the 1950s, the population of the city of Phoenix exploded. In 1950, fewer than 100,000 people called Phoenix their home; ten short years later, over 400,000 people made that claim. Almost all parts of Arizona saw similar growth during the same decade. Demographic projections indicated that one state university, two state colleges, and two junior colleges were not going to be sufficient to handle the growing demand for public higher education in Arizona. Something had to be done. Thus, a movement began for more junior colleges. Yet, the people supporting this idea would take many wrong turns before discovering the right path to follow.

One reason for the wrong turns was that the junior college movement in Arizona lacked a real leader. By all rights, Bob Hannelly should have been that person. He could see the problem coming, and he knew what the answer to the problem should be. When interviewed by Robert Wilcox in the early '80s, Hannelly explained:

I realized that our system was not right. First, there wasn't enough state money going into it, and secondly, there weren't enough junior college advantages for the children of the state. . . . If they lived in Phoenix, they could go to Phoenix College, and if they lived in the Safford area, they could go to Eastern Arizona, but that was it. The children of Yuma and even those in Tucson didn't have a chance at the junior college.

Note the fact that Hannelly saw the need for junior colleges in terms of the "children of the state," not the adults. At least, not yet.

---

[1] As previously noted, John Prince wrote his dissertation on the career of Phoenix Union High School's legendary superintendent E. W. Montgomery. Zeno Johnson speculates that Prince probably saw Montgomery as a role model. Certainly, Prince did not see Hannelly that way. Their two administrative styles were worlds apart.

As dean of one of the most highly esteemed junior colleges in America, Hannelly was often in demand as a speaker at Arizona functions, and his favorite topic was the need for more junior colleges in Arizona. Millie Noble recalls Hannelly "was always pushing. He was talking to the service clubs—Kiwanis, the Rotary Clubs, and all this—that we needed to promote the community college concept. He had a powerful voice in the community. He was very well-known, and he just kept pushing."

Unfortunately (but characteristically), Hannelly stopped just short of advocating a specific solution to the problem. A true academic, he seemed to prefer discussing the problem to solving it. Lawrence Walkup, president of Arizona State College at Flagstaff (later NAU) during these same years, confirms this view. "Hannelly was never a man who stuck his neck out, but he had good insight into junior college legislation. He wasn't a leader in the political arena. . . . He played it safe. He didn't take leadership in issues."

Nevertheless, people in Arizona were listening to Hannelly's message—especially people in Arizona's rural counties. They began to think more and more about the desirability of having junior colleges in their towns to assist their sons and daughters to transfer to one of the state's four-year schools. Of course, the

original 1927 junior college legislation was still on the books, but the rural counties didn't want their high schools to add college-level work; they wanted to establish full-scale junior colleges like Phoenix College and Eastern Arizona. To accomplish this goal, state legislation would be necessary to provide state funding.

In 1956, Harold Giss, a state senator and prominent merchant in the Yuma area, took the first step in this direction. On February 24, Giss introduced SB 142, entitled "Junior College at Yuma or Elsewhere, Permitting Creating." The bill would have provided funding to create a junior college in Yuma and establish machinery for the creation of junior colleges in other areas. Because of its narrow focus, the bill created as many problems as it solved. Not surprisingly, it died in committee. Polly Rosenbaum, whose forty-plus years in the Arizona State House of

Representatives began in 1949, suggests that Giss may even have expected his bill to fail. "He was very adept at knowing how to do things, and he probably introduced that bill knowing that it wouldn't go anywhere but to get people thinking about it."

If that were Giss' intention, then the bill was a success. One person who was thinking about it a lot was Lawrence Walkup, then the dean of instruction at Arizona State College at Flagstaff. He admired Giss personally and did not oppose his proposal, but Walkup didn't

State Senator Harold Giss, Arizona state legislator 1949-73. Photo courtesy of Gerald D. Giss.

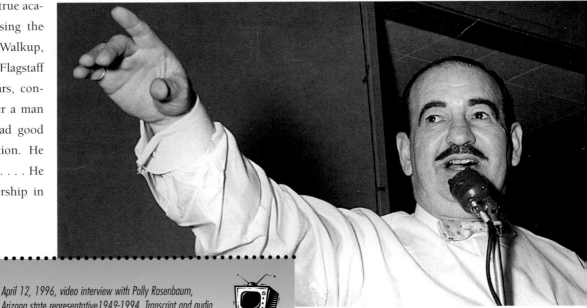

April 12, 1996, video interview with Polly Rosenbaum, Arizona state representative1949-1994. Transcript and audio excerpts available online.

http://www.mc.maricopa.edu/users/M3cdhistory/

like the idea of politicians making policy for higher education. He feared that some kind of pork-barrel legislation establishing junior colleges for political reasons (or as political rewards) might eventually result. For that reason, Walkup decided to convene a committee of prominent Arizona educators to advise the state legislators. To fund this gathering, he applied for a grant from the Kellogg Foundation, which was then operating programs at Stanford University and elsewhere to train future leaders for community colleges.

51

Walkup hosted the conference in Flagstaff from June 18-22, 1956. A significant representation of school superintendents, deans, and other administrators attended, along with State Senators Robert W. Prochnow (who chaired the Joint Educational Study Committee of the legislature) and Harold Giss. After several days of discussions, the group could only agree that establishing a system of junior colleges for Arizona would

J. LAWRENCE WALKUP, *president of Northern Arizona University 1957-79.*

College Plan Needs Study, Meet Agrees

FLAGSTAFF (Special) — Educators who have been meeting here to plan future expansion of Arizona colleges, agreed at a closing meeting yesterday they'd just have to study the subject some more.

"Before we make any recommendation to the legislature," said State Sen. Robert Prochnow (D-Coconino), "more study will have to be made by the joint educational and administrators committee."

Fifteen key educators representing various areas of the state assembled here June 18. They were joined Thursday by Prochnow, who is chairman of the joint education study committee of the state legislature, and the committee.

Discussed was the need to support junior colleges and possible reorganization of the present college system in the state.

The conference was sponsored by Arizona State College, Flagstaff, the W. K. Kellogg Foundation; and the Arizona Association of School Administrators.

The group plans to meet again the last of September or the first of October.

Arizona Republic, June 23, 1956. From microfilm.

be an appropriate and desirable step. To work to that end, the conference participants created the Executive Committee on Education Beyond the High School in Arizona, which Walkup chaired. This committee met again in Flagstaff in October, and Walkup announced the result of a survey he had made of the attendees of the June meeting. Based on the results of that survey, the committee determined a statewide conference was needed to study all sides of the issue more thoroughly. Walkup's committee met again on December 4 at Phoenix College, and several participants (undoubtedly including Hannelly) produced letters asking various legislators to propose the creation of a statewide committee to study the idea of a junior college system for Arizona.

The first signs of opposition then began to appear. The University of Arizona's partisans in the state legislature were determined that the university should not have to compete for students with a completely independent system of junior colleges. To try to avoid that problem, they ignored Walkup's committee's

call for a statewide conference and introduced HB 127 on February 8, 1957. This bill would have empowered the board of regents of the university and the state colleges to take over the state's two existing junior colleges and start more as deemed necessary. The Appropriations Committee eventually recommended this bill for passage, but it was held up in committee and got no further. Walkup speculates that the bill may have failed because the regents themselves did not support this idea. "The board of regents had a lot of [political] clout at that time. . . . It was safe to put [the junior colleges] in their hands, but the board said, 'We've got enough on our hands.' "

The idea of a statewide committee to study a system of junior colleges for Arizona was then proposed. Senate Bill 129 called for "an appropriation to the governor for the purpose of studying the problem of possible locations of junior colleges." The bill passed in the Senate and was introduced in the House as HB 285, but the legislative session was coming to a close. Time ran out, and the bill died in committee.

During the following months, the university and the two state colleges continued to promote the idea that junior colleges should be placed under the authority of the university regents. Lawrence Walkup's *Pride, Promise, Progress* (his history of Northern Arizona University), describes a report that Walkup wrote with Vice President Harold D. Richardson of Arizona State College-Tempe and Vice President Robert L. Nugent of the University of Arizona. They delivered this report to the junior college committee of the regents in 1957. The report recommended that the regents test the waters directly by establishing their own experimental junior college.

When the legislature met again in January of 1958, state representative John Grimes entered the picture with yet another approach. Before being elected to the legislature, Grimes had been a professor of psychology at Arizona State Teachers College in Tempe from 1928-1937, at which time he was named dean of the college. In 1942, Grimes became the founding dean of the summer session, and in 1949, he was made the director of extension, correspondence, and summer school programs. In 1954, he retired from the college and ran successfully for the legislature. Thus, Grimes was a strong advocate for the state's four-year schools, and he believed they should control the junior colleges. On January 17, 1958, Grimes introduced HB 87, which would have authorized the state board of education to set up a study committee. Apparently, the state board was no more enthusiastic about this idea than was the board of regents, and the bill was allowed to expire, but Grimes continued to advocate against an independent junior college system.

Then, the concept of a completely independent fact-finding committee was allowed to come to the fore. On February 13, 1958, the Committee on Education presented HB 238, "relating to education; creating a junior college survey committee to make a survey of junior colleges and related programs for the State of Arizona; providing for the appointment of a director for the survey and other employees and fixing their compensation, and making an appropriation." The proposed survey committee was basically the same one that Grimes had proposed except for the fact that this committee would be completely independent of the regents. The makeup of the committee, however, included the presidents of the state university and the two existing state colleges. That compromise appears to have been sufficient to satisfy Grimes. The bill was promptly passed in both the House and the Senate, and on March 19, the governor signed the bill into law.

This committee consisted of twelve persons, including the three presidents of the four-year schools; the deans of the two existing junior colleges (Hannelly and Guitteau); a member of the Arizona Association of Secondary School Principals; three senators (appointed by the President of the Senate) and three members of the House (appointed by the Speaker of the House). The senators chosen were Robert Prochnow, Neilson Brown, and A. R. Spikes; the representatives chosen were Arthur Schellenberg, Thomas M. Knoles, and E. B. Thode.

When interviewed by Robert Wilcox in 1984, Hannelly recalled that he was delighted with the composition of this committee, but he was even more delighted that the legislature had finally passed education legislation with some money attached to it. "For the first time in my life, I served on a committee which had enough money to operate: $30,000 we had. And you can imagine how a school man perks up his ears at $30,000!"

That money, in part, was to pay for a "qualified professional director" who was not "associated with any state board or institution," a wise stipulation that again prevented the four-year schools from dominating the group. The survey committee met for the first time on March 27, 1958.

Prochnow was elected chairman, and, on June 5, the committee selected Frank R. Lindsay of Sacramento, California, as its director. The committee met seven times, often for two-day sessions, and various subcommittees held additional meetings. The final report was submitted to the legislature in December.

The report that the survey committee produced is filled with tables that indicate projected growth in the state, in the high schools, in the university, etc. These projections confirmed that Arizona's system of higher education was going to be overwhelmed in the next decade. But the report also pointed out,

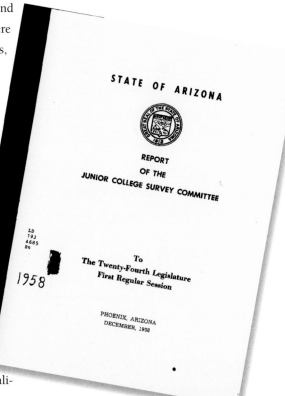

Cover of the published version of the 1958 survey.

Text available online: the "Recommendations" section of Report of the Junior College Survey Committee to the Twenty-Fourth Legislature, First Regular Session.

http://www.mc.maricopa.edu/users/M3cdhistory/

The needs of Arizona business and industry for trained manpower do not require in the instances of many occupations that students complete a four-year curriculum in order to be prepared for initial employment. It has already been noted that sixty per cent of the workers required for the labor force in 1961 can be equipped for employment through training two years or less in length. The institution which has been developed in the United States over the past half century, to perform the dual functions of giving occupational training and the beginning two years of university and college preparation is the public junior college.

This emphasis was significantly different from what Walkup's advisory committee had first recommended. This time, the model of the traditional junior college embraced two-year technical programs in addition to traditional university transfer programs.

However, the junior college legislation met with unexpectedly strong opposition when the state legislature convened in January of 1959. The University of Arizona's partisans had lost the war to keep Arizona State College from becoming a university (see the accompanying text box), and they were determined not to let the junior colleges further infringe on the U of A's turf. Polly Rosenbaum confirms,

In the 1950s, a full-scale war erupted between Arizona State College in Tempe and the University of Arizona in Tucson. Supporters of ASC wanted the state college to be promoted to a state university, but the supporters of the U of A opposed this change—even in the face of the demographic projections that clearly showed that Arizona needed more than one university.

In their history of Arizona State University, Hopkins and Thomas explain how Dr. Ernest V. Hollis, Chief of College Administration for the Office of Education in Arizona, had previously set up a committee to study the matter. In September, 1954, the Hollis report stated, "The State College at Tempe is rapidly becoming a University." The report also criticized "intense rivalry" between the Tucson and Tempe factions. "Where such institutional feuding exists the aggrandizement of the individual institution tends to become the goal, rather than the provision of educational services to meet the needs of the people . . ." In November of 1954, the State Board of Regents accepted Hollis' recommendations that ASC be elevated to university status, but the Tucson forces in the legislature kept this change from ever coming up for a vote.

THE UNIVERSITY WARS, OR TOUCHDOWN IN TEMPE!

Former president of Glendale Community College, John Waltrip was a student at Arizona State College in Tempe at the time, and he remembers the rivalry well:

U of A people didn't want it. It was just a parochial thing, you know. They'd been the university and they didn't want another university here. Very simple. And they didn't want "Arizona" in the name. A lot of the U of A people would have been willing to go along if we'd called it "Tempe University," or something like that, but they really objected to having "Arizona" and "University" both in the title. It was just an attempt by the U of A folks to downgrade [ASC].

In 1958, the junior college bill was pushed aside as the legislators tried to decide whether or not ASC could be renamed as a university. A stalemate resulted, and the legislature adjourned without taking action.

Then, the Phoenix Junior Chamber of Commerce took up the cause. The previous fall, ASC-Tempe had been blessed with a particularly successful football team under the leadership of Coach Dan Devine. To the astonishment of everyone, the team was undefeated in ten games and

March 11, 1996, video interview with John Waltrip, president of Glendale Community College 1975-95. Transcript and audio excerpts available online.

http://www.mc.maricopa.edu/users/M3cdhistory/

They fought it. They contacted alumni and people and said it's bad because it was going to destroy our university system. And I imagine they had a hired lobbyist of some kind, but they didn't lobby me much. They knew I was for it—I was strong for the community colleges. But I am sure people talked to me and said, "Oh, don't you know all the ramifications of this and what it'll do?" And I probably said, "I don't care. It's going to go."

finished its season ranked number twelve nationally. Local boosters began to argue that if the school was capable of producing a football team to rival national universities, then the school, by God, ought to *be* a university!

Realizing that the Tucson forces were too strong in the legislature, the Junior Chamber of Commerce organized a drive to get 40,000 signatures on a petition to force university status for ASC by popular initiative. Arizona State College President Grady Gammage gave his approval in April, 1958, and the fight was on. The name-change proposal went on the November ballot (Proposition 200). Seventy-two percent of the voters turned out, and four out of five voted on the name-change proposal. The vote was 151,135 to 78,693 in favor of the change. Of the negative votes, Pima County (home of the U of A) contributed more than half. Of the state's other thirteen counties, Maricopa passed the measure by an eleven-to-two majority, and ten others favored the change by about three to two. Governor Ernest W. McFarland issued the final proclamation on December 5, 1958. [1]

College football would subsequently reappear as a force in the Maricopa district's history also.

[1] The Arizona Board of Regents approved university status for NAU in 1964, and the legislature approved that recommendation in 1965.

But it didn't go, at least not in 1959. Throughout that year's legislative session, the junior college bill stayed buried in committee. When the legislature met again in 1960, the university wars had been largely forgotten, and the junior college bill finally passed both houses on March 26, 1960. The heart of the legislation, which remains in effect almost unchanged today, allows each county to set up its own junior college system with its own governing board. The local districts are then answerable to a statewide community college board made up of one representative from each county, a member of the board of regents, the state superintendent of public instruction, and the director of the state's division of vocational education. Only the university regents are represented, not the universities themselves. Thus, the new junior college system was given the freedom to follow its own destiny without undue influence from the universities.

Executive and administrative responsibilities are divided among the county boards and the state board. For example, the local boards hire their own faculty and staff and set salaries, but the state board certifies all junior college teachers and approves each local district's annual budget. The local districts and the state board are to work together to find appropriate sites for new colleges, but the state board makes the final selection and holds the title to the land. The local boards hire architects and contractors, but the state board gives final approval of the plans before construction begins. The local districts write their own curriculum, but it must be approved by the state board. And so forth.

The bill stated that funding for junior college districts was to come primarily from two sources. Half should come directly from the state, the exact amount based on the annual enrollment measured in FTSE (Full-Time Student Equivalent); the other half should come from countywide property tax levies. (Unfortunately, the state has never paid its full share, and that problem caused some of Arizona community colleges' darkest hours in the early '80s.)

The plan was so good that even John Grimes voted for the bill, but he requested that the *Journal of the House* contain an explanation of his vote. He said, in part:

A new junior college board will result only in confusion. The State Board of Education and the Board of Regents are sufficient. The survey committee recommended a third board because some members disliked the Regents, and others the State Board. They said they could later put colleges under the State Board when reorganized. The board membership is the worst possible. One from each county fighting for his own county or section bids fair to end in disaster.

Grimes was wrong. He was clinging to William Rainey Harper's belief that the fundamental purpose of junior colleges was to serve the needs of the universities. From that point of view, the junior colleges should have been put under the control of the state regents. But as the following chapters show, the junior colleges were going to follow a very different destiny from anything Harper had envisioned.

1959

They were all used to long hours and hard work, and both were required because the new Maricopa County Junior College District had no operating funds and no paid staff until the beginning of the fiscal year in July, 1963. In spite of the considerable demands of their own careers, these board members agreed to meet weekly for the first six months to stand the district on its feet.

Once the enabling legislation had been approved, the new state board had to be established before any new junior college districts could be created. Polly Rosenbaum remembers that Governor Fannin took special care in the initial appointments to this board:

> *[Governor] Paul Fannin . . . personally talked with the representatives of each county as for their suggestion as to whom they would nominate. And I remember talking with him, and I said, "Democrat or Republican?" And he said, "I don't care. I want the best person for the job." And that was the way they wanted it.*

Hannelly recalls that once the board members had been appointed, he was called upon to help them organize. He told Wilcox:

> *When the state association was formed, the state board hired me two-fifths of my time to put the state organization into operation, and when I got out of there, I had to get the board nominations for an executive secretary, the job that I had been doing. So, I told them Prince would be a good man.*

The first governing board: (from left to right) Jim Miller, Bob Jaap, Bob Easley, Lester Hogan, and Dwight Patterson.

Hannelly's role in Prince's appointment to the state board has long been an object of speculation. Former faculty member Glenn Groenke recalls, "I never knew if Hannelly recommended Prince to get rid of him or if he recommended him because he thought he would be good for the job." Other people speculate whether Hannelly had any influence at all on Prince's appointment. Al Flowers maintains, "Dr. Hannelly went to bat for Dr. Prince to put him out in the state office. And that was a critical factor in Jack Prince getting that job out there."

On the other hand, Prince's daughter Mary Martha discounts the importance of Hannelly's influence. She feels that Joe Ralston, the state board's initial representative from Maricopa County, was more influential. "Joe had worked with my dad off and on. They had known each other since after the [Second World] War. He had watched his career."

One way or another, John Prince left Phoenix College in the summer of 1960 to become the first executive director of the state board. Initially, the state board concerned itself with internal matters of organization, but not for long. Voters in Yuma, Cochise, and Pinal Counties approved the creation of junior college districts in 1961, and Mary Martha Prince recalls that her father soon had his hands full:

> *He drove a lot in those days. . . . I think he established four to five campuses during those years. He worked very hard, he was very diligent. What I found interesting was he was alone. He reported to the board, and he made suggestions to the board—he and Claire Cahill, who was his secretary. . . . But literally, if you read those early minutes, they barely had tables to start out with.*

Maricopa's First Governing Board

Within a year of the passage of the enabling legislation, the Junior College Citizens' Advisory Committee formed for the purpose of organizing an election to create a junior college district in Maricopa County. The election was held on November 6, 1962, and the measure passed by a margin of five to two.

Arizona Republic, November 4, 1962. From microfilm.

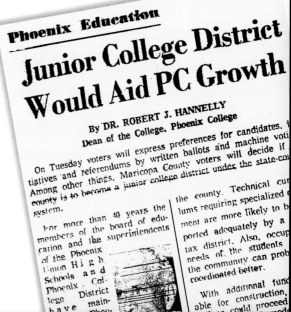

Phoenix Education

Junior College District Would Aid PC Growth

By DR. ROBERT J. HANNELLY
Dean of the College, Phoenix College

On Tuesday voters will express preferences for candidates, initiatives and referendums by written ballots and machine voting. Among other things, Maricopa County voters will decide if county is to become a junior college district under the state-county system.

For more than 40 years the members of the board of education and the superintendents of the Phoenix Union High Schools and Phoenix College District maintain . . . the county. Technical curriculums requiring specialized equipment are more likely to be supported adequately by a tax district. Also, occupational needs of the students and the community can probably be coordinated better.

With additional funds available for construction, could proceed . . .

Robert M. Jaap, Maricopa governing board 1962-68.

Dr. Robert F. Easley, Maricopa governing board 1962-71.

W. James Miller, Maricopa governing board 1962-75.

The county superintendent of education, John Barry, was responsible for appointing the first five people to serve on the new district's governing board:

Robert Jaap was a vice president at First National Bank of Arizona, which actively encouraged its officers to participate in public service. When interviewed for this book, Jaap could not recall why Barry tapped him for service: "I was not in educational circles at the time. I was more in parks' circles at the time. I was one of four or five people who founded the Arizona state parks system, and so my name might have been recognized in that context."

Robert Easley was a physician from the Glendale area and the only original board member to have attended Phoenix College (for one semester after WWII). He had also participated in the Citizens' Advisory Committee. Easley explained that he had been in the same Rotary Club with Glendale's elementary schools superintendent and the principal of Glendale High School. They had heard Easley give a pro-education speech at a Rotary luncheon, and they suggested his name to Barry for the new junior college governing board.

Treasurer for the Del Webb Corporation, Jim Miller was the board member most knowledgeable about financial matters. Al Flowers remembers that the other board members tended to defer to Miller's judgment whenever decisions about money had to be made: "As long as he was sold, we would go to the board meeting, and the rest of them would go along with it. . . . He also was very, very close with the buck. But he was not completely unreasonable, especially if I could spend an hour with him and really hash it out."

Barry's fourth choice for appointment to the new board was C. Lester Hogan, a research scientist and administrator at Motorola. Easley remembers, "Hogan had a fantastic mind. Unfortunately, he didn't have the opportunity to spend too much time with us. He was in the process of building a new electronics plant in France, and he commuted back and forth. So, he would be here for a board meeting and then gone for a board meeting or two. And when he'd come back, he'd have the facility to know what had happened from reading the minutes."

A native of Tempe, Dwight Patterson grew up in Peoria, Arizona, and went to school at

Arizona State College at Flagstaff for three years. He was on the coaching staff there for several years before he married Louise Dobson, of the Dobson Ranch family, and returned to Mesa, where he became involved in the Dobson family business. He retained a strong interest in sports and became something of a local celebrity in 1952 when he convinced the Chicago Cubs to move their spring training camp from Catalina Island to Mesa's Rendezvous Park. Many people credit him with the creation of Cactus League baseball in Arizona.

From this group of individuals—initially strangers to each other—a strong group personality soon emerged.

First, they were all used to long hours and hard work, and both were required because the new Maricopa County Junior College district had no operating funds and no paid staff until the beginning of the fiscal year in July. In spite of the considerable demands on their own careers, these board members agreed to meet weekly for the first six months to stand the district on its feet.

Dr. C. Lester Hogan, Maricopa governing board 1962-66.

Dwight Patterson, Maricopa governing board 1962-75.

Purposes and Programs in Phoenix College by Robert Hannelly, included in the minutes of the December 27, 1962, governing board meeting. Complete text available online.

http://www.mc.maricopa.edu/users/M3cdhistory/

Second, all executive authority for the new district began in the hands of the new governing board. Four of the five were already executives; they were used to making decisions, taking command, and hiring and firing. Months would go by before the first district president would be appointed, and by then, the pattern of the governing board actually running the district had already been well established.

Third, the new board members were all educated, but they were not themselves educators. Of the entire group, only Dwight Patterson had any previous school board experience. Al Flowers makes this point forcibly:

> They dealt in numbers, not in educational values. They didn't even want to talk about them. We used to try to insist upon having an educational presentation at a board meeting, and they finally made us stop that. According to them, we were wasting time. They didn't want to hear about those programs unless they had time to go visit the colleges. . . . It was a typical business-type atmosphere.

The New Board Begins to Function

The five original governing board members met for the first time on December 12, 1962,

in the Kiva Club at the Westward Ho Hotel in Phoenix. They promptly elected Jaap as the chair and Patterson as the secretary.

The first order of business was to orchestrate the district's takeover of Phoenix College. According to the minutes of the meeting December 18, 1962, Hannelly described the college to the new board members (or "greenhorns" as Patterson called them):

> Dr. Hannelly stated that PC has 120 daytime teachers on the faculty, in addition to clerical, cafeteria workers, etc.—all who are gravely concerned with their future. They would like assurance that their salaries will not be less than those already established. The average salary of the teachers at PC is $7,200, and the average training of their teachers is 1.2 years beyond the master's degree. . . . There is a teacher for every 26 students and the ratio for clerical help is 170 students to one employee.

Hannelly added that the enrollment at Phoenix College had grown to 3,400 students in the daytime programs and an astonishing 3,700 students in the evening program. Several terminal two-year courses of study

were available, and fully one-third of the total enrollment was in those programs. An even more remarkable statistic was that 10% of the most recent graduating class had completed their course work entirely at night.

Assuming Ownership of Phoenix College

The PUHS District had a significant investment in Phoenix College, and the PUHS board decided that they could not simply surrender the facilities to the new district. On January 8, 1963, voters within the PUHS district were asked to authorize the sale of Phoenix College. The voters assented and the price tag was set at $2.5 million.

At the meeting following the January 8 election, the Maricopa board resolved that "the junior college program be extended countywide under the supervision of the present administration at Phoenix College, in order that there may be equitable educational opportunity for the students of Maricopa County as far as is practicable, until additional colleges are available." In other words, they wanted to start Phoenix College extension campuses in temporary quarters in the fall of 1963 and later decide where to place new permanent colleges.

But how many extension campuses were needed? Where would they be located? How large should they be? Before Maricopa County had conducted its election to decide a Maricopa county junior college system should be created, the state board had commissioned Arizona Education Consultants (a consulting firm comprised primarily of Arizona State University faculty) to conduct a survey and make recommendations. The survey was entitled *Junior Colleges for Maricopa County*. Dr. Merwin Deever, Director of the Bureau of Educational Research and Services at Arizona State University, was the survey director, and he was assisted by four other faculty and staff members from Arizona State University.

The sixty-page survey provided the new district with a complete blueprint. It included detailed recommendations regarding administrative organization, occupational and vocational education, educational programs, sites, facilities, and financial matters.

A curious element of this document is a heavy dose of university paranoia. The document makes several recommendations designed to keep the new junior colleges from encroaching on the state universities' turf. On page six, the authors state:

> The organization should be such
> that each junior college is planned
> for permanence as a junior college,
> without any possibility of transition
> to a four-year institution. In this
> respect, it would be preferable to
> include in each name the words
> "junior college," or, at least, to list
> on all documents information which
> indicates that each unit is a facility
> of the junior college district.

The report urges the Maricopa district to establish several junior colleges enrolling around 2,000 students each. Clearly, the Arizona State University team wanted to see the competition kept small! Given that Phoenix College's daytime enrollment was

already around 3,400 students during the day and another 3,700 attending the evening program, this recommendation seems almost ludicrous.

Subordination to the universities is further emphasized by the recommendation that faculty should be referred to as "instructors" and traditional academic ranks (professor, associate professor, assistant professor, etc.) should be avoided. Honor societies were to be encouraged, but fraternities and sororities (a privilege of the universities) should be forbidden. The report even takes a dim view of athletics:

> It is recommended that stress on inter-
> scholastic sports be limited and that foot-
> ball teams not be fielded for the first few
> years. There should be heavy stress on
> intramural programs and activities such
> as golf and tennis, which have carry-over
> value in adult life.

The heart of the document suggests the number of junior colleges to be built:

> The survey team recommends that, in
> addition to the Phoenix College site, three
> additional junior college sites be purchased
> immediately. Two others should be pur-
> chased later in 1963. Early in 1963 an
> additional piece of land, five to ten acres
> in size, should be obtained for the County
> Administration Center. . . . The survey team
> recommends that plans proceed rapidly for
> the development of Phoenix College and of
> the three new junior colleges. The other
> two sites should be procured within a year
> and should be retained for junior colleges
> needed within the next ten years.

To pay for these new colleges, the survey recommended a $20 million bond election be held in 1963 to (1) purchase Phoenix College,

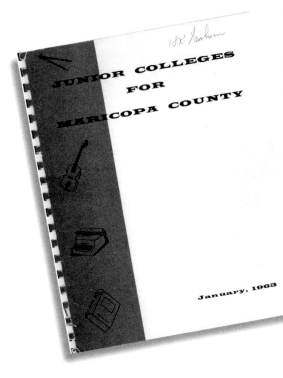

Junior Colleges for Maricopa County, published by Arizona Educational Consultants, 1963. Complete text available online.

http://www.mc.maricopa.edu/users/M3cdhistory/

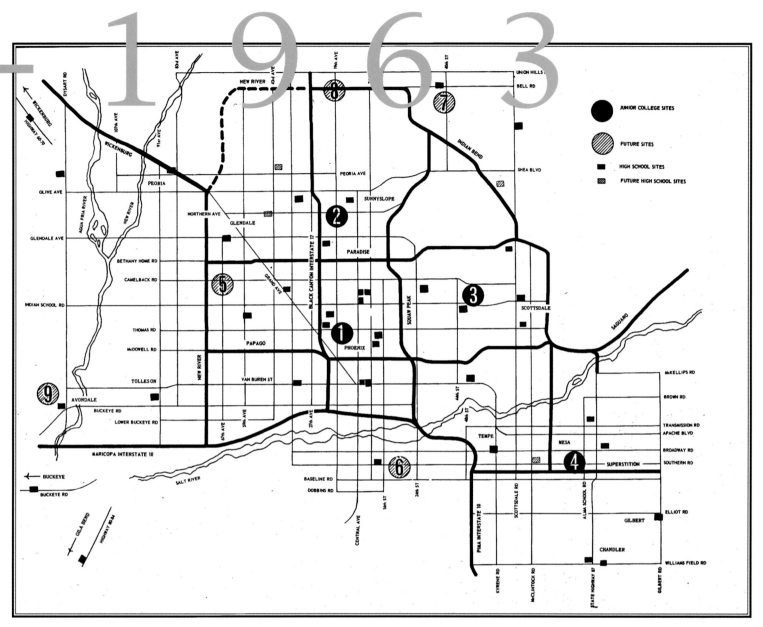

From *Junior Colleges for Maricopa County.* "*Figure 10. Central Maricopa County Junior College Sites, High Schools, and Future High School Sites.*"

(2) build colleges on sites 2, 3, and 4, (3) buy sites 5 and 6, and (4) construct a County Administration Center. "There is real urgency that the four junior colleges . . . be completed by September, 1965, because the high school graduates in that year will exceed the number of 1964 graduates in Maricopa County by 2,000, increasing to more than 10,000."

On January 28, the board accepted most of the survey's recommendations. The district requested the state board find sites for three new junior colleges and investigate the availability of land for others. The board also started the machinery for a bond election, but balked at asking the voters for $20 million; apparently, the board wanted to think further about the money.

Next, the board moved to address the concerns of the Phoenix College faculty and staff. Wisely, board members voted to continue almost all of the current conditions of employment. As an incentive to stay at Phoenix College, each faculty member would be hired by the new district at the next higher step on the salary schedule—a sort of signing bonus to keep faculty from jumping ship. In time, all the faculty and almost all of the staff elected to stay. At this point, all the essential details of the transition had been worked out except one: who would control the district's finances? Up to this time, the PUHS District had handled the financial affairs of the college, so at the meeting on February 11, 1963, the board made its first hiring decision. Robert Taylor was hired away from the PUHS to serve as the district's new business manager. This decision is significant because the more normal pattern would have been to appoint the district president and have that person hire the staff. This out-of-sequence event set a prece-

Robert Taylor, Maricopa district's first business manager.

dent that would cause the district serious problems in later years.

Meanwhile, the search for extension sites had begun. Hannelly's own account of this task sounds a bit like a fraternity scavenger hunt:

> *In the Mesa area, we rented a bowling alley, a funeral parlor, a basketball emporium, and an old church. . . . We came out to Glendale, and we said we can't go all the way out to Glendale because they don't have any space to rent much. So, we rented some space, buildings there near Read Mullan's automobile agency. We called that Read Mullan University. And we rented space in the Jewish Community Center at Fifteenth Avenue and Maryland and various other places.*

The board minutes for March 4, 1963, indicate that the site search really didn't go quite that smoothly:

> *Dr. Hannelly informed the board that the administration was now ready to recommend sites at two locations. He passed copies of a floor plan and a description of property located in the Mesa area. [1] He indicated that the administration felt this was a prime location. . . . The second site recommended by the administration was the Imperial Western Community Center property located at Fifteenth and Camelback. Dr. Hannelly expressed regret that no floor plan was available but explained to the board the advantages of the property. . . . Dr. Hannelly indicated that to date they had not been able to locate a satisfactory site in the Glendale area.*

In the end, the matter of site selection for the Glendale extension dragged on for almost another month and a half and was not resolved completely until the meeting of May 27, 1963.

At the March 16 meeting, the board finally resolved to hold a bond election on May 7, and ask for only $9.5 million, roughly half what the original survey had recommended. According to the minutes, the money would be used for "the purchase of sites 2, 3, and 4 as shown in the survey, the purchase of Phoenix College and improvements therein,

and the building of two new 1,400 student capacity colleges on sites 2 and 3." Later, the figure was raised to $9.75 million.

On March 25, Joe Ralston (who was a regular visitor to the board meetings in his capacity as Maricopa County's representative to the state board) expressed concern about the time remaining to prepare for the bond election. The minutes indicate discussion followed, but Ralston's warning was ignored. The board probably assumed that the public's overwhelming approval of the district's creation would translate into a rubber stamp of approval on the first bond election.

A week later, the minutes reflect that Miller was beginning to worry about the lack of publicity for the election:

> *Mr. Miller informed the Board that he was seriously disturbed over the lack of publicity concerning the bond issue. He observed that while Howard Carroll and John Carpenter were providing excellent [newspaper] coverage of the activities of the Board, there had been a decided omission as regarded the editorial page. While nothing detrimental was being published, neither was anything favorable.*

Miller was right to be concerned about the newspapers. When interviewed for this book, Easley explained the *Arizona Republic*'s attitude towards the bond election.

> *We had some meetings with the editorial board of the* Arizona Republic, *and they asked lots of questions. And we tried to answer them. And we tried to be honest. And one of the editors pointed out to me that even experts did not have all the knowledge in the world, meaning that the*

May 10, 1996, video interview with Robert Easley, Maricopa governing board member 1962-71. Transcript and audio excerpts available online.

http://www.mc.maricopa.edu/users/M3cdhistory/

[1] The building was then known as the Producers' Life Insurance building, formerly a church; today, the building is the home of the Landmark Restaurant.

group that we were getting some of our information from was erroneous. [2] And so later on, we heard—via the grapevine—that they were not going to support us but that they were not going to editorialize against us.

At the board meeting on April 22, the board finally reviewed samples of the publicity materials that had been prepared for the bond election, then just a little over two weeks away, but—regrettably—no one had yet stepped forward to chair a citizens' advisory committee.

Apparently, no one wanted to be captain on the *Titanic*.

On May 7, the voters of Maricopa County went to the polls and delivered a stinging rebuke. The bond was rejected overwhelmingly.

The failure of the newspapers to support the election enthusiastically and the general inexperience of the board members in running a bond election were to blame. Unfortunately, the board decided that the public was really chastening them to be more frugal.

The First District President

Previously, at the meeting on April 8, 1963, the board had finally bothered to name Hannelly as the district's first president. The account in the board minutes is very revealing:

> Motion No. 32. Mr. Patterson moved, Mr. Miller seconded, that Dr. Robert J. Hannelly be retained as President of the Maricopa County Junior College System. Motion carried. Dr. Hannelly was congratulated by members of the board and others present and expressed his appreciation for the honor and the opportunity to serve in this capacity.

By all rights, Hannelly's appointment as president should have created a vacancy in the dean's office at Phoenix College, but the board saw otherwise. The minutes go on to state, "In discussion which followed it was determined that salary for the new post would be established at a later date. Further, that Dr. Hannelly would continue to serve as Dean of Phoenix College."

Hannelly should have put his foot down. Serving as Phoenix College's dean, overseeing three extension campuses, and planning two new colleges was more work than one person should reasonably be expected to do. Also, the board's refusal to set Hannelly's salary at that time was an insult. They took for granted that he would do whatever they told him to do and that he would accept whatever salary they offered.

The problem was that the hard-nosed business types on the board were too impatient to understand or appreciate Hannelly's nonconfrontational style. In his notes on the history of the Maricopa district, Phoenix College faculty member John Goff states that Hannelly may have brought this problem on himself:

> Dr. Hannelly never had an easy time with the governing board. They were not particularly good at treating their chief executive officer fairly. Unfortunately, Hannelly was too much of a gentleman to be forceful enough to put them in their places. Often there was too much of a hat in hand, "by your leave" attitude on the President's part.

The fact that the board members waited four months before appointing Hannelly also gives rise to the speculation that they may not have wanted him for that job initially. When the appointment was finally made, Hannelly was almost sixty-two years old, and some of the board members may have preferred a younger, more assertive candidate.

If so, then why did the governing board offer the job to Hannelly? The most probable reason is that Hannelly had been active with the North Central Association for many years. With Hannelly as president, the board could reasonably expect the district's accreditation to be a breeze. On the Wilcox tape, Hannelly suggests his dual appointment reflected this thinking:

> With Phoenix College's reputation from 1927 and my connection with the brass of the North Central, we made a proposition. I talked to the boys back at Chicago, and I said, "If I personally oversee the extension of credibility and quality to each of these colleges we are establishing, will there be any problem with one accreditation of those colleges?" Well, they said, "How do you expect to extend your influence there?" So, I talked it over with my board here, and . . . the board decided that I would not only serve as president of the district, but I would also serve as dean of Phoenix College as they established these other colleges too, so that when it came time for Mesa and Glendale to be accredited, they would come under the shield of Phoenix College's accreditation.

Eventually, though, Hannelly seems to have had second thoughts about this odious dual appointment, and he decided to speak up. At the board meeting on May 20, he presented reasonable arguments why the board should hire a vice president to share the workload:

2 Easley appears to be referring to the ASU group that had prepared the survey and blueprint for the new district.

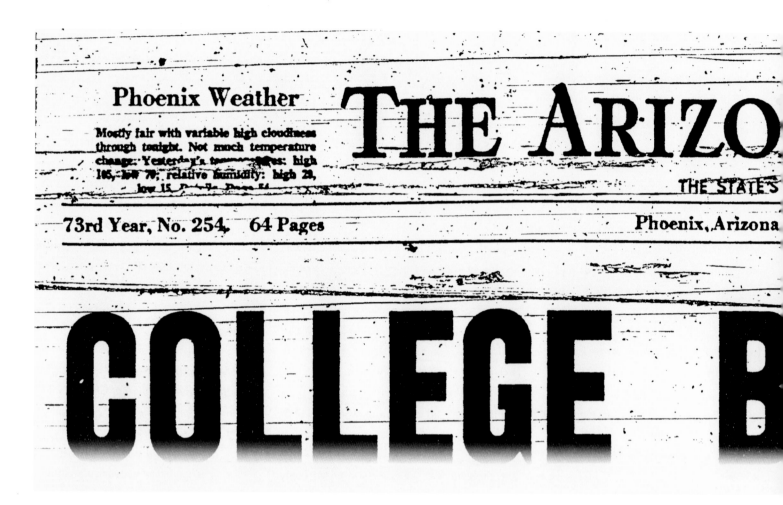

Phoenix Weather

Mostly fair with variable high cloudiness through tonight. Not much temperature change. Yesterday's temperatures: high 105, low 79; relative humidity: high 29, low 15 . . . . Page 54

THE ARIZO

THE STATE'S

73rd Year, No. 254, 64 Pages

Phoenix, Arizona

COLLEGE B

Dr. Hannelly explained to the board that a competent administrator for junior colleges is needed at this time, even though it will cost more to bring in a man who meets these qualifications. Since the county district was established, mail has increased 300%, telephone calls 200%—planning for extensions is being done, personnel hired, etc. Dr. Hannelly presented a list of candidates for the position.

The board then instructed Hannelly to bring in some candidates, but the board does not appear to have been enthusiastic about hiring a vice president. The board minutes for the May 27 meeting show that only one candidate, Dr. Frederick Kintzer, was present at the meeting.

The board met first in executive session—presumably to interview Dr. Kintzer—but no action was proposed on his behalf at the following meeting. The implication is that the board didn't like Hannelly's choice.

Two weeks later, the minutes show that a Dr. Jack Rodgers was present at the board meeting and that the board met first in executive session again. No results of that session are recorded, but the board seems to have found this candidate acceptable. At the meeting on June 27, 1963, Hannelly formally proposed Dr. Jack Rodgers as vice president at a salary of $19,000.

The board accepted the man but balked at the salary and informed Hannelly that they wouldn't pay more than $16,000 for the position. Hannelly was then instructed to offer Rodgers the job for the lesser amount.

Then, the board excused Hannelly from the meeting while they debated the figure for Hannelly's salary as president and dean of Phoenix College. When he returned a few minutes later, the board offered him $17,500—a full $1,500 less than Hannelly had proposed for his own vice president!

In an unusually overt display of displeasure, Hannelly actually declined to accept the board's offer. He asked for time to think it over.

Perhaps sensing the distress of their newly appointed president, the board then elected to recess, and two hours passed before the meeting resumed. What manner of conversation took place in the interval is unknown. Perhaps Hannelly attempted to use some of his usual indirect persuasion to have his

A REPUBLIC

CITY

Today's Chuckle

T NEWSPAPER

day, May 8, 1963.   TELEPHONE: 271-8000   ⊠○   a   Ten Cents

ONDS LOSE

salary increased. When the board reconvened that evening, Hannelly finally accepted the board's shameful salary offer. According to the minutes:

> He stated, however, that in view of the fact that as President he would be called upon to entertain visiting dignitaries, he was requesting that some specific amount be designated as a hospitality fund to be used for this purpose. The members of the Board agreed that this would be perfectly fitting and suggested that he check into the matter further and report to them his findings.

As a scholar, Hannelly might have labeled that final touch a Pyrrhic victory. Dr. Jack Rodgers, however, wasn't impressed. He felt he deserved $19,000, and when he received the board's counteroffer, his response may be inferred from the fact that he is never men-

tioned again in the board minutes. Whether the board simply felt constrained by the failure of the bond or the board was just—to use Al Flowers words—"very close with the buck," the board was certainly not overpaying its administrators.

The district's first six months were history, and the start had been rocky indeed!

Arizona Republic, May 8, 1963. *From microfilm.*

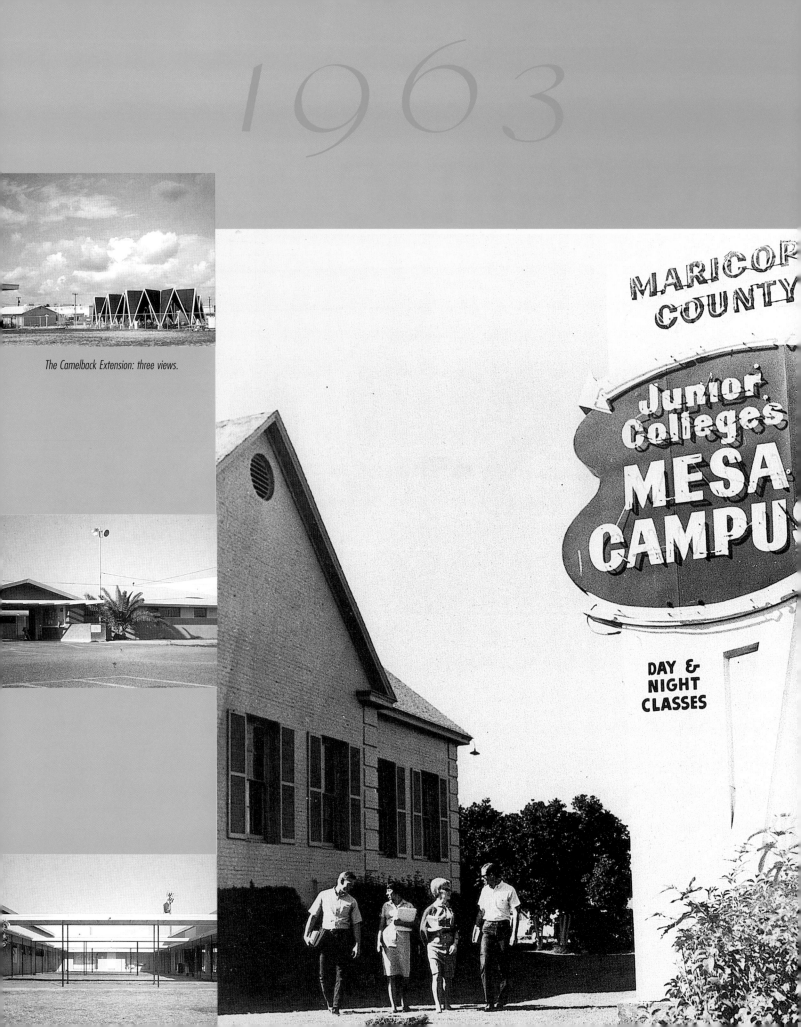

1963

The Camelback Extension: three views.

MARICOPA COUNTY

Junior Colleges

MESA CAMPUS

DAY &
NIGHT
CLASSES

Chapter Seven

1966

Life at the **EXTENSIONS**

The new district's first fiscal year (1963-64) was about to begin, and much remained to be done to prepare the extension campuses to receive students in the fall.

On June 27, 1963, the Maricopa governing board appointed J. Lee Thompson (Hannelly's dean of instruction at Phoenix College), the dean of the two Phoenix College extensions on Camelback and Maryland. Dr. Irwin L. Spector (PC's director of admissions and registrar) was promoted to dean of instruction. PC faculty member William B. Wallace became the new registrar. John Riggs, who had been the equivalent of dean of students at Phoenix College, was made the new dean of the Mesa extension. A Phoenix College counselor, Theodore K. Pierson, took over Riggs' job.

As the summer progressed, the faculty and the new administrators reportedly all pitched in to renovate the temporary facilities for the start of the fall term. Millie Noble recalls, "We worked our buns off that summer. . . . Even the deans, everybody was out there with their hammer and their pliers and their screwdrivers and it was just great."

The Camelback extension was located in a former Jewish Community Center on Camelback Road, near the intersection with 16th Street. The building is no longer standing, but the location was near where Mel Clayton Ford exists today. At that time, the

dealership was owned by Read Mullan. Gene Eastin, who began teaching at the Camelback extension in 1963, remembers why this facility soon acquired the nickname Read Mullan University: "It was so very easy to hear the microphones in the shop saying, 'Car number

The New Team.   Back row (left to right): Ted Pierson, Bill Wallace, J. Lee Thompson, and John Riggs.   Front row (left to right): Jinette Kirk (Mesa's dean of women), Robert Hannelly, Irwin Spector, and Mildred Bulpitt (Phoenix College's dean of the evening college program).

April 19, 1996, video interview with Gene Eastin, Glendale Community College faculty member and Maricopa governing board member. Transcript and audio excerpts available online.

http://www.mc.maricopa.edu/users/M3cdhistory/

The Mesa Extension (the building that is now the Landmark Restaurant).

March 4, 1996, video interview with Jan Boerner, Glendale Community College faculty.   Transcript available online.

http://www.mc.maricopa.edu/users/M3cdhistory/

the week because many faculty worked at both extensions.

According to Moloso, the two extensions functioned more or less as separate entities:

The faculty themselves felt rather divided. There was not any loyalty to the Camelback extension among the

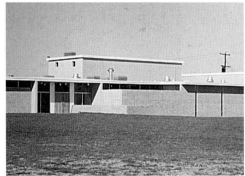

The Maryland extension.

twenty-three, ready to pick up!' 'Mr. So-and-So, will you answer the phone?' and this type of thing that was going on all the time."

Some remodeling was done inside the building, and several portable classrooms were moved onto the property. On the northeast corner was an athletic field, and south of the building was room for parking, but most of the classes were held in the center's gym.

Jan Boerner, who also started at the Camelback extension at this time, recalls, "There were no buffers between the classes; we just lined up chairs, twenty to thirty chairs, in blocks in the gym. We had about ten or twelve classes meeting at the same time. Can you imagine?"

The Maryland extension, which was smaller than the Camelback extension, was located in the Jewish Community Center located at 17th Avenue and Maryland. This facility was newer and currently in use, so the district could use it only on weekdays. The building included an assembly room that seated over 500, an

Olympic-size swimming pool, and tennis and volleyball courts. Phil Moloso, an original hire at the Maryland extension, recalls that the main building was used very minimally, as all classes were taught in portable classrooms:

The Maryland extension was nothing but temporaries. All of the classes were taught and the libraries were in buildings that were attached outside of the Maryland facility. All that we used of the Jewish Community Center itself were the cafeteria facilities and the meeting halls and some of those things. The students used the lounges and things like that, but the classes were taught in temporary buildings.

J. Lee Thompson, the dean of both the Camelback and Maryland extensions, faced the unenviable task of coordinating the activities at both sites. His office was located at the Camelback extension. Once or twice a week, he would travel to the Maryland extension for faculty meetings, but he could remain at Camelback and see most of the faculty during

Maryland people. We felt pretty much on our own, and I think the Camelback people felt pretty well separated, too. There wasn't a lot of communication except within a department to coordinate courses or something like that.

The problems of working between two locations on the west side of Phoenix were nothing compared to those of working on the east side among the numerous locations of the Mesa extension.

The largest single Mesa facility was the former church building at the intersection of Extension and Main (the building that is now the Landmark Restaurant). The administrative offices and the library for the Mesa extension were located in this building. Some rooms were used for classrooms, but several portable classrooms were also moved onto the property to provide additional instructional space.

Ron Yates, who joined the Mesa faculty in the fall of 1964, recalls life in the old church building:

The library was upstairs, and you came up the stairs, and the checkout desk was right in front of you, and the library and the stacks were in a large room to the left. The dean's office was down the hall past the library circulation desk, and there were even a couple of classrooms up there. There was a wonderful feeling of camaraderie

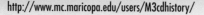

December 6, 1995, video interview with Ron Yates, former Mesa Community College faculty member. Transcript available online.

http://www.mc.maricopa.edu/users/M3cdhistory/

because there were so few of us and because we were kind of squeezed into these facilities that were sort of bursting at the seams.

Jack Twitchell, a Mesa mathematics teacher who started with the district in 1963, recalls the various other locations used by the Mesa extension:

We were downtown, up over a drugstore and what was then Dial Finance. Where Spencer's appliance store is now, at First Avenue, used to be the old Mesa Theater, and our drafting classes and so forth were in the building beside the theater. As a matter of fact, the theater was used a few times for a couple of things because we had no other meeting place. We had speech classes and physics and electronics classes in the old mortuary building, which is now where Nicholas and Killian's law offices are on Pepper Place. The basketball team practiced at the Latter-day Saints Interstake Center on Horne, out to the east. And the fields across from the old church, which are now used by Coury Buick, became our softball diamonds and so forth out there.

All the people interviewed for this book echoed a common theme when describing life at the extensions. Gene Eastin said it very well: "We knew that we were starting something new and big, and we were happy and proud to be a part of it."

The Second Bond Election

The pace of the governing board slowed down once the extensions were staffed and opened, and meetings began to be held every other week. The minutes reflect mostly routine business, but two more staffing changes occurred. James L. Snyder finally agreed to serve as the district's vice president and to supervise the development of new facilities. In addition, Marvin Knudson was hired to handle planning in the area of vocational education.

Mesa's first library in the old church building.

November 30, 1995, video interview with Jack Twitchell, former Mesa Community College faculty member and administrator. Transcript available online.

http://www.mc.maricopa.edu/users/M3cdhistory/

James M. Snyder, first district Vice President, 1963-66.

for the second semester at the extensions were announced. The Camelback and Maryland extensions (which were less than two miles apart) together had enrolled a total of 619 students while the Mesa extension had enrolled only 311. The board must then have assumed that the potential enrollment on the west side of town was greater than on the east side.

Future site of the Glendale campus. The long row of palm trees became an inspiration for the architects.

Marvin Knudson, first district director of semiprofessional education, 1963-64, and executive director of the state board for community colleges, 1964-67.

The first election for a seat on the governing board was also held at this time. The original board members had been appointed to their positions, and as their terms of appointment expired, each had to run for election to remain on the board. In the fall of 1964, Jim Miller became the first board member to be elected to his seat on the board for a five-year term.

During the fall of 1963, the board had begun to think about another bond election. The public had turned thumbs-down on building three new colleges, so the board cautiously moved ahead with plans for only one. At the meeting on December 30, 1963, the board voted to hire Edward L. Varney Associates "to plan and design a new college campus." The location had not yet been decided, but the consensus was to locate the new college in the Glendale area.

The board minutes provide no clues as to why the Glendale site was chosen first, but at the February 24 board meeting, enrollment figures

On March 19, 1964, the date for the second bond election was set for May 2. The plan was to request money to purchase Phoenix College, build one campus in Glendale to open in 1965, and build a second campus in Mesa to open in 1967. The amount was determined to be $4.8 million, roughly half of the previous bond request. Apparently, the board was concerned that the newspapers would not support a larger figure.

Al Flowers, who was then the assistant superintendent of business affairs for the Scottsdale school district, was appalled:

I said to Jim Miller, "You're out of your

cotton-pickin' mind." And he said, "Why?" I said, "Go for double. And if you don't pass it then, double it again. You know, let's get this show on the road! You've got a lot of colleges that are going to come into this county, and if you're going to kowtow to [the press] now, you're dead in the water. You better play hardball with

The People Speak

[the media] at this point, and not be messing around letting them call the shots for you five people!"

The board did not listen to his advice.

Yet, board members did learn from some of their previous mistakes. They organized a better informational campaign, and the newspapers did support the bond actively. As a result, the reduced bond passed easily, and this time, the board members were convinced that the public was endorsing their policy of fiscal tight-fistedness. For the next several

years, the board continued to squeeze every buck until it squeaked.

The New Colleges Emerge

Board members then proceeded with the district's next evolutionary step, that of transforming the extension campuses into colleges. At the end of June, 1964, the state board announced it had selected a

Future site of the Mesa campus.

site at 59th Avenue and Olive for the Glendale college. The P. W. Womack Construction Company owned the land, and the sale price was $3,550 per acre.

The location of the Mesa campus was supposed to be a lower priority, but the Mesa extension's enrollment was picking up faster than expected. At the meeting on December 21, 1964, the board members reconsidered their plans. Board member Dwight Patterson's connection to the Dobson family then proved useful. The Dobsons owned massive parcels of land in Mesa, and Patterson eventually recommended the college's current site between

Mesa and Tempe. Dwight Patterson explains: *We were looking for a site—160 acres— and we were serving Mesa, Tempe, and Chandler. The site we selected was on the border with Tempe, and a mile south of here was Chandler. At that time, we had to have something for Tempe to get their support, and we really didn't know that Mesa was going to grow as fast as it had out east.*

Reportedly, the asking price was only $3,000 an acre.

At the board meeting on April 12, 1965, the new colleges were officially named Glendale Community College and Mesa Community College. The fact that the colleges were both called *community colleges* and not *junior colleges* may seem somewhat surprising because the district was still the Maricopa County Junior College District and the state board still referred to itself as the Junior College Board. (As noted in chapter one, the state-mandated name change from "junior" colleges to "community" colleges did not occur until 1971.) However, Phoenix College had dropped the word "Junior" from its name in 1947. Naming the new schools "junior colleges" would have only created confusion. Meanwhile, the term "community college" had become established nationally, and therefore, the decision to call the new schools "community colleges" was a logical compromise.

The administrative structures of the future colleges were then announced at the May 1965 board meeting. John Riggs was retained as the executive dean at Mesa, but the executive deans at Glendale and Phoenix changed. Speaking to Wilcox, Hannelly explained the changes in this way:

February 22, 1996, video interview with Dwight Patterson, Maricopa governing board member 1962-1975. Transcript and audio excerpts available online.

http://www.mc.maricopa.edu/users/M3cdhistory/

We had Thompson on the job at the Jewish Community Center and Read Mullan University. But for some reason or other, the board didn't want Thompson as head of the Glendale Community College, so I had been holding two jobs: president of the district and administrative dean at Phoenix College. And that was by design—the Board wanted me to hold the two. And I said, "It's about time just to give me one. I'm losin' weight. I have too much of a job going." And so they settled the thing by sending Thompson to my old job at the Phoenix College.

Apparently to no one's surprise, the board announced that Thompson's successor in Glendale would be the executive director of the

state board, John Prince. The district's director for semiprofessional education, Marvin Knudson, then resigned from the district and took over Prince's job at the state board.[1] According to Al Flowers, Prince had been actively campaigning for some time to return to the district: "He worked on it, and had others work on it for him, from his contacts with the state office, state board members, even. A particular one was Joe Ralston, who was a lawyer in town. And Joe was in Dr. Prince's corner, very much so, from the state level."

In fact, many people assumed that Prince was being groomed to become the next president of the district when Hannelly retired in a few years. Millie Noble claims, "I knew about it.

I'm sure a lot of other people must have known. I don't think everybody on the board knew it, but Jim Miller knew it. Jim's the one that said, 'Jack, if you quit the job as executive director of the Arizona community college board and become the founding dean at Glendale, I'll promise you the presidency of the district.'"

Noble's version of the story seems credible because Miller and Prince knew each other socially. They were both members of the RONS Club (Reserve Officers Naval Service Club) in Phoenix. Glendale faculty member John Waltrip was also a member of this club, and when interviewed for this book, he recalled:

The RONS Club is close to Phoenix College, and a lot of Phoenix College people belonged to the RONS Club even if they weren't former Navy officers because the RONS Club had associate members and because it was close. Back in the old days, the Phoenix faculty tended to live close to the college, and so there were a lot of Phoenix College people who were RONS Club members. So it was almost like a Phoenix College club, because of that.

Bob Easley stated in no uncertain terms that he was the one who decided that Prince should become Glendale's first executive dean:

I felt that Phoenix College was a strong organization—Glendale Community College would be a relatively new venture and we needed as much strength there as we could get, and so I chose Jack Prince to come to Glendale Community College and convinced our board members that Thompson should go down to Phoenix College. And Thompson was flattered. He liked that. Jack Prince never said one way or the other, but I think he was happy to get the deanship. So, Jack Prince came to Glendale, and I was very happy about it. I got him out at Glendale.

Prince's desire to return to the district must have been very strong because the move required a substantial cut in pay. According to Prince's daughter Mary Martha, "I remember it was like a three- or four-thousand-dollar cut in salary, and I think the numbers were like twelve thousand down to nine thousand to take that job. It was an item of discussion at home. It was a big cut. My brother was still in college; there were two more kids coming up."

[1] Knudson remained there from 1964-1967 and then served as the president of Sinclair Community College in Dayton, Ohio, from 1967-75. In 1979, he returned to Phoenix and ran unsuccessfully against Linda Rosenthal for a seat on the Maricopa district governing board.

Glendale also acquired a newcomer to the district, Dr. Matt O. Hanhila. He was appointed as the assistant dean at Glendale, a position equivalent to dean of instruction. Speaking to Wilcox, Hannelly claimed that he had known Hanhila for years and was responsible for his getting the job:

We needed a dean of instruction at Glendale, and Hanhila was superintendent over at Paradise Valley, and I called him up. I had known him a long time before. He was an experienced administrator, but not on a junior college level. But he had been effective at Carl Hayden [High School], and he had some pretty tough boys to deal with, so he could take care of that situation very well. And he was very friendly, and they needed this kind of camaraderie around there.

A major reason for hiring Hanhila may have been the fact that his previous experience included opening and equipping two high schools. He fully understood how to start a new school facility.

Matt Hanhila also took a salary cut to make the switch to the Maricopa district. Speaking to Wilcox in 1984, Hanhila explained:

Well, I was a longtime friend of Bob Hannelly's, and I decided I'd like to be in the junior college district, and I just turned in an application for it, and Bob, bless his soul, said, "You'll be an assistant dean." I dropped in salary $3,000 from being superintendent up here in Paradise Valley, but I didn't mind that drop at all. I figured it was an advance as far as I was concerned.

The position of assistant dean was unprecedented, and at that time no comparable position was created at Mesa or Phoenix. The feeling seemed to be that two administrators would be needed because Glendale Community College would continue to function at the two extension campuses until the main campus was completed. Hanhila recalls:

Dr. Prince took Read Mullan U. first semester, and I took Maryland U. . . . then we reversed so we would get to know the teachers and the facilities better. Dr. Prince and I had offices that were adjacent to the secretary's office, and we had joint telephones which we put through a hole in the wall so that we didn't have to have extra extensions. And so, we divided the chores: Jack took the faculty and the curriculum, and I took care of the facilities. Of course, we traded each day all along.

Curiously, the board delayed again announcing Hannelly's role in the new order. The board had clearly filled the position of executive dean at Phoenix, so Hannelly no longer had his dual appointment. Not until the board meeting on July 1, 1965, was Hannelly's status solely as the district's president confirmed.

Al Flowers Joins the Administration

A major restructuring of the district's business office also occurred at this time. In the spring of 1963, the board had hired Bob Taylor as the district's first business director, but the board members had become unhappy

Glendale Community College's first leaders. John Prince, executive dean 1965-67, and Matt Hanhila, associate dean 1965-67 and executive dean 1967-75.

Robert Wilcox's 1984 audio interview with Matt Hanhila. Transcript and audio excerpts available online.

http://www.mc.maricopa.edu/users/M3cdhistory/

"It fell to my lot to decide whether our department chairmen needed the Cadillac or if a Ford would do . . . . Most frequently they got the Ford or the Chevrolet."

with his abilities. The problem surfaced initially at a board meeting in December of that year. Hannelly and Taylor came to the board to ask for $60,000 to supply portable classrooms for the extensions. Taylor's figures weren't exact enough for the board's taste, and the minutes record the following exchange in remarkable detail:

> Mr. Jaap . . . observed that since it was of major importance and due to the amount of the expenditure involved, further consideration was essential. Mr. Taylor asked specifically what the board had in mind in order to prepare for the next presentation. Mr. Miller stated that on any items of this nature the board should be given the dollar value of what is involved. He stated that economics is the lifeblood of the board and in the future he would like to see a proposal such as this in a full-itemized layout, showing the situation as it now exists (to include dollar value), the itemized proposal *and the difference to be expended or saved.* These minutes do not record Hannelly's response to Miller's statement, but Hannelly surely was not pleased. He doubtless felt that education should have been the lifeblood of the board.

With the launching of the new colleges, the board apparently decided that the district needed someone with more experience at handling its "lifeblood." At the board meeting on September 27, 1965, board members authorized a new position, vice president for business affairs, and authorized Hannelly to look for candidates.

Hannelly interviewed only one.

Al Flowers was born in the Catskill Mountains. He began his undergraduate work at a small private business college in Kingston, New York, where he remained for only a year. After the outbreak of World War II, he joined the Army Air Corps and remained in the service for three and a half years. Afterward, he went back to school on the GI Bill: a year and a half at Rider College in Trenton, New Jersey, and another year and a half at Columbia University, where he eventually earned both a BA in business and MA in educational administration.

Al Flowers, district business manager, 1966-78, and acting district president/chancellor 1976-77.

Upon graduation in 1949, Flowers moved to Arizona. At North Phoenix High School, he took over the business education department and taught bookkeeping and accounting. Later, he was promoted to assistant principal for educational services and registrar. In 1958, he became the finance director for the Phoenix Union High School District.

After the community college enabling legislation was passed, the state board awarded Flowers a contract to devise the initial accounting and reporting procedures for all

THE $2,400 MISUNDERSTANDING

The following anecdote—which today has become the stuff of legend at Glendale—may suggest some of the reason the board was unhappy with the way money was being handled in the district at that time. Many versions of this story exist, and they differ greatly in the particulars. The first version here comes from Matt Hanhila, and the second comes from longtime Glendale faculty member Phil Moloso.

Matt Hanhila: *Another funny thing that happened, we didn't have any safe and we didn't have any walk-in place. We had filing cabinets. One day when we were registering—I think it was the second semester we were registering—the filing cabinet was locked and they couldn't get into it for some reason. And so they called on me, the safecracker, to break into the filing cabinet. And I went over and* looked at another one and saw how the lock worked and I got a drill and put in just one punch and it was open. And as I was looking in there, I discovered a money sack in there with $2,400 in it. Nobody knew what it was from. We had no record of it. No nothing. It was just a fly-by-night operation, you know.

Phil Moloso: *In the last year at the Maryland extension, our fiscal agent never deposited the money that was collected for tuition [2] for the second semester. It was found many weeks, perhaps months, later in a closet, undeposited. Nobody'd missed it and no one was concerned. Just hadn't bothered to deposit it.*

[2] The district charged no tuition at this time. The money collected was for student fees.

Arizona community colleges. The job also required him to write a complete guide explaining all the accounting codes, and this guide was used by all the community colleges in the state well into the '70s.

In 1965, Flowers was working for the Scottsdale school system, where he had been employed since 1962. Hannelly approached him, and Flowers was eager to work for the new junior college district, but Scottsdale would not release him in midyear, so beginning in January, 1966, Flowers began to work half-time for both districts.

Al Flowers quickly won over the board members because of his command of their "lifeblood." He also began to involve Hannelly more closely in the district's financial affairs:

> I took Hannelly the first budget I put together, and wanted to go over it with him, and he said, "Thank you very much." I said, "What do you mean, 'Thank you?'" He said, "That's the first budget I've seen. When we started operating under Mr. Taylor, he never gave me a copy of the budget." He should have hauled somebody in there and said, "Where is the budget? And tell me what's in this damn thing!" But he didn't do that. He wasn't even aware of

what was in the budget at that point.
After six months, Flowers announced he'd prefer to work full-time for the district but only on condition that the board appoint a qualified purchasing agent and a qualified accounting supervisor for his staff. At first, the board balked at the idea of hiring additional personnel, but Flowers, unlike Hannelly, would not take no for an answer:

> So I told Dr. Hannelly, "You know, this is something I'd like to do. You know I still

> have an offer of a contract as superintendent at Scottsdale Public Schools for four years." He said, "I've got to talk to them and let them know." I said, "If it's not going to be staffed properly, and if I don't have that kind of authority, then don't count on me. If I didn't have another job, you might have me in a corner, but I still do." I was going to resign at the very next meeting if they didn't do something. But, they went in executive session without me

> and hashed it out and came out and established the positions I wanted. That was a critical point in my staying with the district.

The appointment of Flowers solidified the district's administration at a perfect time for the district. The North Central Association's first accreditation visit was quickly approaching, and the first signs of turbulence in the district's evolution were beginning to appear.

January 10, 1996, video interview with Al Flowers, for district business manager and acting president/chancellor. Transcript, audio excerpts, and video excerpts available online.

http://www.mc.maricopa.edu/users/M3cdhistory/

The only problem was that initially, the faculty was seriously divided as a result of having functioned autonomously at two different locations for three years.

The Maricopa governing board at work. From left to right: Bill Van Loo, Dwight Patterson, Jim Miller, and Bob Easley. Not present: Bob Jaap. On the right, Bob Hannelly. In the background, Millie Noble takes notes.

Just as the new campuses were about to be dedicated, the composition of the governing board suddenly changed. In September of 1966, Lester Hogan resigned unexpectedly due to the relocation of his business to California. John Barry was still the county superintendent at that time, and he offered the appointment to H. W. "Bill" Van Loo, a civil engineer living in Scottsdale. Van Loo was sworn in at the October 12 meeting and within a month was officially elected to the position.

Four days later, the Glendale campus was officially dedicated, followed by the Mesa campus dedication on October 30. Fall registration at Glendale was 4,082 students. Enrollment at the Mesa campus exceeded expectations at 3,850. At Phoenix College, the grand total was 9,832 students (including evening students, which Mesa and Glendale did not yet have).

The new colleges that Van Loo helped dedicate were virtually clones of Phoenix College. In spite of their different facilities, the district's three colleges were otherwise identical. Phoenix College had simply divided itself into three separate institutions. And yet, Mesa and Glendale soon developed very different personalities.

Edward L. Varney Associates' architectural rendering for the Glendale campus.

The Personality of Glendale Community College

The first factor that determined Glendale's personality was the campus itself. Designed by the firm of Edward L. Varney Asociates, the new campus opened complete in every detail and strikingly beautiful. One distinctive feature of the property was a large number of tall palm trees that the architects had incorporated into their designs. The shape of the palms inspired the design of the cement columns that support the school's canopied walkways. (See illustration next page.)

On opening day, the faculty had every reason to feel privileged to move into this beautiful new facility. The only problem was that initially, the faculty was seriously divided as a result of having functioned autonomously at two different locations for three years. Some departments even experienced significant conflicts upon joining forces. Glendale faculty member Jack Hartley, speaking to retired Glendale journalism professor Bob Wilcox in 1984, remembered:

There was one department [head] on each campus—English on Maryland and English at Camelback. And the big problem came when Dr. Prince announced that he was going to have to make [one] appointment as the campuses came together and, obviously, one would be eliminated and one would be kept. And this created, I think, all sorts of hostilities that are still very much a part of the campus today because we're still a sort of Maryland group and there's still a sort of Camelback group, and they simply never melded.

Phil Moloso, another Glendale faculty member who experienced the unification, disagrees with Hartley:

March 29, 1996, video interview with Chuck West, Glendale Community College faculty member. Audio excerpts and transcript available online.

http://www.mc.maricopa.edu/users/M3cdhistory/

The main entrance to the Glendale campus in 1967. The palm trees and the palm-inspired concrete columns became the dominant architectural motif.

Chuck West, who was hired at Glendale in 1965 to set up the chemistry lab, also recalled Prince fondly and noted that Prince was popular because he seemed to treat faculty with high professional regard:

He pretty much left you alone—gave you responsibility, left you alone, and saw to it that you did it. If you did, there were no problems. His office door was always open; you could walk in and you felt comfortable talking to him. . . . He didn't walk around the campus that much, but he had a phenomenal memory for names, and he knew everybody. I didn't know anyone on this campus that didn't like John Prince.

Jack Hartley in 1967.

Well, Jack's not mistaken about the animosity in certain departments, and he happens to come from one of those departments, which is not only big but is probably the most rancorous in that regard. Sure, there were people at war many years afterward, until they retired. But that's true on any campus. So I would say that the origin of disputes among academic people is not because of the disparate campuses, but just because of the antagonistic personalities.

Another determining factor of Glendale's personality was the leadership of its executive dean. John Prince was extremely popular with the faculty. John Waltrip (who later became president at Glendale) recalled: "Prince was a prince. He's one of the finest guys I ever knew. He was one of the most eloquent men that I've ever known. Wonderful public speaker. Great personality, very kind man, generous. We loved him out at Glendale."

Just as Prince respected the faculty's authority, he demanded that the faculty respect his. When interviewed for this book, Glendale faculty member Gene Eastin recalled that Prince was very jealous of his authority: "I liked Prince, but I got the impression that he always wanted you to know that he knew the direction to go better than anyone, and he wouldn't listen necessarily to suggestions from anyone else."

This facet of Prince's personality may have resulted from the way that the Phoenix

Union High School board had apparently been opposed to his move into administration ten years before. Once he began to enjoy some administrative responsibility, he may indeed have been leery of anyone who seemed to want to compromise his authority. Phil Smelser, another early Glendale faculty member, recalls this example of Prince's stubborn streak:

appreciate people pouring gasoline on themselves and lighting a fire." In other words, they shouldn't have argued with him.

In 1968, Prince left Glendale to become the next president of the district (as discussed in the next chapter), and Matt Hanhila was promoted to the position of Glendale's executive dean.

atheism." I'd say, "Well, that's one of those things you talk about when you're talking about the philosophy of religion. That's not an unusual thing, and it's not unusual that students would get upset by that. That's what we're supposed to be doing." Then he said, "Okay." That would be the last that would be said about it.

In this atmosphere, the faculty at Glendale developed a strong independence. At the same time, the school saw a lot of political unrest and an unusual number of bomb threats. Speaking to Wilcox, Hanhila recalled:

April 19, 1996, video interview with Phil Smelser, Glendale Community College faculty member. Audio excerpts and transcript available online.

http://www.mc.maricopa.edu/users/M3cdhistory/

We had a big row about the department chairs. They all get paid in accordance to how many classes they get, and it's a ludicrous system because some department chairmen really have a big job and some don't. For departments like art and biology and business and those that order lots of supplies and have to keep track of a big inventory, a lot of typewriters, computers, that sort of thing, we made the proposal those people should be making more than, say, the philosophy department chair. I make out schedules. All I need is chalk and a chalkboard and a room. I really didn't think that I deserved to be paid the same thing as those guys because they had a really big job and I didn't. Prince just wouldn't hear of it. Five department chairs said, "Well, if you're not going to listen to reason, we're just going to resign." So they did. Five of them. Big departments. I went in to talk to John about that, and I said, "That's silly. These are incredibly talented people you're letting go here." He said, "Well, I just don't

$50,000 DAMAGE AT COLLEGE
'Time For War' Bomb Described

The disgruntled leader of the United Barrio Union (UBU) said he wanted war — so he started one. On April 26 he placed a homemade bomb in the Glendale Community College administration building, testified UBU member Gerardo Rivera.

The explosion caused more than $50,000 in damages.

Rivera told a Superior Court jury yesterday that defendant Jess Lopez, 28, was angered by a proposal to start an ex-offender program at the college. According to the witness, Lopez felt his Chicano group was to be slighted in its receipt of funds for program participation.

THE NIGHT that Rivera and Lopez discussed that proposed program, Lopez allegedly repeated, "It's time for war," and proceeded to construct a gasoline bomb in an empty beer bottle. Lopez took both the bomb and a simulator to

car that carried Lopez and Rivera to the college.

Solares, a scholarship student, was afraid to accompany the two, but agreed to drive them to the school.

Rivera admitted yesterday that he is an ex-convict and former mental patient who has had repeated problems with crime, drugs, suicide and mental breakdown.

The witness agreed to plead guilty to arson charges with a stipulated five year's probation if he testified against Lopez, who is accused of arson and depositing an explosive.

Rivera told jurors that he met Lopez

while the defendant was a "guest speaker" at the Arizona State Prison. Judge Sandra O'Connor refused to let Rivera say what Lopez spoke about, but the witness did testify he was serving a sentence for forgery at the time.

WHEN MEMBERS of the UBU met in Glendale the night before the bombing, all had been drinking beer, but Rivera said he heard Lopez respond to the ex-offender proposal by saying, "They just don't know who they're messing with."

When Rivera said he asked Lopez why the group didn't bomb an individual's house rather than the school, Lopez allegedly answered, "This (the school

bombing) would make the movement stronger."

Although Rivera appeared to show neither aversion nor regrets about helping to cause extensive damage to the school he is still attending, he told jurors he went along with the bombing "to help Jess."

Besides being enrolled as a student, Rivera said under cross examination by defense attorney Calvin Lee, he worked as a college janitor and had access to keys to buildings.

AFTER RIVERA saw and heard the explosion, Solares and Rivera drove near the administration building to pick up Lopez, the witness said. "I asked him how it went, and he said he couldn't get in (the building) but felt he got the job done."

Rivera, 26, is still a student at Glendale College, and testified he earns above average grades. His major is

The Phoenix Gazette
Metro News

Phoenix Gazette for October 5, 1977.

According to Phil Smelser, Hanhila also tended to respect the faculty and rarely interfered in academic matters:

He understood that he was not academically oriented, and he never did any damage to anybody who was. I was department chair of the philosophy department, and I had a couple of teachers that were kind of wild, and there were always students and parents coming in, complaining, especially about religious things. Anyway, he'd ask, "Well, what about this?" Because he didn't know. "I have a complaint here that one of your teachers is supporting

One week we had twelve or fourteen bomb calls in two weeks' time, and I had to make the decision either to close school or not. I attended conferences about this and put together all the information I could get. Most of the time, we never told the students to leave campus. We never turned them loose but once. I was downtown that day and I got a call from the Phoenix police, and then I got a call from the Glendale police, and one from the campus. And I said, "Turn 'em loose." That was 2:00 in the afternoon, and we had the most gosh-awful traffic jam you ever saw.

The Personality of Mesa Community College

The campus at Mesa Community College also opened in the fall of 1966, but the facilities were considerably more modest than those at Glendale. Only three buildings were constructed initially: the student center, the science building, and the maintenance building. Twenty-six portables functioned as the classrooms. The design for the new campus was inspired by traditional southwestern architectural motifs, but the concept was less successful than the concept for the Glendale campus. Early Mesa faculty member Jack Twitchell remembers:

> Horlbeck, Hickman and Associates were the initial architectural firm. The design was truncated pyramids, i.e., slanted walls. And they leaked. And the construction folks didn't seem to have a way to figure out how to keep those slanted walls from leaking because the mortar joints managed to seep. We have worked on that, as a constant problem, for years. Painting the inside of those walls has

Aftermath of the bombing at Glendale Community College, April 26, 1977.

made a significant difference, and we do treat them. As the next buildings began to evolve, the walls began to stand straight on the sides, instead of the slanted walls.

Thus, the Mesa campus was substantially incomplete for its dedication in the fall of 1966. Adding to the unfinished feeling was the fact that Dobson Road, one of the main access roads to the college, was then just a dirt road. Bertha Landrum, who began as a counselor at Mesa in the summer of 1966, recalls, "The sheep had the right-of-way down Dobson Road. It was a sheep trail, so you drive up in the morning and go wait for the sheep to cross and head for the parking lot."

The parking lots and landscaping had also been left unfinished. Imagine, then, what a solid week of monsoonal downpours did to the dirt in the same week classes were scheduled to begin. Jack Twitchell recalled, "We were at least a week, if not longer than a week, late in starting classes because we had nothing but a little bit of gravel and mostly dirt parking. And it rained. And it rained, and it rained. And we spent lots of time sitting in the Student Union, drinking coffee and looking out the south windows, watching the flood." Chuck Evans also remembers the mud: "We had rains after rain after rain after rain, and the parking lots were mud holes, basically. Students would get stuck, teachers would get stuck; everybody was helping one another get out of their mud holes and on their way. It was a dirty time."

1967

Aerial view of the Mesa campus reveals the village of portable classrooms where most of the instruction took place.

As if all the problems with the mud weren't enough, teaching in the old portables had its own problems, too. According to Evans:

> *A great amount of noise transferred from one side to the other through the ducts for the heating and cooling system. And if we had a particularly powerful lecturer on one side, students in both classes, regardless of the need, would hear the lecture from the "dramatic" side, as it were. That was one of the difficulties with holding acting classes or speech classes on one side, because we sometimes had rather powerful delivery, and it might upset somebody who was over there taking a test on the other side, or a teacher who was trying to make some sensitive point, perhaps. . . . But these were things that everybody understood.*

From Mesa's yearbook Jacali for 1967: Sheep grazing near the new campus.

Ironically, the shortcomings of the new Mesa campus had a positive influence on forming the college's personality. Many early Mesa faculty recall that the pioneering spirit they developed while struggling with temporary quarters in downtown Mesa continued after the move to the new campus. Again, people pitched in to make the best of difficult situations.

Another positive influence on the development of Mesa's personality was the character of its founding executive dean, John Riggs.

BUILDING THE MESA CAMPUS

Although the campus opened with only three permanent buildings and twenty-six portable classrooms, planning began almost immediately for the library and another clasroom building. At the board meeting on December 13, 1966, Riggs also convinced the board to construct the gymnasium. Construction on the first two began in March, 1967, and was completed in the spring of 1968. That fall, the football stadium was also dedicated. By the end of 1969, the campus also had a technology building, a social science building, a teacher office building, a business education building, and the gym. The music building was completed in October, 1970. In January, 1974, the nursing building was opened. The liberal arts building was opened for classes in the fall of 1976. The campus remained substantially in that form until the new math building and the remodeling of the student center in the late '80s.

Original main entrance to the student center reveals the sloping walls.

81

1966

John Riggs, seated at right, with his staff in 1967.   Standing (left to right): Associate Dean of Students Theo Heap, Dean of Admissions Roy Owens, and Dean of Continuing Education Stuart Donald.   Seated at left is Dean of Students, Jinnett Kirk.

Bill Holt, who retired in 1996 as Mesa's dean of instruction, recalls that Riggs knew all students by their first names and was involved in every phase of the college:

Dr. Riggs went to every activity that ever happened on this campus during his tenure here. If it was a play, he went to it, [or] a musical, a football game, a wrestling match. This was a student-oriented college. Dr. Riggs would catch a kid walking across the campus and stop him. "How are you doing?" During the week of registration, the kid might say, "Well, I'm trying to register, and I'm having trouble." Dr. Riggs would then walk him around and help him register.

June 27, 1996, video interview with Bill Holt, Mesa Community College faculty and administrator.   Transcript and audio and video excerpts available online.

http://www.mc.maricopa.edu/users/M3cdhistory/

He was extremely well connected to the community because he had been born and raised in Mesa. He was class valedictorian when he was graduated from Mesa High School in 1925. In 1930, he was graduated from Arizona State College in Tempe (now ASU) with majors in physical education and mathematics. He began teaching physical education and math at Mesa High School, and in 1935, he joined the staff of then Gila Junior College (now Eastern Arizona College) in Thatcher. In 1947, he moved to Phoenix College, where he counseled students, taught physical education, and coached football and baseball. He eventually functioned as the equivalent of dean of students under Hannelly. In 1960, he earned his Ed.D. from ASU.

Staged photo of John Riggs greeting students outside of Mesa Community College's original home, now the Landmark Restaurant.

Jack Twitchell confirms Riggs' commitment to students:

And I can remember his saying things like, "The most important thing I need here in teachers is people skills." He would often, sort of jokingly, say something like, "Hell, we've all got so much education we're dangerous, anyway. What we need are people who can work with people!"

Unlike Prince, who guarded his authority jealously, Riggs preferred to be more inclusive in decision-making. Arnette Ward, who was a counselor at Mesa during its early years, recalls:

"[Riggs] did not dictate things. He made the decisions, but somehow I always felt that I was a part of that decision. He would talk with us about different issues before he made decisions."

Riggs had been a coach, and coaching seemed to define his administrative style. Bertha Landrum recalls, "Each of us had our playing spot. He used to call me his quarterback. I mean, he thought of people as having playing positions. And he talked in football metaphors, saying, you know, 'I want you to carry the ball on that.'"

Unlike Glendale, Mesa never had significant problems with bomb threats or student demonstrations. A potentially serious situation did develop around the time of the shooting at Kent State University in 1970, but Riggs and Kirk successfully kept the problem from getting out of hand. The problem began when a group of veterans surrounded the flagpole in front of the student union and cut down the flag because antiwar protesters were threatening to burn it in protest. Bill Holt recalls what happened next:

Jinnett was never one to stray from getting in the middle of whatever goes on, and she was right in the middle of it, and Dr. Riggs came up . . . Apparently the students were really arguing with each other. Looked like it was going to get out of hand. So at that point either Jinnett or Dr. Riggs said, "Would you like to talk about it? Would you like to express your opinions about it?" "Absolutely." So they called for a speaker system, got a microphone, and then they lined them up. Said,

The Arizona Republic, May 7, 1976. This photo shows Mesa students removing the flag from the campus flagpole. From microfilm.

"Those that want to talk about pro-war are over here and those that are antiwar over here," and they started. I think they went all day, and I don't know how long in the afternoon. . . . They timed them, and they had a big long line, and they could come up and speak. I thought it was just a magnificent thing. Never had another issue after that with it, to my knowledge.

JINNETT KIRK'S DEVOTION TO STUDENTS

Jinnett Kirk, Mesa's first dean of students, shared John Riggs' commitment to students. Beginning in 1955, she had been the dean of women at Phoenix College while Riggs had been the counselor of men. When Riggs was named the first executive dean of Mesa, she moved to Mesa as its first dean of students. Her devotion to students often went beyond the call of duty. Bill Holt recalls:

Her memos were precious. You'd get a memo in the mail: "A certain student has been in a car accident and will not be in class. Would you work with the student in their assignments?" A personal memo, signed by Jinnett, typed up: "Help the student. Here's a number to call the student." As a matter-of-fact, there were times I know for a fact that Jinnett Kirk has personally driven assignments home to students that we had here at Mesa. Once, I got her memo, and it said the student's name. I had her in an accounting class, and it asked if I would send work home, and she had somebody that was going to deliver the work. I said, "Well, the student can't come by and pick it up even?" "No, the student can't pick it up." . . . So finally I asked Jinnett—I caught her one day— "Well, how long is the student going to be out?" She said, "Well, she could be out a little while. But I know you'll work with her." I said, "Sure. But, well, a week?" "Well, she may be out thirty days." I said, "Why thirty days?" "Well, I guess I ought to tell you. She's in jail. They picked her up for prostitution, and she got a thirty-day sentence. I know you'll work with her." I said, "Absolutely. I'll work with her." She got out in her thirty days . . .

The Board's Commitment to Athletics

Another fundamental difference in the personalities of the two schools was the way that Mesa developed a much stronger emphasis on athletics than Glendale. Of course, Prince at one time had been a tennis coach, and Hanhila was a passionate handball player, but neither of them focused on athletics to the extent that Riggs did.

Some felt the program at Mesa was actually too strong, but Theo Heap, who was Mesa's first athletic director, disagrees:

> I don't care whether it's athletics or what. If you want the best English program, you go out and hire aggressive people who are really going to build a program. Same thing in science. Dr. Riggs always took that attitude, that we were going to be the best in everything. A lot of people said, "Well, it's just athletics." No, it wasn't athletics. He felt that way about every single program.

May 12, 1997, video interview with Theo Heap, president of Mesa Community College 1978-84. Transcript and audio and video excerpts available online.

http://www.mc.maricopa.edu/users/M3cdhistory/

Another point in favor of a strong athletics program was the widely accepted opinion that athletics were an absolutely essential part of the junior college experience. This belief is stated explicitly in the constitution of the Arizona Junior College Athletic Association, whose bylaws were adopted formally by the Maricopa governing board at their meeting on June 29, 1964. The first section of this constitution states:

The Arizona Junior College Athletic Conference (AJCAC) believes that a well-organized and well-administered athletic program is an integral part of the total educational offerings of each of its member institutions. Accordingly, the purpose of this organization shall be to foster and promote wholesome athletic programs among its member schools. It is dedicated to goals that will assure physical, mental, and social improvement for each participant.

Athletics were considered so important that the governing board took a direct interest in hiring coaches and setting athletic policies at the schools. According to Bob Easley, "The board had retained the right to choose the coaches and the administrators of the district—not that we excluded the advice of the other administrators—we retained that prerogative for the first few administrators and coaches."

An early example of the board's direct intervention in this area occurred at the December 30, 1964, board meeting. According to the minutes:

> *Dr. Hannelly next requested approval of the board to ask the State Board of Directors for Junior Colleges to issue a junior college teacher's certifi-* cate to George D. Hoy. He explained that "Dutch" Hoy had been employed at Phoenix College for 34 years as coach and physical education teacher; that the Phoenix Union High School District had allowed the employment of Mr. Hoy with an AB degree although a Master's was required for every other department. He stated further that the State Junior College District ordinarily would not allow this, however, to take care of teachers of long experience and particular qualifications, they would grant certification in certain cases at the request of the County Board.

This motion was presented by Easley, seconded by Miller, and carried easily.

To have refused to transfer "Dutch" Hoy with all the other Phoenix College faculty to the new district would have been unthinkable. He was a local legend. He had been the athletic director at Phoenix College since 1929. At one time or another, he had coached every sport, including boxing. Clearly, the master's degree requirement had to be waived in his case. But in doing so, the board set another precedent that later became significantly problematic. Where coaches were concerned, their coaching experience was more important than academic credentials.

George D. "Dutch" Hoy, Phoenix College physical education faculty and coach, 1927-1967.

The board occupied itself with athletics frequently during

the Hannelly years. For example, board members took time out from their meeting on December 7, 1964, to congratulate the football team from Phoenix College on having won the NJCAA football championship. Then, on April 12, 1965, the board considered whether the extensions should be granted varsity status to play other colleges in baseball and basketball.

As the time approached to open the new campuses, board members decided the time was right to initiate football programs at both new colleges. At the board meeting on February 28, 1966, $20,000 was budgeted for each campus to start a football program.

Then, at the board meeting on January 9, 1967, the board appointed Carl Rollins as a counselor/football coach at Glendale and Royal Price as a physical education instructor/football coach at Mesa. Unfortunately, Price had not yet completed a master's degree. The minutes state:

> Dr. Riggs explained to the board that some faculty members were concerned about the academic certification of some of the coaching candidates. It was their belief that these qualifications were valid and important and any variance from these standards could be detrimental to the quality of instruction.

Price indicated his willingness to complete his master's degree, and the matter should have ended there, but Jim Miller took strong exception to Riggs' remarks. Miller then requested that his own comments from the January 9 meeting be revised and expanded. According to the February 13 minutes, Miller wanted to be sure the previous minutes included the fact that he had pointed out there "were instructors at PC that did not

have a master's degree. Dr. Riggs commented that none of these men were head coaches." Miller's reply is then recorded in the minutes in unusual detail:

> Seventeen years in a semiprofessional category certainly qualified a person under our schedule to as much as and more than a master's degree holder. It was for this reason that [Miller] had overlooked the requirement for a master's degree—given years on one qualification area compared to 17 years of experience, [Miller] had to give credence to the experience.

In the same meeting, "Dr. Hannelly recommended to the board the employment of Mr. Edgar C. 'Mutt' Ford as the head football coach for Mesa Community College, beginning the 1967-68 school year." A few moments later, Riggs brought in Ford and introduced him to the board. A similar event occurred at the meeting on May 8, 1967. "Dutch" Hoy was retiring from the faculty that year, and the board personally presented him with his certificate honoring him as Professor Emeritus.

During those same years, new faculty were not presented at board meetings, but coaches were. The board's direct involvement with athletics became a major contributing factor to the Artichoke Rebellion five years later.

The North Central Association Pays a Call

1966 was a year of two real milestones in Bob Hannelly's life. In October, the Maricopa district dedicated the first two campuses of the system.

Unfortunately, the other milestone was that on April 30, Bob Hannelly became sixty-five years old.

By all rights, Hannelly should have retired in the spring of 1966.

However, the North Central Association (NCA) accreditation visit had been scheduled for February of 1967, and Hannelly's expertise in that area was obviously needed. By the fall of 1966, though, relations between Hannelly and the board had reached a new low. Bob Easley claims: "Well, there had been a sort of [breach]. . . . We fired one of Hannelly's vice presidents who had been brought in, and I think Hannelly had expected him to be his successor. I've even forgotten the fellow's name. It made a little bit of hard feelings between the board and [him]." (Unfortunately, the board minutes do not provide any clue who this vice president may have been.)

1967 North Central Association Accreditation Reports on Glendale Community College, Mesa Community College, and Phoenix College. *The complete texts of all three reports are available online.*

http://www.mc.maricopa.edu/users/M3cdhistory/

When the NCA accreditation team arrived, Hannelly appears to have been unusually candid about his problems with the board. The team ended its visit in Phoenix on February 21, 1967, and the normal pattern would have been for the team members to present their findings orally, probably to Hannelly and members of his staff, before leaving. What the team said in its oral summary is not recorded, but the team's final report was published in August. Although the document was generally complimentary to the district colleges, the report contains the following:

Disregard of administration prerogatives is further illustrated by two or more instances in which administration recommendations on appointments were overruled and persons appointed who did not meet the qualifications established by the Board. Regardless of the merits of the particular individuals, the procedure by which the action was taken greatly weakened the effectiveness of the administration and the confidence of the staff in the integrity of the Board.

Whether the report is referring to the board's firing of Hannelly's handpicked vice president or to the board's insistence on hiring coaches regardless of their academic qualifications is not known. However, the report goes on to describe the board's general disregard for the authority of its chief executive office, and delivers the following sharp slap to the board's wrist:

The members of the governing board are able men, highly respected in the community, and sincerely dedicated to the welfare of the colleges. Unfortunately, they appear relatively inexperienced in board operation in an enterprise of this size. As a consequence, they have drifted into procedures which are dangerous and have already resulted in reduced efficiency and loss of faculty morale. If they persist, a loss of public confidence is probable.

The NCA team recommended that accreditation be continued for the district colleges but added the humiliating stipulation that a consultant must be appointed "to assist the board

in developing more acceptable procedures, in defining more clearly the central office and campus administrative functions, and improving organization for campus administration. If the consultant is unable to report substantial progress in these areas, a reexamination should be ordered within three years."

Arizona Republic for February 28, 1967.

8 The Arizona Republic

Dr. Hannelly to Retire As District President

Dr. Robert J. Hannelly, president of the Maricopa County Junior College District and associated with Phoenix education, for 40 years, will retire July 1.

H. W. Van Loo, member of the district's governing board, made the announcement last night at a board meeting at Phoenix College. Dr. Hannelly is in San Francisco attending a meeting of the National Association of Junior Colleges.

DR. HANNELLY, who is retiring because of age, will be 66 on April 30. He will remain for at least one year as president emeritus in an advisory capacity to assist the new district president, Van Loo said.

Hannelly began his educational association with Phoenix in 1927 as a math teacher and sponsor of the student association at Phoenix College. He became dean of the college in 1947 and, when the county junior college district was formed, he became its first president in 1963.

MORE THAN 150 persons, mostly junior college district faculty members, attended the meeting because of announcement that a faculty salary recommendation was to be made to the board. However, the salary matter was postponed until the board's March 13 meeting because James M. Snyder, chairman of a joint faculty-administration committee which prepared the recommendations, was out of town.

Also postponed were rehiring of personnel for 1967-68, action on a proposed administrative merit pay increase, reconsideration of special salary benefits for teacher candidates from Maricopa County, and approval of teacher sabbaticals for 1967-68.

DR. ROBERT J. HANNELLY
To Advisory Capacity

No evidence suggests that any board members knew anything about the team's oral summary to Hannelly's staff. However, at the board meeting on February 27—barely a week after the NCA accreditation team had departed—Van Loo announced that Hannelly would retire as of the first of July. The minutes of this meeting then state, "[Hannelly] would remain for at least one year as president emeritus in an advisory capacity to assist the new district president."

The surprising fact is that Hannelly was not present at the meeting. The minutes acknowledge he was than attending the convention of the American Association of Junior Colleges in San Francisco. When interviewed for this book on two separate occasions, Millie Noble stated unequivocally that Hannelly did not know he was being retired until he returned from San Francisco.

The circumstances suggest that the board members were retiring Hannelly summarily as punishment for bad-mouthing them to the NCA team. However, Easley maintains, "We didn't fire him. It was amicable as far as I was concerned. . . . This had been in the discussion of who was going to be where and why. The placement of administrators had been discussed, surely."

Easley's recollection seems reasonable. Hannelly was about two months away from his sixty-sixth birthday (He was born April 30, 1901.) He should have known that once the NCA visit was over, he would not be continued as district president. Also, the minutes of the February 27 meeting contain a detail that tends to suggest the decision to retire Hannelly was indeed "amicable." The board used Hannelly's absence to discuss how the new student center being constructed at Phoenix College was to be dedicated as the Robert J. Hannelly Student Center. If the board felt Hannelly had betrayed them to the NCA, they surely would have opposed this dedication. Perhaps, then, the callous way in which the board chose to terminate Hannelly's employment was just another incidence of their general lack of regard for him, even as they were planning to honor him.

1967

Whatever the truth, Hannelly did remain as president emeritus through the end of the 1968 school year. He was still there when the accreditation team's written report came out. No record exists to document if he took any pleasure in the rebuke which the report delivered to the board. In all probability, he did not.

However, the days when the governing board could walk all over the district president were over. The board members had wanted a strong leader—and they were about to get one.

Bob Hannelly and his portrait commissioned for the Hannelly Student Center at Phoenix College.

1968

MARICOPA COUNTY
JUNIOR COLLEGE DISTRICT

106 EAST WASHINGTON STREET
P. O. BOX 13349
PHOENIX. ARIZONA 85002
252-6661

June, 1968

Dear Graduate:

Now high school is behind you and college lies ahead. Congratulations for graduating and for being ready to enter college!

Your collegiate days can be most exciting. You will make new friends. You will study new subjects under the leadership of thought-provoking professors. You will make all-important career decisions determining the course of your life.

You are fortunate to have available in Arizona a strong higher educational system. Our state universities are excellent. Our junior colleges are excellent, too. Let me describe them briefly.

There are four in the county, one possibly conveniently close to you:

Mesa Community College	Southern Ave. & Dobson Rd.	969-5521
Phoenix College	1202 W. Thomas Road	264-2492
Glendale Community College	6000 West Olive Avenue	934-2211
Maricopa Technical College	106 E. Washington Street	252-6661

Why don't you call or drive to one nearest you?

You can get a sound education leading to further collegiate study or to a good job. You will study with well-educated, carefully selected pro-fessors in well-equipped buildings. You will pay reasonable fees, less than a $100 a year. You can attend classes in the day or at night, making it possible for you to work and attend college, too. Friendly counselors are now available on the campuses to assist you.

Once again, congratulations, and great success in your college work.

Sincerely yours,

John F. Prince
President

John Prince,
district president 1967-76

JFP/vmb

Chapter Nine

1972
Another President, Another College

After Hannelly's retirement was announced in February of 1967, the board quickly turned its attention to the matter of appointing his successor. Board members didn't have to look very far because the logical candidate was in the executive dean's office at Glendale Community College, where he was drumming his fingers on his desk and waiting for the phone to ring.

As explained in chapter seven, John Prince had ample reason to believe he was going to be the next president of the Maricopa district. At least one board member may even have promised him the job outright. But not every member of the governing board admired Prince at that time. In fact, one member actually despised him.

When interviewed for this book, Bob Jaap confessed:

> This is the first time I've really told anybody outside of my own family this story because I'm not proud of it. I regret it. But [Prince and I] became enemies. Not just impersonal toward each other, but we were angry toward each other. Constantly. For no really good reason except that's the way people sometimes do things.

Copy of a letter dated June, 1968, from John Prince to recent high school graduates.

The irony is that for many years before the district had been formed, Jaap and Prince had actually been friends and neighbors. "We lived in the same neighborhood. Our two families were members of a little swimming club for the kids in our neighborhood, which we got together and built. . . . Our wives knew each other," Jaap says.

But after Prince was appointed to head the state board, the friendship between Jaap and Prince began to deteriorate. The problem started because Jaap felt that Prince "just couldn't keep his hands off of us," by which he meant that Prince felt he was responsible

April 26, 1996, video interview with Bob Jaap, Maricopa governing board member 1962-68. Transcript and audio and video excerpts available online.

http://www.mc.maricopa.edu/users/M3cdhistory/

for the Maricopa system. "And that was my and my board's responsibility, and we felt we could handle it pretty good. John felt that what we did was his responsibility, too, I'm afraid." This struggle over turf led one day to a major confrontation. According to Jaap:

> We were having an argument or an opposition on something. I remember what happened; I don't remember about what it happened. I went to John's office. We were talk-

ing about this issue, and . . . we didn't reach any agreement, and the discussion got a little bit heated, and I remember my remark to him. I said, "John, don't look down your nose at us!" That ended our friendship right there. Plunk. It's dead.

The situation deteriorated even further when Joe Ralston, Maricopa County's representative to the state community college board, attended a Maricopa board meeting. Al Flowers recalls that Ralston could be very insistent: "Joe was the strongest member on the state board because he could shout and cuss louder than anybody else."

Jaap felt Ralston was acting not as Maricopa County's representative to the state board but as John Prince's personal delegate to the Maricopa district's governing board:

> [Ralston] was not only acting as one of us—as a board member—he was acting as if he owned us—as if he had the authority to tell us what to do! Anyway, this attorney was interrupting us—interrupting me! I was chairman—interrupt-

ing me at the board meeting, and I finally said to him, "You're not a member of this board. Now, please leave us alone." But he didn't leave. He stayed, and he kept participating in the board meeting, speaking up when he felt like it, that kind of thing. Anyway, that strain stayed, from then on.

Thus, Jaap was not eager to rubber-stamp Prince's appointment as Hannelly's replacement. In fact, Jaap already had someone else in mind for the job: Marion Donaldson, who was then the superintendent of the Amphitheater school district in Tucson, where he had established a considerable reputation as an innovative educator. The son of an old Mesa pioneer family, Donaldson attended Mesa High School and Arizona State

nurturing the development of the Walker School, an innovative elementary school that gained something of a national reputation. During the same period, Donaldson completed his Ph.D. at the University of Arizona. The subject of his dissertation was the history of the Arizona Education Association, and while doing the research, he became well-known in educational circles in Arizona.

Marion Donaldson in 1969.

Even though Donaldson had no previous experience as an administrator on the college level, Jaap remembers that he began to push Donaldson as a viable alternative to Prince:

> *Marion Donaldson is, and was, one of the finest educators in the state of Arizona. He has a beautiful track record. . . . I simply knew him by reputation. We had maybe talked or attended meetings of some kind together, but I knew him well enough to say to the other board members, "I think we should invite this guy to apply."*

The impetus to interview Donaldson may have come from Jaap, but Marion Donaldson remembers that the phone call came from Flowers:

> *Flowers called me, and he said, "The board wants you to apply for the presidency of this district." I hooted. "My God! I've never spent a day in a community college, and you're talking about the presidency?" I said, "What do you want, just an application to make it sound good, that you're looking at a lot of people?" He said, "No; we just want an application." Well, I submitted the application, but I couldn't take that job. I knew I couldn't handle it.*

March 5, 1996, video interview with Marion Donaldson, executive dean of Scottsdale Community College, from 1970-73. Transcript and audio excerpts available online.

http://www.mc.maricopa.edu/users/M3cdhistory/

Teachers College, where he earned his bachelor's degree in 1935. He returned to Mesa High a year later as an administrator and worked his way up to being principal while studying for his master's degree at the University of Southern California in the summer. In 1951, the Amphitheater school district in Tucson offered him the job of superintendent, but initially, Donaldson wasn't interested because Amphitheater was underfunded and its board was in serious disarray. However, the Amphitheater board offered him complete autonomy as superintendent, and he accepted. Between 1951 and 1967, Donaldson made a name for himself by turning around Amphitheater's finances and by

Joe Ralston speaking at the dedication of the Glendale campus, October 16, 1966.

But anyway, I was invited up to the board meeting. When I went in, I went in to the board, and I had a conversation with them, and after I came out, I saw Jack Prince there. I said, "Jack! Are you here for the presidency?" He said, "Yes. I've been invited [to apply]." I said, "My God. If they don't choose you, there's been a real miscarriage of justice. I have no business up here." Jack kind of laughed, and so on.

That next day, Bob Jaap called me and said, "Well, I'm sorry. We gave the job to Jack Prince." I said, "You would have been insane to do otherwise. Well, thanks very much." He said, "Well, wait a minute. We need a vice president for academic affairs. How about that job?" I was flabbergasted again. I said, "I can't do that, really." He said, "We think you can. You've got ideas about education that we want to inculcate here. You and Al Flowers and Jack Prince will make a formidable team here, and we want to offer you the job."

Al Flowers tells the same story differently. According to him, Prince's appointment had always been a foregone conclusion, and the other board members did not share Jaap's enthusiasm for Donaldson. "In executive session, they decided, 'Well, okay. We'll give [Donaldson] a job as a vice president, then, to get you off our backs, Bob Jaap.' That's how he was hired."

However Donaldson came to be appointed vice president, Prince was not happy. Once again, the board had acted as the chief executive officer for the district and compromised the president's authority—as the board had become used to doing to Hannelly. Flowers maintains, "Prince was given a choice: 'You

take him or you don't get the job,' if you really want to know about it. . . . 'You want to be president? Then he gets a job here.'"

Donaldson immediately realized the awkwardness of the situation and went to talk to Prince directly. The meeting did not go well. Jaap recalls, "According to Marion Donaldson, John Prince said, 'I didn't want you; the board selected you,' and Marion has told me that several times."

At the district board meeting on April 24, 1967, the board announced John Prince as the new district president effective July 1. At the same time, the board also accepted the resignation of Hannelly's vice president, James Snyder; according to Tom Garneski (who was then a counselor at Phoenix College), Snyder went on to become the president of a community college in Illinois.

Strangely, the announcement of Donaldson's appointment was delayed until July 6. That fact suggests that Prince may have been working behind the scenes to try to divest himself of Donaldson. Irwin Spector, who was then the district's director of research and curriculum, insists that at one point in this process, Prince actually offered him Donaldson's job. In the end, though, Prince remained stuck with Donaldson.

Prince's overt opposition to Donaldson's appointment was an early indication that Prince was going to be a different kind of president than Hannelly had been. Clearly, he was not going to lie down and let the board walk over him as his predecessor had done.

Cutting his losses with Donaldson (temporarily), Prince then moved to solidify his authority in other areas. When Hannelly was

the district president, the campus head administrators had all held the title of executive dean, a relic of the years when the PUHS superintendent (E. W. Montgomery) had held the title of president of Phoenix College but had had little direct connection with running the college. Under Prince, however, the campus head administrators were renamed *executive deans and vice presidents*, a change which reinforced their subordination to the district president. Under Prince, the campus deans were no longer autonomous administrators; they would report directly to the president of the district.

The Founding of Maricopa Technical College

As John Prince came on board, the district was already in the throes of creating its fourth college, but this one was not to be another clone of Phoenix College.

From the very beginning of the district in 1962, the board seems to have viewed occupational and technical education as being a necessary but regrettable part of the district's mission. Bob Easley explains:

Phoenix College in particular was not interested in occupational courses. [Their] courses had to have a certain aura about them. They were very proud of the RN program, for instance. But they would not have been proud of an auto mechanics course. . . . And we talked about the "garbage pail of education"—meaning to teach the bricklayers and to teach the welders—that we didn't want to be involved with. We felt that the apprentice program of the masons should teach bricklaying, that the welders should teach welding, for example, and that we shouldn't be involved with that. We wanted to offer the two years toward a degree. We thought nothing should be taught except a full-semester course. We weren't interested in any programs that were taught for six weeks and then given a certificate. Courses should be for full college credit, and that was our perceived mission at the beginning.

Still, the district had no choice; the 1960 enabling legislation explicitly defined occupational education as part of the mission for the junior colleges. For that reason, the board had dutifully created a vice president for semiprofessional education and given the job to Marvin Knudson. "Semiprofessional education" was understood to mean preparing medical assistants, secretaries, electronics technicians, etc., but not automobile mechanics, bricklayers, or any other occupation that produced dirty fingernails.

To protect the ideological purity of the junior colleges, the board decided to create a separate technical college. That way, the three junior colleges could keep their fingernails clean while the district could fulfill the state's legislative mandate to provide occupational training.

Of course, the idea of a technical college didn't occur to everyone all at once. The wheels began to turn in the fall of 1965 when the deans from Phoenix College appeared at the October 25 board meeting and presented enrollment projections showing Phoenix College might soon run out of space. According to the minutes, "Mr. Miller indicated that serious thought should be given to redistricting and that perhaps a site [for a technical college] could be chosen somewhere in the perimeter of the Phoenix Union District."

At the next meeting, James Snyder, whose job included overseeing the district's physical facilities, presented a report projecting the district's facilities requirements for the future. After the report, the board began to consider its options, and the following comments appear in the minutes:

> *Dr. Easley stated that, according to the map, the bulk of the students were located in the vicinity of Phoenix College and, because many students have whole or part-time jobs in this vicinity, they prefer to attend PC. He, therefore, thought a downtown campus might be the answer.*

Maricopa's three executive deans/vice presidents in 1966. Left to right: Matt Hanhila (Glendale Community College), J. Lee Thompson (Phoenix College), and John Riggs (Mesa Community College).

At the meeting on January 3, 1966, Jim Miller expressed his continuing anxiety about increasing enrollments. Fall daytime registration at Phoenix College had been stopped at 5,400, and the overflow students had been told to go to the extensions. Projections suggested that PC's daytime enrollment might top 6,000 in the next two or three years. Phoenix College's need for new space was becoming acute.

Al Flowers, who had just joined the district in the spring of 1966 on a part-time basis, began to look at available properties for a downtown technical college. One or two downtown properties were actively considered, but Jim Miller opposed the idea. According to Flowers, the Del Webb company (Miller's employer) was in the planning phase for building the new Civic Plaza, and Miller was acutely familiar with the problems of the downtown area. Flowers comments, "[Miller] thought downtown was the last place you should put anything in this city because it was always going to be a deteriorating situation down there."

Then, the board got an offer it couldn't refuse. Sherman Hazeltine, Bob Jaap's boss at the First National Bank of Arizona, had become aware of a possible opportunity for the college. He told Jaap how the Broadway-Hale Department Stores, Inc., of Los Angeles had acquired an old Phoenix landmark, the Korrick's Department Store at First Street and Washington. The store had been a fixture on the downtown retail scene since before the First World War, but by 1966, the store was hemorrhaging money, and Broadway-Hale wanted to unload it. In fact, the company was willing to give it away. The only catch was that Broadway-Hale owned only half of the land the building was sitting on; the other half was leased. If the district could acquire title to the land that was leased, the district could have a free building.

Jaap brought the offer to the board. District staff members evaluated the building and were impressed with its potential for a new college. Flowers investigated the land leases and learned that they were complicated. All the while, Korrick's was still operating as a department store, and the employees had no idea they were about to lose their jobs.

At the December 12, 1966, board meeting, Irwin Spector, as the district's director of research, presented his latest report. Whether or not the board was enthusiastic about the semiprofessional programs, they were thriving. According to the minutes of that meeting:

[Spector] pointed out that we now have twenty semiprofessional programs, twenty-seven university-parallel programs and five general programs in the MCJCD.

These figures must have impressed even Miller because according to the minutes, "The board seemed to agree as to the educational usage of the downtown facility as indicated in the report attached hereto, that the institution would serve adult, technical, vocational education and retraining programs."

The board moved to accept Broadway-Hale's offer and to refer it to the state board for evaluation and approval. Snyder was then assigned to work up a proposed curriculum

Advertising art for Korrick's Department Store in 1966.

ARIZONA'S LEADING DEPARTMENT STORE

From territorial days, Korricks has stood for continuing progress...ever growing with Phoenix and Arizona.

DOWNTOWN: Washington at First Street, ALpine 8-5911

CHRIS-TOWN: Fifteenth Avenue at Bethany Home Road, AMherst 5-2911

Korricks

Aerial view of downtown Phoenix in the early '70s. The Korrick's building is in the lower right corner. Above it are Symphony Hall and the first phase of the Civic Plaza (completed in 1972). To the left are the Adams Hotel (now the Crowne Plaza) and the skeleton of the Hyatt Regency under construction. Above and beyond to the left may be seen St. Mary's Basilica. Further back is the Phoenix Union High School campus and even Montgomery Stadium. Note that the Civic Plaza does not yet cross over Washington Street. No Mercado — no Bank One Ballpark, either!

There are 4,000 students enrolled in programs with semiprofessional goals or 22% of the entire enrollment of the entire district. The growth of our district in this area may be indicated in that there were only eight semiprofessional programs offered three years ago with an enrollment of less than 400 students.

for a downtown technical college. At the meeting on January 23, 1967, Snyder presented a progress report in which he stipulated that the programs at PC "attempt to serve primarily high school age students in their regular day program" [original emphasis]. The new downtown campus "would attempt to serve primarily those individuals who have left high school and are more than 19 years of age or graduated from high school."

A**ll the while, Korrick's was still operating as a department store, and the employees had no idea they were about to lose their jobs.**

This quotation demonstrates how the district's officials did not yet see Maricopa as a true community college district. In spite of the fact that evening enrollment had been outstripping daytime enrollment for more than ten years and the average age of the students was, accordingly, rising, the district still clung to an institutional model that was already out of date.

Having committed the district to building a technical college in the old department store building, the board did not immediately move to bring the new school into reality. The arrival of the NCA accreditation team in February, 1967, slowed progress on the new college. Then, Hannelly's retirement was announced, and the board was occupied with the search for a new president. Prince won the toss, and then the board focused on the ensuing staff changes and other matters of transition.

In the fall of 1967, the process of creating the new college began to pick up momentum again. Norb Bruemmer, who eventually became the second executive dean of Maricopa Technical College, feels that Prince supported the idea of a technical college more than Hannelly: "Jack was at one time dean of the evening college at Phoenix College, and so he had more affinity toward occupational education than Bob Hannelly. Bob Hannelly was more traditional in his philosophy."

Another factor that might have helped to move things along was that Phoenix—along with many other cities—was experiencing considerable civil unrest. Race riots were becoming common events in major cities during the summers, and Phoenix was no exception. Brad Luckingham's *Phoenix: The*

History of a Southwestern Metropolis states that an episode of "serious civil disobedience" (as it was dubbed by Mayor Milton Graham) in July, 1967, produced the arrests of nearly 300 people. **Tom Garneski** remembers how this situation affected the board's thinking:

> This was all during the period of the LA riots and the Chicago riots, the Washington and Detroit riots, and they were burning cities down. And that was part of the emphasis on getting this Maricopa Tech moving fast. Because we [the district] had nothing to offer. We

 October 11, 1996, audio interview with Tom Garneski, Maricopa district faculty and administrator. Transcript and audio excerpts are available online.

> were offering pretty much all the traditional-type programs at the other colleges, and we weren't doing anything . . . for people in, say, the South Phoenix area as well, who really needed something as well geared to get them moving.

At the board meeting on October 23, 1967, the new college was officially named Maricopa Technical College. (Al Flowers suggested the school be called MIT—the Maricopa Institute of Technology—but the board laughed at the idea.) At the board

meeting on November 13, Dr. Irwin L. Spector was appointed MTC's first executive dean; in proper Maricopa fashion, he was to wear this hat at the same time he continued to wear the hat of vice president for semiprofessional and technical education. Under his immediate supervision, renovations on the Korrick's building then began.

Norb Bruemmer remembers this phase:

> It was still a department store. It still had the cash registers sitting there, all the fixtures were sitting there, empty coat hangers were there, and a lot of dirt and dust.

"The board was kind of lukewarm on occupational education, but they recognized that it's a good thing to do."

http://www.mc.maricopa.edu/users/M3cdhistory/

Irwin Spector, dean of Maricopa Technical College 1967-70.

April 11, 1996, video interview with Norb Bruemmer, dean of Maricopa Technical College 1970-80. Transcript and audio excerpts available online.

http://www.mc.maricopa.edu/users/M3cdhistory/

The board—somewhat uncharacteristically—permitted Spector to make his own administrative appointments. He named Norb Bruemmer, who had been Phoenix College's director of technical education, as MTC's dean of instruction and Tom Garneski, who had a counseling background, as the dean of students. Spector also gave Garneski the job of supervising MTC's general studies program, which would provide the

Maricopa district; so Spector, Garneski, and Bruemmer went junketing to California to look at technical colleges, and based on what they found, they created a new instructional model that they dubbed the "ladder." All of MTC's programs were apparently viewed as ladders. For example, Maricopa Tech began a nursing assistant program, which could be completed in as few as six months. Students who wished to continue could then move up the ladder into the LPN program. From there, they could move farther up the ladder to the RN program at any of the other three district colleges.

The first rung of the ladder for almost all the programs at MTC was the general studies program. Tom Garneski explains this step:

We'd bring them in, people who were really quite deficient in language skills and reading skills and computational skills, and put them into English as a Second Language program and

Reg Manning cartoon from the Arizona Republic as reproduced in the MTC school newspaper, The Prospector, *for September, 1971.*

. . . We converted the display windows into an educational lab. We created that because that was when we had the big computers that had to be air-conditioned and so forth. And we also had some key-punch in the window, so we would cause people to stop and stare.

Unlike Hannelly's dual appointment as district president and executive dean of Phoenix College, Spector's dual appointment was more practical. The technical college was expected to be relatively small, and the district offices were preparing to occupy the sixth floor of the Korrick's building on January 8, 1968. One flight down, he was an executive dean; one flight up, he was a district vice president.

Maricopa Technical College administration in 1970. Left to right: Harry Fletcher (dean of instruction), Norb Bruemmer (executive dean), and Lionel Martinez (associate dean of instruction).

academic underpinning of those courses of study leading to an associate's degree.

Designing the Technical College Curriculum

Renovating the building was one thing; designing the technical college curriculum was another. This was *terra incognita* for the

Tom Garneski, Maricopa Technical College administrator 1970-72.

other kinds of technique-y things, and get them up to where then they could enter the regular program or go into one of the technology programs. . . . The main emphasis was on developmental education, to put people up to where they could function and get into that first ladder of employment.

But the emphasis was not exclusively developmental:

We recognized that the people that we were drawing in from that central Phoenix area and west and south, they were not all to be vocational education-oriented because there were some pretty sharp people in there. So we wanted to have at least a minimal kind of liberal arts program, so that if they wanted to finish up, say, in their first year of liberal arts, we would have a program, all the sociology, history, English, math. . . . They would take the first year there at Maricopa and then they could transfer off to Phoenix College. We had quite a few who did.

Another important innovation at Maricopa Tech was the use of advisory committees pulled from the community to help design the occupational programs. Norb Bruemmer recalls:

We were the first college in the state to work with business and industry in trying to create a curriculum based on performance. We said to them, "What do you want your employees to be able to do?" So we put in whatever industry told us should be incorporated in the curriculum. We developed the curriculum. We'd get them to take a look at it, but we still had the control over it.

In addition to the advisory committees, the school's administrators sought general input

from the members of the Black and Hispanic communities. As a result, the community welcomed the new school enthusiastically. On opening day in September of 1968, the school had over 1,200 students, a record enrollment for any new college in Arizona at that time.

Of course, the "Maricopa Curse" that had provided oceans of mud for the openings of Mesa and Glendale Community Colleges was at work at MTC on opening day, too. Bruemmer recalls, "We didn't have all of our electricity on in all of our areas. So students had electric typewriters and couldn't type, so they played like they were typing. That took about an extra week."

Gene Fazio, who was a charter faculty member teaching English at MTC, recalls the positive environment of the school. For example, MTC employed a grading system that emphasized success: "They had A, B, C, and no-credit, and so you could not have a GPA below a 2.0 at Maricopa Tech." In other words, the ladder led up, not down.

Gene Fazio also recalls that the close quarters fostered positive relationships among the students and the faculty:

The faculty would eat lunch with the students down in the student lounge. It was very close, a lot of contact. You'd see faculty staying there, working with students.

. . . .We taught a night class as part of our day load so that we could have full-time faculty both night and day at the college. We had student activities—we didn't have sports, but we had student activities that were on the weekend. Faculty would be there with the students. It was a very, very close relationship. It would be about as ideal as you could ever want in a college.

THE DEDICATION OF MTC

When the dedication ceremony for MTC was held in the fall of 1968, Bob Jaap was no longer on the board, but he attended the ceremony, and he has this memory of the event:

I still get furious about the following story. Damn. The dedication of that building was held on the north side of the building . . . public area, outdoors. John [Prince] presided. John did not invite me to that event! That is a fact. He invited a friend of his, who was also a friend of mine, by the name of Leonard Huck, [the] president of the Valley [National] Bank.[1]

John invited Leonard Huck to sit in the stand with him, John, for that event. I stood in the audience. I hope you'll excuse me if I become furious again, which I am.

[1] According to Jaap, Sherman Hazeltine, who had been Jaap's boss at the First National Bank of Arizona had brokered the deal with Broadway-Hale Department Stores, so the presence of the rival bank's president was a double insult.

February 2, 1996, video interview with Gene Fazio, Maricopa Tech and Mesa Community College faculty. Transcript and audio excerpts available online.

http://www.mc.maricopa.edu/users/M3cdhistory/

The familial atmosphere of the little college in the old department store and the carefully designed occupational programs quickly began to produce the desired result: employment for the students. According to Garneski, the state's Department of Vocational Education and Department of Employment had full-time representatives at the school to expedite job placements: "As soon as [students] finished a particular program, we had jobs lined up for them right away."

Bill Berkshire said that the job placement often occurred before students completed their programs. For instance, employers would scout the eight-week classes on business machine repair six weeks into the program and ask the instructor for students who knew how to work on typewriters. As a result, many students "didn't finish the course," Berkshire said. "They had the abilities and the competencies to go out and fill that job. So they were gone."

Despite its popularity with potential employers, Maricopa Tech had its detractors from within the district. Garneski recalls that the Phoenix College faculty members in particular were scornful of MTC:

They mocked us. "Can you imagine an institution going into vocational-technical education? Liberal arts and sciences are what we should be doing." And they always referred to themselves as the Mother Campus. And one day, there was one guy who was the head of the physics department and he said that at a meeting

I was in. He said, "But you've got to remember, Dr. Garneski, WE are the mother campus." And I said, "Yeah, and that's where we've got all the mothers!"

Another factor working against MTC's status in the district was the school's name. Berkshire said he would phone employees at other campuses in the district, introduce himself as being from Maricopa Tech, and typically receive the response: "Well, you're not part of the district. Why would you think that we could provide you with any services?"

From Maricopa Tech's newspaper The Prospector for September 14, 1972.

DEBBIE DOES MTC

Gene Fazio recalls how the nearby Fox Theatre was once used for a student orientation:

Remember, this was a slum area, and it was degenerated and stuff. They had the old Fox Theatre, which was a very magnificent theatre, in its declining years, in its last years, before it became the new Phoenix transit bus station. They were having trouble drawing people to downtown to go to the movies, so they turned it into an X-rated theatre.

I remember we had our orientation there. We rented the theatre, we had our orientations. We had a big thing in the student newspaper and we wanted to have a picture of the Fox Theatre and William Percy, the director of student activities, pointing to the theatre saying "MTC Orientation," and the title [on the marquee] was like "Debbie Does Dallas" or something like that. So what we had to do was go back and white-out the original marquee and put in "Welcome to Maricopa Tech." We didn't want "Debbie Does Dallas" down below, you know. We didn't need that as a drawing card.

But I remember that was the big joke. We weren't proud. We were going to go where we could go, and get the most out of it, to serve our students, no matter where. So we went to the porno theatre, and we had a good student orientation. . . . We weren't too proud to do anything.

In 1974, the employees of MTC recommended the word "community" be added in front of the word "college." The school then became Maricopa Technical Community College. **Bill Berkshire** remembers that the change was not universally accepted. "We had some people that were opposed to it. They thought it was getting more into the transfer areas and that we might lose our emphasis on vocational and technical. But we didn't. It definitely helped us."

It certainly didn't hurt. Enrollment continued to expand. Berkshire remembers the school hit its peak during the fall of 1976 when more than 7,800 students showed up to enroll. "People can't believe this—we had students standing outside . . . and the line went all the way around, down the sidewalk, back past where Montgomery Ward used to be, and around the corner. They were waiting to enroll. They were ready to get in. They knew what we offered."

Expanding Partnerships

At the end of its first five years, Maricopa Tech had become almost too successful. In July, 1973, burgeoning enrollment forced the district offices to move out of the top floor of the Korrick's building to new quarters in rented facilities at 903 North Second Street. (In March, 1977, the offices moved again to 3910 East Washington, the site of GateWay Community College today.)

As crowding became a serious problem, MTC began to expand its offerings of classes in satellite centers and on-site at various companies. Associate Dean Lionel Martinez was in charge of coordinating these activities. Soon, he was coordinating more than half of MTC's enrollment at various remote sites. Bruemmer describes some of

MTC STUDENTS VOICE OPINIONS

P.C.   M.C.C.   G.C.C.   S.C.C.

M.C.J.C.D.

Caught In The Squeeze!

A cartoon from Maricopa Tech's newspaper The Prospector *for April, 1971, seems to express the school's uncomfortable position among the other Maricopa colleges.*

May 3, 1996, video interview with Bill Berkshire, Maricopa Tech and GateWay Community College faculty. Transcript and audio excerpts available online.

http://www.mc.maricopa.edu/users/M3cdhistory/

the off-campus programs:

We moved into offering on-site programs out on Black Canyon [Freeway]. Electronics companies were out there. At AiResearch, for example, we had classes in the afternoon for the swing shift before they went on, in the evening for the day shift that had finished, and from ten until twelve for the night shift. We were offering classes in math, English, drafting, almost anything that would be beneficial to them, as well as some pre-GED classes.

An article from the *Scottsdale Daily Progress* December 30, 1975, gives an overview of the scope of the college at this time:

MTCC not only has a central location at 106 E. Washington St., but also spreads out to about 35 other locations in the county. Besides providing its complete college program in the middle of downtown Phoenix, MTCC offers college studies with 15 classes in Buckeye, several technical courses at Phoenix Union High School, automotive courses at its Mechanical Technology Center at 621 N. Seventh Ave., classes at many Valley hospitals and industries, and programs in other high schools and elementary schools throughout the Valley (including Paradise Valley High School).

Thus, MTCC was a great success. Its potential for future growth seemed virtually unlim-

ited because of its ability to grow beyond the confines of the old Korrick's building and offer classes anywhere in the county. Sadly, that potential would not last. With the creation of Rio Salado College in 1978, MTCC's bright future would be rudely eclipsed.

And while MTCC had been establishing itself in Phoenix's reviving downtown area, the district had created another college, one that was destined to turn on its creator in a manner not unlike Frankenstein's monster.

The line of students waiting to enroll at Maricopa Tech wraps around the building in the fall of 1976.

Chapter Ten

The **ARTICHOKE Rebellion**

The planning for what would become the district's most troubled campus had begun innocently around the time that Maricopa Tech was being launched.

The person responsible for setting the wheels in motion was Bill Van Loo, who had been appointed to the governing board in 1966 to replace Lester Hogan. Van Loo readily accepted this appointment because he already had an agenda for the district: "One of my aims in life was I felt [Scottsdale] deserved a nearby community college," he said. "I got with the City of Scottsdale and the Chamber and we formed a committee to develop this. The community was pretty much behind it to try and get something done."

Van Loo could hardly have expected that his pet project would result in a student rebellion that would shake the district to its very foundations.

The infamous Artichoke T-shirt, courtesy of David and Kathy Schwarz.

Al Flowers, the district's business manager, accompanied Van Loo on several scouting trips around the Scottsdale area, and they found that the available sites that were big enough were too far north. Governing board member Dwight Patterson objected to those sites. "You didn't want to go north because there's no kids—they don't live in north Scottsdale, they live in south Scottsdale." (Once again, the junior college is for "kids.")

The Salt River Pima-Maricopa Tribal Council then solved the dilemma. The council was willing to lease to the district a parcel of 160 acres on the Salt River Indian Reservation. The location was far enough south to suit Patterson, but it was on land that bordered Scottsdale's eastern edge, where public transportation was not readily available. Also, the district wanted to purchase the land, but a congressional order prohibited the sale of reservation land. The longest lease allowable was for only 49 years, and the district felt that was not long enough to secure the future of the new college. Stuart Udall, then Secretary of the Interior, persuaded Congress to pass a bill permitting a 99-year lease, and on that basis, Flowers was able to negotiate favorable terms for the district. At the board meeting on April 10, the governing board voted to build Scottsdale Community College on that land.

Donaldson Becomes a Dean

In January, 1968, the district's offices were moved to the sixth floor of the Korrick's building, and relations between Donaldson

The governing board in 1968 (from left to right): Jeremy Butler, Bill Van Loo, Dwight Patterson, Jim Miller, and Bob Easley.

June 27, 1996, video interview with H. W. Van Loo, Maricopa governing board member 1966-72. Transcript and audio excerpts available online.

http://www.mc.maricopa.edu/users/M3cdhistory/

CHANGES ON THE BOARD: 1967

Bob Jaap's term on the governing board was due to expire at the end of 1967, and the prospects for his re-election didn't look good. Faculty felt he had stonewalled their requests for salary increases and advocated forcing them to submit to a process of student review.

Another problem for Jaap developed at the board meeting on August 28, 1967. John Prince arrived with a copy of the newly received NCA report. According to Jaap, a newspaper reporter was present as usual:

John [Prince] then came to the meeting with that report, and then the reporter asked for it, and John looked at me and said, "Should I give it to him?" And I said, "No. I haven't read it yet." I thought I had that right, to read it before I gave it to the paper. But the newspaperman didn't think so.

When the newspapers finally got a look at the report, they found the NCA's criticisms of the board and mistakenly drew the conclusion that Jaap had been trying to hide the bad news from the press. Jaap was then pilloried in the editorial section of the *Republic*.

A faculty delegation approached Phoenix attorney Jeremy Butler to run against Jaap. Butler earned his BA at Yale in 1952 on a Naval ROTC scholarship. After graduation, he spent four years in the Navy, the last two of which as a Navy ROTC instructor at Columbia College. During that time, he also managed to earn a master's in American history. After the Navy, he attended law school at Yale, from which he was graduated in 1959. Arriving in Phoenix, he served as a law clerk for the Arizona Supreme Court for a year before joining the firm of Lewis and Roca as an associate.

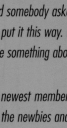

Jeremy Butler, Maricopa governing board member 1968-78.

In the months leading up to the election, Jaap's banking career occupied most of his time and required extensive travel outside of Phoenix. Thus, he spent little time campaigning. He does recall making at least one appearance with Butler at a candidate's forum:

He and I appeared together at the Madison School District PTA meeting. There must have been 75, 80 parents there, and we gave our talks. And somebody asked a question: "Well, why should we vote for either one of you?" And I said, "Well, I'll put it this way. If you like the way the [junior] college district is being run, vote for me. If you want to change something about it, vote for Mr. Butler." Which they did.

In January, 1968, Jeremy Butler became the newest member of the Maricopa district governing board. The board then consisted of Butler and Van Loo as the newbies and Patterson, Easley, and Miller as the veterans.

and Prince deteriorated even further. According to Scottsdale faculty member Glenn Groenke, "They wouldn't even go to the john at the same time. Prince locked the door between the two offices." Al Flowers agrees: "I bet there weren't a dozen words exchanged between Prince and Donaldson in a week's time. Any week."

To keep Donaldson out of his way, Prince assigned him to supervise the conversion of the district libraries to the Library of Congress cataloging system. Library Technical Services was moved into the basement of the Korrick's building, so Donaldson had to spend quite a bit of time in the basement.

Then, Prince got a better idea. In addition to supervising the library project, Donaldson was put in charge of overseeing all the preparations for the Scottsdale campus, and Donaldson was then officially appointed Scottsdale's first executive dean at the board meeting on May 26, 1969.

Recognizing that Donaldson would need help, Prince chose Glenn Groenke, who was then a faculty member at Mesa, to be Scottsdale new dean of instruction. (The irony was surely not lost on Donaldson that Prince was appointing Donaldson's second in command without consulting Donaldson. What goes around comes around.) According to Groenke, "[Prince] said, 'I don't want [Donaldson] to get in trouble out there. I am sending him out there because I don't want him at the district offices, and I want a crackerjack dean of instruction to keep things from getting out of hand.'" [1]

---

[1] Tom Dugan, a longtime Scottsdale faculty member on the counseling staff, states that Donaldson had set up a districtwide committee to make recommendations for his deans of academic and administrative services. Donaldson then surprised and irritated the committee by rejecting its recommendation and announcing Groenke as the dean of academic services. Dugan's story, thus, tends to corroborate Groenke's assertion that Prince intervened directly in this appointment.

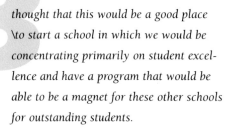

On June 9, office space was rented on North Highland, and Donaldson was shipped out of the district offices. He and Groenke worked there while renovations were completed on a former church building on 82nd Street and Granite Reef. This building became their base of operations for the next year as the new campus was readied to open in the fall of 1970.

Recruiting Scottsdale's Faculty

The district projections for enrollment determined that around 20 full-time faculty would be needed to open the school. According to Donaldson, Prince dictated that 15 of those faculty were to be transfers from the other campuses, and since the Scottsdale campus was expected to draw enrollment primarily from the Mesa campus, the largest number of the transfers was to come from Mesa. Since Donaldson didn't know the faculty, he put Groenke in charge of recruiting.

A bright and idealistic man, Groenke was very sympathetic to Donaldson's desire for innovation. Before joining the district in 1965, Groenke taught English at Arcadia High School. The experience made a deep impression on him. "The last year I worked there in '65, I had 46 National Merit Scholarship winners in my two sections of Honors English," Groenke recalls. He longed for the glory days back at Arcadia High School, and he immediately went looking for the best and the brightest faculty who might share his desire to create a similar educational Eden in Scottsdale:

> I went to Arcadia High School, and picked out Mike Svaco as my math teacher because I had worked with him at Arcadia and I had great respect for him. And I went to Mesa, and I urged Gene Gyurko to be my businessman . . . and I had to fight like hell with Riggs 'cause Riggs

didn't want to let him go. I tried to find the best teachers I could. . . . I liked Ronny Kearns because I had worked with him at the extension center when I was at Mesa, and I asked Ron Kearns to become my history person. And then, another fellow I tried to get was [Bob] Winters, who was a real radical. He was very left and . . . always pushing the far left type of an idea. But I liked him because he read. He would argue, but he would argue intelligently. He's a good reader.

Groenke then submitted his preliminary list to Donaldson, who struck off a few names and interviewed the rest. Bob Winters recalls specifically that during his interview, Donaldson "talked a lot about a democratically run school with students and the faculty running things."

November 18, 1996, video interview with Ron Kearns, Scottsdale Community College faculty. Transcript and audio excerpts available online.

http://www.mc.maricopa.edu/users/M3cdhistory/

Ron Kearns also remembers his interview with Donaldson: "He started out, 'What is your dream? What would you like to be? If you had your druthers, how would you like to. . . ?'"

Kearns had a ready answer:

> I'd always felt there was room for what we used to refer to as a Berkeley of the community colleges, an academically-oriented community college that would be different and that would break away from the pattern that had been established in the other three or four schools. . . . We

thought that this would be a good place to start a school in which we would be concentrating primarily on student excellence and have a program that would be able to be a magnet for these other schools for outstanding students.

The other Mesa faculty all seemed to have had similar visions. If the district could support one school dedicated to vocational and technical training, then the district could just as easily support a sort of honors college.

This same group also seems to have shared a general discontent with Mesa's emphasis on athletics. As Theo Heap indicated previously, Riggs was a competitor and wanted a strong sports program. Riggs had a reputation for never missing a game (or, in all fairness, any other student activity), but he was not the intellectual leader that John Prince had been at Glendale. Thus, faculty who talked with Donaldson—especially the Mesa faculty—walked away from their interviews with the hope that Scottsdale would become a school that emphasized academics, not athletics.

They were wrong.

The Gathering Storm

As the early histories of the Phoenix, Glendale, and Mesa colleges clearly show, varsity athletics were part of the bedrock foundation of the junior college concept.

103

More to the point, the governing board members themselves demanded varsity athletics. Bob Jaap recalls that Dwight Patterson was the main force in this area:

> I remember we had quite a discussion about whether we should have intramural or varsity sports in the community college district. And I remember I was very much in favor of intramurals because it took in the whole student body; he (Patterson) was more interested in the varsity type of thing because it attracted more attention and had a higher level of athleticism. He won the battle. We went along with the varsity idea.

One of the primary justifications for varsity sports was that they supposedly attracted students. Barry Wukasch, who began teaching at Scottsdale in its third year of operation, recalls a presentation that Marion Donaldson once made to the faculty:

> I forget the exact details, but the gist of it was that if you recruit a high school football player, that's so many dollars because money follows FTSE (Full-Time Student Equivalent) and that high school football player is likely to bring his girlfriend with him and three or four friends, and all of sudden, you've got eight or nine new students in the school that you wouldn't have had if you hadn't had football, and eight or nine new students equates to so many dollars in the budget.

Thus, conventional wisdom held that varsity sports were essential to a junior college's survival. Given a choice of a school with a sports program and one without, students would always prefer the one with sports. Varsity athletics would also attract media attention. Winning teams would boost school spirit. Athletic programs would encourage students with marginal academic credentials to enter college and stay in school. Thus, athletics benefited junior colleges in countless ways. A junior college without varsity athletics was simply unthinkable.

That conventional wisdom may have had some validity when junior college students were all 18- and 19-year-old transfer students, but when Scottsdale Community College opened in 1970, many veterans were attending full-time, and many older adults were attending part-time during the day. These students had different priorities. For them, intercollegiate athletics were no longer the priority they had been when members of the faculty had to suit up so the Phoenix Junior College students could form a baseball team in 1921.

The problem was a significant issue because the students paid for the athletic program directly. At this time, in-county students paid no tuition; instead, they were assessed a so-called activity fee that funded—among other things—equipment, supplies, and operating expenses for the teams. In 1967, the governing board had hoisted the fee from $28 to $45 per semester for full-time students. According to the board minutes for May 8, 1967, students had protested the increase, but:

> Mr. Jaap replied that the board was looking for a more equitable system than the present one providing operational and capital funds for the junior colleges. The board felt it was logical for students to pay a larger share than they do now . . . Mr. Flowers stated that the fees for full-time students at Cochise College and Eastern Arizona College, by comparison, were currently $50.00.

The minutes for the May 22, 1967, meeting also reveal that the board was appropriating $23.50 of that $45 for "operational and capital funds." Only $21.50 was actually being returned to the campuses to pay for student activities. Nevertheless, that was $21.50 that students were shelling out for activities' programs, and if the older students didn't choose to participate in the activities, then those students began to wonder why they were being assessed for them.

One way or another, $45 was a significant expense for full-time students at that time, and many students were actively questioning what was being done with their money. On Oct. 23, 1970, Glendale Community College's student newspaper, *El Tiempo Pasando*, published an editorial urging readers to examine seriously the fairness of "spending so much of our money on preparing some students to be pro athletes when nowhere near a proportionate amount is being shared per student in preparation for other careers."

The governing board became concerned about the growing anti-athletics movement among the students. To guard against the

September 19, 1996, audio interview with Barry Wukasch, faculty member at Scottsdale, Paradise Valley, and Rio Salado. Transcript available online.

http://www.mc.maricopa.edu/users/M3cdhistory/

"There was definitely a division between the sports, athletic people on the one hand and a lot of the other people—science and social science people in particular."

possibility of student radicals attempting to disrupt the funding of athletics, the board resolved that expenditures for athletics would be exempted from the control of the student governments.

Thus, the forces were lining up for a major confrontation, and Scottsdale was fated to be the battlefield upon which this war would be fought.

Early Faculty Disillusionment

When the new college opened in the fall of 1970, construction on the campus buildings had not even begun. Instead of starting up in temporary facilities elsewhere, classes were conducted in a cluster of portable buildings arranged in a semicircle at the eastern edge of the property (so as to be out of the way when construction on the first six permanent structures actually began in October). Groenke

dubbed the cumulative effect "a seedy summer camp." Even so, approximately 960 students enrolled for the first semester. They didn't seem to mind the temporary quarters, but faculty members were unhappy. Not only were the portable classrooms a burden, but resources in general seemed to be in short supply. Kathy Schwarz, an original hire at Scottsdale, remembers the problems of setting up her first psychology lab:

> I had been promised an amount of money to set up a lab. Never saw a penny of it. So there I was. Students are enrolled and everything. They're going to learn experimental psychology, and we have nothing. My husband and I would spend every weekend putting together stuff so we could run some experiments. Nobody ever told me there was any money anywhere. So it all came out of my pocket.

The faculty also objected to the way that Donaldson implemented many of his so-called innovations without asking for the advice or permission of the persons affected. For example, Donaldson had promised that the new school would be run openly and democratically. To that end, he proposed an innovative arrangement for the new college's administration building:

> I liked the bank idea of having a big room and desks. Here's the president of the bank and here's somebody else—where students could see the guy and come in and talk to him at any time. So I worked with the

Marion Donaldson, Scottsdale's executive dean 1970-73, in a photo from Scottsdale's student newspaper Our Sheet, November 5, 1970. What Glenn Groenke dubbed a "seedy summer camp" (the portable classrooms) is visible in the background.

Aerial view of the Scottsdale campus as published in Scottsdale's student newspaper Faithe, October 26, 1971. In the bottom part of the picture is the semicircle of portable classrooms that were the school's original facilities while the permanent buildings in the upper part of the picture were being constructed.

architects. . . . [The office] was a huge room; it's still out there—and in the back of the room were three small rooms, so that if anybody needed to have very private conversations and so on, they could retire back there.

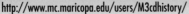

June 26, 1996, video interview with Kathy Schwarz, Scottsdale Community College faculty.   Transcript and audio excerpts available online.

http://www.mc.maricopa.edu/users/M3cdhistory/

The early Scottsdale faculty interviewed for this book all remember this room. Glenn Groenke recalls, "It was pandemonium . . . You couldn't get anything done. You couldn't handle anything. It was maddening."

Donaldson also reorganized faculty. Instead of departments grouped by disciplines, Donaldson grouped faculty arbitrarily by different disciplines. The reason, according to Groenke, was "because that's the way you could get to know each other and other disciplines, etc. Not at all the idea of sharing ideas in your own field."

Groenke recalls Donaldson's policies on typewriters and telephones were equally arbitrary:

Nobody can have an electric typewriter unless it's a dean. The rest can have only manual typewriters. And I could get typewriters from the other campuses . . . [Donaldson said to me:] "Oh, no, the average person couldn't have that." "Well," I said, "how about telephones? Can we have—?" "No, no. We'll have one telephone in the hallway of each

building." "You know, Jeez, Marion, people want to call back and forth—" "No. Hunh-unh." The executive dean's secretary, Jeanie Crop, had a Selectric, xbut nobody else could have a Selectric . . . I mean, weird!

Then came a particularly unhappy surprise: Glenn Groenke was not allowed to become the first dean of instruction as planned. The year before, Groenke's wife had been recruited by Norb Bruemmer and hired as a teacher at Maricopa Tech. The district then had a non-consanguinity policy in effect. When her contract came before the board for approval, board member Jeremy Butler balked because her husband was to be an administrator at Scottsdale. If he were going to be an administrator at Scottsdale, she would have had to leave. Groenke, bitterly disappointed, opted to remain a faculty member.

According to Ron Kearns, Groenke's replacement was "a jock, a football player and jock-sniffer by the name of Larry Stevens. Here

again, nice man, but about as far a cry from what Marion Donaldson said he wanted in a school as you can get." Kearns remembers taking an instant dislike to Stevens:

What started one of the big conflicts was that I walked into his office and saw his list of priorities and number one was a school song, school colors, and a school mascot, and we're trying to get books for our students to read! I'm thinking, "This is my dean of instruction?" When I went back and reported that, people went ballistic, at least the people who supported my point of view.

Tom Dugan feels differently and thinks that Stevens was underrated as an administrator:

Larry Stevens met an awful lot of opposition, even though he was instrumental in starting a lot of occupational programs, the evening program, getting the athletic program started, facilities and what-have-you. He was really a hardworking fellow. But Larry epitomized what they didn't like. He was a former Marine Corps officer, active in the Marine Reserves; he had been a coach; he had played ball for Oregon State; and now he was a very decisive administrator. Larry went through with what the board and Jack Prince and Al Flowers were telling him to do.[2]

[2] After five years, Stevens left to become the president of Tacoma Community College. Later, he became chancellor of the Saddleback Community College District and was a professor at San Diego State University for five years. Most recently, he has been the associate director for the Northwest Accreditation Association.

June 6, 1996, video interview with Tom Dugan, Scottsdale Community College counselor.   Transcript and audio excerpts available online.

http://www.mc.maricopa.edu/users/M3cdhistory/

The Scottsdale faculty received another blow when the student newspaper for November 5, 1970, printed an interview with Donaldson. In direct response to a student's question about the future of sports at Scottsdale, Donaldson stated: "The district board has already proposed a sports program for SCC. Whether we get into big-time sports is a matter of time. We just cannot allow a sports program to drain off funds better used elsewhere. But yes, we will have a sports program."

Students were beginning to voice their concerns, too. On the second page of the same newspaper, an editorial argued strongly against football:

> The greatest menace to us is the war game of football. In this game, people pay money to watch the gory spectacle of twenty-two muscle-bound combatants maiming and wounding each other for the possession of a small oblong of pig skin. . . . Should a school where academic freedom and excellence rule prostitute itself to the god of gladiatorial combat? We think not.

Several other editorials of a similar nature appeared throughout the '70-'71 year. Other articles described how student groups in other states were trying to liberate their colleges from the tyranny of their varsity athletics programs.

Student Government Flexes Its Muscles

Donaldson wanted the student government to be equally innovative:

> I wanted student government to actually have a job, and not just be a ritual that (it) performed. I figured out the things that they could do. For instance, parking was strictly under the students. That included faculty. They were going to tell the faculty where to park.

Donaldson also decided that the students should be in charge of budgeting the money

MEET THE DEANS

Dr. Donaldson, Executive Dean · Dr. Stevens Student Services · Dr. Gyurko Dean Administration · Dr. Snell Dean of Education · Tom Dugan of Counseling Services · Roy Hoyt Financial Aid

Photo gallery of Scottsdale administrators published in Scottsdale's student newspaper Faithe *for September, 1971. Larry Stevens appears in the upper right corner.*

realized from the activity fee. He might have expected the anti-athletics forces to cause some trouble in this area, but he planned to be the student government's adviser, and he may have felt that he would be in a position to talk the students out of any untoward behavior.

During the school's first year, Donaldson worked with student leaders to help them write a constitution. In April, 1971, a student election ratified the new student constitution, and the election for student officers was held during the first week in May. The students chose one of the framers of that constitution, Roger A. Brooks, as student body president. A veteran in his mid-20s who had made the dean's list with a 4.0 in his first semester, Brooks worked in the campus bookstore to support himself and played bridge in his spare time.

In the fall of 1971, the student government set to work allocating its activity fee money. Many of their projects were very meritorious, including the funding of a series of high-profile guest speakers. In the spring of 1972 alone, on-campus speakers included Michael Harrington, Nat Hentoff, Anna Chenault, and Dick Gregory.

The issue of spending money on athletics, however, quickly eclipsed all other concerns. The October 4, 1971, issue of *Faithe* (the name of the student newspaper in its second year) announced that Donaldson was appropriating $24,000 of the activity fee money to buy equipment and uniforms for next year's varsity teams, which would include golf, tennis, cross-country, basketball, and track.

The students were furious. Donaldson had already promised that the student govern-

ROGER BROOKS WINS

Roger

John

Roger Brooks was elected to the office of Chairman during the recent Student Government elections. Roger tallied 178 votes, or roughly 2/3 of the votes cast.

A mere 26 votes decided the fate of the highly - contested Co-Chairmanship. John Annerino was the winner with 129 votes, defeating competitor Steve Fenderson.

Don Marsh recieved 89% of the votes to take the office of Treasurer. There were 218 votes cast, with the write-ins totalling 25.

Fifty-five percent of the votes put Rita Giordano into the office of Scribe, over number-two girl Kathy Rottas.

A total of 264 votes were cast, about 1/4

ment would decide how the activity money was to be spent. They fumed that he had no regard for the constitution he himself had helped to write.

On October 18, 1971, *Faithe* reported that the students were organizing to hire a lawyer and sue the district—if necessary—to regain complete control of their funds. When the Scottsdale faculty met on October 20, the members voted unanimously to express their support for the student government's position.

Scottsdale's new student body president, Roger Brooks, then took an extremely bold step. In November, he somehow managed to wrangle an invitation to speak to the state legislature's subcommittee investigating state tax expenditures. The November 29, 1971, issue of *Faithe* contains the following report:

> Brooks expressed his concern for the costs of athletics on the community college campuses. "I believe that our community colleges are going to be in deep trouble in the very near future if the excessive expenditures for intercollegiate athletics are not brought under control," Brooks stated. . . . Brooks was "very pleased" with his meeting with the subcommittee. "They were very receptive and interested," Brooks said. "They have asked that we take a poll to question students as to what they feel they most want to spend money on at our college," he added.

Roger Brooks' address to the legislative subcommittee as published in Scottsdale's student newspaper Faithe for November 29, 1971, is available online.

http://www.mc.maricopa.edu/users/M3cdhistory/

The legislators' suggestion to poll the students was not easy to ignore, and in December, Donaldson agreed to the survey. Copies were given to students when they registered for spring classes.

By this time, the district was becoming alarmed over student opposition to athletics, and on January 13, 1972, the district invited representatives of student governments and administrators from all over the district to attend a daylong convocation to discuss the activity-fee policy. Al Firestein, Chief Civil Deputy of the Maricopa County Attorney's office, was the keynote speaker. He reiterated the district's claim that the activity fee money was district money, not student money. On January 24, 1972, *Faithe* quoted from a speech Brooks apparently made early in this meeting:

> What we ask is that the Maricopa County Community College District institute a new policy giving the students of the various colleges greater control over their activity fees. This is the kind of challenge we can use to make our schools places where free men learn what it means to be citizens in a democracy. By taking this initiative now, our district can show the way for educators across the country.

But Brooks' appeal went unanswered. The same article from *Faithe* reports that Brooks had decided the convocation was a complete waste of time.

On February 21, *Faithe* printed an editorial by Brooks in which he announced the results of the student poll taken in December:

> In the poll taken during registration we in student government attempted to find out just how much support we had in our fight with the district to gain student control of student funds. Ninety-one percent of the students presently registered at Scottsdale Community College believe that **students should determine how their activity funds are spent**. This may not seem like a revolutionary idea, in fact, it seems pretty logical, so logical that ninety-one percent of the students at this college agree. But in downtown Phoenix a thriving bureaucracy doesn't agree. They believe that students are in college **not** to learn how to become self-governing citizens in democracy, but to be folded, spindled, mutilated and manipulated by the bureaucracy downtown. [original emphasis]

Brooks added that only 15% of the students polled had voted in favor of varsity sports.

Feeling his oats, Brooks now took another bold step. On February 29, 1971, the United States Senate had passed the so-called Harris amendment to the Higher Education Act. This amendment recommended that students be extended full voting powers on governing boards and boards of trustees at colleges and universities. Brooks took his cue, and went to the March 13, 1972, meeting of the governing board to propose the board add two students as voting members. Brooks brought with him letters from Senator Harris and Arizona luminary Barry Goldwater both expressing support for Brooks' proposal to the board.

The board minutes show that Brooks was received politely but coolly. Dr. Paul Wright, who had replaced Bob Easley on the board in the fall of 1970 (see accompanying text box), recalls:

> As I remember, in Roger Brooks' presentation he also wanted that student to be a voting member. We said, as a board, "No way." We were elected; we're not going to bring somebody else on the board and give them an equal vote just because they're a student.

Brooks probably knew the board wouldn't go along, but he may not have cared. His real objective may have been simply to study the governing board in action. Brooks was experimenting, flexing his political muscles, and trying on the spotlight for size.

The Artichoke Election

In the spring of 1972, two other events further stirred up the students' ire and helped to set off the coming rebellion.

The first problem was the opening of the new library. Donaldson had planned for a large library, and, according to him, an unusually large budget for buying books. "We actually opened with more books in our library than

any community college in Arizona had opened [with] before. Twenty thousand volumes. That's a lot of volumes. Most libraries at other colleges begin with seven or eight thousand volumes and are then built up over

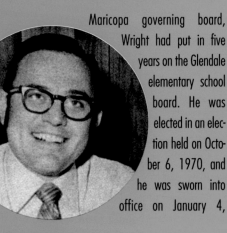

CHANGES ON THE BOARD: 1970-71

Dr. Robert Easley had decided to leave the board when his term expired at the end of 1970. A close friend and colleague, Dr. Paul Wright, replaced him. Wright was a dentist in the same office building where Easley once had his medical practice, and like Easley, he too had been a student at Phoenix College. But Easley had been there only one semester, and Wright had been there for a full two years before transferring to ASU. Before running for the

Paul Wright, Maricopa governing board member 1971-76.

Maricopa governing board, Wright had put in five years on the Glendale elementary school board. He was elected in an election held on October 6, 1970, and he was sworn into office on January 4,

Ken Badertscher, Maricopa governing board member 1972-77.

1971. Just as Dr. Easley had been a supporter of Prince, Dr. Wright was, too:

I had known Dr. Prince and had had him as an instructor when I went to Phoenix College. I'd been a student of his. . . . He was a great instructor. He had a lot of enthusiasm. I thoroughly enjoyed him. I was very pleased when went on the board and he was the president.

In 1971, Bill Van Loo also decided he would not run again when his term expired at the end of that year. At Van Loo's suggestion, his friend Kenneth Badertscher announced he would run for Van Loo's seat. Badertscher grew up in Ohio and did his undergraduate work at Ohio State, where he received his BS in business administration with a major in accounting in 1961. In 1963, he moved to Arizona, and in 1969, he went to work for the Arizona/Colorado Land and Cattle Company, which had acquired the Cohen/Van Loo Engineering Company several years before.

Badertscher had no previous school board experience, but he had been active in various civic organizations. Even though no other candidate declared for the election on October 5, the voters in the Scottsdale area must have liked Badertscher a lot because even running unopposed, he garnered 6,094 votes. He was sworn into office on January 3, 1972, just as the problems at Scottsdale were beginning to spill over into the public arena.

One other change in district leadership occurred on July 1, 1971. J. Lee Thompson was named district director for educational projects and research, and Dr. William E. Berry assumed the position of executive dean of Phoenix College.

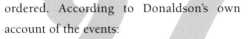

the years," he said. Those 20,000 volumes, however, didn't begin to fill up all the shelves, and when the building was dedicated on April 16, 1973, the library appeared to be understocked.

The new gymnasium, dedicated on the same date, was fully equipped.

The second problem occurred when the student government had tried to allocate several thousand dollars of the activity-fee money for scholarships for American Indian students. Donaldson quashed that initiative because scholarship money was readily available from the federal government and elsewhere.

ordered. According to Donaldson's own account of the events:

I discussed this matter with the student body president [Brooks] and we agreed that the best way was to choose a large committee of students, faculty, staff, and administration to decide on the best procedures. The student body president suggested I make the selection of those to serve. I chose four students, including the president, two faculty, two staff members, and two administrators.

The committee met April 28 and decided it would do two things. The first was to invite suggestions from all students, faculty and

For the students, this flyer was the final straw. According to Scottsdale faculty member Bob Winters, "The word quickly began to circulate among the students and faculty that this would be a chance to express their strong disapproval of what had happened with the [American] Indian scholarships."

The day of the mascot and colors meeting, Donaldson was unexpectedly summoned to the district office. In his absence, the meeting quickly got out of control. Bob Winters supplied the following eyewitness account:

People were having fun. There were about six or seven faculty there and twenty-five or thirty students, and they put on the

"Athletics, Control of Funds, and Related Areas: A Statement of the Facts" by Marion G. Donaldson, Executive Dean, September 20, 1972. Full text is available online.

http://www.mc.maricopa.edu/users/M3cdhistory/

ballots rutabagas, artichokes, and the granite reefers [a road near the Scottsdale campus is named "Granite Reef Drive"]. And they realized immediately that they had two competing vegetables, or a fruit and a vegetable, and that would be disastrous and split the vegetable vote, so they quickly got behind the artichoke.

Photo published in the Scottsdale student newspaper The New Leaf for September 25, 1972, shows the empty library shelves that so incensed the students.

According to some reports, Donaldson had even threatened to shut down the whole student government if the members persisted in this idea.

Thus, students were looking for ways to express their discontent when Donaldson announced the formation of a committee to pick the school's mascot and colors so that uniforms for the school teams could be

staff by placing suggestion boxes in the student center. Once these were in, the student body president would form a subcommittee to select the three best mascot-and-color combinations and submit those to the general student body to make the final choice. A flyer was placed in the student newspaper inviting everyone to "participate" in making suggestions and to "attend" the meeting of the subcommittee to be held on May 3.

Word of the subcommittee's choices spread quickly around the school. Kathy Schwarz remembers:

I knew this little gal who was helping me out in the lab. She came running back to my office and she was just ecstatic. She said, "You'll never guess what we did!" I said, "What did you do?" She said, "We just voted on our mascot and our school colors!" I said, "What are they?" She said, "The artichoke and pink and white." I said, "Oh, my God!"

Donaldson returned from his meeting at the district office later that afternoon. He remembers:

> After it was all over, Roger Brooks came in and said, "You know what name they chose? The artichokes! Pink and white for the colors!" I hit the ceiling, only in the fact that I saw this as a direct attempt to denigrate one of the programs on this campus. "These colleges are comprehensive colleges," I said to myself. "They include everything. They include programs for the athletes, but they also include programs for the musicians and for the dramatists and for the artists and for the academically inclined and all of that. You cannot exclude athletics; otherwise, Scottsdale will be a pariah among the schools and all of our students will have to go to other colleges." So I said, "You cannot do this. No. I will not allow it."

The following day, May 4, Donaldson sent the original steering committee a memo declaring the committee's decisions null and void. Donaldson also refused to sanction the planned general student election to choose from among the steering committee's recommendations. Donaldson's memo was too little and too late. Enterprising students had already made up signs and papered the school with them. The signs featured a picture of a defiant artichoke and proclaimed, "PINK AND WHITE—JUST RIGHT!"

Over Donaldson's objections, the students held the election anyway, and on May 8, 229 votes were cast: 175 students voted for "artichoke" as a mascot and 130 voted for "pink and white" as school colors. At the time, about 2,000 students were enrolled at the college, so the number of votes cast hardly represented a majority of the students. Using that fact as an excuse, Donaldson was true to his word and nullified the student election. Then, he reconvened the original steering committee:

[They] accepted my judgment about the election, with no objection from the student representatives, and decided to postpone any further efforts to choose a mascot until the following fall. Because uniforms had to be ordered, [the committee] voted on three possible combinations. Blue and white received the highest number of votes, largely, I believe, because no other community college in the state used this particular combination of colors.

WHY THE ARTICHOKE?

Out of all the vegetables in the garden, why was the artichoke the choice of the Scottsdale students? Ron Kearns claims to know the answer:

It's a fun kind of story because it goes back to one of my teachers at Phoenix College named Bruce Smith, who was a psychology teacher. You know how you meet two or three professors in your life that turn you around and excite you? He was one of them. We first started here in 1970. Faculty are always complaining about the quality of students and things like this. Bruce had written a little monograph, somewhere along the line, that started out—because he got tired of hearing people complaining about students— "While toiling in the rose garden of education, you must always remember that the cash crop is rutabagas." That kind of caught on at this campus, and we started talking about some of these students as rutabagas . . . well, nobody knows what a rutabaga is, so it went to artichokes. . . . So the students came up with the Artichoke, the Farkels [characters from TV's Laugh-In], the Granite Reefers, and [the Scoundrels] . . . But the students picked, out of that, the Artichokes. Because, as we said, "The community's not going to be too keen on the Granite Reefers. It's going to give the whole image we don''t want over here.' And Scoundrels? I never could understand that one. The students said, "Hell, everybody's a Panther or a Bulldog or this or that." So the Artichokes.

Then they voted for pink and white, because they figured if we had to have a football team, by golly, if they were wearing pink and white, they'd better win!

So it's really Bruce Smith at Phoenix College who got the whole Artichoke thing going.

Donaldson's version of these events suggests that the students meekly acceded to his will, but the truth is just the opposite. The students had already retained a lawyer, Fred Lemberg, to help them gain control of their funds, and on August 7, he filed suit in Maricopa County Superior Court on the students' behalf. The suit asked the court to stop the college from purchasing athletic equipment and uniforms without the student government's approval and to force the district to accept the artichoke as the school mascot and pink and white as the school colors. The suit named Marion Donaldson, John Prince, the district governing board, and the State Board of Directors for Community Colleges as defendants.

On August 28, Superior Court Judge Jerry H. Glenn began the formal hearings on the suit. Al Firestein defended the district's position, and testimony concluded after two days. On Friday, September 1, the ruling came down.

The students lost.

The court order, dated September 1, 1972, stated: "The Court finds that the college administration of Scottsdale Community College did not act improperly in expending money for athletics without the consent of the designated representative of the Associated Students." Further, the college administration "had the power to rescind the action of the committee before an election had been called by the college." The order refers to a referendum election intended "to bind the college administration" which is found to be invalid.

The defeat went down hard with the students, who felt the justness of their case was obvious. Regardless of the court's decision, they strongly believed that the district had wronged them, and John Prince became their new enemy. Donaldson recalls, "Roger Brooks spent a lot of time in my office. . . . He said, 'Dr. Donaldson, we like you. It's that Jack Prince we're after. We're after him.'"

First, though, the students had to raise the money to pay their legal expenses. To that end, Brooks and the other student government leaders used student activity funds to have commemorative T-shirts printed. The first fall issue of the student newspaper—rechristened the *New Leaf*, a not-so-subtle reference to the artichoke—includes a photo-

graph of the T-shirts being sold in the student union. In the same newspaper, Brooks asks for student support to hold another mascot and colors election.

The Hired Gun

Meanwhile, John Prince felt he'd had enough. The situation at Scottsdale was clearly out of control, and he sent for Tom Garneski, then the dean of students at Maricopa Tech. According to Garneski:

Dr. Prince just simply invited me in for a discussion one day and asked me if I would take over the dean of students' job on a very troubled campus. That's all. He said, "I just want you to go over there and do anything you can to help clear up those problem they're having." He did not specify what I was to do. He said, "I've just got confidence in you, Tom, and I want you to go over there and straighten things out."

Garneski had been effective as the dean of students at Maricopa Tech, where many had expected that the students would be hardened, rebellious inner-city students. Prince may have felt that Garneski was one of the

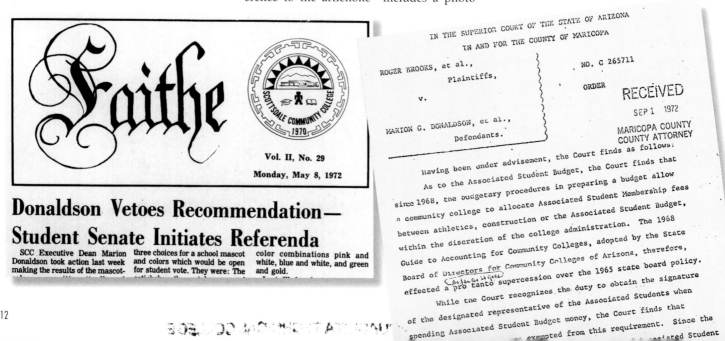

Faithe

Vol. II, No. 29
Monday, May 8, 1972

Donaldson Vetoes Recommendation—
Student Senate Initiates Referenda

SCC Executive Dean Marion Donaldson took action last week making the results of the mascot-

three choices for a school mascot and colors which would be open for student vote. They were: The

color combinations pink and white, blue and white, and green and gold.

IN THE SUPERIOR COURT OF THE STATE OF ARIZONA
IN AND FOR THE COUNTY OF MARICOPA

ROGER BROOKS, et al.,
        Plaintiffs,

    v.

MARION G. DONALDSON, et al.,
        Defendants.

NO. C 265711

ORDER

RECEIVED
SEP 1 1972
MARICOPA COUNTY
COUNTY ATTORNEY

Having been under advisement, the Court finds as follows:

As to the Associated Student Budget, the Court finds that since 1968, the budgetary procedures in preparing a budget allow a community college to allocate Associated Student Membership fees between athletics, construction or the Associated Student Budget, within the discretion of the college administration. The 1968 Guide to Accounting for Community Colleges, adopted by the State Board of Directors for Community Colleges of Arizona, therefore, effected a pro tanto supercession over the 1965 state board policy.

While the Court recognizes the duty to obtain the signature of the designated representative of the Associated Students when spending Associated Student Budget money, the Court finds that exempted from this requirement. Since the

reasons that Maricopa Tech never experienced any significant discipline problems during its first few years.

Of course, the students at Scottsdale knew immediately why Garneski was being sent there, and they were ready for him.

Tom Garneski's arrival on campus as acting dean of students on Monday, October 2, became a full-blown media event. Garneski recalls:

> It was amazing. Television cameras from KOOL and all the TV stations, and I walked into this student center. There were the students demonstrating at the tables, and they had everything set up, protesting and such. . . . I would go up to students and say, "Why all this demonstration and such?" And then they would go into a diatribe, "We need more emphasis on the educational program and look what they're doing. They're building gymnasiums and athletics and all the emphasis is in the wrong direction and we need change." And some of that even went beyond that—it was very hostile, belligerent kind of behavior.
>
> And so I would ask a student. I would say, "Well, can you tell me your name? I am Dr. Garneski. Can you tell me you name? I am the new dean of students." And they wouldn't say who they were. They all shut up. They would not give their names. And I just said, "Well, you know, if you really believe in what you're doing, I'd think you'd be proud to tell me who you are." And they caught all that on the cameras, and they played it back on the evening news, and it made the students look like a bunch of asses. . . . I lost some battles, but I won that first one, and I think that's where they got this idea that I might have been a hired gun.

Scottsdale student newspaper The New Leaf, September 11. 1972. "SHIRTS OFF TO STUDENTS—A thrilled SCC student eagerly reviews the infamous artichoke T-shirts being sold in the student center, profits from the T-shirts, which were conceived, designed, and purchased for distribution by a group of SCC students, are being used to pay for court costs and lawyers fees."

Scottsdale's student newspaper The New Leaf, October 9, 1972

Editors' comment

Assignment: SCC

Good morning Mr. Garnosko . . . and so Tom, your mission should you decide to accept it, is to finally terminate all artichoke activities at SCC before students raise the necessary funds for a court appeal. Should the appeal be successful, we here at the District would lose much of our coveted power. Good luck Tom, and of course should you fail, we will disavow any knowledge of your existence. This caption will self destruct in five seconds.

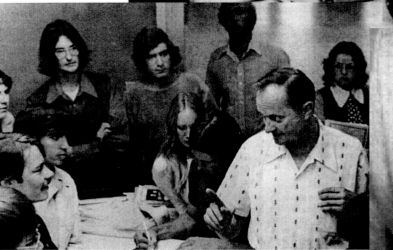

Scottsdale's student newspaper The New Leaf, October 9, 1972. "Dean Garneski admonishes SCC students for their participation in the sale of Artichoke T-shirts. Garneski took the names of those behind the counter for possible disciplinary actions. None of the individuals involved admitted to any of the charges leveled by Garneski."

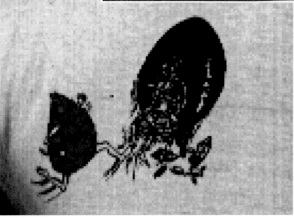

This design appears on the front of the artichoke T-shirts. An artichoke kicks a football, which is bursting at the seams and spewing forth all the money inside.

According to the October 9th edition of the *New Leaf*, Garneski then moved to stop the sale of the T-shirts:

> *Acting Dean of Students Thomas Garneski informed those students selling Artichoke T-shirts Wednesday that according to district policy they were operating illegally in refusing to stop the sale of T-shirts. When asked what course of action would be taken, he said the students were subject to suspension. He did not say they would be suspended, however, and he said that he doubted anyone would be arrested.*

Garneski then took on the student government, which by then had adopted a policy that no faculty, administrators or outsiders of any kind could attend meetings except by invitation of the student body president. As the official advisor to the student government, Garneski was not going to be denied, and another embarrassing confrontation occurred. When he learned of a clandestine meeting, Garneski barged in and sat down:

> *They were going to enact something and they didn't want me to be aware of it, and Roger Brooks said, "We're going to take a vote on this first." He said, "I would like to propose a motion that Dr. Garneski be declared persona non grata." And they seconded and voted, and I was declared persona non grata. And I just ignored them and sat there. And then Roger Brooks turned to someone and said, "Sergeant at arms, do your duty." And I was going to deck him if he touched me because I was furious. Underneath, I was furious. But he wouldn't do it. He didn't come over. And I just told them right there and then, "If anyone touches me, that will constitute assault, and you are disrupting the educational process by holding illegal meetings to conduct business of student*

> *government." And that just shut them down right there.*

The intimidation only strengthened the students' resolve. The second mascot and colors election was held from November 13-15, 1972, and the results were announced in the *New Leaf* on November 20. Nearly half the students voted this time—a total of 994 ballots cast—and the artichoke received 764 votes, or 76.8% of the total. The colors pink and white were selected by 559 votes, or 56.2%.

Again, Donaldson declared this election unsanctioned and refused to acknowledge the results. Blue and white became the school colors by default (because the uniforms had already been ordred), but the athletic department decided to adopt the Drover as the school mascot. (The name apparently came from the Drover Foundation, an organization of boosters that athletic director Larry Philpot had created to provide additional financial support for the Scottsdale teams.)

The students were undaunted. According to Ken Badertscher:

> *[Brooks] would be at every [governing board] meeting. And since we were always at the local campuses, when we went to Scottsdale, he would be there with all of his folks. Some of the meetings ended up being long drawn-out affairs because we would listen and let them talk. . . . They wanted to talk about doing away with athletics—not just at Scottsdale, but everywhere. They didn't believe that the community colleges should be conducting athletics.*

In effect, the students had declared war on the district.

Donaldson's Exit

Late in January of 1973, Donaldson threw in the towel:

> *Things were getting really out-of-hand, as far as the college was concerned, and nearly every day there was something in this paper, or . . . in the Tucson papers, and I talked to Jack. I said to him, "I've got to leave here, Jack, but I need a job." He said, "You take this job, and we'll put Ray Cattani (dean of instruction at Mesa Community College) out there." I think I would have been fired anyway. I'm not sure. It was just that it seemed to me that I wasn't serving any useful function on the campus anymore.*

The official announcement was made at a special meeting of all faculty and staff on February 8. Shortly after, John Prince invited Tom Garneski to another meeting. Garneski recalls:

> *I was in effect asked if I was interested in taking over as president of the campus. [Prince] didn't come right out and say it, but he implied that it was mine if I wanted to ask for it. And I said, "No. If we get a new president coming in, I would like to see that president come in without carrying a lot of past burdens with him . . . Perhaps I should go, too. It will be a clean slate, and someone else can come in and be successful." And then he said, "Okay, Ironside, I want you to be my new vice president for educational services."*

Donaldson was absorbed back into the district, where he worked on the computerization of the library catalog and other projects. But he remained there only one year:

> *Jack (Prince) called me in sometime*

Dean of Scottsdale College quits dissension-torn campus

Arizona Republic, February 9, 1973

Dr. Marion Donaldson, founding dean of Scottsdale Community College, unexpectedly announced his resignation yesterday at a faculty meeting. It is effective immediately.

The 63-year-old administrator will trade positions with Ray Cattani, who is director of the Allied Health Planning Project in the Maricopa County Community College District's administrative main office.

The Scottsdale campus has been torn with student dissension since the college opened in 1970, but Donaldson would not indicate whether this is his reason for leaving the post.

Cattani will serve as acting dean while a special committee be... lect son...

Dr. Marion Donaldson

Born was su... theater son pri... trict in 1...

In 196... head th... district's... Scottsdal...

Since... lege has... over stu... ignate t... college against intercoll gram fo

The c... touching student...

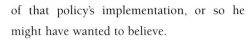

Cattani named SCC dean

Dr. Ray A. Cattani, 43, was appointed executive dean of Scottsdale Community College, effective July 1, by the college governing board.

The Maricopa County Community College District Board of Governors named Cattani acting dean at the college Feb. 12 after Dr. Marion Donaldson resigned the post in the wake of the heated artichoke court battle.

Scottsdale Daily Progress, June 6, 1973.

District president Dr. John Prince said Cattani's yearly salary would be "in the neighborhood of $25,000." He said Cattani and the district still are negotiating a final figure.

Prior to his appointment as acting dean, Cattani had been director of the district's Allied Health Curriculum Project — a post now held by Donaldson.

Dr. Cattani has been with the district since 1963, when he was a chemistry instructor at Phoenix College. He went to Mesa Community College in 1966 where he became the Dean of Instruction one year later.

Dr. Cattani lives at 3910 S. Grandview in Tempe, with his wife, Irene, and their four children, Keith, Kent, Kyle, and Kathleen.

Cattani

---

around March or April or May of '74, and said, "Marion, I'm going to ask you to take early retirement." I was really astonished because I thought I was doing some pretty good work for him. I didn't really say, "Why? Why, Jack? Why?" I had a little too much pride for that . . . I didn't say, "Jack, you know what you're doing? You're cutting me off at sixty-four, and you're denying me at least one more year, and probably more, of eventual Social Security." But I didn't. I didn't think that far ahead. It has really made a difference. Jack stayed on until he was over 65, and so he was able to take advantage of that increased Social Security deal that I didn't get.

The Foundation Cracked

On his way out the door, Donaldson might have tried to take comfort from the fact that his departure from Scottsdale had done nothing to calm down the disturbances there. After all, the district's pro-athletics policy had really fomented the rebellion. Donaldson had merely been the instrument

of that policy's implementation, or so he might have wanted to believe.

In reality, Donaldson shared a full measure of blame along with the rest of the district's administrators who hadn't yet figured out that the students weren't "kids" anymore.

The students in the Scottsdale student government were not children, and they were not acting like children when Donaldson had summarily appropriated the $21,000 for sports. Quite the opposite, they had been trying to spend their activity-fee money in surprisingly mature and responsible ways: to fund a superlative lecture series, to build a child care center, to provide scholarships for American Indian students, etc. Thus, Donaldson's preemptive strike to head off the student government's possible denial of funds for uniforms and equipment was the key mistake. He should have simply followed the procedures in the student government constitution that he himself had helped to draft. Even if the student government had

refused, the Drover Foundation or some other source could have taken up the slack.

For that reason, the Artichoke Rebellion represents a major turning point in the district's evolution. At long last, the district administration was aware that the students weren't "kids" anymore. From that time forward, students would begin to have an active voice in determining the district's future direction.

In other words, the community part of "community college" was beginning to take on a whole new meaning.

Chapter Eleven

Aftershocks

Donaldson left Scottsdale in January of 1973, but Roger Brooks remained. He had planned to transfer to ASU and complete a degree in accounting, but his plans were changing. Appearing before the governing board and the state legislature had excited him. He had also learned how to manipulate the newspapers, and before leaving Scottsdale, he decided to make one more play for media attention.

tions—everything—and the district still overrules us. Our only course of action left is to recall the board's Scottsdale representative, Ken Badertscher. Maybe this will get some result."

This announcement reveals two important elements of Roger Brooks' personality. First, he was vindictive. He wanted to punish those who opposed him. Second, Brooks was becoming much more politically astute. Due

College board recall tried

A recall attempt began Wednesday night to remove Kenneth R. Badertscher, Scottsdale's member from the Maricopa County Community College District Governing Board.

More than 100 signatures had been collected by noon today mainly through the efforts of students at Scottsdale Community College (SCC) who are spearheading the recall drive.

According to Roger Brooks, student president at SCC, Badertscher has ignored the wishes of a vast majority of individual taxpayers by voting for athletic funds rather than supporting academic subjects.

"I don't believe I have failed to represent the

district taxpayers," Badertscher said this morning, "and up to this point I haven't heard any direct comments that they are displeased with my performance on the board. I believe the recall movement is unjustified."

Petitions listed charges including Badertscher's support of "unnecessary and exorbitant appropriations of tax monies and consistently voting in favor of establishing and maintaining a semi-professional intercollegiate athletic program requiring unreasonable, wasteful expenditures."

Further complaints claim the SCC governing board member has not supported necessary funding for academic programs such as vocational education, science and English.

SCC students became embroiled in a fight with the administration in 1971 when they attempted to resist the establishment of an athletic program.

They filed a suit in the Maricopa County Superior Court last year to determine whether students have the right to run their own campus activities. The court found all rights and responsibilities to rest with the school board.

In order to hold a recall election, Brooks said 20 per cent of the registered voters who voted in the last election must sign petitions. Based on 6,000 votes in the 1971 community college district election, 1,200 signatures are needed to force the election.

From the Scottsdale Daily Progress, for April 5, 1973.

The Educational Subcommittee of the House had promised to mount an investigation of spending on athletics throughout the district, but the chair, Representative Robert Hungerford, was not moving fast enough for Brooks. Hungerford seemed to be backing away from the issue and urging students to settle the matter through the district. His frustration showing, Brooks was quoted in the April 9, 1973, issue of the *New Leaf:* "We've tried everything; publicity, elec-

to the poor voter turnout at the last governing board election, only 1,200 petition signatures would be required to force Badertscher's recall. Brooks may simply have decided to force a recall election because of its apparent ease. The article in the April 9 *New Leaf* ends ominously with a quote from Brooks: "Whatever happens, we will throw the district in a turmoil."

Brooks then created the Committee for Responsible Community College Spending and began circulating a flyer featuring a car-

The Maricopa governing board in 1974. Standing from left to right: Dwight Patterson, Jeremy Butler, and Paul Wright. Seated left to right: Ken Badertscher and Jim Miller.

September 14, 1996, audio interview with Ken Badertscher, Maricopa governing board member, 1972-77. Transcript available online.

http://www.mc.maricopa.edu/users/M3cdhistory/

"Here I was in a situation where I had run for office unopposed and the next thing I know, I'm embroiled in the middle of an A-number One...!"

toon of an angry, muscle-bound artichoke. The flyer lists Badertscher's crimes and ends with these words:

> Two weeks ago, Mr. Badertscher and another Board Member from Glendale, Paul Wright, voted to make "Drover" SCC's mascot. "Drover" was the choice of forty athletes. Artichoke was selected by 750 students! . . . Mr. Badertscher and the Board thought they had quietly killed the Artichoke two weeks ago when they voted for "Drover." Mr. Badertscher, you took on the wrong vegetable! [original emphasis]

Not surprisingly, Brooks ran the recall effort as if he were campaigning against Badertscher for a seat on the board. More than once, the two of them were invited to various radio stations to debate the issues on the air. Brooks'

The Fighting Artichoke from the flyer published by the Committee for Responsible Community College Spending.

strategy was to portray Badertscher as favoring varsity athletics above all else, but Badertscher maintained he was neither for nor against athletics:

> I wasn't opposed to athletics any more than I would have been opposed to theater or any other peripheral things that might be done at the schools outside of the normal. Our whole idea was to open up to the community what they wanted. Actually, the community as a whole wanted athletics. The football games were supported by the community.

On May 18, the Maricopa County Recorder announced that the recall petitions didn't have enough valid signatures. On June 14, Richard Lang—who had been elected to succeed Brooks as Scottsdale's next student body president—announced that he'd received a letter from the superintendent of schools stating that the deadline for assembling the required signatures had expired, and therefore, no recall election would be held.

Was Brooks disappointed? Probably not. The recall attempt had really been only a dress rehearsal for Brooks' future political career. He learned much in the process. For instance, he learned a lot about the right ways and the wrong ways to use student help. Student workers had been used to gather signatures for the recall petition, but the students had been too enthusiastic, and a significant number of the signatures had been

judged invalid. In his next campaign, he would use students to much better effect. Also, Brooks had used the recall effort to establish his public image as an opponent of wasteful spending on the part of the community college district. He was planning to cash in on that investment later.

And what elective office was Brooks planning to campaign for? He had already made up his mind to run for a seat on the Maricopa County Community College District Governing Board. The board members had denied him that honor once, and he was determined to show them that he was not to be denied. He knew that governing board elections were not heavily contested, and a seat on the governing board could then be used as a springboard to the state legislature. From there, the sky was the limit.

Also, Brooks wanted a seat on the governing board so he could properly settle an old score. All during the Artichoke Rebellion, Brooks had steadfastly blamed John Prince for all the unrest at Scottsdale. In the *Arizona Republic* for October 8, 1972, Brooks declared, "It may sound strange, but it is the school administration and Dr. John Prince . . . that are disrupting the campus. Dr. Prince, as president of the district, should be concentrating on seeing to it that the students of this college are getting an education. Instead, Dr. Prince has directed the student government be silenced in retaliation for suing the district."

Al Flowers insists that Brooks' hatred of Prince was really personal. Sometime after the lawsuit and before the second student mascot and colors election, a confrontation between Brooks and Prince had occurred. According to Al Flowers:

> Prince used to meet with the student body

presidents from the colleges—I don't even know if it was once a month, but periodically—and sit down with them, and talk issues with them, and what-have-you. Brooks showed up with a lawyer who was giving free service to them at that point, too. Ted Jarvi. Prince told [Jarvi] he could not stay in the meeting; he had to leave because it was just for the student body presidents. Brooks said, "If he leaves, I leave." Prince threw them both out, in effect. A long time later, Brooks told me, "That was the beginning of the end for Prince, because I wouldn't stand being treated that way in front of my peers." That stuck in his mind, and he hated Prince over that.

Brooks might have considered running for the board as early as the fall of 1973, but his opposition would have been Dwight Patterson, a founding board member who was very popular in the community because of his connection to Cactus League baseball. Brooks must have realized that he had no chance to unseat Patterson, so he opted to bide his time. That decision turned out to be fortuitous. The battle over athletics in the district then took an unexpected turn that greatly improved Brooks' position.

Out-of-State Recruiting for Athletics

Meanwhile, the students were still waging war on varsity athletics in the district. The students were attacking on two fronts: the practice of out-of-state recruiting and the

practice of awarding athletic scholarships. Both turned out to be easy targets.

Out-of-county and out-of-state recruiting were unknown at Phoenix College before the Maricopa district was created. Ken Stites, who played football at Phoenix College in 1959 and 1960 and later became head football coach there, confirms, "When I played in 1959, I can't recall any player that was an out-of-state player. All of our kids were local high school [kids]."

Once the junior college enabling legislation of 1960 took effect, more junior colleges came into existence, including two more in

April 24, 1997, video interview with Ken Stites, Phoenix College and Mesa Community College faculty and coach. Transcript and audio excerpts available online.

http://www.mc.maricopa.edu/users/M3cdhistory/

Maricopa County alone, and suddenly, the supply of local athletes was no longer sufficient. Theo Heap, Mesa's first athletic director and later president of Mesa, recalls that coaches were encouraged to recruit aggressively inside and outside the county: "Our first goal was to get the people locally, but we went other places, too. In fact, we brought in kids from all over. Some of our track kids came from Jamaica. We had people from Pennsylvania."

Alan Benedict, Mesa's athletic director and chair of the physical education department, describes how the process usually worked:

In 1972, we could recruit everywhere. We could make phone calls, write letters, travel. Not that we had any budget to go travel across the country to recruit; we didn't do that. We could go down to Tucson; we could go up north to some of the smaller high schools. We really had no restrictions as far as student athletes that were brought to this campus.

Lacking a travel budget, the coaches would often utilize a sort of "old boy" network of coaches in other states to recommend promising high school athletes play for Maricopa schools. Ken Stites recalls that Paul Widmer (Mesa's second head football coach) had grown up in Pennsylvania and still had many friends there. When Stites was coaching at Phoenix College, he would kid Widmer about his out-of-state players: "I'd call them up. 'Paul! Where'd you get this guy?' He'd laugh. 'Oh,' he says, 'He wanted to major in southwest history.' That was his line he'd always give me."

Another source of out-of-state players was Arizona State University. Ken Badertscher confirms that ASU regarded the district sports programs as active partners with the university:

ASU, for example, would be looking at a kid to come to play football. They may

October 14, 1996, audio interview with Alan Benedict, Mesa Community College faculty and coach. Transcript available online.

http://www.mc.maricopa.edu/users/M3cdhistory/

"When Scottsdale opened up, the basketball program brought the focus of something negative. The young men that they brought out there to play basketball were not the best citizens."

1973

have recruited the kid, and for some reason they didn't feel he was ready, and so they would refer him over to us, and he would end up coming to Scottsdale Community College to be on the campus and he did play football there. And also in baseball, that was fairly common at the time. It wasn't like it is now where after a couple of years they'd go pro. They referred to us as almost a farm team for ASU, in baseball and also in football.

These out-of-state players quickly became a source of resentment because they were perceived as taking places away from local athletes. Alan Benedict protests that this perception was false:

> *We also had no team limitations, so in the early '70s, we might dress out over 100 kids at home. We had them lined up from the 20 [yard-line] to the 20. Our president, Dr. Riggs, had a philosophy that every kid who wanted an opportunity should be given an opportunity, and we would keep them on the team.*

At Scottsdale, however, the situation appears to have been different. Glenn Groenke recalls, "Some of the people in the community would get very angry because their boys wouldn't be able to play because they would have gotten somebody from Jamaica or somebody from New York, and they said, 'Isn't this supposed to be community college? Aren't our guys supposed to play there?'"

Bob Winters, a longtime Scottsdale faculty member, recalls an incident that the opponents of out-of-state recruiting at Scottsdale often cited:

> *They had a basketball court, and local kids were playing basketball and actually got thrown off the basketball court. There was*

a basketball coach, and he said, "This court is for the team," and the entire team is from out-of-state, so local kids were not allowed to play on the basketball court. That seemed an odd idea for a community college, so that just added more fuel to the fire.

The other problem with out-of-state recruiting was the practice of awarding those players athletic "scholarships." Officially, the district did not award scholarships of any kind.

September 27, 1996, audio interview with Bob Winters, Scottsdale Community College faculty. Transcript available online.

http://www.mc.maricopa.edu/users/M3cdhistory/

The governing board, however, did authorize each college to grant a certain number of fee waivers. For local students, that waiver didn't amount to much, but for out-of-state students who otherwise would have been assessed full tuition, the waivers amounted to serious money. An article in the *Arizona Republic* for July 24, 1974, noted that between 500 and 600 of the 630 students participating in sports on district campuses had received tuition waivers.

In addition, out-of-state athletes usually needed money for travel expenses and living expenses. Alan Benedict explains where that money came from:

> *We had some scholarship dollars. None of it at that time was provided by the district; all monies were raised from the community. Coaches were allowed to assist in finding an apartment or a house or someplace where the guys could live. . . . We would have some people that would donate dollars to a scholarship fund, and then we*

would use those funds to distribute to some of the athletes.

Larry Philpot, Scottsdale's first head football coach, learned how the scholarship game was played while serving as an assistant coach at Mesa. At Scottsdale, he wasted no time in appealing to the community for support, and as a result, the Drover Foundation was formed. An article in the May 7, 1973, issue of the *New Leaf* explains that the Drover

> **"Mike Svaco went down to the district one day and was pushing for intramural sports, and he said Prince told him, 'Any faculty member who gets in the way of intercollegiate sports will be run over,' something like that."**

Foundation, "is made up of Scottsdale citizens who have come together to assist the SCC Athletic Department build a program that will enable it to compete and rank highly in the Arizona Community College Athletic Conference." The president of the Drover Foundation was listed as John H. Conner, then also president of the Scottsdale Rotary Club. Philpot was the secretary and treasurer. The article further states that donations for the previous year had amounted to approximately $9,000.

Armed with this kind of money, the coaches would go and recruite athletes. As Alan Benedict explains, some of the recruited athletes "were not the best citizens."

> *The best way to recruit out-of-state is go visit the kid, go visit his parents, go visit his home, go visit the environment in which he grows up. Get some background on the individual before he comes out to you, an area where it's 100% different. We're not allowed to do that, so what*

College to pay dorm $3,000 owed by 6 basketball players

By GORDON ROBBINS

SCOTTSDALE — Scottsdale Community College will pay room and board debts of approximately $3,000 run up by athletes attending school on federal Basic Education Opportunity Grants, according to Larry Philpot, college athletic director.

The debts were incurred by six unidentified basketball players housed at the privately owned La Mancha Dormitory in Tempe, 10 miles from the SCC campus, Philpot said.

Philpot said an installment on the debts will be paid Friday, with the money coming from SCC financial scholarship aid funds.

He blamed the existence of the debts on SCC basketball coach Ivan Duncan.

"We're not breaking any National Junior College Athletic Association rules in helping the kids," Philpot said.

The use of funds at SCC and in the Maricopa County Community College District currently is the subject of an informal probe by Sen. David Kret and Reps. Robert Hungerford and Americo Carvalho, a l l Scottsdale Republicans.

Allegations regarding wrongful use of funds at SCC and in the county college district have been made by Richard Lang, SCC student body president. One of Lang's allegations is overspending for athletics at the various district colleges.

The federal grants were provided the athletes on a basis of need, according to Russell Bloyer, SCC dean of students. The six are black athletes recruited from underprivileged areas of eastern cities, according to one source.

The grants totaled $1,100 to $1,400 per student, Bloyer said. In addition, the students were provided jobs under a federally financed work-study program, he said.

Bloyer said it is uncertain how the funds granted the students were spent.

Philpot blamed Duncan for the debts. "Duncan was irresponsible in handling the kids brought here," Philpot said.

Duncan resigned as basketball coach at Scottsdale Community College Feb. 18 and has said he will leave at the end of the semester in June. He referred to a controversy on out - of - state recruiting at SCC in a statement made at the time of his resignation.

Continued on Page B-2

From the Arizona Republic for April 4, 1974.

up the apartments, in many cases. They're going to end up stealing food and other things. They're going to end up in trouble, and you're going to end up as part of it.

Soon, these problems at Scottsdale began to find their way into the newspapers. Recruited from the Eastern United States, several basketball players were living in apartments in nearby Tempe. In April of 1974, the newspapers reported that six of

$3,000 debt

Continued from Page B-1

Duncan could not be reached Wednesday for comment.

Duncan's resignation occurred about the time school officials began a series of meetings to find a solution to the financial plight of the athletes.

"The athletic department has seen a wrong by a former coach and we are attempting to correct it," Philpot said.

One source involved in the meetings said a major difficulty of the students is finding transportation to school and work-study jobs because the dormitory is so far from the campus.

The source also said the athletes were provided meals at the Tempe dormitory but often were unable to take advantage of the meals because of the transportation problem.

SCC Dean Ray Cattani and Bloyer said last week they and other administrators personally are attempting to solve the problem by providing the students with rides to and from the campus.

La Mancha Dormitory administrator Annette Gyles refused to discuss the debts with newsmen but Bloyer said La Mancha officials also are providing transportation for the athletes.

information we get might be from a phone conversation, might be communication from a coach. Usually the coaches don't tell you everything, anyway, because they're trying to get the kid out of there on his way, and you can't find out anything about the environment in which he grew up. So you're getting a strange package, and so is he.

That problem was exacerbated by the fact that the district colleges were never designed to accommodate out-of-state athletes. As Ken Stites explains:

If you have 20 people on your football team that have no money or little money, on financial aid, living in apartments, living right on the edge of every dime that they have, you're going to have serious problems. They're going to end up tearing

these athletes owed about $3,000 in back rent to the La Mancha Dormitory. When the story broke, Ivan Duncan, who had been Scottsdale's head basketball coach for the first two years of the team, resigned. An editorial in the *Scottsdale Daily Progress* for April 10, 1974, states:

> *The buck should not stop with Duncan, however. It should be passed to Philpot, who was his boss. And it should ultimately reside with Dr. John Prince, president and chief administrator of the district . . . We believe that it is time for the board to tell Prince that his policies should be changed. Athletics have a valid place in education, but not at the expense of the academic budget, which is what has happened in the Maricopa County Community College system.*

The Drover Foundation gallantly announced it would pick up the tab for the students' back rent, but then the whole situation took a very unfortunate turn. On April 17, two of the students involved in the La Mancha debacle were arrested and charged with raping a 17-year-old girl, and the newspaper accounts all emphasized the fact that the players were on financial aid.

Scottsdale student body president Richard Lang did a little checking, and on April 30, the *Arizona Republic* revealed that 18 athletes at SCC had earned only a total of 54 hours of academic credits during the first semester of the '73-'74 school year. The same eighteen had also earned 159 hours of physical-education credit. According to the article:

> *Lang said 27 percent of the academic credits earned by the athletes are in a reading course. Lang claimed that without*

Arizona Republic *for April 18, 1974.*

physical-education credits most of the athletes would be ineligible to participate in sports at the school and "perhaps ineligible to collect the federal funds which are to be used for their educations."

A story in the *Arizona Republic* for June 6, 1974, revealed even more details of this mess. One of the students charged with the rape was a six-foot, ten-inch basketball player who had been recruited out of his high school in New York in the middle of the eleventh grade. In January of 1973, he had enrolled at Scottsdale as a part-time student taking fewer than six hours. According to the newspaper:

> *He had no high school diploma, no general equivalency degree (GED), was not an "ambitious student" still in high school and was too young for the "maturity" status given by the district to some 21-year-olds who cannot otherwise qualify as college students because they have neither a diploma or a GED.*

Even so, he was entitled to enroll as a part-time student taking less than six credits. Apparently, he was working on his GED, which he earned on October 4.

In the fall of 1973, he enrolled as a full-time student. He still wasn't qualified because he hadn't yet earned that GED, but his previous enrollment as a part-time student made him technically a "continuing student" and, therefore, exempt from the entrance requirements for full-time students. When the GED was granted, his status was upgraded to that of a "regular student," and he was then eligible to play for Scottsdale.

On November 22, 1973, he played his first game as a starting center. During the ensuing season, he averaged a promising fifteen points and nine rebounds per game. Unfortunately, the basketball season ended in February, and then he got into trouble. In addition to being charged with rape on April 17, he was also to be arraigned on two counts of second-degree burglary on June 14.

Roger Brooks must have been feeling very smug, much like a prophet who had just accurately predicted the winner of the Kentucky Derby.

The public was outraged. John Prince tried to put a good face on the affair. The June 6 article quotes him as saying, "[The arrested stu-

College board bars recruiting of athletes out of state, county

Arizona Republic, July 23, 1974.

By ATHIA L. HARDT

The Maricopa County Community College District board Monday night prohibited out-of-state or out-of-county recruiting of athletes.

The board also said that in the future, no out-of-state or out-of-county student will be given a waiver of the $45-per-semester attendance fee charged by colleges within the district for any reason other than financial need.

Currently, fee waivers are granted to nearly all athletes and also to many other students for achievements in fine arts, academics or other activities, district administrators say.

Dr. John Prince, district president, said the board action does not affect commitments already made to students for the 1974-75 school year.

"It really becomes effective in a year," he said.

Scottsdale Community College students who have fought out-of-state recruiting of athletes said after the district board meeting that the new policy is "a first step" towards ending what they see as overemphasis of athletics in the colleges.

The board action expanded a recommendation by Prince that sought to ban use of private or public funds for out-of-state recruiting. That recommendation was criticized by SCC students as being ineffective.

But Todd Schwartz, SCC student body president, said that although the board's action "is not what we were looking for, it's a lot more than we expected."

Richard Lang, former SCC student body president, said he will make recommendations for amending the new policy "on several small points."

But he added, "It's a good first step for the board to take. The board has stated its intentions."

Continuing what is supposed to be unwritten current policy, according to

Continued on Page A-18

for financial aid, the same as any other students. The coaches were supposed to discourage potential out-of-county athletes from coming to the district unless they had at least $1,000 of their own money to use for expenses. Ken Stites confirms, "We would do that. Every single kid. Then you'd pray, 'Please get a thousand dollars!' because you wanted them to come."

Thus, the end of out-of-county recruiting and private scholarships for athletes did not turn out to be the end of varsity athletics in the district. Still, the unseemly spectacle caused by the six athletes at the La Mancha had given the district a significant black eye. And waiting in the wings, Roger Brooks was ready to turn the district's distress into political capital for himself.

dent] came in and got his GED and that's the important thing . . . Look at some of the positive things." Privately, however, Prince was fed up. At the board meeting on July 22, 1974, the board formally banned all out-of-state recruiting and even out-of-county recruiting of student athletes. The ban specifically prohibited the use of public and private funds for this purpose. The board also reconfirmed that fee waivers could be granted only on the basis of financial need.

The anti-athletics forces greeted this ban as a victory, but in reality, little changed. Coaches were not allowed to make the initial contract with out-of-county students, but coaches were still permitted to give a sales pitch to any student who contacted them first. As Ken Stites explains, the coaches could easily work around that restriction:

> The more you got beat, or the more fanatical or desperate you got, the more you'd find a way for those kids to get in contact with you, if that's what it took. In other words, maybe I would say, "No, we didn't call the kid. He called us." But I might have called somebody else over there to tell him to call us. You see what I mean? Look, let's face it. That was an unenforceable rule.

No private money could be used for scholarships, but out-of-county athletes could apply

1974

Critic Of Community College District Wins Election To Its Board

A critic of the Maricopa County Community College District was elected to the district board yesterday and said a first duty will be to compare administrative costs with similar costs in business.

Roger Brooks, 27, former student body president of Sc[...] leg[...] La[...] th[...] Sc[...]

Br[...]

The votes will be canvassed next Tuesday.

Harold Gade, who supervised the election, said the turnout was lower than he expected. Dysart and Ruth Fisher, two of the westside polling locations, reported only seven votes each.

citizens would be out voting in the Peoria District bond election the same day.

Without Sun City, Mrs. Lakin had 596 votes and Brooks 314. About 1,415 of the 2,325 votes cast in the election came from Sun City, returns show.

BROOKS, an accountant for Lovett's Paint and Body Shop, said his election "will [t]urn the board around."

He believes Jeremy But[...] will generally vote in fav[...] of reduced athletic a[...] administrative costs and K[...]

Badertscher, another board member, may do so at times.

"That makes three out of five much of the time," he said. Butler and Badertscher could not be contacted.

Brooks led the fight three years ago to name the Scottsdale College mascot the Artichokes, with colors of pink and white. It was a protest against alleged over-

the district has since moved to eliminate that recruiting

Brooks said a first duty would be determine if the administration costs are in line with similar costs in Valley businesses. He has charged the district has been wasteful.

A PART-TIME student at Arizona State University, Brooks said he spent $400 on the campaign, while Mrs.

1 before completing his five-year term. The new member normally would begin his term in January, but Richard Harris, Maricopa County schools superintendent, has said he would probably appoint the victor immediately.

"The very first thing I'm going to do is write a letter to the Sun City paper," Brooks said. "Those people out there elected me and I want them to know I'll keep my campaign promise to reduce costs."

Roger Brooks didn't have a snowball's chance of winning election to the governing board in 1974. Jim Miller was going to be up for reelection in 1974, and Brooks could not have unseated him any more easily than Dwight Patterson. But suddenly, Brooks' problem was solved. Effective August 1, Jim Miller resigned from the board.[1]

An election to fill Miller's seat was announced for October 8th, and Brooks threw his hat in the ring immediately. The situation was perfect—instead of having to face a popular incumbent, his only other opposition would be Maxine Lakin, a businesswoman who had also served on the Phoenix Union High School District board from 1964-69.

Brooks analyzed the electorate and devised a clever strategy for his campaign. First, he capitalized on the board members' relative anonymity. His newspaper ads were headlined, "Five Men Spent $26 Million on Our Community Colleges Last Year . . . Can You Name Two of Them?"

Phoenix Gazette for October 9, 1974.

Two newspaper ads from Roger Brooks' campaign. The one on the right was published in the Sun City News-Sun on October 4, 1974. The one of the left was published in the Arizona Republic on October 8, 1974.

Roger Brooks, Maricopa governing board member 1975-78.

Second, he targeted his constituency in Sun City. For several years, Sun City residents had wanted Glendale Community College to offer extension classes in their area, but Glendale had ignored their request. As a result, many residents were complaining that their tax dollars were supporting the district but the district wasn't providing anything in return. An article from Sun City's October 4, 1974, *News-Sun* enlarged on Brooks' reputation as an opponent of wasteful spending and repeated his campaign pledge to work to establish community college extension courses in Sun City.

Third, Brooks used student workers very effectively. Although no longer a student at Scottsdale, he had continued to maintain his contacts there, and more than fifty SCC students were organized to canvass for him door-to-door. Two years later, an article from the *Arizona Republic* published October 4, 1976, stated that the students were not entirely volunteers and quotes Todd Schwarz, student body president at Scottsdale in 1974, as saying that student government funds were used to pay for Brooks' campaign materials and to pay some students by the hour to work on Brooks' campaign. "I received a directive from the student senate telling me to expend funds for the purpose of electing Roger Brooks to the governing board," Schwarz said.

Brooks, naturally, denied that student funds were spent on his campaign—but by then, it was too late.

On October 8, 1974, Brooks' campaign strategy was aided by the usual low turnout for district governing board elections. When the ballots were counted, Brooks had won 1,353 to 972. The *Phoenix Gazette* on October 9, reported, "The winner's strongest support came from Sun City, which had the largest turnout. . . . Without Sun City, Mrs. Lakin had 596 votes and Brooks 314. About 1,415 of the 2,325 votes cast in the election came from Sun City, returns show."

Brooks on the Board

Brooks asked Maricopa County School Superintendent Richard Harris to appoint him to the board immediately to fill the seat vacated by Miller. Harris agreed, and Brooks was sworn into office on November 12 to fill out the remainder of Miller's term. (Brooks was sworn in again on January 6, 1974, when his own term actually began.)

One of his first priorities was to take care of some unfinished business at Scottsdale. At the board meeting on December 9, Brooks offered a resolution calling for the board to recognize the artichoke as the official mascot

[1] The reason for Miller's abrupt departure from the board was not announced, but it may have been poor health. On June 26, 1975—barely a year later—after playing a round of golf at the Olympic Club in San Francisco, Miller collapsed and died.

of Scottsdale Community College. Jeremy Butler seconded Brooks' resolution, and the vote was unanimous. In article from the *Phoenix Gazette* for December 10, Paul Wright is quoted as saying, "the board will be thrilled not to have to sit and listen to this year after year."

An office in the district headquarters had been set aside for the use of board members, and Brooks quickly appropriated this space for his personal office. Prince's daughter Mary Martha recalls:

I remember going, when the district offices were on Second Street, going into the district offices and there was Roger Brooks. I asked my dad why he was there. [Brooks] had just gotten an office in the district office across the [hall], and Dad said, "He sits there all day and watches me. It's an untenable situation." This went on for two years.

From this office across the hallway from his hated enemy, Brooks launched a full-scale investigation, looking into anything he could use against John Prince. According to Ken Badertscher:

I think Roger spent a lot of time at the offices. Prince or Al Flowers came to the board and said, "We don't mind giving Roger information, but we don't want information going exclusively to one board member and not to all." So we voted and set a policy that Roger would have to come through the board to get information, that he couldn't just go in

and say, "Give me this. Do that," and tell people to do things for him. They would have to be put together in a package that could come to the board itself. And I think the reason that came up is that he was just driving people crazy, and he was looking for dirt. . . . He was acting more like an internal auditor than he was a

"Artichoke Emperor Peels," an interview with Roger Brooks published in Maricopa Tech's school newspaper The Prospector, November 19, 1974. Text available online.

http://www.mc.maricopa.edu/users/M3cdhistory/

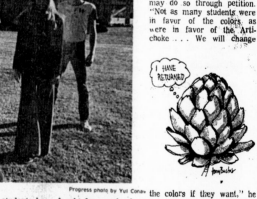

SCOTTSDALE COMMUNITY COLLEGE student body president Todd Schwarz, wearing an "Artichoke" t-shirt, gives a sign of triumph today as the vegetable officially becomes the school's mascot. SCC students have fought for nearly three years to have the artichoke designated as the mascot.

Top right
Phoenix Gazette,
December 10, 1975.

Above
Scottsdale Daily Progress,
December 10, 1975.
Photo by Yul Conaway.

College Artichoke Finally Has Day; 'Pink' Left Pending

Gazette 12-10

By LOUISE GACIOCH

The "dye" not quite cast in the artichoke issue at Scottsdale Community College, although the vegetable has been officially recognized as the school's sports nickname and mascot.

The dainty pink and white colors selected in earlier elections could change, Todd Schwarz, student body president, declared today.

ALL FIVE Maricopa County Community College District Board members voted last night to recognize the artichoke, resolving a 2½-year-old controversy touched off

by student government leaders.

The board recognized the artichoke as selected by students in two elections in 1972, which were later voided as "unofficial" and unrepresentative of student opinions. In both elections, 67 per cent of the those who voted favored the artichoke, said Roger Brooks, former SCC student body president and now a member of the board.

The college administration's decision voiding the elections was upheld in Maricopa Superior Court in 1972.

BROOKS' resolution to the board last night called only for recognition of the artichoke. "Perhaps I should have worded it differently . . . It's a matter for the students now."

Dr. Paul Wright, board president, agreed the colors are up to the students.

Schwarz is empowered to call an election or students may do so through petition. "Not as many students were in favor of the colors as were in favor of the Artichoke . . . We will change

I HAVE RETURNED

the colors if they want," he said.

HE SAID 62 per cent of those voting in the last election wanted pink and white while 76 per cent favored the artichoke.

Turn to ⬤PINK, Page B-2.

(Concluded from Page B-1)

A new election would be called when existing athletic uniforms wear out and paper and envelopes are used up. The Artichoke will be used as a symbol on school paraphernalia, he said.

Scottsdale College had once used the "Drovers" as mascot, but the board last year recognized "no mascot," and the school has since been without a name.

THE ARTICHOKE has been a student symbol of protest against alleged overspending on athletics in the district.

Wright said last night the artichoke issue has dragged on too long. "The board will be thrilled not to have to sit and listen to this year after year."

Dwight Patterson, another board member, said he sees no harm in recognizing the mascot since "students next week may decide to change the name to the 'Skunks'."

BOARD MEMBER Jeremy Butler, who seconded Brook's resolution, warned students to phase in use of the artichoke as a symbol "so there is not additional cost to the taxpayers."

"Do you think we can phase it in over the next 10 years?" quipped Dr. John Prince, district president. He later said the decision is "unkind . . . It brings derision to the athletic program."

Larry Philpot, SCC athletic director, declined to comment on the decision. "I have no reaction at all," he said.

SCHWARZ SAID the decision assures the students a greater voice on campus, but does not end the symbol of the artichoke: "Fighting for cuts in athletic spending."

Brooks said the decision represents "a major turnabout in the attitude of the board."

board member, and rather than policy matters, he was dealing directly in day-to-day situations.

During the board meetings, Brooks would use whatever information he had found to try to embarrass Prince. According to Al Flowers, Prince often played into Brooks' hands:

> Brooks came in with an agenda against Prince in every board meeting. It was hot pursuit. It was terrible. But the rest of the

Prince warned over records

Maricopa County Community College District Board Member Roger Brooks said Monday he will seek the dismissal of MCCCD President John Prince if Prince continues to refuse board members' access to district records.

Brooks, the former Scottsdale Community College student body president who was elected to the district board in October, said he would call for the dismissal of the district president for "insubordination and unlawful acts."

Brooks said Prince violated state statutes in October when he issued a directive to all district personnel instructing them to deny Brooks access to district records.

Brooks was prohibited from looking into personnel records in a situation in which there had been a charge of hiring discrimination against the district and he was denied access to official Scottsdale Community College enrollment records.

Prince has confirmed that he has denied Brooks access to the records.

Prince today maintained the state statute governing board members' responsibilities calls for the board to act in concert and the statute does not give individual board members access to the records.

Prince said that he will ask the entire MCCCD board for guidelines to govern the release of information to individual board members.

Brooks said the law clearly defines the board's responsibilities saying board members' must employ all means including gaining information, to fulfill their responsibilities.

"There is no privileged information to an elected board member," Brooks said.

In a letter to his fellow board members, Brooks asked the board to support the existing laws and if Prince continues "to obstruct" the board in its duties, then he must be dismissed.

"Hired officials have no right telling elected officials what to do when public tax funds are at stake," Brooks said today.

Scottsdale Daily Progress, December 17, 1974.

board didn't really control it, and they should have. [Brooks] would ask a few innocuous questions, and Brooks was good with the numbers. He studied the reports; he studied everything. He would ask Prince these questions, instead of asking me, and Prince didn't shuffle it to me,

because he was the president, you know? Prince would finally end up giving him answers, and Brooks would nail him to the wall. They wouldn't be correct. He would prove it, in open board meetings. But Prince would never want to back down, or say, "I don't know. We'll find out for you." Or, "Ask Flowers. That's what we hired him for." He wouldn't do that. Prince believed that the president should know more than any staff member about an operational area. So it became a terrible situation in board meetings.

Prince's strategy for dealing with Brooks' attacks was to try not to let the man knock him off center. Bill Berry, who observed the struggle firsthand, recalls:

> My view of Jack's position on Roger was that he did not want to lower himself to

March 19, 1997, video interview with Bill Berry, president of Phoenix College 1971-89. Transcript and audio excerpts available online.

http://www.mc.maricopa.edu/users/M3cdhistory/

fight in the ditch with Roger. He just continued to try to ignore him. . . . He did absolutely refuse to face Roger and deal with him. He just kept resisting whatever Roger wanted him to do. It was a terrible, terrible time in the district. Everybody became apprehensive about themselves and their positions.

Up to this point, Brooks was waging essentially a one-man campaign against Prince, but that situation changed before the end of the year. Paul Wright announced that he had decided against running for reelection:

It was at a time we were getting into everybody suing for everything. . . . We would go to a board meeting and they'd usually hand out at least one, two, three subpoenas. As I remember, there would be a janitorial person suing because they were getting into discrimination cases, and if you didn't give somebody a raise, somebody else said, "Well, I should have gotten that raise." Everybody was filing suits for everything. . . . I just lost interest because of the legal things that were going on, so I decided there must be other ways to spend my time.

Prince's wife was furious. "When I decided not to run, I heard that Mrs. Prince made the statement that I had really stabbed Dr. Prince in the back by not running," Wright recalls.

BROOKS PAYS HIS DUES

Brooks did not forget about the people who had elected him. In addition to having the artichoke anointed as Scottsdale's official mascot, Brooks also caused the development of the Bell Plaza Center, a satellite campus run by Glendale Community College in the Bell Plaza Professional Building. On January 6, 1976, the ribbon-cutting ceremony was held, and Sun City residents could at last take extension classes in their own neighborhood.

July 3, 1996, video interview with Paul Wright, Maricopa governing board member 1971-76. Transcript and audio excerpts available online.

http://www.mc.maricopa.edu/users/M3cdhistory/

Brooks wasted no time in finding a suitable candidate for Wright's seat on the board. He turned to Bob Robertson, an employee of Western Electric. At that time, Robertson was 32 years old and a graduate of Glendale Community College, where he had been student body president in 1971—the same time as Roger Brooks at Scottsdale. Tom McCarthy, an attorney, opposed Robertson, but the race was really no contest.

Again, a low voter turnout worked to Brooks' advantage. Only 1,554 votes were cast—out of a potential 100,000 eligible voters—and Robertson won by a little more than half.

A week later, however, the entire election was almost thrown out because of a procedural error. Janice McIlroy (now Janice Bradshaw), an assistant to Prince, discovered that the Maricopa County Elections Department left out an entire precinct eligible to vote, an area called Windrose, where approximately 500 voters had never even been given ballots. Hope briefly flickered that the district might be able to void the entire election, but in the end, the Maricopa County attorney's office decided the district did not have that power. Tom McCarthy could have disputed the election, but he decided that another election would not be worth the expense. So the election stood.

Then, Prince received another blow. In October, Prince's longtime supporter Dwight

Patterson announced that he would resign from the district board in order to accept an appointment to the state board of regents. At the governing board meeting on December 9, 1975, Mesa developer Ross Farnsworth (an old friend of Patterson's) was sworn in to complete the remainder of Patterson's term. Ironically, Farnsworth had been a student at Mesa High School when Marion Donaldson had been the principal there. For that reason, Prince might have worried that he was not gaining an ally on the board.

As Prince looked ahead to 1976, he could not have been pleased. The makeup of the board had changed quickly and dramatically. All the old-timers were gone. Brooks and Robertson would be sure to oppose Prince at every opportunity. Farnsworth did not appear to be his friend, and Butler and Badertscher couldn't be counted on for their support, either.

John Prince's Last Six Months as President

At the meeting on January 13, 1976, Robertson was sworn in as a board member. Al Flowers remembers Robertson favorably:

He was a Vietnam veteran, older guy, and had a lot of good about him. I never considered him an evil person at all. However, he had very strong ideas about students' rights, and he had a father-in-law who

Brooks essentially ran the same campaign over again, as this campaign ad for Bob Robertson shows. Notice that the ad copy has been recycled from Roger Brooks' campaign ads from the year before. Ironically, though, Roger Brooks himself is now one of the "Five Men" that the ad attacks.

MCCCD election may be disallowed

The Oct. 7 election of Robert Robertson to the Maricopa County Community College District governing board may be disallowed because of an omitted precinct.

According to Janice McIlroy, assistant to district president John Prince, the county elections department failed to include the Windrose precinct in a list of those qualified to vote in the election. Approximately 500 persons registered in Windrose were not given a chance to vote.

Albert Firestein, chief deputy of the county attorney's civil division, has discussed the problem with college district officials, and he is researching the possibility that the election may be void because of the oversight.

The county attorney's office also is studying whether district officials have the power to disallow the election and whether one of the candidates have to contest the results

before another election is called.

Robertson, a former student body president at Glendale Community College, won the election with 825 votes. Glendale attorney Tom McCarthy received 569 votes, while write-in candidate Muriel Small received 76 votes.

When asked this morning whether he planned to challenge the election, McCarthy said "I'm considering it, but I've made no definite decision."

McCarthy said he had "advisers looking into" the procedure of challenging the election. He said he campaigned in every section of Precinct 3, which involves the northern section of the county and a small part of Scottsdale, but he was "unable to tell whether it (Windrose) would have made a difference in the total votes."

Scottsdale Daily Progress for October 14, 1975.

was a Chicano, so he had strong feelings about Chicanos, and Blacks. He was very liberal. He was rather typical of the '60 student-type thing. But, at the same time, Bob was holding down a full-time job at Western Electric.

Robertson tended to follow Brooks' lead, and the two of them continued to oppose Prince and look for ways to embarrass him at board meetings.

When the board met on February 10, Brooks and Robertson nearly pulled off a coup. Together, they held up what should have

Ross Farnsworth Named to Vacancy On Colleges Board

Ross Farnsworth, co-owner of a retirement community development firm here, has been named to the Maricopa County Community College District board, it was announced Friday.

The appointment, by County School Supt. Richard T. Harris, also of Mesa, is for the unexpired term of Dwight E. "Pat" Patterson of Mesa. Patterson resigned recently to accept membership on the Arizona Board of Regents, upon appointment by Gov. Raul Castro.

The term which Farnsworth will finish runs until Dec. 31, 1978. The college board is made up of five members, elected for five years from districts within the county, with one member elected each year in special elections held in October. It presides over affairs of all the junior colleges in the county, including Mesa College.

Farnsworth and his brother, Jay, are associated in the family's Farnsworth Realty and Development Co., here, developers of Dreamland Villa and the now-in-progress Sunland Villa retiree areas east of the city, as well as other enterprises.

A native of Mesa, he went through Mesa schools and holds bachelor and master degrees from Arizona State University. He is active in the Latter-day Saints Church and has taken a leading role in many community activities and projects. He and Mrs. Farnsworth are the parents of 11 children.

ROSS FARNSWORTH

been the routine renewal of administrative and support contracts for the '76-'77 year. The issue was that one of those administrators, John Prince, would be 65 years old when his contract expired on August 1, 1976. [2] Previously, the legislature had set 65 as the normal age of retirement and stipulated that any employee desiring to continue employment beyond that time must make a formal application to the governing board at least six months before that retirement date. Brooks claimed that Prince had not made such a request and therefore

would have to be retired as of August 1. The vote stalled with Brooks and Robertson on one side and Badertscher and Farnsworth on the other. (Butler was absent from this meeting.)

A special meeting of the board was called for February 14, 1976. The minutes reveal that Jeremy Butler was doing his best to avoid a showdown. First, Butler moved and Brooks seconded a motion that the administration prepare for the board a report on the number of administrators employed by the district. The reason for this motion was to throw Brooks a bone; he had been making noise in the press that the district already had too

many administrators, and the legislature had been demanding that the college trim its budget. Brooks obviously welcomed Butler's support in this area. Then, Butler moved and Farnsworth seconded a motion to extend Prince's contract beyond his 65th birthday. Brooks and Robertson predictably voted no, but the motion passed anyway. The minutes state:

> *Mr. Butler stated that the district will be going through a period of transition from one leadership to another. He noted that Dr. Prince has accumulated leave and if it is his wish to take it, it is possible that there will be an interim head of the district during the 1976-77 year. Then, Butler moved and Brooks seconded that the administration should appoint a search committee "for the purpose of screening applicants for the position of president of the community college district . . . the position to begin on July 1, 1977." Motion carried.*

In other words, Butler continued Prince's

Bob Robertson, Maricopa governing board member 1976-81.

contract for one more year but, at the same time, placated Brooks by urging Prince take the year on leave while the search for a new president progressed. This incident would

[2] Prince was born July 28, 1912.

not be the last time that Butler would act to try to save the district from public embarrassment.

In the spring of '76, the board became entangled in the student government elections at Scottsdale. A new student political party, Students for '76, had mounted the first strong opposition to the Artichoke candidates. The defeated Artichoke candidates were claiming election fraud. Charges and countercharges of interference were thrown around, and the matter was dropped in the board's lap at the meeting on April 12. The arguments dragged on into June, exhausting everyone, particularly Ross Farnsworth, who recalls, "We held 15 hours of hearings on this one election thing. . . . We went through so much fighting and so many things, it was a burden trying to come and do all this besides all the regular business of the board, too."

Then, in June, a particularly nasty controversy erupted over an issue at Phoenix College. The board approved the hiring of Ray Laing, the former head football coach at Phoenix's Central High School, for a faculty position in the math department. Apparently Bill Berry, president of Phoenix College, had wanted Laing for a coach, but at that time, the physical education department had no faculty openings. The math department had a vacancy, and Laing had sixty hours of credits in math—or so Berry thought. The math teachers didn't want Laing's appointment forced on them, and when they looked more carefully at Laing's transcript, they discovered that he did not have the required number of hours to teach math.

Prince stood behind Berry and claimed that Laing did have the necessary credits. Once again, faculty protested that the district was

MCC's Prince Sweats Job?

By JIM WALKER

Dr. John F. Prince, president of the Maricopa Community Collge District, today said reports that he would be asked to resign "have been leaked to the press in an attempt to discredit me."

PRINCE

PRINCE SAID "any change in my position as president must be handled in a' public board meeting and no formal action has taken place."

Board member Roger Brooks said Dr. Prince's name was brought up during an executive session last week at which all board members were present. He would neither confirm nor deny that Prince would be asked to resign, citing a state law providing confidentiality in personnel matters discussed in executive session.

Brooks did say the matter would probably be discussed in a special board

Turn to ●PRINCE, Page B-2

Phoenix Gazette for July 23, 1976. From microfilm.

emphasizing athletics at the expense of academics. Formal grievances were filed against John Prince, William Berry, and William Wallace, the Phoenix College dean of instruction. Once again, the board meetings degenerated into long, drawn-out shouting matches. Glenn Groenke, who was the district faculty president at the time (and no particular friend of John Prince's), recalls one of these sessions:

I called Prince on the carpet. It was very hard for me to do. And the faculty was

vehement, and I remember that board meeting, because I was so nervous, and I stood up there and I called Prince a liar— I didn't say he was a liar, I said, "That's not the facts, sir," in front of the board . . . He said that what they did was legal and right, and the faculty took an opposite opinion with this coach. . . . It wasn't the first time that Prince had bent the truth or interpreted things the way that was most beneficial to him.

Once again, Brooks used the occasion to call for Prince's resignation, and this time, others took up the cry, too.

The matter was finally resolved at the board meeting on August 10. Laing was permitted to transfer to the physical education department at Phoenix.[3] John Prince, however, was conspicuously missing from this meeting. According to Al Flowers:

We were on North Second Street then, in rented facilities. I just stayed there on nights when we had board meetings, preparing and getting stuff together. I never even went out to eat before the meetings, generally. Prince came in about five-thirty, quarter-to-six, or so. Prince came into my office, and he said, "You run the board meeting tonight. I'm not staying." I said, "What do you mean?" He said, "I'm not staying. I'm not going to put up with any more of that stuff from Brooks. I don't intend to attend any more board meetings." I said, "How can you be president, Jack, if you're not going to attend any board meetings?" He said, "Don't worry. I'll go over everything with you, and you will represent me, and you'll

---

[3] In an article published in the *Arizona Republic* for August 15, 1976, Prince commented derisively about the Laing controversy, "There's been more bloodshed over that than slavery."

run the board meetings. I'm not going to those board meetings and put up with what I have with Brooks on all this stuff." I said, "Well, I think that's a dangerous decision. You better think about that."

Well, we had a pre-session on some personnel item [the Laing issue], and it was in Prince's office, and the board members showed up . . . I think the board meeting started at seven and they showed up [at] six, to six-fifteen. I went down because I was supposed to be involved, and they asked, "Where's Jack?" I said, "Well, he was here earlier." Then they pursued me. They said, "Where's Jack?" I said, "Well, I don't think he's coming. I think maybe a couple of you board members better call him tomorrow and have lunch with him and talk to him." I really didn't even want to convey such a message to them. So we went in and had the board meeting, and I put the budget through, and all that sort of thing, and he did not come back.

In fact, he never came back to another board meeting. They met with him, and they tried to work out some kind of an agreement, and he always said, "I'll work out any kind of agreement, but I'm not going to attend board meetings and put up with this stuff." Even his supporters had to say, "You can't be president of the district and not attend board meetings."

Arizona Republic for August 15, 1976.

They sat down with me a couple of times, and—it was a Saturday meeting—finally I said, "Well we've got to make some decisions here. We can't go on like this. You're the acting president, as of right now. Jack, apparently, is never going to come back to a board meeting as long as Brooks is there, so he's out."

Jeremy Butler remembers that he tried to talk Prince out of his decision not to attend further board meetings.

I told him that if he wanted to stay, I would vote for his staying, and he told me in effect that he'd had enough, that "Life's too short," or something like that, whatever the cliché was at the time, and he wasn't going to stick around.

Predictably, Brooks was jubilant and insisted that Prince's contract be terminated immediately. Al Flowers claims he intervened:

I really raised hell with [Brooks] then. I insisted the board honor [Prince's] contract—even though, from the fiscal area, I almost would have had to say, under any normal circumstances, "If you don't work, you don't get paid." I kept him on the payroll for a whole year without him doing anything. Never appeared, actually. He was, however, given consultant-type assignments to complete and report to the board in writing. I felt I owed it to the man. I think he was completely mistreated, and the older board members should have taken

that control early in the game. I never should have gotten to that point. He put in a lot of years, the whole bit. It's a cliché to say, "He earned it. He had it coming," and all those kinds of things. It was just a mistreatment of a human being that never should have occurred.

Effective August 16, Al Flowers became the district's acting president. The board conferred upon Prince the title of President Emeritus, and Prince remained on the payroll until the end of the '76-'77 school year.

Brooks had won. He had brought down his hated enemy, but the victory would not turn out to be the stepping-stone to the bright political future that Brooks had wanted. Within two years, Brooks would be gone from the board and sentenced to serve time in jail.

And the real turbulence was only just beginning.

1976

ROSS FARNSWORTH, a member of the Maricopa County Community College Board, announces that A.W. Flowers will become acting district president Monday. He will replace Dr. John F. Prince, who will assume other district duties. Flowers, a former Scottsdale School District assistant superintendent, is the MCCCD's current executive vice president for business services. Board members (from left) are: Roger Brooks, Kenneth Badertscher, Farnsworth and Robert Robertson.

Flowers gets MCCCD post

By BONNIE FOSTER

A.W. Flowers today was named acting president of the Maricopa County Community College District and will assume the duties now assigned to Dr. John F. Prince, the current president.

Prince's new title will be president emeritus.

The changeover, announced during a special meeting of the MCCCD board, is effective Monday.

Flowers now is executive vice president for business services.

He will serve in his new position until a permanent president is selected. The board did not indicate when a president will be named.

Board member Ross Farnsworth, who introduced the two resolutions making the reassignment, emphasized that the action was requested by Prince. There have been reports that board members last month asked him to relinquish his duties.

The decision was voted on by board

son, Kenneth Badertscher and Farnsw Neither Prince nor the fifth board me Jeremy Butler, were present at the me

New duties assigned to Prince, wh retire from the district next year, i various public relations duties, prir appearing at several meetings on beh the district plus other duties which mi assigned by the board.

According to the resolution, Princ retain his present office space, secr services, use of a district car an executive title.

Flowers' duties presumably w assumed by Robert Little, currentl district's business manager.

Flowers, who served from 1962 to 1 the Scottsdale School District's as superintendent for business services, the MCCCD in 1966. He previously ser finance director and assistant bu manager for Phoenix Union High Scho the Phoenix College System. From 1 1958 he was assistant principa educational services for North Phoeni

1977
Chapter Thirteen
Interregnum

Al Flowers should have said no. The whole district was suffocating in an atmosphere of contention and mistrust. The Laing affair had completely eroded faculty confidence in the district leadership. All the wrangling over athletics and student politics had exhausted and demoralized the board—all except for Roger Brooks, of course, who was jubilant at having crushed the "tyrant" Prince. He had indeed fulfilled his threat to "throw the district in a turmoil."

In the meantime, facilities had been deteriorating in the three years that the district had been choking on artichokes, and another bond election to fund capital improvements was long overdue. At the same time, the national economy was also deteriorating. Inflation was on the rise. The legislature's portion of the district's annual tab was shrinking while the faculty were demanding bigger and bigger salary increases. An accreditation team from the North Central Association of Schools and Colleges was scheduled to arrive in February, 1977—always a stress-producing situation at best. At the same time, the district had to organize a search for a new district president just when the district was generating some of the worst possible publicity.

Scottsdale Daily Progress for August 14, 1976.

Adding to the strain, the board—predictably—gave Flowers the honor of running the district and managing all of its business affairs simultaneously and for roughly the same salary. He explained, "As long as they were paying Prince, they wouldn't even consider putting another salary on. So they paid me an extra fifty bucks a week. I acted in both capacities."

Flowers' most immediate problem was the faculty. Some of them were not happy that he had been appointed acting president. They felt he simply held too much power. When Flowers had assumed control of the district's financial affairs in 1965, he had also acquired many of the responsibilities that would normally have been given to a director of human resources. He was the one to negotiate for the district in the meet-and-confer process with the faculty. Al Flowers recalls, "With the faculty, we had lots of knock-down-drag-outs, but always with real respect, and we were always able to come to a mutual decision as to what we'd present to the board." Then, Flowers would turn around and represent the faculty in negotiations with the board. As a result, he often found himself in the unusual—possibly even unethical—position of representing both sides in different phases of negotiations. Thus, some faculty felt that Flowers already had too much power and that the role of acting president would only exacerbate the situation. Gene Eastin recalls, "He was the one who seemed to put the block

on all our salary negotiations, and he was disliked seriously because of that. He was the one who always said, 'No, we can't afford it. You don't do this, and you don't do that, and we can't do this, and there isn't enough money,' and all that."

To try to mollify the faculty, Flowers named Walt Morrison as the district's new vice president for educational services. A faculty member at Mesa, Morrison earned both his bachelor's and master's degrees from Northeast Missouri State University. He began his teaching career in 1963 at Westwood High School, where he taught political science and history and watched Mesa Community College begin in storefronts on Main Street. In 1965, he began teaching part-time in Mesa's evening college, and in 1968, he was appointed to the Mesa faculty full-time. At the time of his appointment to the district, Morrison was also working on his dissertation in the Adult Education Doctoral Program, Higher Education, at ASU.

At Mesa, Morrison became a popular faculty leader. He was active in faculty governance, and in 1972, he was also elected department chair for social sciences. In 1975, he was elected president of the district faculty executive council. Flowers felt that by appointing Morrison the district's new vice president for educational services, the faculty would feel they had their advocate on the district level.

Next, Flowers set the wheels in motion for a bond election. The last one had been held in 1969 for $9.8 million. The only other bond election had been the original 1964 bond election for $4.9 million. This time, Flowers wanted the district to ask for $20 million, including nearly $8.8 million to complete the Mesa campus. The board scheduled the election for December 15, and Flowers set about trying to sell the idea to the public.

Unfortunately, the timing was all wrong. The tax rate in Maricopa County had already been set to jump from 59 cents to 71 cents per

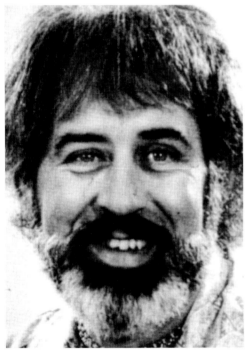

Walt Morrison, Mesa Community College faculty and president of Rio Salado College 1978-79.

$100 assessed valuation. Still, Flowers did his best to put a good face on the issue. The *Chandler Arizonan* for August 18 quoted Flowers:

> *"It should be noted," Flowers said, "that the Arizona State Legislature reduced the aid to this district by $1 million this year in spite of the fact that the enrollments have increased over 25 percent in the past*

two years. . . . Maricopa County has experienced tremendous growth in the past several years and the Maricopa County Community College District has offered a quality education for a minimal cost to students and taxpayers. There are approximately 50,000 students participating in the educational programs in the five colleges in Phoenix, Mesa, Scottsdale, and Glendale and more than 90 outreach locations. If these low-cost educational opportunities were not available to many students, they might well become the unemployable and cost the taxpayers many more dollars in the unemployment or welfare systems."

Sadly, the public did not agree. The *Scottsdale Daily Progress* editorialized on September 22:

> *The Maricopa County Community College District plans to have a special bond election this year. It is thinking of asking approval of a $20 million issue to meet construction needs for the next six years. Considering the district's potential growth, this is not an excessive figure. But considering how much district taxes have gone up when compared to other taxes, and when we include ability of homeowners to pay, $20 million is too much.*

The omens were all bad, and sadly, the bond was put on indefinite hold.

Even so, the district went ahead with a few construction projects, including a new home for the district offices. The district administration had been leasing office space in five different buildings at three different locations since moving out of the Korrick's building. In July, the district finalized plans to acquire a warehouse and offices located at 3910 East Washington—the site that would eventually

become home to Maricopa Tech (later renamed GateWay Community College). The acquisition of the East Washington site saved the district about $676,000 in lease payments over a ten-year period.

What Goes Around Comes Around

Managing the district's finances was relatively easy compared to the growing problem of Roger Brooks. Intoxicated by his success in felling Prince, Brooks was starting to run amuck. Al Flowers recalls that Brooks regularly threatened to fire anyone who opposed him on any level:

> *He would call some of my staff in and threaten to fire them on the spot unless they hired some girlfriend that he had, or something. I remember one day, he came in and he said, "Those goddamn presidents are all undermining you. Why don't you fire every one this afternoon, and I'll back the action and get a majority of the board on it. Fire them all! Put new people in there. They're not beholden to you." I said, "You're out of your mind, Brooks! You don't do things like that in an organization like this!"*

Brooks' behavior also began to attract attention outside the district. Ross Farnsworth speculates:

> *Dr. Prince certainly was respected and was in Rotary One Hundred and sat right there with some of the Republic and Gazette owners and publishers in the Rotary and so on. They weren't very happy when he resigned and Brooks and Robertson were kicking it up. I think they started checking him out through reporters. I don't know that to be a fact. I just know that the reporters watched him carefully.*

A BOOST FOR THE PERFORMING ARTS

No bond election was held in 1976, but some new construction did occur anyway. One of the most remarkable projects was the construction of four Performing Arts Centers, all completed more or less simultaneously in the fall of 1977. To fund this construction without a bond election, Al Flowers and Joe Refsnes (of Refsnes, Ely, Beck) worked out an innovative financing plan to sell $4.7 million in revenue bonds, which the district's food services, bookstores, and student fees pledged to repay.

Jeremy Butler regards these buildings as one of the governing board's finest achievements during that time:

One of the things that I personally was the proudest of that we did is that we decided that each campus—well, each of the so-called "main campuses" at the time—would have a performing arts auditorium. I was in the forefront of that effort. . . . My memory is that what we said is, "Each campus" being Mesa,

Scottsdale, Phoenix, and Glendale, "we will grant you a certain amount of money, all about essentially the same"—and I don't know whether it was one million or two million dollars—"and you build whatever kind of auditorium you want, theatre that you want, within certain general guidelines."

All four facilities were completed in the fall of 1977. Each was planned to contain about 18,000 square feet of space, and each campus was involved in the planning. The centers at Mesa, Glendale, and Scottsdale were all planned as more or less conventional proscenium theatres, but under the leadership of longtime theatre director John Paul at Phoenix College, the facility there was planned as an open stage that revolved, with entrance aisles under the audience.

Specifically, Max Jennings, a reporter for the *Arizona Republic*, published three exposé articles on Roger Brooks and the situation at Scottsdale. In the first article, published September 27, 1976, Jennings painted a grim picture of political terrorism on campus:

Students at Scottsdale Community College have made artichokes into political stew and a onetime student into a school board strong man. They've intimidated administrators to the point that some of those who are supposed to be running the community college admit it's become impossible for them to do their jobs.

Jennings quoted Tom Garneski: "I was intimidated, and I was even informed much later that one student was out to get me, and that the student had followed me in a vehicle and was following my route of activities every day."

June 25, 1996, video interview with Jeremy Butler, Maricopa governing board member 1968-78. Transcript and audio excerpts available online.

http://www.mc.maricopa.edu/users/M3cdhistory/

Arizona Republic *for September 27, 1976.*

Administrators at Scottsdale college gag on militant Artichoke

BY MAX JENNINGS

SCOTTSDALE — Students at Scottsdale Community College have made artichokes into political stew and a onetime student into a school board strong man.

They've intimidated administrators to the point that some of those who are supposed to be running the community college admit it's become impossible for them to do their jobs.

Those administrators are more than a little interested in student government elections beginning today and running through Wednesday.

The students will be choosing between a relatively traditional student

slate calling itself Students for '76 and a more controversial group known as the Artichokes.

Administrators don't take sides in public. Secretly, many of them don't want the Artichokes to win, because the Artichokes stand for Roger Brooks, and to the administrators, Brooks stands for trouble.

Most of the previous top administrators have quit at one time or another — more than a dozen in the five years the college has been open. They don't like the atmosphere, among other things.

Brooks, who is often given credit for keeping the campus revolution

brewing at SCC, has said of the present students:

"I have never seen any group more independent than that student government in Scottsdale."

Brooks has a basis for comparison. In 1972, the 24-year-old president of the student body at SCC, he initiated a protest against athletic spending at the college that resulted in students choosing the artichoke as the school mascot and pink and white as the school colors.

Administrators and the district board balked at the mockery and refused to recognize the artichoke, but after a court suit and years of

wrangling, the board finally accepted the selection of one of the strangest school mascots in the nation.

College administrators and some faculty members didn't like Brooks then and they dislike him even more since his election to the board in 1974.

Brooks, the board member, wields more clout now than when he was president of the student body, administrators and some teachers say.

They didn't let their names be used when they are critical. They admit they are afraid of his power.

One thing students, administrators and board members agree on: Politics is so much a part of campus life

that the educational process is being hampered.

Said Tom Garneski, a former acting dean of students who now teaches at Mesa Community College: "It was a contentious atmosphere constantly."

Garneski admitted that he feared student power when he was on campus in 1972.

"I was intimidated, and I was even informed much later that one student was out to get me, and that the student had followed me in a vehicle and was following my route of activities every day," Garneski said.

Continued on Page A-4

In the same article, Jennings focused on Roger Brooks' power:

> Brooks, the board member, wields more clout now than when he was president of the student body; administrators and some teachers say. They don't let their names be used when they are critical. They admit they are afraid of his power. . . . But the most common complaint against Brooks, who is unemployed, is that he promotes his own projects directly with students instead of going through channels, leaving district administrators wondering whether they are dealing with students, or with Brooks.

The second article in Jennings' miniseries appeared in the *Arizona Republic* for October 3, 1976. In this one, Jennings continued to emphasize the fear that Brooks was causing among district employees:

> More than a dozen teachers and administrators have contacted reporters for the Arizona Republic in the past week to complain about the political climate they say has been created by the District's board of trustees. But almost without exception, they have refused to let their names be used with the criticisms because of fear they will lose their jobs. Most complain about Roger Brooks.

On October 4, 1976, Jennings concluded his series with a description of Roger Brooks' 1975 visit to a Scottsdale political science class taught by Robert Winters. Allegedly, a tape recording was made of Brooks' presentation, and excerpts were presented in the article:

> "The deans of students disrupt student government. That is their sole function. The deans of students at Phoenix College—they have three of them—don't do anything. We don't need a dean of stu-

Barbara Hitchcock's campaign brochure.

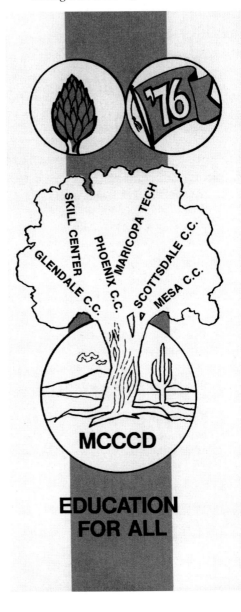

dents at any of the colleges." Brooks told the students, according to the tape: "I definitely came out here (to the class) for political reasons. There is no doubt about that." Brooks also told the students, according to the tape, that once a majority bloc was obtained on the board, "You will see a mass exodus of coaches from Mesa (Community College)."

Changes on the Board: 1976

Jennings' articles were timed to coincide with the next governing board election, scheduled for November 2. Ken Badertscher's term was expiring, and he had no desire to run again: "[Serving on the board] became more of a chore. I enjoyed the first few years on the board, and when Roger got on the board, it became more of a chore than anything else . . . The tail end is just kind of foggy for me . . . That part of it I just blanked out."

Four candidates announced their intention to run for Badertscher's seat. Apparently, Jennings' stories had affected public opinion because a news story in the *Arizona Republic* for October 4, 1976, emphasized that contention on the board was a major issue in the campaign:

> Four candidates for a seat on Maricopa County's community college governing board say they hope to make peace as well as policy on a board torn by conflicting educational philosophies . . . . All the governing board candidates claim to be independent and say they hope to put an end to the infighting.

Brooks hoped to elect a third board member who would give him a majority bloc and send the coaches fleeing from Mesa. His candidate was Cecelia Kline, who had a background in journalism and business and car-

ried the Artichoke Party's endorsement. Three other candidates also ran, among them Barbara Hitchcock, who was often identified as the anti-Artichoke candidate, a label that she rejected. The October 4 article observed,

"Mrs. Hitchcock said that, as the only candidate who has not been connected with the community colleges as a student or administrator, she could be a peacemaker on the governing board."

PROFILE: BARBARA HITCHCOCK

A native of Pennsylvania, Barbara Hitchcock earned her undergraduate degree in English at Allegheny College, near Erie, Pennsylvania. She then attended Boston University, where she earned her master's degree in English in one year. Directly afterward, she found a part-time job in New York at a high school in which she assisted five different teachers. The next year, 1940, she was hired to teach English, drama, and speech at the high school in Bedford, Pennsylvania. Later, she moved to Philadelphia, where she taught high school English, social studies, and business arithmetic for five and a half years. She then married and left the classroom once and for all when her husband was transferred to Waynesboro, Virginia. In 1968, her husband was transferred to Arizona, where he worked as an executive for Honeywell.

Hitchcock became active in the Scottsdale branch of the American Association of University Women, where she was approached about the possibility of running for the community college governing board:

> I said, "Well, it certainly sounds like what I would love, and I would certainly feel that I

am qualified for that because I've always been interested in education. I regard myself as an educator. I have never been on a school board, but I always wished that I could be on a school board sometime."

She agreed to run, but she realized that she faced an uphill struggle. Support for the Artichokes seemed to be very strong:

> They thought they had Cecilia as a shoo-in, and she was recommended by Jonathan Marshall because he was always strong for students' rights and all this stuff and an honorary Artichoke, and they thought they had it all sewed up—and I did too! But I went around, and I worked really hard. And the people that elected me were the Mormons and the Rotarians. I'd be playing bridge with a friend, and the husband would come home for lunch, and he'd say he'd been hearing about me. They were plugging for me at these various meetings. And all the people who were sick of these shenanigans.

September 26, 1996, video interview with Barbara Hitchcock, Maricopa governing board member 1977-92. Transcript and audio excerpts available online.

http://www.mc.maricopa.edu/users/M3cdhistory/

The election was held on November 2, 1976, the same day as the general election, and Hitchcock was not expecting to win. She recalls how she finally heard the results of the election:

I remember sitting and listening to the radio or the TV the night of the election, and I said to my husband, "I'm writing my concession speech." I never intended to win. I didn't think I had a ghost of a chance. And pretty soon, he said, "You'd better write another speech." It was the greatest shock.

Hitchcock's victory seemed to signal that the general public was growing weary of the contention on the board. Following the election, Badertscher, Butler, Farnsworth, and Robertson—but not Brooks—jointly wrote a letter to the editor of the *Phoenix Gazette*. The letter, which appeared in the December 6, 1976, edition, tried to reassure the public:

The Members of the governing board come from different backgrounds, professions and outlooks. Contrary to recent stories in the newspapers, no one member dominates our deliberations.

Each of us votes our conscience on the various difficult issues that reach us. Our meetings are open to the public, and we are sure that people who attend those meetings would confirm that most of the votes are unanimous, with occasional dissents by individual members. We believe that the decisions can be made only in a climate where vigorous discussion is encouraged. . . . [The responsibility to provide education for our citizens] rises above any disagreements between members of the board and members of the administrative staff.

The NCA Visit

In February, 1977, the NCA accreditation team arrived for its visit. The team was not happy with what it found, particularly that so many of the 1967 accreditation team's recommendations had not been heeded. The final report states:

It is difficult for members of the valuation team to understand why a substantial number of the concerns which exist today were reported by earlier North Central Association teams which visited the District in 1967. It would have seemed that over a ten-year period of time such concerns could have been addressed and resolved. Much of the great potential of one of the largest community college districts in the nation appears to have been dissipated as a result of the failure of the Governing Board to address seriously these most important issues. It is of great concern to the present evaluation team that steps should not have been taken to resolve these matters.

The main concern continued to be the conduct of the governing board, which was too much involved in the administration of the district and not sufficiently involved in setting educational policy:

As a result of this lack, the Governing Board all too frequently finds itself in a position of reacting without precedent to immediate issues rather than attempting

North Central Association Accreditation Reports of visits to Mesa Community College, Phoenix College, Glendale Community College, and the Maricopa District in February, 1977. The complete texts of all four reports are available online.

http://www.mc.maricopa.edu/users/M3cdhistory/

to respond to such issues in accordance with precedent or in a deliberate way so as to provide policy guidance for the district administration and staff when they are required to address such issues as they recur in the future.

Worse, the NCA report cited many instances of unnamed board members regularly exceeding their legal authority and meddling directly in the affairs of the individual campuses. The team that visited Mesa reported:

The greatest concern of the administration, faculty, and students [at Mesa] is the functioning of the Governing Board of the Maricopa County Community College District. There were several reports that one or two members of the board allegedly interfered in the day-by-day operation of the college. For example, it was reported that on one occasion a student failed to pass her courses and was dropped from the nursing program. She appealed directly to one of the board members who ordered the student reinstated. There were other instances cited whereby a board member visited the college without prior authorization of the whole board and acted in a unilateral fashion. This, if true, is not only interference in the administration of the college but also blatantly illegal according to the Arizona state laws.

The NCA team saw this kind of interference as symptomatic of a much bigger problem:

Throughout the visit to the district office and to the three colleges, the problem of Board/administration relationships and the need to define respective roles and responsibilities was a matter of continuing concern. . . . Members of the evaluation team, because of the very vocal nature of criticisms of the Governing Board/admin-istration relationships, felt compelled to examine rather carefully the status of these relationships during the visit. A review of the administrative structure indicated that such structure is presently not well defined and that as a result of this situation, there is confusion as to line and staff relationships throughout the entire District.

In view of these problems, the NCA team recommended that the district be put on a short leash. Accreditation was extended for six years only, instead of the usual ten. But even more embarrassingly, strings were attached. The district was ordered to submit to "limited focused visits each two years, directing attention to relationships among the Maricopa County Community College Governing Board, the MCCCD central administration," and the individual colleges.

The threat was veiled, but no less a threat: The district had to show progress within two years or risk having its accreditation yanked.

The Search for a New President Begins

Meanwhile, the board had to initiate a search for a new district president. But before advertising the job nationally, the board apparently seriously considered giving the job to Flowers permanently, and in the process, the board did something almost unbelievable. To gauge what reaction a Flowers presidency might evoke, the board decided to hold an open meeting and allow district employees to say whether or not they favored Flowers for district president. An article in the February 9,

1977, *Arizona Republic* explained the reason: Board members Roger Brooks and Robert Robertson said they expect Flowers to be hired unless unforeseen problems arise. "If there's no objection, it's going to happen tomorrow night," Brooks said Tuesday. Robertson said the board has been "extremely well satisfied" with Flowers' performances since August, when he assumed the acting presidency in addition to his regular duties as executive vice president for business services. . . Robertson said the consideration of Flowers grew out of a study session last Saturday. "That's when the board members started noticing that we had a man in the district that fit the qualifications," he said.

The next day (February 10, 1977), the *Arizona Republic* supplied the following report:

Arizona Republic *for February 9, 1977.*

County colleges to weigh retention of acting chief

By CECELIA GOODNOW

The governing board of the Maricopa County Community College District has scheduled a special meeting today to decide whether to offer the district presidency to acting president A. W. "Al" Flowers.

Board members said Tuesday night they will seek advice of students, instructors and administrators at the 5:30 p.m. meeting in the district office, 903 N. Second Street.

Board members Roger Brooks and Robert Robertson said they expect Flowers to be hired unless unforeseen problems arise.

"If there's no objection, it's going to happen tomorrow night," Brooks said Tuesday.

Robertson said the board has been "extremely well satisfied" with Flowers' performance since August, when he assumed the acting presidency in addition to his regular duties as executive vice president for business services.

Flowers replaced Dr. John F. Prince, who was stripped of his duties as president and named president emeritus after friction developed between him and the board.

Robertson said the consideration of Flowers grew out of a study session last Saturday. "That's when the board memberss started noticing that we had a man in the district that fit the qualifications," he said.

Board President Jeremy Butler said, however that no decision has been made on whether to hire Flowers or advertise the vacancy nationwide.

"The matter is completely open as far as I'm concerned." he said. "I'm really

A. W. "Al" Flowers

Continued on Page B-12

The audience was overwhelmingly opposed to such a move. The district should be certain it hires the best possible person, even if that person is Flowers, many speakers said. Others complained that failure to solicit would deny equal opportunity to minority groups. . . . Board members Roger Brooks and Robert Robertson had predicted Tuesday night that barring unforeseen objections, Flowers would be hired after Wednesday's meeting. "I did not expect what happened tonight," Brooks said later.

The decision to let Al Flowers' fate be decided in an open meeting was simply unconscionable and demonstrates just how rudderless the board really was at that time. Flowers should have told the board to take a hike, but he shrugged off the snub:

"Newspaper articles indicated I was getting the job. It scared the faculty." He vehemently denies he ever even considered accepting the job.

The national search then began in earnest. According to Flowers, the district was already receiving inquiries:

There was a lot of interest from around the country in this job out here because of contacts around the country and community college people, I guess. We got letters and phone calls from some of the contacts, including from Dallas. "When are you going to open up that job?" I said, "Are you interested in applying?" "Yeah, I think I might be. What's it going to pay? Where's the job description?" Well, we really didn't have that.

At this time, the board members also decided to change the job title from president to chancellor. They also changed all the executive deans into presidents. The new titles were officially adopted at the board meeting on March 8, 1977.

As the hiring process began, the renovations on the building at 3910 East Washington were completed, and the district administration moved into its new home, christened the District Services Support Center. On March 22, 1977, the Board held its first meeting in the new facility.

By that time, applications for the job of district chancellor were arriving. Hitchcock recalls that she, Jeremy Butler, and Hal Naumoff (a faculty member) screened all 160 applications for chancellor. They then selected the most promising applications, and all the board members read those.

Butler recalls that not all of these applications could be taken seriously:

> If they kept those records, you would get a lot of chuckles out of looking at the applications. The one that sticks in my mind. . . . We asked for a photograph, and there was one guy who sent his in wearing dark glasses and standing with his Volkswagen in a T-shirt someplace. People just responded incredibly to our job offer and advertisements.

The search continued into the summer. The *Arizona Republic* for June 22, 1977, announced that the short stack had been cut down to a list of seven candidates. Interviews with these candidates had already been scheduled and were expected to continue through July 7. Robertson announced optimistically that a decision was expected by July 23.

Not surprisingly, Brooks and Robertson tried to influence the process to their advantage. Flowers suggests that they even tried to work out some kind of arrangement with Bill Berry, then president of Phoenix College:

> One or both of them approached Berry—and this I can't prove, and Berry may have a short memory, or won't want to have a memory—about asking him some leading questions—I know; I was told this directly by Berry at the time—It was an attempt to find out philosophically, "Are you going to work with us, and how are you going to work with us?" They found out Berry wouldn't be controlled.

When interviewed for this book, Berry did not recall the events that Flowers mentions. However, Berry did recall:

> Ironically, I had had Bob Robertson [as a student]. . . . He became a friend of mine at GCC. He was a student there. So,

although I didn't relish the situation, I was always Roger and Bob's friend. They liked to call me and talk to me about, "What's supposed to be going on in this situation?" Well, that put me in a horrible situation.

On July 21, 1977, the newspapers announced that four of the seven were out of the running: Dr. William Berry, executive dean of Phoenix College; Dr. Alfredo De Los Santos, director of institutional planning and bilingual education of the Southwestern Educational Development Laboratory in El Paso, Texas; Dr. Laurence Lauth, president of Wutheville (Virginia) Community College; and Dr. Omar Scheidt, president of Cypress (California) College.

Those left in the running included Dr. Konnilyn Feig, dean of the college of arts and

---

THE PRESIDENT BECOMES THE CHANCELLOR

Al Flowers claims the idea originated with him.

> I told them that I thought the college people ought to be presidents, and they said, "Well, how many damn presidents can we have in this district? Have one at each college, and you're a president, too? That's going to be a little confusing." I said, "Well, the title should be different at this level. You really should have a chancellor. We're getting big, and we're going to be very big. They all should be presidents of their colleges."

Barbara Hitchcock claims that the idea actually came from her.

> In fact, I got rid of the term "executive dean" at the colleges for the presidents. They came and asked me to please [change their title]. They'd

go to meetings and nobody would know who they were. And they were college presidents. So I got all that straightened out. All by myself. I mean, I pushed it and it happened.

However, the person who actually suggested the idea first was Robert Hannelly. According to the minutes of the October 24, 1966, governing board meeting, "Dr. Hannelly explained his request to change the titles of executive deans to Presidents and the President of the District be changed to Chancellor of the District. After some discussion the item was tabled until information could be obtained from other junior colleges over the nation." The board then seems to have treated Hannelly's suggestion in the same manner they treated almost all of Hannelly's suggestions, and the matter never came up again while Hannelly was president.

County college district names new chancellor

By CECELIA GOODNOW

Dr. Paul Elsner. vice chancellor for educational services at Peralta Community College in Oakland, accepted an offer Tuesday to head the Maricopa County Community College District.

Elsner's selection as chancellor of the nation's fourth-largest community college district was announced at a governing board meeting Tuesday night. Elsner met with the board before the meeting to decide whether he would accept the job offer. He will be paid $55,000 a year and will start in late October.

Elsner said later he was attracted to the district because of its potential for growth. By attracting new types of students, the district can forestall declining enrollment, he said.

"I think we're going to have to individualize instruction more, gear ourselves up for the older and returning students," he said. "I think we need to link up educational experiences with work experiences."

Elsner has experience with varied types of students, having served since June 15 as acting president of the Peralta district's College of Nontraditional Studies. He said he helped secure accreditation of the school, which gives students academic credit for skills they already have and focuses on subjects such as child development, drug abuse and care of the elderly.

"I'd say one of my skills would be to come into new situations, sometimes politically difficult and emotionally charged situations, and bring order," he said.

Board president Jeremy Butler said the board unanimously selected Elsner, based on his broad experience and ability to handle difficult problems.

Elsner, 43, was one of three finalists for the job, which attracted 137 applicants. Other top contenders were Dr. Jan LeCroy, vice chancellor of the Dallas Community College System, and Dr. Konnilyn Feig, dean of the College of Arts and Sciences at the University of Maine at Portland.

The district's top administrative post has been vacant since last August, when the board removed Dr. John Prince.

Since then, A.W. "Al" Flowers, deputy chancellor, also has served as acting chancellor. The board considered making Flowers the permanent administrator last February, but protests from some employes prompted the board to advertise the vacancy. Flowers did not apply.

Elsner has served as vice chancellor at Peralta since 1971 and was director

Continued on Page B-11

sciences at the University of Maine at Portland; Dr. Jan LeCroy, vice chancellor of the Dallas County Community College System; and Dr. Paul Elsner, vice chancellor of educational services of the Peralta Community College District in Oakland, California. The article in the *Arizona Republic* added the information that Roger Brooks and two other board members intended to visit the applicants' home campuses within the next three weeks.

Jeremy Butler commented on this phase of the process:

> The main traveling circus was Brooks, Butler, and Robertson. The thought was we would see [the candidates] not only in

More about Chancellor for district

Continued from Page B-1

of educational services for two years before that.

He was the director of the State Board for Community Colleges and Occupational Education for the State of Colorado for two years. From 1965 to 1967 he held several positions at San Jose (Calif.) City College. He was dean of students, director of instructional resources and director of research and development.

He began his career as dean of instruction for the Junior College District of St. Louis in 1964, and also has taught at a high school in Wyoming and a community college in Minnesota.

He received his educational doctorate from Stanford University, his master's degree from South Dakota State University and his bachelor of science degree from the University of North Dakota.

Dr. Paul Elsner

Arizona Republic for Aug. 17, 1977.

> their natural surroundings but we would talk to other people who had worked with them in their natural surrounding.

Paul Elsner recalls being invited to Phoenix for an initial screening interview and then a second trip to Phoenix to meet with the board members. Then, the "traveling circus" came to Peralta to meet him on his home turf. Elsner felt then that he was a good match for Maricopa's needs:

> I was in the middle of Berkeley. This was a very troubled, radicalized area. I was involved in a lot of committee work and a lot of mediating processes. . . . I think I had a pretty good reputation with that. They had had some difficulty here with the Artichoke movement and all those other types of things, and I think that might have been one of the features they might have been interested in, that I was a listener, and most of the time I was able to get things done through mediation or other kinds of processes.

Jeremy Butler agrees that the Maricopa governing board was very interested in Elsner for this reason:

> We were looking for—I think actually it was Roger Brooks who kept after this and said— we were looking for somebody who would be a healer, someone who could bring together the disruptive forces that had affected Scottsdale and the whole district there for several years.

The board met on Saturday, August 13, 1977, and made its final selection. They offered the job to Dr. Paul Elsner. He then flew to Phoenix on August 16 and met with the board in executive session to iron out the details. Shortly thereafter, Jeremy Butler announced that Elsner had accepted the job.

And with that announcement, the interregnum was over. The board felt that it had found someone who could effectively calm things down and avoid stirring up more conflicts.

They couldn't have been more wrong.

1977

T he most important fact about the Maricopa district's new chancellor was that he was a complete outsider. Bob Hannelly had been on the faculty at Phoenix College since 1927. Al Flowers had managed the business affairs of the Phoenix Union High School district since the '50s. John Prince had been a student, a faculty member, and a dean at Phoenix College. But Paul Elsner came from a completely different world.

Born in 1933, he was the youngest child in a family of Minnesota farmers. College education was not part of the family tradition. He recalls attending family gatherings in which no more than one or two people out of a group of fifty or more would ever have been near a college. "In rural small-town northern Minnesota, that's not unusual."

Elsner's education began in a one-room school in northern Minnesota. In high school, he played football well enough to earn a scholarship to Macalester College, a private liberal arts college in St. Paul. "It was what we called a 'sweeping scholarship.' You could help out in the equipment room." He stayed for a semester, which he claims he did not finish, and then joined the Army. The

Paul Elsner, chancellor of Maricopa district 1977-99.

January 10, 1996, video interview (the first of three) with Paul Elsner, Maricopa district chancellor 1977-99. Transcript and audio and video excerpts available online.

http://www.mc.maricopa.edu/users/M3cdhistory/

Korean War was in progress, and he decided to volunteer instead of waiting for the draft.

Following his two-year hitch in the Army, Elsner decided to return to college courtesy of the GI Bill. This time, he enrolled at the University of North Dakota, where he eventually earned a bachelor's degree in English. Why English? "Didn't know what else to do, and I started taking courses in the English Department, and I liked them, and I decided that's what I wanted to do. Also, I had heard that there were jobs for male English teachers that were placed really fast out in the rural North Dakota schools."

Actually, he found employment as an English teacher at a high school in Wyoming, not North Dakota. He taught for one year and then enrolled in a one-year master's program at South Dakota State College. He continued to teach English while serving as a teaching assistant. Upon completion of his master's degree, he found employment in the English department at Austin Junior College, in

Austin, Minnesota, where he stayed from 1959 to 1962 (the year the Maricopa district began). Like Phoenix College, Austin Junior College also dated back to the twenties and focused on transfer to a four-year university or college.

In 1962, Elsner discovered a pamphlet describing the Junior College Leadership Program at Stanford University, one of several programs that the Kellogg Foundation had set up at various universities to train future community college administrators. (The Stanford program also had funded Lawrence Walkup's conference on the future of higher education in Arizona in 1956.) Elsner applied and was accepted as a Ph.D. candidate. At that time, however, he was not thinking about moving out of the classroom. "I thought if I went to Stanford, I could be an English department chair, which is as high an aspiration as I had."

However, the Kellogg Foundation would not pay for courses in the English Department, so

Elsner's educational plans began to change. George Spindler's class on cultural transmission pointed in a new direction:

> *Cultural transmission was powerful. Actually, [Spindler] did it through sort of disassembling his empirical research on the Menomonee Indians in Wisconsin. How an ethos, a culture, is transmitted through family, through symbol, through validation, personal validation . . . even validation of masculine roles in the culture or in the family or the unit. It was just like everything came alive.*

Spindler's class impressed on Elsner the idea that everyone lined up at the same starting line, "but when the pistol was fired, not everybody had the same chance. That was a powerful concept." He began to envision the community college as a force that could help to even out the playing field.

Elsner needed to support himself financially during the second year of his program. Stanford staff assisted him in landing an appointment at San Jose City College, where he once again taught English. This school was very different from the world of Austin Junior College due to the presence of a strong vocational program. For the first time, Elsner found himself teaching remedial composition courses:

> *In fact, I liked remediation actually better than the composition because I liked the integrity and the honesty of the students. Then, I sort of related to the students—there were GIs, for example, that would be in there, and I related to them. I said, "This stuff isn't as bad as you think it is. It's a big obstacle to a lot of people, and you can get over this. Let me help you get over it, and let me work with you in getting over it. We'll all get over this*

thing together," type of thing. They related to that.

Elsner completed his doctorate at the end of the summer of 1964 and moved himself and his family to St. Louis, Missouri, where he served as general dean of instruction for the one-year-old community college system.

There, Elsner made the acquaintance of Dick Richardson, another beginning dean. Together, Richardson and Elsner shared a common vision and argued for a curriculum that would address the needs of St. Louis's substantial, underserved minority population. They expressed their ideas in an article published in the *Junior College Journal* in December, 1965. The article was entitled, "General Education for the Disadvantaged." The first paragraph reveals that Elsner's vision of the junior college in 1965 had moved away from the traditional emphasis on bringing the university to the small town:

> *A distinguishing feature of the community junior college has been its open door admission policy. The popularization of higher education has resulted in an influx of marginal students who increasingly view the junior college as a logical extension of the secondary school. The junior college, consequently, is torn between the necessity of maintaining standards to guarantee the employability and transfer-*

ability of its graduates, and the knowledge that it constitutes the last opportunity for formal education some of its students will ever have.

Richardson went on to become a professor of educational leadership and policy studies at Arizona State University. When interviewed for this book, he didn't remember much about writing the article with Elsner, but he did remember the context in which he and Paul collaborated on this piece:

> *There was considerable debate within the [St. Louis] district in those days about whether the college should serve students who had not graduated from high school and who weren't adequately prepared to take on the kinds of courses that we offered. I think along with that there was a lot of sensitivity to being perceived as an institution that was not respectable because of the students it served.*

How those kinds of concerns would have made the Old Guard at Phoenix Junior College shudder! Elsner believes that his commitment to broadening the mission of the junior college to include serving underprepared students was a direct result of the influence of the Kellogg program:

> *I think we [Kellogg fellows] helped set some of the ideological premises of moving away from transferability. Now, this is*

June 2, 1997, video interview with Dick Richardson, Arizona State University professor. Transcript and audio excerpts available online.

http://www.mc.maricopa.edu/users/M3cdhistory/

no small burden because this has caused some degree of alienation from traditional academic people, of whom I am a part. At the same time, there are strains and tensions of how much we should do in terms of a social agenda and so forth. How much outreach we should have? How much distance education we should do? All these overlay what was a very respectable collegiate core.

Paul Elsner's wife returned to graduate school at Stanford in 1966, and Elsner again found employment at San Jose City College, where he remained for two and a half years as an administrator. There, he helped to run a successful bond election. He then accepted an offer to become the state director of the new community college system in Colorado, where he supervised the transition from local districts to a statewide system.

In 1969, Elsner moved to the Peralta Community College District in Oakland, California, where he was eventually appointed vice chancellor for educational services and president of Vista College, a nontraditional college in inner-city Berkeley:

It tended to take on populations that normally weren't served by the traditional colleges, such as handicapped people, and people who were at some risk in the society. It took senior adults; it took people who were in the human services network . . . It was kind of a storefront, street-college type operation.

Vista College was fully as turbulent as Scottsdale at the same time, but the turbulence resulted from different causes. The local community in Oakland had wanted a traditional campus, but Vista was the last college to be established in the Peralta system,

and the resources were not available to build a conventional campus. "When they went to a nontraditional solution, the community itself said, 'This is not a bona-fide solution for us.'"

The Peralta district suffered from many internal problems as well. "I used to say that I went through at least two transitional governments and one Banana Republic up there. This is Berkeley, okay?" Under Elsner's leadership, the college turned around, gained enrollment, and became a community asset. From Peralta, Elsner came to Maricopa.

Restructuring the District

The district that Elsner inherited in the fall of 1977 was already the nation's fourth largest, serving somewhere around 50,000 students annually. Sadly, the district was still very much in disarray when Elsner walked in the door. Dick Richardson summed up the situation from the point of view of an outsider who knew Maricopa in those days:

Paul inherited a very traditional, not very distinguished community college district that had a very ingrown administration, a very ingrown faculty, and not a reputation for much excellence in very many places. . . . He knew what urban districts could and ought to be, and there was just no even remote resemblance between the community college—and its leadership— when Paul arrived here in '77.

Elsner rolled up his sleeves and set about a substantial reorganization of the district administration in three specific areas: long-range strategic planning, human services policies, and the highly centralized decision-making structure.

First, Elsner introduced long-range strategic planning for the district. He recognized the

Max Tadlock in 1969. No stranger to the Maricopa district, Tadlock had been hired as a consultant to help organize the district's 1969 Charrette, a conference on the future direction of "community and continuing education."

need for demographic predictions through the year 2000 to help guide decisions about future growth. To this end, he turned to another outsider for assistance, Max Tadlock, with whom Elsner had previously worked on the master plan for Colorado's community college system.

Second, Elsner had the district adopt personnel policies more consistent with common practices in business and industry. To this end, Ron Bush (another stranger to the district) was announced as the new vice chancellor for human resources at the governing board meeting on February 14, 1978.[1]

---

[1] At the same meeting, Elsner announced two more outsiders would be joining his administrative team. Dr. Alfredo De Los Santos was appointed as Elsner's vice chancellor for educational development and Charles Allan became the district's first director of computer services and information systems.

PROFILE: ART DeCABOOTER

While in seminary as a Benedictine monk, DeCabooter earned his BA in philosophy with a minor in English at St. John's University in Collegeville, Minnesota, in1964. Subsequently, he went through four years of theology and was ordained. He became active in the ministry at St. Gregory's monastery in Shawnee, Oklahoma. St. Gregory's also runs a private, Catholic, two-year, liberal arts junior college, where DeCabooter was eventually appointed dean of students. During this time, he went to Indiana University and earned an MA in student personnel work and an Ed.D.

Art DeCabooter, president of Scottsdale Community College 1977 to the present.

After leaving the priesthood, DeCabooter became dean of students and later president of Blackhawk College, East Campus, in Kewanee, Illinois. According to DeCabooter, "Blackhawk had programs that reflected the community. We were in an agricultural area, so we had ag. science, ag. business, and we had horse-judging teams, swine-judging teams. . . . It was a little different."

After about eight years there, he then applied for three different college presidencies advertised in the *Chronicle of Higher Education.* One of these was Scottsdale Community College. DeCabooter explains what happened next:

> Thanksgiving of '77, my wife and I and all three of our children came out here to visit my parents, who had lived out here for ten or twelve years. My dad came out with Cudahy Packing Company when it moved from Omaha. But I came out to visit because my dad was having some significant heart problem. I went back home after Thanksgiving, and there was a phone message—the Monday after Thanksgiving—from the Maricopa District: Could I be on a telephone interview?

The telephone interview never took place. A day or so later, DeCabooter was summoned back to Maricopa for an interview in person:

> At that point, it was before Christmas, and the district was having its Christmas party just for the district personnel. I went in there and there were so many people I thought it was the whole district. . . . This guy came in and sat down beside me—didn't introduce himself. . . . Then, [someone] came in and got this guy, and they left. I said, "Who was that guy?" "Well, that's the chancellor. You don't know him?" I said, "I don't know him from Adam."

That incident was followed by a four-hour interview with Elsner, and on December 27, 1977, DeCabooter was officially hired as Scottsdale Community College's first president.

> When I came, I told my wife we would keep the packing boxes because I didn't know how stable this job is. Because the college is only six and a half years old, there have been three [deans] already, so it's kind of a vociferous place. . . . But I got here, and it was going to be a time that the campus was either going to come together or totally explode.

To date, he remains the only president that Scottsdale has ever known.

Elsner credits Bush for innovating the district's wellness program, employee assistance program, and flextime for clerical and staff employees.

Elsner also commissioned two outside consulting firms to recommend a restructuring of the district staff and administration. The first study, the Ashauer Study, examined the various jobs being performed by the district employees other than the faculty. Elsner explains: "You wanted to hire a custodian, you hired a custodian. You didn't necessarily know what salary they were going into." A series of job classifications, based again on business and industry models, was then implemented. The second study, the Hay Study, recommended adjustments in compensation for district employees other than faculty.

Third, Elsner moved to decentralize district decision-making and make the campuses more autonomous. Under John Prince's leadership, the district's administration had become highly pyramidal, a fact which Prince himself freely acknowledged in a revealing article published in the *Chronicle of Higher Education* for December 13, 1976:

> Mr. Prince, who helped establish the community-college system in Arizona, is an advocate of strong central academic and fiscal control. "The Arizona community-college law established a district, and funds are granted to that district," he says. "The intense centralization of the Maricopa County district grew out of that law and the administration of guys like me."

Art DeCabooter, whom Elsner appointed to head Scottsdale Community College in late 1977, recalls this system well:

When I came to the college, all the maintenance and operations reported to the district; security reported to the district; the bookstore reported to the district; the food services reported to the district; all the carpenters and all those people reported to the district; the fiscal office reported to the district . . . it was really interesting.

Elsner realized that this system produced administrative gridlock more than anything else. "[It] essentially assumed that all the smart people were at the central office, and less able people were at the colleges because the colleges would wait for what they could get approved by the district." According to DeCabooter, this intense centralization also contributed to the contentious atmosphere in the district at that time:

There was a real animosity when I came here between the college and the district. Not just this college; all the colleges in the district. There were people from the district office who didn't dare come out here. I'd go down to the district for a meeting, and some of these people (who I don't really want to mention) would tell me, "Well, those SOBs out at the colleges . . . " I'd say, "Well, geez, I'm one of them!"

Reversing this tendency did not happen overnight. As Elsner began to return budgetary and executive authority to the campuses, he met more resistance from the individual colleges than he had expected: "People tended to want to defer to central office people making the decision."

As Elsner moved to make the campuses more autonomous, Arnette Ward, who began her district career as a counselor at Mesa, vividly recalls that when a new president had to be selected for Mesa, a delegation from Mesa

approached Elsner with the idea of letting them recommend a candidate. Elsner accepted the idea and let the school put together a committee of students, faculty, and administrators. Then, Elsner made a believer out of everybody by actually accepting the committee's recommendation.

In this way, decentralization slowly began to be accepted.

Elsner and Flowers

Elsner's biggest problem initially was taming the governing board. Early in Elsner's tenure, the board decided to show him who was boss. The board may have become concerned about all the outsiders Elsner was hiring and ordered

March 8, 1996, interview with Art DeCabooter, president of Scottsdale Community College 1977-present. Transcript and audio excerpts available online.

http://www.mc.maricopa.edu/users/M3cdhistory/

him to retain Al Flowers as the district's money man. Flowers remembers the board members were most insistent on this fact:

They said, "We're protecting the district." The board was united on that. "You've got the numbers. People will get in trouble over these dollars and cents, and your end of it runs smoothly, and you give us the reports, and we feel comfortable, the state board feels comfortable . . ." You know, went through all the litany and said, "We're protecting the district. It isn't that we're doing anything to him; we're protecting the district. How do we know how long he's going to stay here even?"

In spite of his intentions to the contrary, Al Flowers thus became Marion Donaldson to Paul Elsner's John Prince. Flowers remembers that the results were less overtly hostile, but no more successful:

> So Paul came in . . . didn't speak to me for about two months, I guess. . . . He was pretty busy, too, coming into the new job, and I'm sure he got stories, pro and con, pertaining to me. Mostly, the con would be "dictatorial." That type of thing, I'm sure. Even from friends that I got along with.

Into the Maelstrom

On the night of November 8, 1977, Elsner attended his first board meeting as Maricopa's new chancellor. Immediately, he found himself right in the thick of two potentially explosive problems.

The first was fallout from the North Central Association's accreditation report. The faculty were very concerned about the NCA's threat to yank Maricopa's accreditation. To force the governing board to clean up its act, the faculty had retained the services of an attorney, Osmond Burton, Jr., and circulated a carefully worded petition demanding that board members accede to the NCA's recommendations. At the previous board meeting,

signed copies of the petition had been presented to the board. A total of 424 district faculty, staff, and administrators had signed their names. An article from the October 26, 1977, *Phoenix Gazette* indicated that the board was fully aware that the petition was a prelude to a potential lawsuit.

The petition begins, "THE UNDERSIGNED, certificated employees of the Maricopa County Community College District, teachers and/or administrators, within said District, respectfully submit this petition to the end that conditions within said District, both educational and administrative, shall be stabilized and improved."

The petition boldly accuses board members of violating some of the provisions of the Arizona Revised Statutes and the policies of the State Board of Directors for Community Colleges. The petition also accuses unnamed board members of violating Arizona's open meeting laws and directly interfering in campus affairs. An unnamed board member is accused specifically of attempting to "direct the activities of District personnel upon the five campuses of the District by personally communicating with both faculty and administrators, mandating specific action, and threatening censure or termination of employment by the District in the event of failure or refusal to comply with his mandates." The report further accused unnamed students on an unnamed campus of trying to do the same because of their association with this unnamed board member. The petition then reminded board members that failure to follow the NCA's recommendations could jeopardize continuance of the district's accreditation.

The night Elsner arrived for his first board meeting, the faculty were there in force to

Phoenix Gazette for October 26, 1977.

The Phoenix Gazette

Wednesday, Oct. 26, 1977   **Section D**   □   Pages 1 to 22

COLLEGE BOARD 'EXCEEDED AUTHORITY'
Teachers Raise Threat Of Suit

By JIM WALKER
Gazette Education Reporter

Maricopa County Community College board clerk Roger Brooks said today he has been told that if the district does not act on recommendations in a faculty petition, a suit will be filed.

The petition, which has more than 411 signatures representing 70 percent of the permanent faculty, alleges the board has exceeded its authority and calls for changes.

Brooks said he was told last night "the petition is a prelude to a lawsuit if the district does not act on the demands in the petition by its Nov. 8 board meeting."

BROOKS DID NOT reveal his source, but said "it is a reliable source at Scottsdale Community College."

Attorney Osmond Burton Jr., who will present the petition to the board tonight, said in the absense of board action a suit is "a possibility," but said no decision has been made. "My clients haven't decided what action to take" if the board does not initiate some action. He added that "there are lots of possibilities" at this point.

Burton said the petition is an attempt to see if concerns of the faculty and administrators can be worked out. "This is quite serious and thretens to undermine the morale of the district and make it the laughingstock of the nation," Burton said.

Board President Jeremy Butler described the petition

as "not detailed" and "difficult to respond to."

"I'm not opposed to anyone who wants to present a petition on matters that concern them, but I am a little disappointed that they did not wait until the new chancellor, Dr. Paul Elsner, is here to present it to him."

BURTON SAID "these matters concern the board and not Dr. Elsner. He is only going to inherit the problem, but the problem is with the board. These concerns have been going on for more than a year and they just can't be postponed. It will take Elsner six months to know what's going on."

Board member Barbara Hitchcock called the petition "most unfortunate" and "not the best way to handle the problem." Another board member, Bob Robertson, said he hadn't seen the petition "but I would like to meet with those who circulated it and see what their concerns are."

Board member Ross Farnsworth said "I haven't seen it (the petition) yet but an attorney called me last week about some problems of the faculty, students and administrators at Scottsdale Community College and wanted to talk about them. I was advised by our legal counsel that meeting alone might compromise my position as a board member."

ALL BOARD members except Brooks received such

hear the governing board's response to the faculty petition. The board had a response ready, but it was not one that the faculty were going to like. The minutes for this meeting show that two resolutions had been prepared in advance. One reaffirms Resolution No. 3186, from August 24, 1976, which states in part that board members want "all employees and group representatives of employees to follow and exhaust all administrative remedies and procedures before requesting Governing Board involvement . . . and that all requests for any Board action be transmitted to the Governing Board through the Chancellor . . . " The other resolution essentially acknowledged in principle the recommendations made by the NCA report without admitting any improprieties on the part of the board itself or indicating any changes were going to occur.

Neither resolution addressed any of the specific complaints raised in the petition or promised any of the specific reforms that the faculty had demanded. In other words, the board members were trying to stonewall the faculty. Had the governing board adopted those resolutions that night, the faculty probably would have responded by suing the district—and Elsner had no intention of letting that happen, especially on his first night on the job. The minutes document that neither of the prepared resolutions were formally proposed. Instead, "Mr. Farnsworth asked Dr. Elsner to take the two Resolutions and come back with recommendations."

The implication is that Elsner had intervened to try to head off a lawsuit and find a better way to handle the situation.

The second prickly problem that night was not so easily resolved. A major confrontation

County probing mileage claims by community colleges official

By ART GISSENDANER

The Maricopa County attorney's office is investigating allegations that records concerning mileage-expense claims filed by Roger Brooks, Maricopa County Community College District board member, were falsified.

Brooks, however, said the investigation is indicative of an impending power struggle between him and fellow-board member Ross Farnsworth.

He charged the investigation was initiated either by Farnsworth or board president Jeremy Butler to embarrass him publicly and ruin his chances to become board president when Butler steps down next year.

Otis Brown, chief investigator for the county attorney, said an investigation of

Brooks' mileage claims is under way but refused to go into details.

District records show that Brooks has been reimbursed more than $2,000 for more than 13,000 miles of driving within the district during the past year.

Monthly mileage vouchers filed by Brooks were as high as 2,759 miles for the month of September, for which he received $413. Approval of Brooks' mileage claim for October, amounting to $456 for more than 3,000 miles, was delayed at the board's Nov. 8 meeting until Nov. 22. The delay came after Butler requested more information on the claim.

The delay followed the board's adoption of a policy limiting the amount

Continued on Page A-4

Arizona Republic *for November 18, 1977.*

was shaping up between Roger Brooks and Jeremy Butler over the approval of Brooks' travel vouchers.

Brooks had been submitting greatly inflated vouchers every month, and everyone knew the reason. In spite of his statements to the contrary, Brooks had been unemployed since he had become a board member. He claimed that he was an accountant for a local body and paint shop, but in reality, he had no visible means of support. Instead of holding down a job, Brooks had been spending all his time at the district office, where he had been searching the district records to find ways to trap Prince. Ross Farnsworth recalls:

Once, [Brooks] made a motion to have the board be paid. We squashed that. Then he brought up, "Well, all right, we won't pay the board. We should be on several com-

mittees and we can pay the committees and appoint ourselves." It was a ploy to do some of the work of the board but call it "committees" so that he could be paid.

That idea didn't go anywhere, but Barbara Hitchcock remembers that Brooks and Robertson tried to work other angles:

They all had credit cards for gas and stuff. The first thing after I was elected, Roger and Bob walked me down somewhere and they were going to break me in. "We're going to get you some credit cards!" And I said, "Oh, no, you're not. No credit cards for me. I'll do my expense accounts."

Hitchcock remembers that Brooks even went so far as to pressure people at the district to loan him money: "Floretta [Awe, director of nursing and allied health for the MCCCD]

149

gave him $600. 'Well, why did you give it to him?' 'Well, he's a board member!' Well, she shouldn't have, of course. He was definitely sticky-fingered."

Eventually, Brooks noticed that no one was verifying board members' travel expense reports, so Brooks began to milk the cash cow. Al Flowers quickly became suspicious:

> [Brooks] was faking mileage reports because he couldn't get paid any other way. He would have had to have been driving all day and all night, half the time. So I turned it over to the president of the board [Jeremy Butler]. I said, "I can't disprove that he wasn't out there driving. He signs it, but it ain't so. He couldn't be sitting in that office as much as he is and still be out there driving, see?" The president of the board said, "He's signing them personally?" I said, "Yeah." He said, "You have to take it, on that basis. He's a board member. If he's swearing to it . . . " So he said, "Don't you do anything at this point."

At the November 8 board meeting, Butler refused to approve payment of Brooks' latest travel expense claim, and at the same meeting, the other board members passed a motion limiting travel expense claims for local travel to no more than $25 per month.

Elsner could only watch helplessly as this little drama began to erupt in the press. On November 16, 1977, the *Scottsdale Daily Progress* broke the news that the Maricopa County attorney's office was looking at Brooks' mileage reports. Apparently, Brooks had claimed travel amounting to 2,367 miles in August (for reimbursement of $355.65); 2,759 miles in September ($413.85); and a whopping 3,041 miles in October (for $456.00). In this article, Brooks protested his innocence:

> *Brooks told the* Progress *Tuesday the claims "are legitimate and every bit of that mileage is accurate and made as part of my job as a board member. . . . I guess I could be accused of taking my job too seriously, but that's about all," Brooks said.*

A similar article appeared in the *Arizona Republic* for November 18 and raised the question of how the county attorney had become involved in the matter:

> *Farnsworth denied calling in the county attorney's office, saying it is the board president's responsibility to do so. Butler refused to comment on who called in the county attorney or who suggested the $25 limitation. Brooks also denied allegations by some district employees that he was living off his mileage checks from the district. "That's incredible. I am self-employed as an accountant for small businesses," he said.*

Unable to do anything about Roger Brooks' problems, Elsner focused instead on the problem of how the governing board should respond to the faculty's petition. The next board meeting was held on November 22, and the agenda revealed that board members were considering adoption of a document entitled "Code of Ethics and Responsibilities for the Governing Board." The minutes of the November 22 meeting indicate that the following discussion occurred:

> *Mr. Butler said this [code] was self-explanatory. Dr. Elsner stated he felt the document was written in the spirit of public accountability and that he would like the Board also to be mindful of ARS 15-679, as well as general responsibilities. He stated this code is meant to foster public accountability and that the policy is intended for observance by the staff and*

> *other personnel as well. Robertson moved for acceptance. Motion carried.*

The copy of the board minutes in the district's law library includes a copy of this code prefaced by the following "justification":

> *Members of the Governing Board have requested that a Code of Ethics and Responsibilities be drafted by the Chancellor for their consideration; the attached code addresses both the legal responsibilities of the Governing Board and the general, ethical responsibilities under which the Board can effectively function. It also acknowledges the recent concerns of the faculty and other interested groups and attempts to clarify the Board's interpretation of its respective roles, both as a total governing body and as individual Board members.*

Whether or not Elsner's code would have been enough to keep the faculty from suing will never be known. The faculty grievances were momentarily overshadowed by events reported in the *Arizona Republic* on the morning of November 26, 1977: Roger Brooks had been arrested.

The day before, the county grand jury had handed down four counts of indictment accusing Roger Brooks of embezzling public funds and one count accusing him of submitting a false claim to the district. The newspaper stated:

> *Brooks was arrested at 8:30 AM Friday in a west Phoenix diner by Ed*

Campion and Dave Corey, investigators assigned to the special operations bureau of the county attorney's office. He was booked at the sheriff's department and appeared before Superior Court Commissioner John F. Sullivan, who released Brooks without bond. He will be arraigned at 8:30 AM next Friday. The arrest followed a four-week investigation by the county attorney's office.

The false claim mentioned in the indictment was for $616, which Brooks explained was for a trip to San Diego that he had taken over the Labor Day weekend. Brooks claimed that he took the trip to meet certain people at San Diego City College for the purpose of "conferring with student government leaders and school administrators." Campion had contacted people at San Diego City College, and according to them, Brooks had not put in an appearance there during that time. So, where had he been?

On December 3, Brooks appeared for his arraignment in Maricopa County Superior Court and pleaded innocent to all counts.

The trial was then set for January 19 (although Brooks later won a postponement to April 21).

On December 13, the governing board met as usual and formally voted against accepting Brooks' October mileage claim. Brooks surmised that Butler was probably the one who had turned him in, and Brooks went on the offensive. The article from the *Arizona Republic* for December 14 describes what happened next:

> *Brooks said after the vote that he followed normal district procedure in filing for reimbursement. He read a prepared statement calling for a "thorough investigation of Butler's activities during three out-of-state trips he and Butler made during district chancellor selections. On each of these occasions, Mr. Butler saw fit while traveling at district expense, to make a social visit to an old college chum in Oakland, California, to visit relatives in Portland, Maine, and to conduct private business with a client in Dallas," the statement said.*

Butler subsequently admitted that he was the one who had notified the county attorney's office of the problem concerning Brooks' Labor Day junket to San Diego. He also said that he had been expecting this challenge from Brooks:

> *Butler said he discussed his travel expenses with investigators shortly after the investigation of Brooks and will turn over his expense vouchers to the county attorney's office today. "I did what I thought was in the best interest of the district. Some may see it differently. I am not an evaluator, that is the county attorney's function," Butler said.*

Elsner's name was almost never mentioned during all of the activity regarding Brooks and Robertson. He had arrived on the job only weeks before and could do no more than stand on the sidelines and shake his head in disgust.

Arizona Republic, November 26, 1977.

Brooks is indicted as embezzler

Board member charged after probe of mileage claims

...ANER

...ed member of ...ommunity Col-...een indicted by ...n four counts of ...s and one count ...laim to the dis-

...ed at 8:30 a.m. ...enix diner by Ed ...orey, investigators ...tions bu-

reimbursed more than $2,000 for more than 13,000 miles Brooks said he drove within the district during the past year.

Monthly mileage vouchers filed by Brooks were as high as 2,759 miles for September, for which he received $413. His mileage claim for October, amounting to $456 for more than 3,000 miles, has yet to be approved by the board.

Campion said the investigation is continuing and that Brooks could face addi-

apparently made no appearances" on that campus.

"He (Brooks) hasn't said where he went in San Diego but we know for a fact he didn't visit the college," Campion said. Campion said he didn't know if Brooks had any relatives or friends in San Diego, but added that learning of Brooks' ties there is part of the continuing investigation.

Brooks' September mileage claim includes a 14-mile trip to Sky Harbor Airport from his home on Sept. 2 and a

1977

Brooks Denies Fund Charges; Politics Claimed

By JIM WALKER
Gazette Education Reporter

Roger Brooks today denied charges that he had embezzeled funds from the Maricopa County Community College District and claimed he is a victim of "a blatant attempt to ruin me politically."

ROGER BROOKS

Brooks, a district board member, was indicted by the county grand jury on four counts of embezzling public funds and one count of submitting a false claim to the district regarding a trip he took over the Labor Day weekend to San Diego at a public expense of $616.

He claims the charges "insinuate that I have falsified my mileage claims and that I live on this money. It certainly seems strange to me that I have been filing these claims for a year and there never has been any question from anyone."

Part of the investigation into the reimbursement expenses paid to Brooks include his mileage vouchers, according to investigators assigned to the special operations bureau of the county attorney's office. But none of the current charges relate to these vouchers.

HOWEVER, INVESTIGATORS said Brooks could face additional charges, possibly on these claims.

District records show Brooks was paid more than $2,000 during the past year for the 13,000 miles he said he drove on district business, or the first two years on the board he said he never did turn in any travel vouchers for mileage.

Some monthly mileage claims were as high as 2,759, for which he filed for September and for which he was reimbursed $413. His claim for October, which has not yet been paid by the board, includes nearly 3,000 miles, which would amount to a payment of $456.

"IT IS OBVIOUS that the entire investigation itself is a political motivation of smearing me and causing me to be held in public contempt. Brooks said. "It is sad to say but it has obviously been orchestrated."

Board travel, both in state and out of state as well as mileage vouchers, had been under study for more than a month. At the Nov. 8 meeting board president Jerry Butler proposed changes in the amount board members could receive for mileage per month for district business. He also asked that there be a more explicit explanation of who was contacted and what business was conducted.

BUTLER RECOMMENDED that planned mileage travel vouchers in excess of $25 receive prior board approval. Brooks made the motion based on those recommendations and the policy went into effect immediately.

Brooks denies the county investigators' claim that during his trip to San Diego he did not go to San Diego City College. He said he did go to the campus, located near Balboa Park, but would not disclose whom he talked to or what the specific reason for the trip was.

He said he followed district policy and notified Butler a week before he left that he was considering a trip to San Diego City College "for the purpose of conferring with student government leaders." He said Butler approved the trip.

HE SAID HE also visited Deputy Chancellor Al Flowers to tell him of the trip and that Flowers approved it, that motel reservations were prepaid, as were airline tickets, by the district and that he received a cash advance of about $250.

Brooks said his travel to the five community college campuses, plus the district office, skill center and Sun City extension campus, "is considerably more than other board members because I confer with a lot of students and administrators to find out what's going on in the district."

Phoenix Gazette Nov. 28, 1977.

Chapter Fifteen

1978
Trials and *Tribulations*

The Roger Brooks indictment completely overshadowed Elsner's debut as the new chancellor of Maricopa, but Elsner soon managed to bring himself into the spotlight.

As 1978 began, enrollment projections for the spring term took a sudden nosedive. As spring registration was approaching its final phases, district statisticians projected enrollment would be down a whopping 9% from the fall term. In a district press release, Walt Morrison tried to put a good face on the problem:

> "It is traditional for enrollments to drop off for the spring semester," Walt Morrison, vice president for educational services for Maricopa County Community Colleges said. "In addition," he stated, "we are experiencing a leveling off period after a surge of high enrollments for the past two years. Things are getting back to normal." Community college enrollments have soared for more than two years due to high unemployment and special economic pressures. There is also a big decrease in GI Bill enrollments as the veterans from the Korean War no longer have educational benefits. "At this time," Morrison said, "we have a full-time student enrollment of 26,318 and the total head count of full-time and part-time students is 44,619."

Elsner was not pleased. Declining enrollments meant declining FTSE (pronounced "Footsie")—an acronym for Full-Time Student Equivalent, the formula used to determine the state's annual share of the community college expenses. Declining FTSE meant death for an institution—the Phoenix Union High School District was already on the verge of closing the old Phoenix Union campus because of declining enrollments.

Elsner had no desire to be the first Maricopa chancellor to close colleges.

The bad news about spring registration came just when Elsner was preparing his first address to the faculty at large. The occasion was the annual all-faculty convocation at Phoenix College. He decided to try to rally the faculty by impressing on them the importance of turning around the enrollment figures. To drive home the point, he announced that from now on in Maricopa, "FTSE's the name of the game!"

Rather than a loud cheer of collegial support, a deafening silence followed Elsner's battle cry. Several faculty from Glendale recall being absolutely horrified. Chuck West recalls the moment well:

> I think the thing that really started off bad with the chancellor was his speech at Phoenix College, in which he challenged the faculty and said, "FTSE's the name of the game." . . . The faculty interpreted that as not being concerned with the quality of education but only with the number of the students that were coming in order to get the funding.

Phil Smelser remembers reacting even more strongly:

> [Elsner] made some grievous misstatements, and one of them was, "FTSE is the name of the game." Well, that's their name of the game—that's not our name of the game! The whole attitude built from there that this guy had very little interest in what goes on in the classroom. He's an empire builder. That permeated the whole thing, and everything he did was viewed in that light.

Conrad Bayley recalls how a number of faculty were afraid for what this remark would do to the district's public image:

> Everybody literally sucked in their breaths at that one time. "Who is this person that would say something like that in public? There are newspaper people here, there are television cameras here, and we just don't want that image to be something that people hear!"

The more faculty thought about the implications of Elsner's little catch phrase, the more they thought it sounded like a threat. Just what did he have in mind? Did he want to increase class sizes to increase FTSE? Did he want to do away with low-enrollment, special interest classes that didn't generate enough FTSE? Did he want faculty to water down their assignments or lower their grading standards to make courses more popular and generate more FTSE?

Following the convocation, Elsner made ceremonial get-acquainted visits to each of the campuses, but his reception everywhere was less than cordial. Kathy Schwarz remembers Elsner's visit to Scottsdale:

> *I will never forget his speech at Scottsdale when he came out to meet the faculty. By God, he was going to run it like a business and he was going to do this and he was going to do that and the faculty all looked at each other and said, "Uh-oh. Interesting times ahead!" That raised the red flag.*

Martinez Joins the Board

In January, Jeremy Butler left the board, and Bob Martinez, a Phoenix attorney, took over his seat. Like Van Loo before him, Martinez arrived on the board with an agenda.

Community leaders in south Phoenix had endorsed Martinez's candidacy in return for Martinez's promise to see that the district's next community college would be located in south Phoenix. They'd had enough of Maricopa Tech's offering courses in schools and church basements. "They wanted bricks and mortar," he explained. Hardly had Martinez taken his oath of office than Brooks and Robertson approached him and pledged their support for a college in south Phoenix—the price for which was Martinez's support for their initiatives. With Martinez in their pocket, Brooks and Robertson would then have had their long-hoped-for majority on the board, and they could have then done anything they wanted.

Bob Martinez, Maricopa governing board member 1978-83.

However, Martinez was not in anyone's pocket. With Brooks under indictment and his future on the board uncertain, Martinez was thinking ahead. With the support of Brooks and Robertson, Martinez was in a position to have the south Phoenix community college created almost immediately, but he wisely decided to wait. "We could have voted on it on the first night. [But] I wanted to be the swing vote. I wanted to build support before we voted. You want to have as much support as you can going in. I didn't want it to be Bob Martinez's boondoggle or pork barrel."

Martinez presented the community's desires to Elsner, who was in favor of a college for south Phoenix but not at that time. The population figures did not yet indicate sufficient strength for a full campus to be located in south Phoenix. The big problem was the lack of a sufficient number of high schools to serve as feeder schools. Also, a permanent campus in south Phoenix would have required a bond election to raise the capital funds, and Elsner felt the public would not have endorsed the sale of capital bonds at that time.

The College without Walls

Another reason why Elsner was not eager to launch a new college in south Phoenix at that time was that he was already at work on a different solution to the same problem.

Elsner was looking hard at the district's crazy quilt of off-campus and outreach programs. Each college was running its own evening college division that sponsored extension classes on campus and off campus in local high schools and other remote locations. In several instances, notably at Mesa and at Maricopa Tech, the schools also supplied instructors to offer classes on-site at various large businesses, such as Motorola and Intel. In addition, the District had been offering classes by radio and television since about 1953. And yet, these various off-campus programs had a lot of problems.

Jan Baltzer explains the problems with the television courses:

> *It was an absolute nightmare from a coordination standpoint because there were five*

February 23, 1996, interview with Jan Baltzer, district administrator. Transcript and audio excerpts available online.

http://www.mc.maricopa.edu/users/M3cdhistory/

colleges, and so we had to make sure we got the course listings in all five schedules. We were still handing out cards in the gym for registration. So we had to have staff that would work registration—because we had our own little table at registration—at every single college. . . . Of course, they were at all different times, and all different ways that those were done, so we had to coordinate that. We got five sets of rosters that had to be administratively merged, but we couldn't really merge them because the credit came for each different college.

Lionel "Marty" Martinez, who was then responsible for all the evening programs at Maricopa Tech, observed that individual campuses, often started and then terminated courses capriciously with little regard for the needs of the community being served:

> From Maricopa Tech, I ran programs one year in Wickenburg, and we did very well. Then the next year, Phoenix College said, "You can't run them there anymore because we're going to do them because they're academic courses." "Okay." So they ran them. The third year, Phoenix College, or whoever was running that program, decided not to offer anything at Wickenburg, and I get the call from Wickenburg, and it was too late for me to do anything. So here you had a community that nobody was specifically in charge of, and so they're serviced one year,

or two years, and then they're not serviced, and nobody knows why.

Also, the existing coursebank structure was an obstacle in itself because each course was tagged with a code that indicated which college had developed that course. When Maricopa Tech wanted to offer a course that had Phoenix College's code on it, Martinez would have to secure Phoenix College's permission first:

> My contacts at Motorola would call me, and they'd give me four or five courses they'd want, and I'd say, "Okay. Well, we can offer this one, but I've got to call, and it'll help me if you'll call Scottsdale so I can run that one," because it had "SCC" behind it. "We have to call Phoenix College to get their permission," because it had "PC," and all those. The question I got back from business at the time was, "Don't you guys work at the same place?"

Elsner was well aware of these problems:

> We didn't have a particularly well-coordinated extension into the community; it was heavy on some fronts and not enough on others. There was very little consistency to it. We had cooperative education programs and all kinds of other things, and people were stepping over one another in some of these outreach programs.

The problem was the lack of coordination among all these outreach programs. As a

result, they were not realizing anywhere near their potential enrollment. If that problem could be solved, then the district's problem with declining enrollment could be turned around very quickly. The solution was to bring everything together under one roof.

And Elsner knew exactly what sort of roof that would be: a nontraditional college such as Vista College, the one he had run for the Peralta district.

Actually, the idea of a nontraditional college had been proposed in Maricopa before. According to an article in the *Scottsdale Daily Progress* for March 5, 1976, a faculty committee had been studying the idea and had even presented a recommendation to the governing board:

> Nontraditional education should be separated from Maricopa County Community College District campuses and organized as a distinct division, the MCCCD Nontraditional Education Committee proposed this week. An overview of nontraditional education was presented to members of the MCCCD governing board and faculty by Dr. Francine Hardaway, chairman of the committee, and Bill Hughes, an intern doing research for the committee. Nontraditional education, which includes broadcast classes over radio and television, is offered on all MCCCD campuses, Hughes said. He indicated nontraditional education appears to operate better under a separate division, according to research he compiled.

Elsner remembers that this committee had even contacted him in the course of their research:

> They were corresponding with me and kind of laid out the frustrations that they

March 11, 1996, interview with Lionel "Marty" Martinez, district administrator. Transcript and audio excerpts available online.

http://www.mc.maricopa.edu/users/M3cdhistory/

had had because they couldn't get any-body to listen to them. I gathered that there were some smaller groups that were working toward that, and there was a high degree of frustration. People wrote to me and told me that.

The nontraditional approach offered a solution to another problem as well. Elsner remembers, "The issue of bonding was not a big, popular, item on the tip of the tongue of every board member. I didn't get the impression that anybody wanted to put on a major capital program for anything." The storefront approach represented a way to launch a new college very inexpensively.

In fact, Elsner may have been thinking about starting a nontraditional college for Maricopa almost as soon as he walked in the door. In an article published in the *Scottsdale Daily Progress* for December 16, 1977 (a little more than a month after Elsner had been on the job), Elsner described his long-range plans in these terms:

> *"There has been planning, but it's been segmented. There has been no definitive set of guidelines for development. During my early tenure I'll be proposing some long-range planning objectives to give us a road map to the future." Expansion doesn't necessarily mean new buildings, he said. Such ideas as a college without a campus, a college in unused industrial property leased as classroom space, may be considered.*

Somewhere around this time, Walt Morrison—whom Elsner had retained as his vice chancellor for educational services—remembers when the planning really began:

> *At some point—I don't remember, now, exactly when it was—I went to a meeting in California for the district. I was there for three days and two nights, maybe. Dr. Elsner came over there to the meeting. He was probably making a speech or something, which is not unusual for him. Anyway, we talked, and he said he wanted me to stay over there and go to the districts there and study their campuses like Rio was to become.*

Morrison cannot remember exactly, but he thinks that the meeting was a League for Innovation conference probably at Coastline Community College, which was the nontraditional "college without walls" that the Coast Community College District had developed:

> *After the meeting was over, I was there probably another two days, looking around, asking questions . . . when I got a call: "Call Dr. Elsner." I did. He said, "I want you on the next plane back here." I was. He said, "Now that you're here, you're going to start a nontraditional college, and I want the organizational plan. It has to include all off-campus programs, a single budget, its own administration, ding-ding-ding-ding. Now go in there and sit down and do it, and have it ready for Tuesday," or whatever. So that's what I did.*

Acting on Elsner's instructions, Morrison sketched out a rough draft and submitted it to Elsner, who then worked out the imple-

February 16, 1996, video interview with Walt Morrison, district faculty and administrator. Transcript and audio excerpts available online.

http://www.mc.maricopa.edu/users/M3cdhistory/

mentation plan. The key element of the plan was to bring together under one roof all the existing extension classes, outreach programs, on-site course offerings, and television and radio classes—in short, everything that was "off the curb" at any of the existing colleges. Existing administrators and staff would be reassigned to coordinate the administration of these offerings.

To house the new venture, the district would simply rent office space as needed, just as the district was already renting classroom space in locations all over the county. The result would be increased efficiency, less confusion, and greater service to the community and to business. And since the changes were primarily administrative—the courses were already staffed and being taught—the whole change could occur almost overnight. The nontraditional college could be open for business by the fall of 1978.

For the first two months of 1978, Elsner seems to have held these cards very close to his vest. In an article published in the *Arizona Republic* for May 8, 1978, Elsner claimed that only he, the three vice chancellors; the president of the faculty executive council (Bud Morris), and a representative from Tadlock (the company that was doing Elsner's long-range planning) were involved initially. The first time the governing board was let in on the secret was at a study session on February 28. To present the details, Elsner had Walt Morrison present organizational charts to explain how the school would be administered. At that session, Morrison heard for the first time that the school would be called Rio Salado Community College.

Soon after that meeting, Elsner previewed the new college at a meeting of the presidents' council. The response was mixed. John Waltrip, who was then president of Glendale, was in favor of the idea. "What the hell? You've got a new boss, and he wants to try something. So you look for ways to support him." Privately, Waltrip welcomed the creation of Rio for another reason. Roger Brooks' pet project, the Bell Plaza Center in Sun City, had become a thorn in Waltrip's side. Full-time faculty at Glendale didn't particularly want to drive from Glendale to Sun City to teach the courses, but the Glendale faculty association had protested when part-time faculty were hired to staff classes offered during the day. Waltrip welcomed Rio because it would take that problem out of his hands.

Norb Bruemmer, president of Maricopa Tech, was outraged. Extension courses and classes being offered on-site at various manufacturing plants and large businesses generated more than half of Maricopa Tech's FTSE. Rio threatened to have a catastrophic effect on MTCC's enrollment. Lionel Martinez recalls how Bruemmer broke the news to his staff:

When he made the announcement to the faculty at Maricopa Tech, it was downstairs in one of the conference rooms, and everybody knew "Rio," but they didn't know what it meant to them. Norb explained to them what Maricopa Tech would lose, and he cried. He said, "I worked so hard to build it up, and in one fell swoop, it's taken from me."

At the governing board meeting on March 14, 1978, Rio Salado College was announced to the public for the first time. At this same meeting, Walt Morrison was appointed as the new college's founding president. The following day, the *Arizona Republic's* article described the event and included a revealing detail:

The college's administrative offices will be located in south Phoenix. . . . The board also voted to institute a study on the feasibility of locating a site for a permanent Rio Salado campus. "This has been long overdue," said board member Robert

Arizona Republic *for March 15, 1978.*

Martinez. *"There has been a petition drive started by residents in this area and I hope this will be the start of a permanent campus."*

Thus, Rio Salado was initially being touted as the college that the people in south Phoenix were demanding.

The same article goes on to stress that setting up the new college was estimated to cost a mere $2 million, which would be taken from the district's unrestricted cash reserves. Obviously playing to the taxpayers, Elsner then contrasts a mere $2 million with the cost of starting a full campus. "Elsner said his executive council chose the college-without-walls concept to avoid the initial cost of about $60 million to construct a permanent facility. He said this concept would provide a 'testable model while other alternatives are being looked into.'"

So far, so good. But the next sentence in the article caused district faculty to gasp:

"Elsner said in an effort to keep costs down, only visiting instructors would be used and full-time faculty would work on a voluntary basis as advisers or in a developmental capacity."

Community College is approved for south Phoenix

3-15-78 AR

By ART GISSENDANER

The governing board of the Maricopa County Community College District approved establishment on Tuesday of a sixth college to serve south Phoenix and other areas in the primarily southwestern portion of the county.

Rio Salado College is scheduled to begin operating this fall under the "college without walls" concept, with classroom space to be rented in existing structures that are easily accessible to students. The college's administrative offices will be located in south Phoenix.

Walt Morrisson, former acting vice chancellor for educational services was

The board also voted to institute a study on the feasibility of locating a site for a permanent Rio Salado campus.

"This has been long overdue," said board member Robert Martinez. "There has been a petition drive started by residents in this area and I hope this will be the start of a permanent campus."

District Chancellor Paul Elsner said Rio Salado College is the result of a week of intensified study by the chancellor's executive council.

"This is a very significant development for the district. We will re-allocate our resources to keep costs down, but

to providing services to everyone within our financial constraints."

Initial financing for the college will be in the sum of $2 million from the district's unrestricted cash reserves.

Al Flowers, executive vice chancellor, said target enrollment for the college is 2,500 students, which is expected to produce $300,000 in student fees, $1.25 million in state aid for operating, and $337,-000 in capital funds from the state.

"The state aid, if realized, would reduce the tax rate about 4 cents because the money would come into the operational funds," Flowers said.

Elsner said that although the college's

nix, the school would serve Sun City, Buckeye, Litchfield Park, Apache Junction, Carefree and other areas not served by the district's other five colleges.

Elsner said his executive council chose the college-without-walls concept to avoid the initial cost of about $60 million to construct a permanent facility.

He said this concept would provide a "testable model while other alternatives are being looked into."

Elsner said in an effort to keep costs down, only visiting instructors would be used and full-time faculty would work on a voluntary basis as advisers or in

Elsner was starting a new college that wouldn't have any full-time faculty? What on earth was he thinking?!

That statement only confirmed the faculty's worst fears since the "FTSE's the name of the game" speech. A college-without-faculty was a declaration of war!

On April 7, the *Arizona Republic* described the faculty's view of Rio Salado:

> Maricopa County Community College teachers on Thursday denounced the proposed Rio Salado College as a hoax on south Phoenix residents and said they'd fight to stop its opening this fall. "We condemn in the strongest possible terms a decision by the governing board to establish the so-called Rio Salado College," teacher spokesman Gene Eastin said in a press conference. "South Phoenix residents think they will be getting the same education that other students are getting, but they won't. The residents of south Phoenix are being deceived," Eastin said.

And then to cover all the bases, Eastin also denounced the way that Rio had been developed in secret as a clear violation of the state's open meeting law.

The uproar continued in the newspapers for the next several days. The Faculty Executive Council decided to poll the full-time faculty to see how they felt about Rio. The results of the poll were not conclusive, but they were not in any sense favorable to Elsner. According to an article that appeared on May 8, 1978, in the *Arizona Republic*, over 400 teachers did not even respond. Of those that did, more than 200 teachers wanted the council to initiate some kind of legal action to protest Rio. Fifty teachers came out in direct opposition to the college being started at all.

1977

Proposed Rio Salado College is a joke, county teachers say

By ART GISSENDANER

Maricopa County Community College teachers Thursday denounced the proposed Rio Salado College as a hoax on south Phoenix residents and said they'd fight to stop its opening this fall.

They contended the college was being established without a campus as a means of securing additional state aid. They further complained that the decision to proceed with it was made before a feasibility study can be completed.

"We condemn in the strongest possible terms a decision by the governing board to establish the so-called Rio Salado College," teacher spokesman Gene Eastin said in a press conference.

"South Phoenix residents think they will be getting the same education that other students are getting, but they won't. The residents of south Phoenix are being deceived," Eastin said.

"We have an attorney looking into the matter and we are advised there may be a basis for a lawsuit to stop the project. If so, we plan to file such a suit," he said.

Rio Salado College, approved by the board during a March 14 meeting, meant to serve south Phoenix and other unserved areas in the county using the "college without walls" concept.

Although the administrative office will be located in south Phoenix, classroom space will be rented in existing structures that are easily accessible to students.

State aid is paid to the district on the basis of full-time student enrollment. However, credit is given for part-time student enrollment, meaning that two half-time students would generate the same amount of state aid as one full-time student.

Arizona Republic for April 7, 1978.

South Mountain Is Proposed as Brooks Goes to Trial

Meanwhile, the community leaders in south Phoenix were beginning to have second thoughts about Rio. On paper, they were getting a new college, but in reality, everything would stay the same as before.

Lionel Martinez explains their concerns:

> Remember, we were already running classes in the elementary schools and high schools, which aren't really adapted for adults. The chairs are small, tables are low, and that kind of stuff. So the leaders of south Phoenix really got irritated . . . . I was asked a lot of questions by some of the south Phoenix leaders. "Are you going to build a building?" "Well, no, we're going to rent facilities." "Well, where else are you going to run classes?" "Well, in the elementary schools, in churches, et cetera."

Attending classes at Phoenix College had never been a real option for south Phoenix residents. The reason is that south Phoenix was more isolated from the rest of Phoenix than it is today. As Lionel Martinez explained, Phoenix College might just as well have been on another planet:

> If it rained, Central [Avenue] was the only bridge that used to last. I mean, you were virtually isolated. You'd have to go to Tempe to get across, and the bus system in those days . . . It's not great now, but it was terrible then.

158

There was no way. It's still a pain to catch a bus from south Phoenix to go north to catch a job. Some of these people spend ten, twelve hours a day trying to get to a six-, eight-hour job. They just travel all the time.

So, the pressure on Bob Martinez was beginning to build. The people of south Phoenix wanted their own community college, and they deeply resented the fact that the district had tried to put one over on them with this Rio nonsense.

Furthermore, Roger Brooks' embezzlement trial was about to begin. If Brooks were to be convicted—a possibility that seemed very likely—he would be removed from the board, and Martinez would not have the votes he needed to create the south Phoenix college. For that reason, Martinez decided not to wait any longer.

At the governing board meeting on April 18, 1978, Roger Brooks stunned everyone by formally proposing the creation of what he then called South County Community College. Following the announcement, Brooks said the matter would be voted on at a special meeting to coincide with a scheduled study session on the following Saturday, April 22.

Needless to say, the announcement came as a complete surprise to Farnsworth and Hitchcock. As reported in the *Arizona Republic* on April 19:

> *Board members Ross Farnsworth and Barbara Hitchcock, visibly stunned by the motion, objected to considering a location for a campus without awaiting the results of a $50,000 feasibility study[1] to determine the educational needs in areas the minority community leaders were*

unserved by the district. . . . [Farnsworth] called Brooks's motion a "slap in the face." "I'm offended at the very way this was brought about. We need the study to make an intelligent and fair decision," Farnsworth said. "This way it makes us look like we're opposed to something for south Phoenix."

The article from the *Republic* also mentions an appearance that evening by Dr. Lawrence McHenry, executive consultant of the Phoenix NAACP:

> *He said minorities in south Phoenix were concerned over the establishment of a full-service campus that would offer the same educational [services available] on other district campuses. . . . McHenry said he was not opposed to Rio Salado but insulted because they were not consulted when the college-without-walls program was established. "No one asked us if we wanted Rio Salado," he told the board. "We're not knocking it, but Rio Salado was a slap in our faces that we will take. But we need a full-service campus."*

But the person who felt his face had been slapped the hardest was Paul Elsner.

According to Hitchcock, "Elsner was fighting it like crazy because they hadn't asked him! It was a terrible thing for a board to do. A terrible thing! And he was shocked and very upset. . . . He wasn't told in advance." Elsner's anger can be gauged in part by the fact that

Educators defend 'floating campus' for south Phoenix

BY ART GISSENDANER

The "College Without Walls" concept has been the target of criticism and skepticism since Rio Salado College was established more than a month ago.

Some educators and community leaders feel the college was approved with alarming swiftness and have raised serious doubts concerning the validity of the Maricopa County Community College District board's deliberations and the concept.

District administrators feel the resultant tremors from within the district and community questioning the methods used in establishing the college is a result of misunderstanding and fear and has almost completely subordinated the importance to the county of a college-without-walls concept.

Rio Salado, they say, was conceived with the intent that it would serve the entire county by giving the mobility to classes that potential students may not have.

This will be done, district officials say, by renting space in existing structures located in areas exhibiting the greatest student demand.

The district will look for space in high schools, junior highs and elementary schools, offices, store fronts and businesses.

District Chancellor Paul Elsner said the college's mobility will enable it to test educational needs in south and southwest Phoenix, Sun City, Chandler, Mesa, Tempe, Apache Junction, Para-

dise Valley, Carefree, Buckeye, Goodyear, Litchfield Park, Gila Bend and Wickenburg.

The district already has initiated a $50,000 study to determine which areas need educational servicing and why. The study conducted by Tadlock and Associates, a California-based consultant firm, is still in progress.

Elsner said Rio Salado will work in conjunction with the study in determining on an "as need" basis the areas of growth and those needing educational services.

"Rio Salado and the study will tell us where the growth and need of the entire Valley is before we move to a permanent solution like $35 million worth of concrete," Elsner said.

Rio Salado became the district's sixth college March 14 after a week of intense planning sessions unknown to everyone except the board and the participants.

The participants, according to Elsner, were himself, the three vice chancellors, Carl Morris, president of the faculty executive council and a Tadlock representative.

Teachers and community leaders were caught by surprise when the college was approved and openly criticized the board and the administration for the lack of communication.

Elsner admitted he made no effort to notify the district's 731 faculty mem-

Continued on Page B-2

Arizona Republic for May 8, 1978.

his name disappears from the newspapers for the next several days.

On Thursday, April 20, Roger Brooks' trial began in Maricopa County Superior Court, Judge Val Cordova presiding. The *Arizona Republic* for Friday, April 21, reported that Brooks' girlfriend, Ardath W. Maturo, would be testifying for the prosecution. Brooks' attorney admitted that Brooks had not only paid her airfare and hotel bill, but also that she and Brooks had shared the same hotel room in San Diego.

---

[1] The reference here is to the Tadlock study, the results of which had yet to be announced.

MARICOPA COUNTY
COMMUNITY COLLEGE DISTRICT

3910 E. Washington St. / Phoenix, Arizona 85034
P. O. Box 13349 / Phoenix, Arizona 85002
(602) 244-8355

May 2, 1978

Representative Earl Wilcox
State Representative, District 22
Arizona House of Representatives
Phoenix, Arizona 85007

Dear Representative Wilcox:

I am in receipt of your letter of April 26, 1978, and I
appreciate your generosity and confidence in me. I wish
to make it clear, however, that the resolution establishing
the South Mountain Community College was written by Mr.
Brooks. It was at his urging that the matter came before
the Governing Board and his pursuasion was instrumental
in the passage of the resolution. For this reason I felt
it only proper that his role in this regard be acknowledged.

Thank you for your support in this matter, and your offer
of assistance is most appreciated.

Sincerely,

Robert L Robertson

Robert L. Robertson
MCCCD Governing Board President

RLR:jbh

*from J. Hales file—
never given me*

This letter from Bob Robertson to Arizona State Representative Earl Wilcox indicates that South Mountain Community College was entirely Roger Brooks's idea. Note the stationery is out-of-date; Bob Martinez has succeeded Jeremy Butler, but Butler's name appears as board president.

Brooks' attorney, Garrett Simpson, offered the following explanation:

> Simpson said Brooks wanted to look into allegations that consulting firms hired by school districts were charging exorbitant prices but doing no work. Simpson said Brooks was to have a covert meeting with an unidentified informant. He said Brooks was booked into the wrong hotel and the meeting fell through. The lawyer told jurors that because it was a holiday weekend, Brooks could not rearrange his airline reservations for an immediate return

to Phoenix. Simpson said Brooks, therefore, spent the rest of the weekend in San Diego and "partied" with Ms. Maturo.

According to the *Scottsdale Daily Progress* for April 21, Jeremy Butler and Al Flowers were called as witnesses for the prosecution on the first day. The trial continued on the next day, Friday.

On Saturday, the vote to establish the new college did not materialize. Brooks and Robertson were the only ones who showed

District OKs college for S. Phoenix

By ART GISSENDANER

A college campus for south Phoenix was approved Tuesday night by a 3-2 vote of the Maricopa County Community College District's governing board.

The college, to be called South Mountain Community College, is scheduled to open in the fall of 1980. A site for the college has not been selected.

Board members Roger Brooks, Robert Robertson and Robert Martinez voted for the college while Ross Farnsworth and Barbara Hitchcock voted against it.

The board's action climaxed a tense week of speculation on whether a campus would be approved to serve residents of the southern and southwest portions of the county.

The motion to establish a campus in south Phoenix was first made by Brooks during an April 18 meeting. Action was delayed until last Saturday but that meeting was canceled when only two board members showed up.

The SMCC campus is the second established by the board within a month. Recently, the board approved the Rio Salado college, a campus-without-walls concept, that initially had been planned to serve south Phoenix, along with the rest of the county.

The board approved the college despite a terse warning from Dr. Cliff Harkins, the district's representative to the state community college board.

Harkins told the board that it was approving a campus without following criteria established by the state board.

"In order to establish an additional campus the local district must prove to the state board there is a need," Harkins said. "The district must guarantee an enrollment of 500 full-time students and offer a reasonable site which will be approved by the state board."

Harkins said the district must follow the state board's criteria or run the risk of losing the $500,000 in capital outlay to build new campuses. He said the district must also put up $1 million toward the college.

Harkins joined Farnsworth and Mrs.

Continued from Page A

...cock in asking to delay vote until May 10 when the boa[rd w]ould receive a report from Max [Tadl]ock, who is assessing the district's educational needs.

More than 70 people attended the meeting, which was punctuated by shouts from the audience in favor of the college and rounds of applause for those who spoke for it.

Mrs. Hitchcock attempted to have the motion tabled until after the May 10 Tadlock report but her motion was defeated. She warned that "railroading this resolution through will result in legislative backlash that could be detrimental to south Phoenix."

The board voted after listening to nearly three hours of emotional pleas from legislators, community and student leaders who emphasized the importance of a campus for south Phoenix.

Sen. Polly Getzwiller, D-Casa Grande,

...[w]ith M[rs.] Hitchc[ock's] [legi]lative [acti]ons at [the col]lege [she] warne[d th]e boa[rd th]a[t] it [did not] appro[ve a] cam[pus] it [might] miss its [ch]ance with [the S]enate and House Appropriations committees.

She said the population in the area has increased substantially and no form of higher education is available to them.

"We feel like the time is right for us to be considered for a community college," she said. "I am sorry to hear Mrs. Hitchcock's resolution because I've discussed this in the Senate and I've experienced no backlash."

Mrs. Getzwiller agreed with earlier statements that no outside study was needed to see that south Phoenix had an educational need.

The board was admonished repeatedly for violating the rights of south Phoenix residents by not making a comprehensive education readily accessible.

Arizona Republic for April 26, 1978.

up for the study session. Hitchcock and Farnsworth both deliberately stayed away; Martinez claimed later that he got the meeting time wrong.

On Monday, April 24, Ardath Maturo testified. According to the *Arizona Republic* published on May 2:

> Mrs. Maturo testified that Brooks never mentioned to her that the trip was for district business, and that he was out of her sight only a few times during the entire trip. She claimed Brooks, in addition to taking her and her daughter to the zoo, Sea World and other attractions, also gave her $200 to spend.

On Tuesday, April 25, Brooks' trial continued. The *Scottsdale Daily Progress* for that day reported that Bob Robertson appeared to explain that the district had no formal guidelines to govern travel by board members

when Brooks made his trip to San Diego. "Robertson also testified as a character witness for Brooks. 'If there's an example of what a board member should be, it's Mr. Brooks,' Robertson said."

That night, the board met as scheduled and voted to approve South Mountain Community College (as it was then named). Predictably, the vote was 3 to 2. On the following day, the *Arizona Republic* described what happened:

> More than 70 people attended the meeting, which was punctuated by shouts from the audience in favor of the college and rounds of applause for those who spoke for it. . . . The board voted after listening to nearly three hours of emotional pleas from legislators, community and student leaders who emphasized the importance of a campus for south Phoenix.

Lionel Martinez recalls that many faculty members voiced opposition to the new college at that meeting:

> The faculty tried to block South Mountain. I can tell you what some of them said at the board meeting. They said things like—and I got angry with some of those remarks— "The people down there"—I'm quoting, now—"don't want a community college. They don't need one. They can come to the other ones. They don't need one." But the people from South Mountain area were there and said, "We need one. We deserve one. We demand one!"

On Wednesday, April 26, Brooks' trial continued. On this day, Brooks' attorney presented a sworn statement from James M. Veletz, a writer for the *Phoenix New Times*. Veletz claimed that he had promised Brooks to set up a meeting with a man named Stephen Douglas, who would then give Brooks proof that some unnamed consulting firm had overcharged the district (*Scottsdale Daily Progress*, April 26, 1978).

On the same day, Paul Elsner issued a statement—the first time that the newspapers report his response to the board's creation of South Mountain Community College. Surprisingly, he had decided to support the new college. However, the newspaper doesn't say what the price was for his support. According to Bob Martinez, Elsner asked for Martinez's support for Rio in exchange for Elsner's support for South Mountain: "You support this. I'll support South."

Apparently, the trial did not continue on Thursday and Friday. The newspaper accounts suggest that the next day of court action was Monday, May 1. On this day, Brooks himself finally took the stand and elaborated on his story that he was secretly investigating possi-

Brooks Found Guilty; Loses Board Position

By EDYTHE JENSEN
Gazette Courts Reporter

The embezzlement conviction of a Maricopa County Community College Board member "will show public officials that if they are enterprising in their offices, they can be crushed," said Garrett Simpson, attorney for Roger Brooks.

Brooks, 30, was found guilty late Tuesday of four counts of embezzlement and one charge of presenting a false claim in connection with a trip he made to San Diego at taxpayers' expense.

Simpson said today that Brooks made the trip to investigate alleged wrongdoing on behalf of another official. A meeting he was supposed to have with an informant on

BROOKS

Turn to ●BROOKS, Page B-2

Phoenix Gazette *for May 3, 1978.*

1977

BROOKS FOUND GUILTY

(Concl. f   Page B)

the coast fell through, and Brooks admitted spending the Labor Day weekend vacationing and sightseeing with his girlfriend.

"I am surprised and shocked the jury found me guilty," Brooks said today. "I expected that I would be acquited."

Although college district credit cards were used to finance the more than $600 in expenses for the trip, Brooks said he never turned in an official claim to his supervisors.

Testimony during Brooks' trial showed that if an individual doesn't turn in the claim by the end of the fiscal year (which would be June 30), he must pay back the funds used.

Simpson said Brooks had no intention of filing a claim and "just assumed he would have to pay the money back once he discovered he could accomplish no district business in San Diego."

UNDER STATE LAW, Brooks' office became vacant upon his conviction. Maricopa County School Supt. Richard Harris will appoint his replacement. Although Simpson said he will appeal Brooks' conviction, those proceedings will have no bearing on his immediate replacement, district officials said.

ior Court Judge Val Cordova w   ntence the defendant May 30. Simpson said that at a pre-sentence hearing community members will vouch for Brook's reputation as a hard working administrator.

"These were very poor charges to bring to trial," said Simpson. "Because there was never a showing of guilty intent. At best, it was a technical offense — he took his duties too seriously."

BROOKS TESTIFIED he was investigating a possible conflict of interest against Al Flowers, executive vice chancellor for the district. The witness said he suspected that consulting firms were being paid exhorbitant fees by the district for little work and that Flowers had a financial interest in those consulting jobs.

Brooks' girlfriend, 24-year-old Ardath Maturo, was the state's key witness. She said Brooks never mentioned the business nature of his trip and that they spent the entire weekend vacationing.

Deputy County Attorney John Birkemeier argued that Brooks never intended to go to any district-related meetings in San Diego.

BROOKS SAID, "There was no intent on my part to defraud the district or divert funds. I went over there in the performance of my duties as a board member."

He said his investigation resulted in an audit report of an assisting agency involved with federal funds which indicated that services were not performed by the agency for which it was paid more than $10,000.

ble conflicts of interest on the part of Al Flowers (*Phoenix Gazette*, May 1, 1978).

On Tuesday, May 2, the trial went to the jury at noon, and after eight hours of deliberation, Brooks was convicted of four counts of grand theft by embezzlement and one charge of presenting a false claim. Sentencing was set for May 30.

On May 4, Thomas J. Saad, the director of administrative services for the community colleges' state board, sought a legal opinion as to whether Brooks' seat on the board was then vacant. The state attorney general, John A. Lasota, Jr., returned the opinion that Brooks was not out of a job until his sentencing on May 30.

Brooks did his best to forestall the inevitable by appealing his conviction. On May 17, Brooks petitioned the Arizona Supreme Court to dismiss the charges against him, and on the following day, Thursday, May 18, the court issued a temporary stay against the sentencing which was to have taken place on May 30. A hearing was scheduled for June 13.

On the night of Thursday, May 18, Roger Brooks appeared in his capacity as a board member to hand out degrees at Phoenix College. Several newspaper articles protested this action. The *Arizona Republic* ran an editorial entitled "An Obscene Exit."

Brooks' appeal was eventually denied, and on June 27, Judge Val Cordova sentenced Brooks to twelve weekends in jail, five years probation and $1,500 restitution for legal costs. According to the *Phoenix Gazette* for this date:

> The judge also imposed an unusual term to Brooks' probation—"that you not cohabit with a female unless she is your wife." [1]

2 "Open and notorious cohabitation or adultery" is a Class 3 misdemeanor in Arizona (ARS §13-1409); in 1977, it had been reclassified from being a felony.

162

Cordova told the college official that one of Brooks' major personality flaws "is your propensity for relationships with females without the benefit of wedlock. As an elected official, you should have been as Caesar's wife—above reproach." Cordova noted that a few days after Brooks' conviction in May, the defendant moved in with a different woman.

Brooks' attorney vowed to appeal the conviction, but apparently, no appeal was ever made. Brooks served his sentence and then disappeared from Maricopa's history completely.

The judge's unusual sentence had one other effect on the district. According to Mesa's former dean of instruction Bill Holt, "About that time, several of our administrators got married real quick."

Gazette Staff Photo by Rick Glass

BROOKS OFFICIATES AT CEREMONIES

Maricopa County Community College board member Roger Brooks (center), convicted May 3 on embezzlement charges, assisted in conferring degrees on 817 Phoenix College graduates Thursday night in the college auditorium. With him on stage were William E. Berry (left), executive dean of PC and Pedro Gomez, president of Associated Students. Brooks was granted a stay on sentencing by the state Supreme Court so he could retain his seat on the board while preparing an appeal. The top court has scheduled a hearing on the appeal June 13.

Phoenix Gazette for May 18, 1978.

An Obscene Exit

As they march across the auditorium stage of Phoenix Community College to receive their diplomas Thursday night, the 817 graduates will have a distinction they may want to forget.

They will shake hands with, and receive their diplomas from, a convicted felon.

It is no doing of the college, nor of the Maricopa County Community College Board.

It is the doing of board member Roger Brooks, convicted earlier this month on three counts of embezzling tax funds, and one count of filing false travel claims.

Because technically, Brooks still is a member of the college board until he is sentenced May 30, he insists on being an honored guest and participant at the graduation. And there seems to be precious little anyone can legally do about it.

Except, of course, to appeal to Brooks' conscience.

By flaunting himself this way, Brooks undoubtedly is satisfying an ego and a seige mentality which was his undoing.

But he also is bringing shame to a decorous and solemn occasion and inflicting embarrassment and hurt on young people who celebrate their graduation with pride.

It is an unfitting personal obscenity by Brooks, the chiseler, toward college students who have come to expect better.

The only spectacle that could compare with Brooks' climactic public appearance would be for the Arizona State University business school to confer an honorary doctorate on land fraud kingpin Ned Warren for his financial expertise.

Arizona Republic for May 17, 1978.

Restraint on love life of ex-college official is imposed by judge

By FRANK TURCO

An ousted member of the Maricopa County Community College District Board who used taxpayers' money to take his girlfriend to San Diego was ordered Tuesday not to live with a woman out of wedlock for the next five years.

The unusual order was part of a five-year probation sentence Maricopa County Superior Court Judge Val Cordova imposed on Roger A. Brooks, 30, for his conviction on charges he embezzled public money and filed false expense claims. Brooks is unmarried.

Brooks, who lost his seat on the board when the sentence was imposed, also was ordered to spend the next 12 weekends in the county jail and to repay the county $1,500 for legal fees.

Cordova said he was disturbed because Brooks charged taxpayers for his pleasure trip, on which he stayed in

Arizona Republic for June 28, 1978.

163

1978

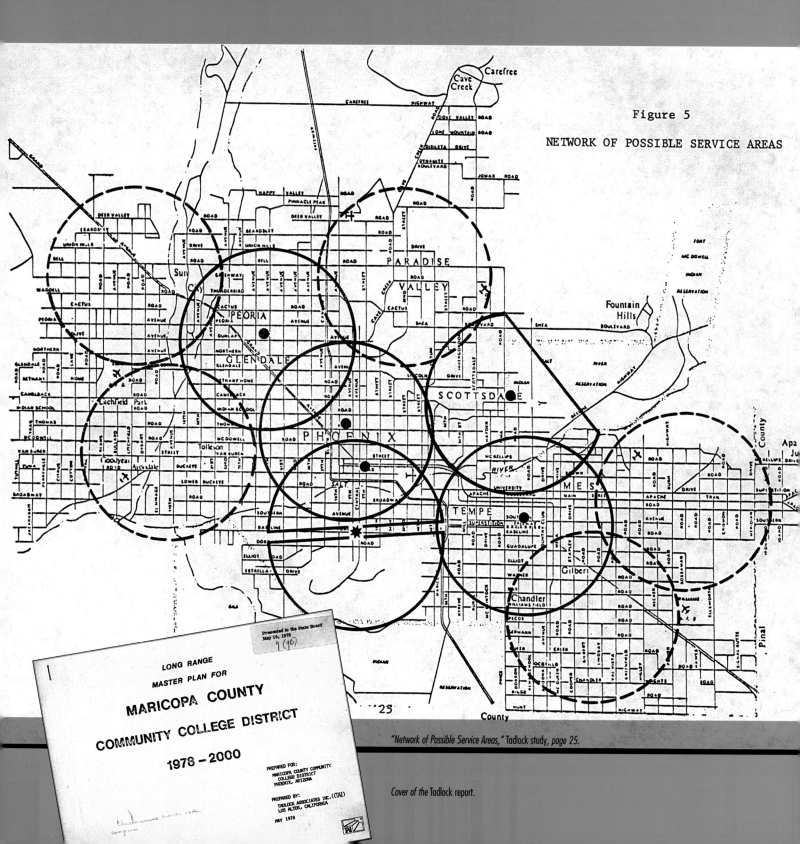

Figure 5

NETWORK OF POSSIBLE SERVICE AREAS

"Network of Possible Service Areas," Tadlock study, page 25.

LONG RANGE

MASTER PLAN FOR

MARICOPA COUNTY

COMMUNITY COLLEGE DISTRICT

1978 - 2000

PREPARED FOR:
MARICOPA COUNTY COMMUNITY
COLLEGE DISTRICT
PHOENIX, ARIZONA

PREPARED BY:
TADLOCK ASSOCIATES INC.((TAI)
LOS ALTOS, CALIFORNIA

MAY 1978

Cover of the Tadlock report.

Chapter Sixteen

1979
The **Battle** of the **Rio Salado**

Nothing seemed to be going Paul Elsner's way. The announcement of Rio had been a public relations disaster. The board had completely ignored the new code of ethics by creating South Mountain without so much as a "by-your-leave." The faculty was screaming for his head on a plate. Right about then, he really needed a little support.

Right about then he got some.

Max Tadlock and his company, Tadlock Associates, Inc. (TAI), were ready to announce the findings of their demographic survey of the district. The report might even have been ready earlier, but the sudden announcement of South Mountain on April 18 and the board's subsequent approval on April 25 had required Tadlock's people to wear down the erasers on their pencils. Somehow, the report was ready for the board to see on May 15, 1978.

Long Range Master Plan for Maricopa County Community College District, 1978-2000. *Full text available online.*

http://www.mc.maricopa.edu/users/M3cdhistory/

Tadlock begins by defining terms. The colleges in Glendale, Mesa, and Phoenix are dubbed Regional Campuses destined to sustain a maximum daytime FTSE of 5,000. Scottsdale, South Mountain, and Maricopa Tech are called Special Service Campuses with a maximum daytime FTSE of 2,000. Rio Salado is neither, but "a system, not a place or a faculty, for delivery of educational programs and services through alternatives to the campus."

Based on the district's previous patterns of enrollment, Tadlock establishes the following formula for growth: When the population of a given service area reaches 170,000, then the district should establish a "core" campus that can handle about 6,000 enrollments. A "core" campus will include classrooms, labs, a library, a student-services area, offices, and physical education facilities but not stadiums, etc. When a service area population exceeds 285,000, the "core" campus should be expanded to a full-service campus to include expanded vocational/technical training facilities, expanded physical education and sports facilities, more parking, etc.

Tadlock then defines the potential service areas in Maricopa County through the year 2000. He does so by imposing a series of twelve-mile-wide circles on a county map. (See the accompanying diagram.) Four of the circles represent the existing service areas of

Glendale, Phoenix, Scottsdale, and Mesa Community Colleges. Other circles represent the service areas that would eventually require Chandler-Gilbert, Paradise Valley, and Estrella Mountain Community Colleges. The other two circles take in the Sun Cities area and the east Valley area.

In the lower center of the map, two mutually exclusive half-circles represent the service areas of Maricopa Tech and South Mountain. The half-circles are Tadlock's way of hinting that Maricopa Tech should become part of the newly proposed South Mountain campus, a suggestion which seems to reflect Tadlock's complete lack of understanding of the forces that had necessitated South Mountain in the first place.

Based on projected growth within those service areas, Tadlock forecasts that the district will need five Special Service Area Campuses in operation by the year 2000. The first two are Scottsdale and the proposed South Mountain/Maricopa Tech consortium. The next campuses should be the Litchfield/Goodyear area campus in 1990, the South Mesa area campus in 1995, and the North Phoenix area campus in 2000. (Ironically, those three campuses were eventually built, but not in that order and not on that timetable.)

In the report's conclusion, Tadlock endorses Rio but strongly disapproves of South

Study Urges 4 New Campuses For College District

Four new campuses should be added to the Maricopa County Community College District in the next 20 years to meet growth demands, according to a comprehensive master plan which would restructure the current system.

A South Phoenix campus, already approved by the board, is the first priority, followed by a campus in the Litchfield-Goodyear area by 1990, south Mesa-Tempe by 1995 and north Phoenix by the year 2000.

The plan, developed by Tadlock and Associates, a California-based planning and consulting firm, was presented to the district board Tuesday night ahead of schedule. The study, presented by Max Tadlock, indicated strong support for the Rio Salado Community College, a "college without walls" system to provide classes throughout the county using leased space.

THE BOARD TOOK no action on the plan.

Tadlock said the district should be restructured in the next 20 years to provide three regional campuses and five smaller special service campuses to serve the rapid population growth in the county.

He recommended the district follow through with its current building program to bring all campuses in the system up to the 5,000 full-time student equivalent capacity, which roughly equates to about a 10,000 actual student load due to part-time students and evening division attendance.

Three campuses — Mesa, Glendale and Phoenix College — would serve as the three main regional centers under this plan. Scottsdale does not have the "population draw" necessary to develop

to this level, Tadlock said, based on growth projections for the next 25 years.

SCOTTSDALE would be developed into a special service area campus such as Maricopa Tech, downtown. In addition, the planned South Phoenix campus would be a sister school to Maricopa Tech and provide a special service campus at two locations connected by a shuttle bus.

The South Phoenix location would provide academic and liberal arts courses while Maricopa Tech would provide the vocational and occupational courses for this area.

Based on population figures, the Glendale area will double in the next 20 years and the Litchfield-Goodyear area will more than double putting extreme pressure on Glendale Community College and Phoenix College, according to the study.

The report indicates planning and site acquisition must begin now for the Litchfield-Goodyear campus, Tadlock said.

THE MESA-TEMPE area "will be another Phoenix with 623,000 people by 2000," Tadlock said, and will need a campus by 1995.

In comparison, Scottsdale Community College will be able to handle the growth in that area in the next 20 years, he said.

In other action, the board heard complaints from the minority and handicapped coalition at Phoenix College that they needed a special services center on campus. The group, which picketed the office prior to the meeting, will confer with district officials today on the request.

The board also approved a 7 percent

raise for classified employees, 8 percent pay hike for maintenance workers, 7 percent for food service employees, supervisory and technical staff and a 6.3 percent wage hike for professional and administrative staff. The approved pay increases amount to $732,590.

BOARD MEMBER Roger Brooks, who was convicted of embezzling district funds for a trip to San Diego, participated in the meeting and said he had no intention of resigning his seat. He said that when he is sentenced May 30 he will have to forfeit the position but intends to continue his duties until then.

He said that he intends to repay the $615 cost of the trip "as I said all along, but I was advised by counsel not to do so until after the trial," Brooks said.

Phoenix Gazette for May 10, 1978.

Mountain. Tadlock likes Rio's potential for serving the entire county and filling the bare spots between service areas. But Tadlock argues the demographics are all wrong for South Mountain and the community lacks the resources to support a full-service campus. Tadlock even goes out of his way to debunk the idea that South Mountain can be an engine of future development for the community:

> *History does not show that a community college campus in and of itself will be a magnet to attract the financial forces needed for significant change in a community. Only major university campuses seem to have this impact.*

For Elsner, Tadlock was all good news. Tadlock's seal of approval on Rio vindicated its creation, and Tadlock's thumbs-down on South Mountain gave Elsner all the ammunition he needed to kill it then and there—not

that Elsner needed any additional ammunition. South Mountain couldn't possibly be built without a bond election to raise the capital funds, and a bond election was completely out of the question at that time. And the state board was probably not going to approve the new college anyway. The board members had looked at the same data as Tadlock and come to the same conclusion: the service area was not sufficient to sustain a full-size campus.

Furthermore, Elsner had every right to kill it. The creation of South Mountain had been a flagrant affront to Elsner's authority as chancellor. Pulling the plug would serve notice to the board not to pull a stunt like that again.

Remarkably, though, Elsner chose not to withdraw his support for South Mountain.

For years before coming to Maricopa, he had been committed to the idea that the community college should serve the underserved. If the community wanted a college badly enough to storm the sacred ramparts of the governing boardroom, then he was not going to stand in their way. He was well aware, in the words of Langston Hughes, of the dangers of a dream deferred. He'd dealt with those problems before at Vista College. He had no idea yet how the district could bring it off, but somehow, South Mount Community College was going to happen.

Even so, the governing board's misconduct could not be allowed to go unanswered. A June 7, 1978, memo from Elsner to the governing board members contains the following:

> *I recall the governing board's adoption of a Code of Ethics shortly after my arrival and certain matters pertaining to Chancellor-Board relationships that I emphasized upon entering into contract with the board. I am going to assume that*

From left to right, Walt Morrison (Rio's founding president), Richard Elton (area coordinator for Sun City), Jane Freeman (Sun City resident), and Lionel Martinez (Rio's founding dean of education).

these will be the topic of my reaching some "understanding" with the board at a future work session in July, based on my assessment of some serious and potentially detrimental effects of recent board actions.

Rolling on the Rio

The new nontraditional college was expected to be up and functioning by the fall of 1978, so Walt Morrison and his crew had to scramble over the summer to make it happen. First, the main administrative positions had to be staffed.

Lionel Martinez was one of the first to come aboard. At Maricopa Tech, he was already in charge of all the off-campus programs that Rio was going to swallow up. He figured he might as well be swallowed up with them:

> So Walt called me, and I met with him. He showed me the staffing chart and the organizational chart, and I said, "I want to be the dean." He said, "I'll think about it." I knew he couldn't turn me down. Hell, I knew all the programs—I knew everybody. So, a week later, he called me, and that was it.

Martinez was appointed Rio's first dean of education and given charge of all areas represented by traditional, classroom delivery.

Rio then created a dean of alternative education to handle nonclassroom modes of instruction, and that job was given to Joyce Elsner, who actually started work about a month after Rio began offering classes. She holds a bachelor's in child development from Long Beach State College (now Cal State, Long Beach), a master's in child development and family studies from the University of Arizona, and an Ed.D. in community college administration from UCLA. For the three

years before she came to Maricopa, she was with California's Coast Community College District, where she participated in the creation of Coastline Community College (the nontraditional college that Morrison had been told to study just before he had been put to work creating Rio).

Joyce Elsner, Rio Salado and Glendale Community College administrator.

Walt Morrison recalls the overwhelming problems of starting up a new college in less than six months:

> All the problems, all the leases, all the hiring, all the staffing, computers to buy, and on and on and on . . . I didn't get a lot of sleep. But it was new, it was different. I mean the old adrenaline was up and everybody was running and it was really hectic. The district rented the second story of a building at 2300 North Central Avenue. It was an insurance company building, and we moved in. They got a college.

MIDNIGHT REQUISITIONS

Lionel Martinez recalls the difficulties of setting up the offices for Rio:

> As a system, the district moved slow. I'm talking SLOW. If you ordered a desk, maybe in six months you'd get it. It was a very slow process.
>
> Anyway, we found a place to open up our offices on North Central, and it had some desks, but we needed more office stuff. So one day, I got my pickup truck, and Walt Morrison—the president—and I went down to the district office, and we looked around, and we stole chairs. If there were four chairs, we stole one and put the other three together. Spaced them. We loaded the back of my truck at the district offices. Yes. Eleven o'clock at night.
>
> So we "relocated" some desks, chairs. Then, I still had keys to some rooms at Maricopa Tech. We needed more chairs. So, if you arranged it right, you took one or two chairs here—you didn't get greedy—and you rearranged it. People would say, "Something's different," but they wouldn't know what was different. So we furnished some offices for people, and we had a good time doing that. This went on about two weeks. We worked in the daytime, so we had to do the moving at night—and there are some respectable deans around here who worked for me at the time that helped in all of that!

By some miracle, the new college opened on schedule, and the district felt the impact almost immediately. An article in the *Scottsdale Daily Progress* for September 18, 1978, reports that districtwide enrollment was up for the fall term. The headcount for the district was about 55,600, an increase of

about 4,600 over the previous fall. The enrollment figures at all of the other district colleges were down—not surprising since Rio had siphoned off all their off-the-curb programs. However, the overall enrollment for the district was up, and therefore, Rio had fulfilled its promise of generating new enrollment.

In November, Walt Morrison appeared before the board and announced Rio's final attendance figures for the fall term. Classes were being offered at 118 different sites. A grand total of 7,950 students enrolled in academic courses, and more than 14,000 students enrolled in noncredit courses of various kinds. The most striking statistic is that 75% of these students had never before attended a community college (*Phoenix Gazette*, November 15, 1978).

New Faces of 1978

During the same time, several changes in district leadership occurred.

In June, Richard Harris, the Maricopa County Superintendent of Schools, met with Barbara Hitchcock and Bob Martinez to discuss Brooks' replacement. Harris presented six candidates he had already interviewed and invited Hitchcock and Martinez to comment. Their choice was William Schindel, a retired U.S. Army colonel living in Sun City.

Schindel had excellent credentials, including a bachelor's degree in civil engineering from the University of Pittsburgh and a law degree from Fordham University. He had served on school boards while living in Long Island, New York, and for eleven years, he had worked for Frederick P. Weldersum Associates, a New York architectural firm, for whom he had helped design and build schools. He was an ideal choice.

In the meantime, Ross Farnsworth (who had been appointed to the board back in December, 1975, to complete Dwight Patterson's term) decided not to run when that term expired at the end of 1978. In an

William Schindel, Maricopa governing board member 1978-80.

article in the *Mesa Tribune* for July 19, 1978, Farnsworth gave the following explanation for his decision. "There have been controversial and some frustrating times, but I certainly realize this goes with this kind of board, and it was not a consideration in my not running again. . . . Because I have a large family, I feel I must take care of that obligation at this time and let others serve in this capacity who have more time for it now."

When interviewed for this book, Farnsworth gave a different reason. The "inane hours" spent dealing with the student government problems at Scottsdale had worn him out:

> *If they'd have come in and said, here's a tough issue and we're faced off, and let's make that decision—okay, I could fight that through. But to sit for all those hours! It would delay a lot of things. We'd have so many nonessential long meetings or lengthened meetings because of this kind of thing . . . . I just couldn't put up with all that time and what I thought was inane talking about it.*

Dr. Grant Christensen, a prominent Mesa dentist, was elected to replace Farnsworth in January of 1979. Eventually, Christensen served two terms of service, the first from 1979 to 1985, when Phyllis Muir defeated his reelection attempt. When her term expired, he ran again and was reelected. His second term was from 1989 through 1995.

September 5, 1996, video interview with Ross Farnsworth, Maricopa governing board member 1975-79. Transcript available online.

http://www.mc.maricopa.edu/users/M3cdhistory/

January, 1979. Paul Elsner thanks Ross Farnsworth (left) for his term of service to the Maricopa district.

January, 1979. Maricopa governing board president Bob Robertson (right) administers the oath of office to Grant Christensen, Maricopa governing board member 1979-84 and 1989-95.

Helena Howe, president of Mesa Community College, 1974-78.

In addition to the changes on the board, two other changes in leadership also took place in 1978. Helena Howe, who had replaced John Riggs as president of Mesa in 1974, took a year's leave of absence to work at the Department of Health, Education and Welfare in Washington, DC. She eventually stayed there, and in 1979, Theo Heap became Mesa's third president.

Also, the board named Dr. Raúl Cárdenas as South Mountain's founding president. Cárdenas is a native of Del Rio, Texas. He earned his bachelor's degree in education from Saint Mary's University in San Antonio and began teaching in a junior high school in Del Rio. Two years later, he moved to El Paso and taught in a junior high school there while he worked on his master's degree at the University of Texas at El Paso. In 1971, Cárdenas became the registrar at El Paso Community College, where he remained for five years and started on his doctorate at the University of Arizona on a Ford Fellowship. In 1976, he became the vice chancellor for student affairs at UC Berkeley, the position he held when he was tapped for the presidency at South Mountain.

Theo Heap, president of Mesa Community College, 1978-84.

Raúl Cárdenas, president of South Mountain Community College 1978-1999 and Paradise Valley Community College 1992 to 1999.

The intention was to name him well in advance of the college's anticipated start in the fall of 1980, so that he could participate in all the preliminary planning. Also, Elsner correctly anticipated that the new college would be a hard sell to the state board, and Cárdenas would be needed as Elsner's point man on that team:

> Paul and I went to a meeting in Tucson, and we made our presentation as to what it was we wanted to do at South. The board was not very pleased to see us. There were some members on the board who felt that there was no need for a college in that area. They said it was duplicating services, it should never exist, and so on. . . . One of the things they told me was, "You have to go back there and really show community support. You need an

advisory committee." So I said, "Okay. I'll go find an advisory committee to help me."

As events would develop, that advisory committee eventually saved the project and set a very important precedent for the development of future colleges in the district.

A Quality War

During the summer, the faculty regrouped its forces, and as Rio began its first fall term, opposition to the upstart college heated up again. For district faculty at other colleges, the issue was the quality of the courses being offered. When interviewed for this book, Glendale faculty member Chuck West explained, "What we were concerned with, and what I was concerned with, was the quality of the education being delivered through Rio Salado. . . . We were concerned that the reputation of our students would be damaged when they went to the university, and maybe they would stop accepting credits, this type of thing." Glendale faculty member Gene Eastin agreed. "We perceived that the quality of the classes was not as good as ours. The teachers that were hired, the visiting staff to teach these, were not as good teachers as we."

Walt Morrison found that suggestion infuriating:

> When the same people were teaching the same classes in Mesa the year before, they

were good. When they came over and signed a Rio contract, all of a sudden they were scabs, they were dumb—over the summer they had lost their mental capacity to teach! Good Lord. I mean, when they signed a contract that didn't say Mesa on it, they were fundamentally unsound. The department chairmen right here on this campus had gone out and done their evaluations and given them high marks. Okay? And six months later, they were brain-dead! It hurt a lot at the time.

Rio attempted to answer some of the district critics directly, but the results were not entirely successful. Ted Humphrey, the chair of ASU's philosophy department, was invited to evaluate Rio's philosophy department. Unfortunately, he concluded that 51 courses should not have been offered and the credentials of five of the instructors were suspect.

March 12, 1996, video interview with Raúl Cárdenas, president of South Mountain Community College 1978-92 and president of Paradise Valley Community College 1992 to 1999. Transcript and audio excerpts available online.

http://www.mc.maricopa.edu/users/M3cdhistory/

Then, the *Arizona Republic* for November 17, 1978, revealed that a student reporter for the Glendale Community College student newspaper, *El Tiempo Pasando*, had attended a Rio philosophy class called Selected Problems of Religion. The instructor was the Reverend Oliver Swaim of the First Assembly of God Church in Mesa. The Reverend Swaim's section was subtitled "The Work of the Holy Spirit." The article went on to state:

> *[The student reporter] said he identified himself to Swaim as a reporter and pro-*

Is This A College?

THE Maricopa County Community College District was leading with its chin when it decided to open "a college without walls," sometimes known as an "alternative college."

The idea was to produce an informal institution that ignored such subjects as Latin, medieval history and trigonometry. Higher education would be taken to the people, with classes being held in empty stores, church lounges and other available spots.

The decision led to the creation of the Rio Salado Community College, named for a non-existent river and offering a curriculum that apparently falls short of accepted standards.

There was a recognized danger in throwing out structured curricula. Standards might well be lowered. But the district board decided to run the risk. That decision is now being scrutinized.

Recently Dr. Ted Humphrey, chairman of the philosophy department at Arizona State University, was asked to evaluate the courses should not be offered, and that five instructors hired to teach philosophy classes had not submitted resumes that would allow a determination of their qualifications.

Then it developed that a minister was preaching religion under cover of a course in philosophy. No one knows what will be revealed next about the "alternative college."

The idea of universal education, government sponsored, is one of the propositions on which the United States was founded. Certainly everyone should be offered as much education as he or she can absorb.

But it is folly to lower collegiate standards in order to achieve this goal. And it is even greater folly to breach the constitutional wall between church and state by turning philosophy classes into religious exercises.

Obviously the board, the administration and the faculty of the county's community district should take

Arizona Republic, *November 20, 1978.*

quickly shifted to a television course that had been developed by Mesa instructor Robert W. Smith, then the chair of Mesa Community College's philosophy department. The course was entitled Philosophies of World Religions, for which Smith had authored a series of six booklets under the collective title *The Bits of Silver Series*. Again, Ted Humphrey was hired to review the books and the videotapes. At the end of February, 1979, Humphrey issued a report to the board. According to an article in the *Arizona Republic* for April 12, 1979, Humphrey concluded the books "fail to use standard scholarly techniques of reference, acknowledgment and permission," a polite way of accusing Smith of flagrant plagiarism. The district's embarrassment was acute. The books were immediately pulled at Rio and at Mesa, but once again, Rio sustained a black eye.

Meanwhile, Ron Kearns, a history teacher at Scottsdale Community College and one of

Arizona Republic, *December 18, 1978.*

ceeded to tape the class. Not only were prayers said, but personal testimony of religious experiences were related by at least three members of the class. . . . "It didn't seem like a philosophy class, but a religious service," he said.

Alarmed, the Maricopa district's philosophy instructional council then met to examine the Rio courses. A representative from the ACLU was called in, and the judgment was that Swaim's class probably violated state and federal laws prohibiting the establishment of religion. The issue was further clouded because the class was being taught at the Reverend

Swaim's church and the church was receiving a fee from Rio for hosting the class there. The class was subsequently discontinued, but Rio's critics were far from satisfied.

In December of 1978, the governing board formed a committee to investigate religious studies offered by Rio, and the focus

Rio Salado barbs show district's ills, faculty leaders say

By ART GISSENDANER

When Rio Salado Community College opened its doors this past fall, it was thrust into the role of the much maligned stepchild of the Maricopa County Community College District.

District administrators steadfastly have defended the "college without walls" concept, saying that criticism — the most damaging of which has come from faculty members — has been unfair.

Faculty leaders who have been most critical say they are not opposed to the college's concept, but say their complaints are symptomatic of longstanding district ills that have festered into a "cold war" between the faculty and administration.

Both groups agree there is a serious lack of communication within the district. Administrators say conditions are improving, but some faculty leaders say conditions are getting progressively worse.

The crux, teachers say, is that the administration consistently has failed to seek faculty views before making decisions that directly affect the faculty.

Televised MCCCD Class Called 'Flim-flam job'

A televised history course offered by Rio Salado Community College is a "flim-flam job" and threatens the reputation of junior colleges, a Scottsdale Community College teacher charged today.

Ron Kearns, an SCC history teacher, said ne is considering filing suit to stop the Maricopa County Community College District from offering the three-credit-hour televised Rio Salado history course.

The course, United States History, is broadcast in two half-hour segments each week over a commercial Phoenix television station.

Kearns teaches a three-hour U.S. history course at SCC. Students are required to attend three 50-minute class periods a week, he said.

The television course is "of questionable historical significance" and should only be a one-credit class, Kearns said.

"It's shameful for an educational institution taking state money and putting on something like this and calling it education," Kearns said. "I really think this is destructive and I really think that it's against everything the (state) Legislature is interested in and that's quality education."

Kearns, chairman of the MCCCD History Instructional Council, said administrators sidestepped the council and offered the course without its approval, which is a breach of district policy. The council was not even told the course would be offered, he said.

Kearns said the quality of the Rio Salado course does not compare with the three-credit U.S. history course he teaches.

"The (Rio Salado) students are given workbooks and assignments, but they are told they don't have to hand them in," he said.

"And I think the students are being tricked into thinking they are getting the equivalent of a three-hour course," he said.

Kearns said he is not opposed to radio and television classes, but "it has to be done so its credibility isn't threatened like this."

Kearns is among a number of SCC faculty members who are concerned about the quality of radio and television courses being offered by Rio Salado, the Maricopa County college-without-walls created by the MCCCD board last year. Many faculty members, however, are reluctant to make public their criticism.

A common faculty complaint is that courses for Rio Salado are being approved by administrators without consulting faculty members.

Jane McGrath, an SCC reading teacher, said faculty members learned Rio Salado had proposed offering academic survival skills and memory and concentration classes over radio or television next fall without consulting faculty members.

But the MCCCD Reading and Instructional Council, composed of faculty members representing all MCCCD campuses, met Thursday with administrators, she said.

"I was assured yesterday that nothing would be done without the knowledge and approval of the instructional council," McGrath said. "Fortunately, our problem has been solved."

Walt Morrison, president of Rio Salado, said the televised history course was approved by an instructional council 10 years ago.

He said the course is of equal quality to a history course taught in a classroom.

Rio Salado can offer any course — in a classroom or on radio or television — that has been approved by district instructional councils, he said.

The college, however, would have to seek approval from a council if it proposed modifying or creating a course, Morrison said. Offering the history course over television does not constitute a modification of the class, he said.

"The way the material has been delivered has never been a concern of the instructional councils, at least not up until this point," he said.

Rio Salado has six college-credit radio and television courses this spring. Enrollment in the courses totals 750 students and more students are expected to enroll, a Rio Salado spokesman said.

Rio Salado this spring has 6,119 full- and part-time students, but more students are expected to register. Officials had projected that the college would have 20,000 students this spring.

Scottsdale Daily Progress, January 26, 1979.

---

the godfathers of the Artichoke movement, announced that he was planning to sue the district to stop Rio from offering a television course called United States History. The course required students to view two half-hour television segments per week. According to an article in the *Scottsdale Daily Progress* for January 26, 1979, Kearns thought students were being ripped off because he taught the same course at Scottsdale, where students were required to attend three fifty-minute lectures per week. According to Kearns, "The (Rio Salado) students are given workbooks and assignments, but they are told they don't have to hand them in. . . . And I think the students are being tricked into thinking they are getting the equivalent of a three-hour course."

Similar controversies soon turned Rio's faculty and staff into district pariahs. Walt Morrison well remembers how he became a Wanted Man: "People that knew me wouldn't even talk to me. It got pretty hairy. It was not a fun time.

Oh, yeah. Hell, people I used to go out and have a beer with wouldn't even talk to me."

Inevitably, Rio staffers began to suffer from a siege mentality. Rio staff member Ken Roberts called it the Rio Syndrome. When Joyce Elsner heard him use that term for the first time, she asked him to explain:

I said, "Ken, what do you mean? What's that?" He'd cross his arms across his chest, and say, "When people ask you, 'How are things at Rio?' you go, 'Why do you want to know?!' And the body language says, 'Why do you want to know?' as well as your voice." We found that we did do that. You'd go to a district meeting and you went with your guard up. . . . It took the organization some time to work that out because of the intensity of the feeling.

April 18, 1997, audio interview with Joyce Elsner, Rio Salado and Glendale Community College administrator. Transcript available online.

Ambush

Throughout the spring term, district faculty made angry speeches at board meetings and circulated petitions urging Rio be shut down.

The climax of the organized faculty opposition occurred on the night of April 24, 1979—a confrontation that marked a major turning point in the history of the Maricopa district as a whole.

Ken Roberts and Lionel Martinez tell the story better than anyone else:

ROBERTS: There was a core of very, very vocal faculty that were making appearances at the board, really chastising the board and Dr. Elsner about starting Rio because of this lack of quality. Lionel got word that there would be a contingent at

> "You'd go to a district meeting and you went with your guard up."

http://www.mc.maricopa.edu/users/M3cdhistory/

the board, an organized contingent, to really make an aggressive criticism on quality.

MARTINEZ: Al Flowers called them the "rump group" out of Glendale Community College.[1] Chuck West and his group. So, I made a number of calls. I called in about fifty markers that night. I had some good

April 11, 1996, video interview with Ken Roberts and Lionel Martinez. Transcript and audio excerpts available online.

http://www.mc.maricopa.edu/users/M3cdhistory/

area deans, and I told them what I wanted. I said, "I want people that will stir you emotionally." I called the mayor of Guadalupe, José Linares was his name, at that time. I said, "Have we done you good?" He said, "Oh, hell, yeah, Marty. You have." I said, "Have we served your people?" "Yeah." I said, "I need you to say some stuff." "I'll be there."

ROBERTS: Then Lionel went to talk to Joanie Thomas, the board secretary, and told her he needed some help because he had people coming to talk that were old, and disabled, and tired, and coming off shifts, and really couldn't stay late, so we needed to show them courtesy and let them speak first. So, Lionel got all the citizens' interim cards, got all his speakers' cards arranged, and—plop—they were on top of a stack that must have been a foot tall. So the first speaker was an old gentleman—I still remember him—in a walker. Must have been eighty-five or ninety. Walked up to the microphone and really thanked the board for Rio providing him with education that he didn't have access

before. He was taking courses, and it saved his life. Then off he would go, and then an elderly couple up in a wheelchair. She had taken a sewing class, I think, at one of the high schools, in their home ec class, and made her husband a jacket, and was crying that night at her sense of pride of learning how to sew, at her age, and made her husband a jacket, and she was crying. Then off she would go, and disabled people would come up. There was just wave after wave of people that you couldn't refute. You really couldn't criticize the quality of instruction, given how important it was to them in their lives. That went on until one o'clock in the morning.

MARTINEZ: José Linares went a little bit far. He said, "And Mesa Community College never [did anything for us]! And no other damn college [ever did anything for us]! And then, there was Rio!"

ROBERTS: And the Glendale people were sitting there paralyzed. You could certainly not make a scene with this old gentleman talking about how it saved his life. You couldn't stand up and say, "But I don't care." So . . .

MARTINEZ: There were people from Guadalupe who were there that night, and said, "It's the first time we have service."

ROBERTS: Yeah. "The first time we've ever had a college."

MARTINEZ: I remember the dean at

Phoenix College, Bill Wallace. He said, "Hey, Marty, how much did you pay them?" I said, "Not a damn thing, Bill." It was beautiful, especially when that lady started crying. In fact, I almost cried too. But she was sincere, and that was the most important thing.

As is the case with most stories of the Good Old Days, the details of this story seem to have improved with age, but the substance of the story is corroborated by an article in the *Mesa Tribune* for April 25, 1979:

> During public testimony, a three-hour parade of Rio Salado supporters, including senior citizens, handicapped persons and part-time teachers praised the college's efforts to offer programs in the community that had not been available before. The school was credited with providing education for those who before had no opportunity to take classes because of transportation problems. Vennie Reylea, a visually impaired woman explained that the dress she wore and the outfit her blind husband Mel had on were made by her in a Rio Salado sewing class for the sightless. Toby Stubbs, a Honeywell employee who teaches at Rio Salado, said providing courses taught by working professionals rather than by theorists gives a new dimension to the education. He said he resents implications that part-time teachers are inferior.

Thus, the faculty attempt to ambush Rio at the board meeting failed. It was a minor victory at best, and the complaints against Rio did not go away, but the tide of resistance had been turned. Rio was here to stay.

---

[1] The reference is to the notorious Rump Parliament, the members of the House of Commons who remained after Oliver Cromwell had forcibly removed his dissenters; this group then brought about the execution of Charles I in 1649.

The Notorious T-Shirts

Unfortunately, a regrettable incident nearly spoiled Rio's moment of triumph. Lionel Martinez, Walt Morrison, Joyce Elsner, and Jan Baltzer all recall the events:

MARTINEZ: Mr. Robertson, the governing board member, made a comment. He was at a meeting somewhere with ASU, and he was quoted in the ASU paper, the State Press. He said, "Rio Salado's just a pain in the ass." Those were his words. They were in sub-headlines. So we were very offended about that. Our first anniversary was coming up. The troops were down. Everybody was putting in sixteen, seventeen hours a day, six and seven days a week. Nobody was bitching about it, but we were getting tired.

MORRISON: And they all said, "Hey, it's our anniversary. We passed our first year. We deserve a party." So I said, "Well, okay. Sounds like a winner to me. We need to blow off some steam and pat ourselves on the back and all that sort of thing. Okay. I can go for that. I've got a good-sized townhouse. Fair. Some room in the back for a patio area. Behind the wall. That kind of thing. I'll throw some beer in the thing, and some pop, and buy some ice, and get some whatevers, and we'll just go over and visit and lie to each other and tell ourselves how great we are and all that stuff."

ELSNER: So we said, "Okay. We really should do something obscene." See if we could get everybody up again because we were just exhausted. So I said, "Ken, we need a T-shirt. We'll get everybody a T-shirt." We cooked up the slogan.

MORRISON: It sort of became an everybody-was-coming-in-uniform kind of thing. Anyway, administration in the district was told, "Come on down," or invited to come.

Board member Barbara Hitchcock then came to the party with her husband. As she recalls, she was the only governing board member who attended. When she arrived, she discovered everybody wearing a T-shirt proclaiming, "YOU BET YOUR ASS! RIO'S GOT CLASS! (AND FTSE TOO!)"

ELSNER: We thought we were coming to a beer bust. Then, of course, we couldn't take them off—that would be more obscene!

MORRISON: Shortly thereafter, Paul called me in, and he had a complaint. . . . Elsner said, "That's not what you should have done as a college president. You shouldn't even have gone. If they go off and do that sort of stuff, well, as the college president, you're not supposed to be a part of it." Well, one thing led to another, and I told him, "Well, it's my team. If I'm not part of it, I shouldn't even be on it." And from that time on, my fat was kind of in the fire.

Photo of the Rio T-Shirt.

Exhaustion is blamed

Rio Salado College president quits

By BEVERLY MEDLYN

Walt Morrison, Rio Salado Community College's founding president, has resigned because of exhaustion.

"It's basically a case of burnout and exhaustion, which is pretty common for college presidents who start up institutions," said Paul Elsner, Maricopa County Community College District chancellor.

Lionel Martinez, dean of education at Rio Salado, will serve as acting president. A national search will be launched for a new president, and Elsner said he hopes to hire someone within two to three months.

Morrisn founded the controversial "college without walls" in August 1978. Since then, he has had to defend the concept of alternative education to legislators and to faculty members employed at other schools within the district.

He submitted his resignation Friday. After talking with board members over the weekend, Elsner accepted it Monday, effective immediately. Morrison was placed on administrative leave with pay, at a $39,000 annual salary, until he returns to classroom teaching in January at Mesa Community College.

Morrison said through a district spokesman Monday he had no comment. Employees who work with him said the resignation surprised them, but added that they had noticed his fatigue in recent months.

Morrisn was called before the House and Senate education committees in August to defend the need for the college, which operates without a campus. At that meeting, faculty members from other colleges who had previously criticized Rio Salado surprised committee members by saying they supported the school because of changes that had been made.

Some legislators and faculty members believed the school's mission could be accomplished through existing district colleges. Since then, some of Rio Salado's courses have been reassigned to other colleges.

Arizona Republic, October 16, 1979.

BALTZER: It was very frightening, and those of us who were responsible for the T-shirts felt very badly and didn't quite know what to do. You've got to remember, too, that most of us were a whole lot younger than we are now. And we really had not intended any disrespect or intended to offend anybody. We really didn't intend anybody but us to see them. We were pretty bloodied. It was pretty bloody by that time.

Eventually, Paul Elsner decided that even though Rio was a nontraditional college, it needed a more traditional president. Lionel Martinez remembers the ax fell around the middle of October, 1979:

MARTINEZ: I was working one day. It was about four or five in the evening. Walt said, "You stay here until I get back. Paul wants to see me." So he left to see Paul at four o'clock, whatever time the appointment was, and I waited. I thought, "Oh, damn, I'm going to have to be here a couple hours at least," and so I hung around, and

he was back in about forty-five minutes. He was crying. He had tears in his eyes. I said, "Walt, what's the matter?" He wouldn't talk to me. He said, "Paul wants to see you." He walked out to his car and left, and so I went to see Paul, and Paul told me that he had let Walt go, and that he wanted me to take over as the acting president.

Thus, Rio's survival was a bittersweet victory, but the impact of Rio Salado College on the whole direction of the district was clear. After the night when the community had turned out *en masse* and held the board captive for three hours to lavish praise on the upstart college, everyone could see that the district was evolving in new directions. As Ken Roberts explained:

That night, there was the beginning of a shift—not only in mission but in modality. We still had a junior college mission, but that night we really began looking at alternatives—compressed courses, courses in the middle of the night, distance deliv-

ery. . . . But that night really defused public, organized criticism of Rio. I mean, it still persisted, certainly. It still does today. But never as organized or as public, I don't think, since that night.

Lionel Martinez remained as Rio's acting president until Myrna Harrison became Rio's next president in 1980.

1979

Board Will Build New College Without Bonds

The Maricopa Community Colleges Award has voted unanimously not to seek voter approval in November of a proposed $25 million bond issue, but does intend to begin development and construction of South Mountain Community College.

The bond issue would have included site acquisition and construction of the South Phoenix campus with $11 million of the bond money in the next two...

accumulate $7 million in capital funds in the next two years for some construction.

The board agreed that at this time it would be best to follow a "pay as we go plan" for the initial phases of South Mountain Community College, recognizing that this would eliminate any construction at the other campuses at this time.

FLOWERS SAID the district has $1.5 million in capital funds and...

This $5.5 million would be used to buy a site and start classroom construction with the $2 million in revenue bonds earmarked for a student center and parking lot facilities.

Chancellor Paul Elsner indicated that the district could put up some relocatable classroom buildings, but Flowers noted that these might not be well received in South Phoenix. Flowers said he will sug...

part of the student center could be used for classrooms.

South Mountain is scheduled to start classes by the fall of 1980.

Flowers told board members it would be possible to pass a $25 million bond issue and not raise the tax rate due to bonded indebtedness.

Board member Ross Farnsworth...

that building and land are going to go up in two years — but to jump into a bond issue now without adequate time for educating the public who are going to vote on it is unwise."

HE SUGGESTED a formal citizens review committee to examine the long-range and short range goals of the district and make a recommendation to the board before...

20 to... years climat... Gann... make... year,... lot to... now."

Clif... ber of... munit... told... that "... ing b... kind...

Chapter Seventeen

1979

The *Insurrection* and *What Followed*

While the battle over Rio Salado raged on during the 1978-79 school year, Elsner managed to keep a low profile. His attention seemed to be focused primarily on two other problems: planning a defensive strategy against the looming threat of taxpayer revolt, and figuring some way to pay for the newly created South Mountain Community College without running a bond election.

Defensive strategy was necessary because the annual inflation rate was accelerating, exceeding 10% for the first time in 1978. Partly as a result, Arizona taxpayer groups were beginning to agitate for property tax reform along the lines of California's notorious Proposition 13, a grassroots initiative which the voters had approved in June, 1977, by a margin of two to one. Overnight, property tax rates in California had been capped at 1% of assessed valuation and rolled back to 1975-76 levels. Statewide, property tax revenues fell by an estimated $6.1 billion—a reduction of about 53%. Proposition 13 further limited any future tax increases to no more than 2% annually and required such tax

Phoenix Gazette, August 30, 1978.

Fall, 1978, Maricopa governing board members (left to right) William Schindel, Bob Robertson, and Barbara Hitchcock. The other board members that year were Ross Farnsworth (replaced by Grant Christensen in January, 1979) and Bob Martinez.

increases to be authorized by two-thirds of the legislature.

The taxpayers sang hosannas, but the state's educators wept openly. Today, many people feel that California schools have never fully recovered from that blow.

Fearing some kind of copycat initiative in Arizona, Elsner began taking a hard look at how the district had been raising its property tax rate every year. At the board meeting on June 20, 1978, the board began considering some economies to try to reduce the need for further increases. A little liposuction on the operating budget produced $1 million in savings, but Flowers quickly transferred that money to the district's capital budget (*Phoenix Gazette*, June 21, 1978). At the meeting on July 18, the board removed another $1 million by economizing on the district's computer budget over the next three years. No more fat remained to be trimmed.

On July 25, Carolyn Warner, Arizona's superintendent of public instruction, delivered more bad news: Over the next two years, Arizona was going to have to spend about $25 million to bring Arizona schools into compliance with the 1973 federal mandate requiring all federally-funded programs not to discriminate against the handicapped. The state had until 1980 to comply. The result promised to be $25 million less for school

operating funds during the next three years.

The fall attendance figures helped a little. Thanks in large measure to Rio, district FTSE was up about 500 to an estimated 29,458 for the 1978 fall term, a number worth an additional half a million dollars in state aid. Escalating inflation, however, effectively neutralized the impact of this increase in state funds. Indeed, increased enrollment was a mixed blessing because the district's facilities were already being strained to the breaking point. South Mountain was not the only capital improvement project that the district needed at that time.

Taxpayer revolt was beginning to make its presence felt in Arizona. The district would simply have to find other ways to pay for its capital improvements.

Then, Elsner's own consultants presented him with another unanticipated expense. Arthur Aschauer and Company completed its study comparing administrative job categories and staff salary levels to similar categories and salaries in other schools nationally. The report recommended a total of $98,000 in salary increases and $182,000 in increased fringe benefits for 103 administrators. The November 15 issue of the *Arizona Republic* suggested the board's response was tepid at best.

For a while, Elsner flirted with the idea of risking a bond election, but then came the chilling news that in Kingman, Arizona, the voters had turned down the Mojave Community College District's request for a paltry $9.5 million bond. Taxpayer revolt was beginning to make its presence felt in Arizona. The district would simply have to find other ways to pay for its capital improvements.

That money would be added to $3.5 million in cash reserves that the district had already realized from previously announced austerities, plus interest earned on those reserves and other district funds. The grand total amounted to approximately $22 million.

Sadly, that money would not be enough to fund a full-size campus for South Mountain. The *Republic* reported:

> The largest project proposed was construction of a "scaled down" South Mountain Community College. Plans originally called for construction of a $14.5 million to $16 million college that

would house 2,500 full-time day students. The current plan would cut enrollment in half and cost the district $8.4 million. That figure would include land acquisition, construction, and purchase of operating equipment. "Should South Mountain not have the ability to generate 2,000 to 3,000 full-time students, we would cap off that phase and go no further," Elsner said.

All of this fiscal belt-tightening played well in the press, but the threat of a Proposition 13-style initiative in Arizona still weighed heavily on Elsner's mind. The original junior col-

MCCCD Board OKs freezing budget

A resolution not to spend "one dollar more" in 1979-80 than this year's $49.1 million budget was approved unanimously last night by the Maricopa County Community College District Board.

Dr. Paul Elsner, MCCCD chancellor, said the proposed hold-the-line budget is in reaction to the tax-cutting mood created by California's Proposition 13 and President Carter's proposed "austere" $532 billion federal budget.

Board president William Schindel said the district's property tax rate of 87 cents per $100 assessed valuation should not increase if the budget is frozen at this year's level.

Scottsdale Community College and other district faculty members would get cost-of-living raises next year under the proposed budget, but they

would not advance along salary schedules, Schindel said.

The district offered $1,000 cost-of-living increases for faculty members earning $14,000 or less and $950 pay increases for those making more than $14,000.

The faculty last week [...]

Ron Bush, vice chancellor for employee relations, said today, however, the wage offer is more than the 1.5-percent increase claimed by the faculty.

Employees [...] or less would [...] ary increase, [...] than $14,000, [...] percent, he [...] about it (the [...] great deal of [...] Bush said. [...] he proposed [...]-s will try to [...] ercent by

Phoenix Gazette for January 30, 1979.

Scottsdale Daily Progress for January 31, 1979.

Elsner and Flowers went to work and somehow managed to produce a capital improvement budget without a bond election. According to an article in the *Arizona Republic* on January 17, 1979, the district would issue $4.2 million in revenue bonds, which would underwrite some new construction. That money would be added to the district's expected annual capital fund money from the state ($135 per FTSE, or about $3.5 million).

Maricopa College Head Pledges No Budget Hike

Phx Gazette 1/30/79

Maricopa Community Colleges Chancellor Paul Elsner today said he is recommending that the district not increase its operational budget next year.

"I will be recommending to the board tonight that we not increase the current $49.1 million operations budget one penny next year, although we are expecting a 3 to 4 percent increase in students and have had a 9 to 10 percent inflationary rate," Elsner said.

"We are going to do with what we've got," Elsner emphasized.

If current expenses were left intact, "it would cost us $4 million to $5 million more next year," he said.

DISTRICT ENROLLMENT increased from 48,000 to 56,000 this year and "we expect well over 60,000 students next year," he said.

Although it is too early to project what effect the "hold the line budget" [...] have on the tax rate, he said "it

justment for all employees below $14,000 and a $950 increase for all employees above $14,000," he said.

He said the faculty representatives have not formally responded to the offer, but have requested more budget information. Elsner said he expects some negative reaction to the proposal.

"But it's not as if we were holding the budget and freezing salaries, he said. "We're offering a cost-of-living adjustment. It's a solid offer."

Recommendations for budget guidelines Elsner said he will propose to the board at 7 tonight are:

● Cutback of administration overhead expenses by "3 to 4 percent," which will mean consolidation of administrative positions and reassigning of some duties.

● Eliminate duplication in some administrative functions.

lege legislation had intended that half of the junior colleges' annual funding should come from the state, but the state's share had shrunk to somewhere around one-quarter. Thus, the colleges were dependent on property taxes for nearly two-thirds of their budget. A Proposition 13 in Arizona would have surgically removed about a third of the community colleges' funding. The result would have been a catastrophe—everything the faculty feared most: low-enrollment programs would have been canceled, class sizes would have been increased, and even some full-time faculty would have been fired.

Consequently, Elsner thought long and hard about the district's operating budget for the following fiscal year and made a bold decision: instead of risking the end of the world by raising the property tax rate again, he would freeze the operational budget for the following year. In an article in the *Phoenix Gazette* for January 30, Elsner acknowledged his fear of a Proposition 13 on the November, 1980 ballot. He refused to promise that a stable budget would mean the tax rate would stay the same (because of inflation), but at least, everyone could see that the district was doing its best to slow the rate of annual tax increases. At the same time, he would increase the portion of the budget allocated for faculty salaries to provide "economic adjustments" that amounted to an average salary increase of 6% for all faculty.

The plan was sound—maybe even brilliant—but if Elsner had been expecting the faculty to applaud, he should have known better. Twice before, he had failed to calculate the effect of his announcements on the faculty. The first time had been his ill-conceived "FTSE's the name of the game!" speech. The second time had been his surprise announce-ment of the new college-without-wall-or-full-time-faculty. The third time was a charm. As chronicled in chapter one, Elsner's announcement ignited open faculty rebellion.

However, the district's capital plan did win a favorable reception at the state board. The *Arizona Republic* on March 4, 1979, explained that the state board had decided that the south Phoenix population couldn't support a full-size campus, but Elsner's South Mountain Lite plan had more appeal.

In spite of faculty outrage, the governing board went ahead on March 13 and voted to implement the Aschauer study recommendations. The next day, the *Phoenix Gazette* reported on the board's action and noted how angry faculty members had directed their fury at Rio, which by then had become a symbol for everything faculty thought was wrong with the district. About 250 people, most of them faculty members, were present. Eleven faculty members had addressed the board directly, unanimously characterizing Rio Salado as unnecessary, expensive, and the reason for the deteriorating quality of education in the district. Faculty members criticized a change in direction away from traditional academic and vocational courses, the 20% increase of administrative support personnel while decreasing full-time faculty, increases in part-time faculty, administrative decisions made without consulting faculty, and insufficient pay increases for faculty.

On March 17, 1979, the *Arizona Republic* carried the news that the state board's ad hoc committee studying South Mountain had decided to recommend the state board approve the creation of the south Phoenix college, but with an insulting stipulation:

An ad hoc committee on Friday approved the concept of South Mountain Community College but slapped a two-year moratorium on construction of permanent buildings at the south Phoenix facility. The committee, whose members also serve on the state Board of Directors of Community Colleges, voted 3-2 to recommend the campus to the full board today. The development restriction was presented in a motion by Joe Almar, Yuma County representative to the board. He said the two-year incubation period would give the state board a chance to assess student use of the campus before authorizing investments in permanent facilities. He said it would hedge against possible cuts in state funds for community colleges.

In other words, only portable classroom buildings were authorized for the first two years—a clear vote of no confidence in the college's future. Raúl Cárdenas, South Mountain's president, heard what the ad hoc committee had decided and called an emergency meeting of the community advisory committee he had formed several months before. Cárdenas recalls:

I said, "Look, folks. First of all, they're not going to meet here. So those of you who live in this area, we need to first make a good showing, so we're going to have to travel all the way to Casa Grande [1] to do that. Second, we need to let the majority leader of the House and the Senate know that, indeed, there are some issues. Maybe they can get to the governor, and see if the governor can do something about getting people to move on this."

To make a long story short, come Saturday morning, I would venture to say

---

[1] Casa Grande is more than an hour's drive south of Phoenix.

that the state board was really shocked . . . to see all the people from the south Phoenix area in the audience. By then, as I understand it, the governor had already made some phone calls because he had appointed some of the board members.

The account of the meeting in the *Arizona Republic* on March 18, 1979, confirms that the meeting was packed, and even some local political celebrities had driven down to Casa Grande to support the new school:

"The Maricopa County Community College District has worked out a way to finance South Mountain," said [Phoenix City Councilman Calvin Goode]. "I hope you will heed what that board has recommended to you.". . . South Phoenix citizens complained that the portable-building clause would inject an element of failure into plans for the college. . . . The resolution to approve the college was amended gradually through the course of discussion until only a clause requiring committee review of construction projects remained.

The final go-ahead for South Mountain only intensified the faculty's fury. On March 25, 1979, the *Arizona Republic* described the final confrontation with the governing board:

Wearing red armbands and carrying placards, more than 250 angry Maricopa County Community College School District

College board OKs South Mountain plan: building ban rejected

By SUSAN CAREY

COOLIDGE — The state Board of Directors of Community Colleges Saturday approved without restrictions establishment of South Mountain Community College.

Conceptual approval, which came at the board's monthly meeting at Central Arizona College, gives the Maricopa County Community College District the go-ahead for its seventh campus.

Responding to a vocal coalition of south Phoenix residents and legislators, the board threw out a proposed two-year moratorium on permanent buildings at the south Phoenix campus. The site for the school has not been selected.

The building restriction was part of a resolution approved Friday by an ad hoc committee of state board members studying the college. It was presented to the full board Saturday.

Joe Atmar, Yuma County representative to the board, introduced the restriction because he said the need for the college has to be demonstrated before an investment in permanent structures is made. He also said the moratorium will be a safeguard against possible legislative cutbacks in community college funding.

Opposition to the building restriction was overwhelming.

Sen. Alfredo Gutierrez, D-Phoenix, pointed out that the state board already has the authority to review, revise or reject construction plans submitted by community colleges.

"An immense amount of control is already built into your system," he told the board. "To further place a restriction is unnecessary in terms of your concerns."

Phoenix City Councilman Calvin Goode concurred. "The Maricopa County Community College District has worked out a way to finance South Mountain," he said. "I hope you will heed what that board has recommended to you."

The building restriction was part of a resolution approved Friday by an ad hoc committee of state board members studying the college. It was presented to the full board Saturday.

Joe Atmar, Yuma County representative to the board, introduced the

Arizona Republic, March 18, 1979.

faculty members demanded higher salary increases at a district board meeting Tuesday. But after several hours of emotional arguments, the board voted 4-1 to retain its original plan on salary hikes. Bob Robertson cast the only dissenting vote.

Outraged faculty demanded action. But what to do? As explained in chapter one, a strike was out of the question. The faculty looked around for some kind of higher authority to whom they could appeal for justice, someone or something with sufficient power to force the district to come to its senses. The courts? No, the district had already crushed the students when they had sued back in 1972. The

state legislature? Hardly. The lawmakers were behind Elsner all the way.

And then, almost miraculously, the faculty's prayers were answered: The accreditation team from the North Central Association was scheduled to arrive for the first of the two-year follow-up visits mandated by the 1977 accreditation report. From April 9-11, the team members would be in Phoenix, and they clearly had

Phoenix Gazette for March 28, 1979.

Faculty Fails In Protesting College Raises

By LORI RABINOWITZ
Gazette Reporter

Wearing red armbands and carrying placards, more than 250 angry Maricopa County Community College School District faculty members demanded higher salary increases at a district board meeting Tuesday.

But after several hours of emotional arguments, the board voted 4-1 to retain its original plan on salary hikes. Bob Robertson cast the only dissenting vote.

UNDER THE PLAN, faculty members earning less than $14,000 annually will receive a $1,000 raise and those making $14,000 and more will receive a $950 raise.

The district's program would boost salaries 4.8 percent on the average. The faculty was seeking a 10.5 percent hike.

District officials said a confrontation by teachers at a board meeting has not occurred for several years on as large a scale as it did Tuesday night.

THE BOARD RESPONDED to the faculty's criticism by cutting speakers short — an action which brought repeated hostile remarks from the audi

College Teachers Protest Salaries For Visiting Accreditation Team

By LORI RABINOWITZ
Gazette Reporter

A four-foot-high wooden tombstone was erected today near the Glendale Community College administration building to dramatize the faculty's concerns over salaries and district administrators.

The tombstone is meant to be displayed for members of the Interim Review Committee of the North Central Association of Colleges and Schools. The accreditation agency is making a periodic visit today to GCC as well as to Mesa Community College and Phoenix College. The purpose is to investigate concerns expressed by faculty members and others at the colleges.

THE ACCREDITATION agency usually visits colleges every six years unless there are special problems warranting a two-year interim visit. Two years ago it was reported that there were complaints about the Maricopa County Community College District administration, district officials said.

Faculty members picketed at all the community college campuses today to demonstrate their "solidarity" in their protests about the district's administration, said Al Shipley, faculty meet-and-confer negotiating chairman.

At the heart of the controversy is the district board of education's $688,000 ceiling on salary increases for 714 full-time faculty members.

SHIPLEY SAID the faculty is opposed to taking the $688,000 because there is a $3.5 million carryover in this year's budget and $3 million in student funds remaining.

District officials said the carryover funds are expected to be used for capital expenditures with a $22 million building program.

Phoenix Gazette, April 10, 1979.

the power to make the board sit up and pay attention! To emphasize the seriousness of their plight, faculty members would picket to attract the media and embarrass the district during the NCA visit. The teachers would tell everyone how Elsner was running the district into the ground. The NCA team would be overwhelmed by the justness of the faculty's case and force the district to accede to the faculty's demands.

Or so they hoped.

Strangely, very few faculty members who were present at the time recall any details of the NCA visit. Glendale faculty member Phil Smelser is one of the few. He remembers that he was one of the people that the visitation team interviewed. "They interviewed maybe thirty people, perhaps. Activists, on several campuses, as I understand," he says.

The faculty put on a vigorous show and forcibly presented its grievances to the NCA team, but in the end, the NCA team did not embrace the faculty's cause. The written report did not arrive at the district until the end of May, but the team would have made an oral presentation of its findings before leaving town. Therefore, the team's findings would have been known at the time.

Gazette Staff Photo by Ebby Hewerlander, Chief Photog

...mmunity College faculty president Charles West holds ...at was erected in front of the school this morning, then rem... ...enance shed by order of the college dean. The teachers pla... ...est marker back up this afternoon, when they will set up p...

THE TOMBSTONE IS UNVEILED

A photograph accompanying an article in the *Phoenix Gazette* for April 10, 1979, reveals the plywood tombstone for the first time:

A four-foot-high tombstone was erected today near the Glendale Community College administration building to dramatize the faculty's concerns over salaries and district administrators. The tombstone is meant to be displayed for members of the Interim Review Committee of the North Central Association of Colleges and Schools. . . . Faculty members picketed at all the community college campuses today to demonstrate their "solidarity" in their protests about the district's administration, said Al Shipley, faculty meet-and-confer negotiating chairman.

When interviewed for this book, Chuck West was shown a copy of this photo as it appeared in the newspaper. He grimaced, and then commented:

Oh, God. The true story about this is I didn't know it was there. I came on campus one day, and I went into the cafeteria for coffee, and somebody said, "Have you seen the tombstone?" We were drinking coffee. I said, "What tombstone?" He said, "Well, somebody erected a tombstone on our campus out here." I said, "Where is it? I'd like to see it." There was a reporter there. Somebody said, "Well, they've moved it over to the compound." I said, "Well, I think I'll walk over and look at it." The reporter says, "I'll go with you. I want to photograph it." So we got over there, and he said, "Lean on the tombstone. I want to take a picture of it." He did. That's how that came about. I knew nothing about it; I was not involved in creating it. But what it did for me with the faculty . . . all of the radicals of the faculty said, "Hey, this is our man!" They thought that I was behind this.

181

In sum, the team found that the district had been making significant efforts to ameliorate the problems outlined in the disastrous 1977 report. The team approved of Tadlock's *Long Range Master Plan* and other efforts to clarify the district's goals and administrative policies. The report also lauded the outreach initiatives represented by Rio Salado and South Mountain Community Colleges.

Regarding the governing board, the team seemed much happier (no doubt because Brooks was no longer there):

The team wishes to congratulate the current members of the Board of Trustees on the marked improvement in this area of concern. The adoption of its Code of Ethics and the clarification of the Chief Executive Officer role of the Chancellor has established the basis for improved Board concentration on matters of broad policy making and its discharge of other appropriate legal responsibilities.

Referring to the current upheaval in the district, the team refused to take sides and, instead, rapped all parties over the knuckles:

It is obvious that all elements of the College and District community need to be sensitive to the possibility that a prolonged period of severe tension is not conducive to servicing the best interest of either students or the community. The team shares the concern of faculty and administration over the negative feeling

tones that appear to have deepened in recent times. The team recommends that a major reexamination of attitudes and perceptions be undertaken so that a common base of shared respect and mutual professional concerns can be reestablished in order to address collectively the major problems facing the District.

Noble sentiments, but not what the faculty wanted. Their frustration unabated, the faculty members continued informational picketing even after the team left town, and the board members continued to be unmoved.

Elsner Throws Down the Gauntlet

The NCA's comments on the Code of Ethics seem to have been unduly optimistic.

According to an article in the April 19, 1979, *El Tiempo Pasando*, the Glendale Community College student newspaper, Bob Robertson had taken a page out of Roger Brooks' old play book and tried to initiate an audit of the chancellor's travel expenses. Robertson apparently approached some unnamed district staff members directly for information. The student newspaper claimed it had obtained a copy of a memo that Elsner fired off to district staff on March 19 to warn them not to "take directions from individual governing board

members unless [the request] comes from the chancellor's office." Robertson was quoted as saying: "As an elected representative of Maricopa County it is my obligation to remain informed of all areas of district business so I can help set policy for the district. I find it ironic that a reporter is able to secure a memo—which I might add, none of the other board members knew about—without going through the chancellor's office." Robertson charged that the memo is "evidence that Elsner is not honoring the code of ethics, a code of ethics which he wrote."

Robertson's reference to the code of ethics must have infuriated Elsner. In the code's section entitled "Procedural Responsibilities," the second item stipulates that "all requests for materials from District employees for any Board action will be transmitted to the Governing Board through the Chancellor and that Governing Board members will request information and action through the Chancellor." So, Robertson clearly violated the code by requesting an audit of the chancellor's travel records be sent directly to him. Then, Robertson chose to mock the code by suggesting—with rather tenuous logic—that Elsner was also in violation of his own code

Phoenix Gazette, *April 21, 1979. From Microfilm.*

College Pay Question Scheduled For Vote

ALL EDITIONS

By JEFF SOUTH
Gazette Education Reporter

A stalemate between the Maricopa County Community College District and its faculty may be broken next week when teachers vote on a proposed new salary package for the 1979-80 academic year.

The package would give the 721 faculty members a pay raise of nearly $1 million, officials said today. The district's previous offer was $688,000.

The district increased its offer during a meet-and-confer session last week, negotiators disclosed. The Faculty Executive Council then agreed to put the sweetened proposal to a vote by the rank and file.

FACULTY MEMBERS will vote Monday and Tuesday, said Alvin Shipley, chairman of the faculty bargaining team.

"Personally, I feel that more money

is there (in the district budget) and should be made available" for faculty pay raises, Shipley said.

However, the council passed the proposal to the teachers because it represents "something of a concession" on the part of the district, he said.

The community college district's governing board says it is in a "hold-the-line" position on expenditures for the coming year.

because the student newspaper had obtained a copy of the memo without, apparently, going through Elsner's office to do so.

Furthermore, Robertson wasn't the only board member who was ignoring the code. Rio staffer Jan Baltzer recalls:

We got lots of backlash against Rio, board members siding with faculty and staff, people calling board members and telling tales—in effect, interfering in day-to-day business. They just were out of control. I can remember Barbara Hitchcock walking in my office and asking me to see rosters and asking to see numbers. That's just not acceptable. None of our board members would think of doing that today.

By this time, Elsner began to despair that the governing board was ever going to play by the rules. Perhaps for this reason, he elected to try to end the faculty insurrection by sidestepping the governing board and going directly to the faculty with an offer of a 7% pay hike. However, even this direct action failed. The *Mesa Tribune* reported on April 25 that the faculty at all the campuses had voted to reject Elsner's offer. The voting was 488 to 107; at least 100 district faculty apparently abstained. At the previous night's meeting, the governing board approved the faculty salary budget at Elsner's figure of $988,000 anyway. This meeting was also the same night as the three-hour marathon on behalf of Rio Salado. The salary vote had followed at midnight.

front page of the *Mesa Tribune* was headlined: "Teachers unite against district chief." Rather than a news story, the story by Hal DeKeyser summarized the war to date: "Teachers in the sprawling Maricopa County Community College District are angrier and more united than ever in the 16-year history of the system. The focus of their fury is Rio Salado College and its creator, Chancellor Paul Elsner."

The article continued with criticisms of Elsner from Bob Robertson and new board member Grant Christensen:

"My real disappointment in Elsner is I can't believe he could establish a program like that at Peralta and then make the kind of mistakes that have been made here," Robertson said. Dr. Grant Christensen, Mesa board member, said off-campus programs never should have been taken away from the traditional campuses. He said poor and rapid planning increased administrative cost.

Angry College Board Rejects Mediation, Sticks To Pay Plan

By JEFF SOUTH
Gazette Education Reporter

Accusing picketing faculty members of unprofessional conduct, the governing board of the Maricopa County Community College District today refused teachers' appeal for federal mediation in contract negotiations.

District officials said the $1 million pay raise they offered at the bargaining table last week is as high as they plan to go.

SOME BOARD members, angered by the faculty's protest activities, even suggested cutting the salary increase to the district's original $668,000 offer "We should not reward unprofessional conduct," member Robert Martinez said.

The action, taken at a board meeting which lasted from 5 p.m. Tuesday to 2 a.m. today, enraged faculty members. They had voted 488-107 to reject the district's $1 million offer, saying it was too low.

Alvin Shipley, chairman of the teachers' negotiating team, said faculty leaders were to meet this morning to discuss the matter.

Faculty representatives say they have not ruled out a possible strike.

IN ANOTHER controversy, the district board today voted to reinstate with modifications a community college course titled "Human Sexuality."

The course came under attack last fall for its allegedly explicit approach to sexual experiences. The board then discontinued the class. Teachers

subsequently filed suit on grounds of academic freedom.

The board today approved an advisory committee's report allowing the individual college campuses to decide whether to offer the sexuality course.

"IN EFFECT, THIS returns to the president at the local level (the college) the responsibility to appropriately supervise this and other courses," said Dr. Art DeCabooter, president of Scottsdale Community College.

He said each college is "sensitive to

Turn to ● MEDIATION, Page B-2

Arizona Republic, April 25, 1979. From microfilm.

In the *Tribune* article describing this meeting, Bob Martinez took a jab at Elsner:

Board member Robert Martinez criticized Elsner for delivering the second offer to faculty members without board approval. "I'm a little upset that the chancellor found it necessary to exceed his authority in the salary offer," Martinez said. I hope this doesn't set a precedent." He said approval would mean that the governing board rewards intimidation, picketing and name-calling.

The district seemed to have achieved a complete meltdown. On Sunday, May 6, 1979, the

On May 10, the Phoenix College Faculty Association took out a half-page advertisement in the *Arizona Republic*. The headline read: "What Is Really Happening to Maricopa County Colleges?" The text was a fairly explicit attack on Elsner, although he was mentioned only once by name. The ad summarized all the previously heard charges but emphasized that administrative costs in the district had increased dramatically since Elsner's arrival. Regarding Rio, the ad noted that "more than twice as much goes to administration there than it does at Glendale, Mesa or Phoenix Colleges." The ad summed up the faculty's case at the end:

Maricopa County is experiencing a marked increase in property values. There is money available to operate five high quality

WHAT IS REALLY HAPPENING TO
MARICOPA COUNTY COLLEGES

- **Since Phoenix College was established in 1920**
  teachers there could pride themselves on providing outstanding two-year college programs. A quality faculty cooperating with an enlightened administration built a district that received national recognition for excellence. Things began to change. The appointment of Dr. Paul Elsner as chancellor in 1977 accelerated the process. The faculty has become increasingly concerned about these new directions. Until now citizens have only heard the administration's side of issues. District teachers want you to know the harm now being done to your colleges.

- **Creation of Rio Salado Community College.**
  Rio Salado was established to provide college courses to "underserved" areas in the county. The faculty applauds this concept. They are, however, disturbed by shockingly high administrative costs (in proportion more than twice as much goes to administration there than it does in Glendale, Mesa or Phoenix Colleges) and the harm done to existing campuses by removing well-established programs to Rio Salado.

- **Diverting funds to build a new college campus.**
  The administration intends to build South Mountain college <u>without</u> voter approval. A bond issue has been the traditional method for voters to express their wishes for or against new school construction. While teachers are not against a new campus, they object to the diversion of large sums from the five existing campuses to create a new college. The administration has bypassed any citizen participation at the polls. The president of this new college and his assistants have been paid approximately $64,000 and the school has yet to enroll its first student.

- **Increased use of part-time faculty.**
  The chief ingredient of high-quality college education is a well-trained, dedicated, full-time faculty. A strong faculty is the vital force in achieving educational excellence. Teachers are profoundly disturbed as are other concerned citizens at the ever-increasing use of part-time, underpaid teachers.

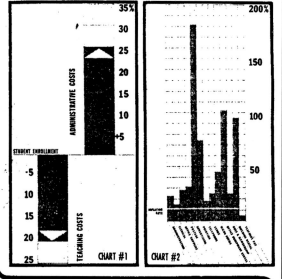

- **An overgrown bureaucracy.**
  Just as in many governmental functions, Maricopa County College administration has ceased to be efficient. It devours an ever-increasing portion of each tax dollar. Chart #1 illustrates this.

- **The administration increases spending on itself.**
  Last year the amount that the administration devoted to advertising went up 182 percent. Chart #2 indicates the administration's priorities. If the increase in the costs of the items shown here had been held to 10.5 percent (this year's inflation figure) they could have saved $1,18 ,813.00.

- **Concerning the budget.**
  Maricopa County is experiencing a marked increase in property values. There is money available to operate five high quality schools if the administrative fat is trimmed and old educational priorities re-established. The administration, with disregard for the democratic process, has diverted funds from quality educational programs in order to assist building a new college. Register your disapproval now. Once ground is broken for the new campus the camel will have its nose under the tent. There is no way to keep last year's 49.1 million dollar budget, build a new campus and continue to pour money into Rio Salado without further sacrificing educational excellence at the five established colleges.

THIS ANNOUNCEMENT PAID FOR BY THE PHOENIX COLLEGE FACULTY ASSOCIATION

Dr. Barbara C. VanSittert, (president)
A. A. Dutton   Bruce Smith   Helen H. Holnan

Arizona Republic, May 11, 1979.

schools if the administrative fat is trimmed and old educational priorities re-established. The administration, with disregard for the democratic process, has diverted funds from quality educational programs in order to assist building a new college. Register your disapproval now. Once ground is broken for the new campus the camel will have its nose under the tent. There is no way to keep last year's 49.1 million dollar budget, build a new campus and continue to pour money into Rio Salado without further sacrificing

educational excellence at the five established colleges.

The text did not specify how to register that protest, but the implication seemed to be that people would do well to call their respective governing board members and demand Elsner's removal.

By then, the school year was over, and the insurrection had run its course. The weary board decided that after its meeting on May 12, it would not meet again until the end of July.

And then, as a sort of going-away present, the board delivered Elsner one last slap in the face. Al Flowers unintentionally was responsible.

During the six-week break ahead, Elsner had plans to go to Harvard to attend a summer institute. But before Elsner left, Al Flowers wanted to settle the matter of his own position in the district. In spite of the fact that he and Elsner had worked well together in their first year—the plan to finance South Mountain out of thin air was nothing short of a master stroke—he still felt uncomfortable because the governing board had forced him

College chief calls teachers' ad inaccurate

By HAL DeKEYSER
Tribune staff writer

A half-page advertisement by Phoenix College teachers claiming rising administrative costs in Maricopa Community Colleges is inaccurate, according to the district chancellor.

Dr. Paul A. Elsner said administrative costs have declined 3.2 percent with the district's $49.1 million budget. He said he froze salaries of 24 administrators this year after a study showed they were earning more than their counterparts in industry and in comparable districts.

"We also rank currently the lowest in the state for administrative costs," Elsner said.

The teachers and administration have been battling for the past two months. Faculty leaders have been especially critical of the establishment of Rio Salado and South Mountain colleges, which some claim has taken money that could have gone to salary increases.

Faculty raises this year averaged 3.3 percent according teachers and 7 percent according to the administration, which includes longevity increases.

Half-page newspaper ads in Phoenix newspapers last week purchased by the PC faculty association charged that two campuses established since Elsner became chancellor in 1977 have boosted administrative costs about 25 percent.

It also claimed that South Mountain was authorized without voter approval, and that money spent for advertising has climbed 182 percent — up $1,188,813.

But Elsner counters that Rio Salado, the controversial "college without walls," has the lowest per-student cost of any in the district, between $1,200 and $1,300. Traditional campuses such as Mesa Community College average about $1,700 per student, he said.

The projected per-student costs for Rio next year is $1,047, he said.

"I think our administrative efficiency is probably the best in the country," the chancellor said. "I wish they (faculty) would have come to me or Al Flowers (vice chancellor for business). We would have given them some accurate information."

Please turn to page A-10

on Elsner. Flowers perhaps thought that Elsner could improve his position if he were allowed to appoint his own business director, someone who did not have a long-standing previous relationship with the board. Flowers had remained the additional year at the board's insistence, but the year was up, and the year had not exactly been pleasant. He told Elsner that he was leaving and that he had another offer:

Mesa Tribune, May 13, 1979.

I wanted to move to Prescott anyway, and I had the number-two job sewed up at Yavapai Community College. Much less money, but it was a nice town I would like to live in. . . . They gave me a short window up there because they wanted to get with it. Elsner said, "Well, you're working with the board because I'm going to be at Harvard at that program. So you work it out with them

Continued from page A-1

The faculty also misrepresented the process of authorizing new colleges by saying South Mountain was passed without voter approval, Elsner said. It doesn't work that way.

"South Mountain didn't require voter approval," he said "We're on a pay-as-you-go plan. The governing board voted 5-0 to establish South Mountain."

Elsner said had a bond issue been required, there would have been an election. The money for South Mountain and the rest of the district's $22 million capital budget this year comes from "money the district already has or anticipates on collections from our normal enrollment growth."

That building budget also includes $7.8 million for four Mesa Community College projects and construction at other campuses, he added.

Kent Ord, public relation director for the district, said he doesn't know where the faculty got figures claiming a 182 percent advertising increase amounting to $1,188,813.

Those costs formerly were picked up from various budgets affecting areas, including veterans, continuing education and night schools, he said. and never have been lumped **together previously**.

"We never before in this district have put together a comprehensive plan for informing our various publics throughout the county of the programs that we have," Ord said. "It had never been a priority before."

The district has produced radio and television advertisements which run just before registration citing classes available and emphasizing how easy and inexpensive they are to obtain. Ord says the district also has sought public service space and changed to a "more effective way of communicating."

Much of the controversy in the district can be traced to teacher dissatisfaction with salaries, Elsner said, but teachers aren't as bad off as they would have the public assume.

"Faculty salaries rank as high as any

multicampus district in the nation," he said. "They're $3,700 more than the national average. We have faculty with cumulative earnings that make $41,000 a year by teaching nights and summers . . .

"My feeling is, the public doesn't know that."

He also challenged faculty contentions that the district was wasting money on an expanding bureaucracy.

"I've got to be convinced were a 'spending' district when we have the second-lowest tax rate in the state (among community colleges), the lowest unit cost, the lowest proportion of money into overhead and administration, and we're making concerted efforts to reduce the overhead."

Of 721 full-time district teachers, Elsner said 391 earned more than $25,000 last year, 125 had salaries above $30,000 and nine were paid more than $35,000. Maricopa's average is $22,000 he said, which is $5,000 more than the nearest Arizona district, Pinal.

"I get pressure from the community on salaries," Elsner said. "A Motorola engineer, a graduate engineer working 12 months will make $18,000 to $20,000 a year, (working) 40 hours a week in a very structured time-clock basis."

Elsner said that next school year he plans to focus on increasing handicapped projects, getting building projects under way and pushing occupational education, from which he says the district is getting most of its growth.

He also said the traditional campuses would be offering off-campus courses again, and that college presidents are meeting to work out which courses should be taught by which college. Faculty leaders had complained that programs they spent years developing were stolen when Rio Salado formed.

"I want them to move off-campus — get back into the community," Elsner said. "I think people feel more restricted of being able to get off campus than they really are."

because you run the board meetings while I'm gone, anyway, so work it out."

After Elsner was gone, Flowers approached the board:

> *I asked them for a release. William Schindel said, "Well, how many more years do you want to work?" I said, "What does that have to do with it?" He said, "Well, answer it." I said, "Well, at least 'til I'm 62." "Well, how many years is that?" "Four more years." So they went into executive session, came out, and voted me a four-year contract.*

Flowers immediately realized the insult. Paul Elsner's contract was for less than four years:

> *You talk about embarrassment! They didn't ask me if I would accept it, even. But they said, "We're protecting the fiscal integrity of this district, and that's why we're taking this action, you know." Well, it's hard to say you shouldn't do that, but that's not the proper way to do it, those kinds of things.*

He then called Elsner at Harvard and tried to put the best face possible on what had happened. Elsner received the news calmly, almost without interest. During the time away from Maricopa, Elsner was conducting the sort of reexamination that the NCA report had recommended. His attempt to resolve the faculty deadlock through direct intervention had failed. The board members had never stopped flagrantly disregarding the code of ethics, and one board member had even mocked him with a perverted interpretation of that code. The faculty remained in open revolt.

He perhaps concluded that he, like Oedipus, had become the unclean thing that had brought the plague down upon the city.

Elsner Makes His Move

Elsner was back in Phoenix for the board meeting on the night of July 31, 1979. The occasion was a regular meeting held at the District Services Support Center on East Washington Street. The meeting began late at 7:26 in the evening with an executive session to discuss personnel matters. The public meeting then began at 8:07 PM.

The board began by approving the minutes. Next, Robertson was asked for the secretary's report, but he indicated he had nothing to report. The next item was the chancellor's report, but Elsner made none. The representative of the state board, Harkins, had a few informational items, but nothing of great importance. His report was followed by several routine reports: an upcoming meeting of the Arizona Association of District Governing Boards, a faculty report, a student government report, and a citizens' forum during which no citizens had anything to say (a refreshing change from the diatribes that characterized the spring term).

The next item on the agenda was the equally routine matter of the approval of the agenda itself. The board minutes state:

> *Dr. Elsner recommended that the following items be added to the agenda: II.H., Extension of Leave of Absence for Helena Howe, II.I., Chancellor's Resignation, and II.26 (A-26), Vouchers. There being no objections, these items were added to the agenda.*

Apparently, the additions to the agenda were made so quickly that everyone was caught off guard. Those in attendance began to look at each other: What was that second one again? Did he say the chancellor's resignation?

One after the other, the routine items were acted upon as the suspense began to build in the room. Six relatively minor items were dispatched in short order until the three items Elsner had added to the agenda were reached.

Calmly, he presented the request for Helena Howe's leave of absence to be extended. So moved. Motion carried. And then, the room grew very quiet. By then, everyone had had time to reflect on what Elsner had said. What was he up to this time?

The spotlight focused on him, Elsner began to speak. The governing board minutes contain the following account of what happened next:

> *Dr. Elsner reviewed accomplishments during his year and one-half as Chancellor, and indicated the period had been the high point of his professional career. He told the Board that in the interest of continuity in the district, facing a year which potentially has similar kinds of divisiveness that occurred last year, and because of some specific involvements at the board, faculty, and other levels, he was submitting his resignation in the best interest of the district. Dr. Elsner indicated this resignation would be effective upon the appointment of a permanent Chancellor.*

Sue Carey, writing for the *Arizona Republic,* described the reaction: "The announcement visibly shocked district administrators, faculty and residents attending a meeting in the district's headquarters at 3910 E. Washington. . . . He delivered his resignation announcement in a calm manner and did not elaborate."

(II-G)

IN-LIEU OF MILEAGE PAYMENTS FOR 1979-80 - Dr. Elsner recommended that
all personnel except executive personnel be removed from in-lieu
mileage allowance payments and be placed on straight mileage reimbursement
based on a recently completed study. He noted that approval of this
recommendation would eliminate in-lieu mileage payments to fourteen
positions.

MOTION

MOTION NO. 4287

Dr. Christensen-M, approval of in-lieu of mileage payments for 1979-80
as recommended. Motion carried 4-1; Mr. Robertson voted no.

(II-F)

EXTENSION OF LEAVE-OF-ABSENCE FOR HELENA HOWE - Dr. Elsner recommended
extension of Helena Howe's leave-of-absence for one additional year,
with the recommendation that she be allowed to return to an
administrative position with the district at a dean's level salary
at the end of that period. He indicated as part of this recommendation
that the position of President of Mesa Community College will be announced
as open immediately, and that a search will be undertaken to find a permanent
replacement for Dr. Howe.

He commended Theo Heap for the excellent job he has done as acting
president of the Mesa campus, and he encouraged Mr. Heap to apply for
the position.

MOTION

MOTION NO. 4288

Dr. Christensen-M, approval of an additional one year leave-of-absence
for Helena Howe, with the stipulation that she be allowed to return
to an administrative position with the district, at a dean's level
salary, at the end of the one year period; and that the position of
president of Mesa Community College shall be advertised immediately.
Motion carried 5-0.

(II-G)

CHANCELLOR'S RESIGNATION - Dr. Elsner reviewed acomplishments
during his year and one-half as Chancellor, and indicated the period
had been the high point of his professional career. He told the
Board that in the interest of continuity in the district, facing
a year which potentially has similar kinds of divisiveness that
occurred last year, and because of some specific involvements at
the board, faculty and other levels, he was submitting his
resignation in the best interest of the district. Dr. Elsner
indicated his resignation would be effective upon the appointment
of a permanent Chancellor.

AR 8/7/79

'Divisiveness' is factor

Community college chie resigns post unexpected

By SUE CAREY

Paul A. Elsner, chancellor of the Maricopa County Community College District, surprisingly announced his resignation Tuesday night.

Elsner, a 45-year-old resident of Phoenix, has been chancellor since November 1977. He said he will continue in his $55,-000-a-year job until a successor is appointed.

Elsner said he is quitting rather than "face another year of potential divisiveness with specific involve-

every possible attempt to d him from his action," Schind

He said the resignation ered orally, and the board received it in writing.

Al Flowers, executive vic lor, said the resignation sudden and out of the blue

Under Elsner's chancel district created Rio Salac Mountain community coll dertook a $23 million o program.

Elsner said he consi those decisions milestor trict.

"I regard the last ye the height of my profe

Chapter Eighteen

1981
The **Healing Process** Begins

Bob Martinez broke out in a cold sweat. Elsner's resignation put all the plans for South Mountain Community College in jeopardy because the state board had not yet approved a site. South Mountain's opponents might yet find a way to block the new college. When interviewed for this book, Martinez stated, "I needed [Elsner] to get South Mountain through the state board."

As Elsner quietly explained his reasons for resigning, Martinez searched the faces of the other board members. He thought Robertson was about to move to accept the chancellor's resignation as soon as Elsner stopped speaking. If so, Hitchcock would oppose the motion, but how might Schindel and Christensen vote? Christensen had been very negative toward Elsner in the press, and Schindel had taken a lot of abuse from the faculty over Rio and the faculty raises. If they voted with Robertson, then Elsner—and South Mountain—would be history.

Elsner finished his remarks, and before anyone else could speak, Martinez grabbed the floor and moved to table the matter of the chancellor's resignation for further consideration. Probably still in shock, the other board members agreed, and the motion carried 5-0.

The meeting continued according to the agenda, almost as if nothing had happened. Elsner asked for and received approval of curricula. A Phoenix College biology class field trip to Alaska was discussed. Elsner suggested that the board needed to establish an advisory committee to oversee the radio station, KMCR. All those in attendance sat squirming, waiting for the meeting to end so that they could express their reactions to Elsner's announcement. The end came at 9:22 PM.

More than one newspaper reported that Elsner left the meeting room immediately, went to his office, closed the door, and refused to speak to anyone.

Reporters then swarmed around the board members to garner their reactions. Art Moore of the *Mesa Tribune* talked to Grant Christensen, who said the announcement was completely unexpected. "I was surprised. I had no indication he would resign," he said.

> Christensen said he could not pinpoint any reason that may have prompted Elsner's resignation, but he felt there was not much friction between Elsner and the board. "It's true the board has not voted unanimously on several items, but I felt there was not that much dissension between Dr. Elsner and the board," he said.

Sue Carey of the *Arizona Republic* talked to William Schindel, who was similarly taken aback:

> "I think the board is going to make every possible attempt to dissuade him from this action," Schindel said. He said the resignation was delivered orally, and the board has not received it in writing.

Neither Barbara Hitchcock nor Bob Robertson were quoted in any of the newspaper accounts, but when interviewed for this book, Hitchcock said she never took Elsner seriously. "My impression is that he enjoyed the dramatics."

Jeff South, the education reporter for the *Phoenix Gazette* caught reactions from some of the faculty in attendance:

> "He may be looking for a vote of confidence from the board," suggested Chuck West, president-elect of the faculty association. Another faculty member interpreted the resignation more bluntly:
> "I think it's all a ploy. Elsner just wants to get the board behind him so he can talk tough at the bargaining table." But other officials disagreed. They said Elsner already has the board's full support. And they said the determined tone of Elsner's announcement indicates he is serious.

Was the resignation merely a ploy? Not according to Elsner:

Chancellor's bid to resign splits board

By SUSAN CAREY

Governing board members were split Wednesday over whether to honor Paul Elsner's unexpected request to resign as chancellor of the Maricopa County Community College District.

One member said he will vote against releasing Elsner from his three-year, $165,000 contract. Another said he favored releasing him and a third said he wanted to find out why Elsner asked to resign.

Elsner, 45, shocked district administrators, college presidents and faculty members at a board meeting Tuesday night when he announced his desire to leave the post he has held since November 1977.

Board members have the authority to make Elsner honor his contract, which will expire in December 1981.

In announcing his resignation, Elsner said he did not want to face "another year of potential divisiveness with specific involvements at board- and faculty-level." He also said there had been "strained relationships" within the district but would not elaborate.

However, some faculty members contended that the "divisiveness" Elsner is feeling is of his own making.

The board unanimously deferred action on the request until an Aug. 14 board meeting.

Board member Robert Robertson of Glendale said he will vote to allow Elsner to resign.

"Paul's insight into the problems of the district are pretty accurate and it's regrettable but it may be in the best interests of the district that we have somebody else at the helm," Robertson said.

Robertson said controversy surrounding some of Elsner's actions may have spurred the decision. As examples, he cited creation of Rio Salado Community College, disagreement over a human-sexuality course and stormy salary negotiations with instructors.

Board member Robert Martinez, a Phoenix attorney, said he will vote against releasing Elsner from his contract.

"It would be a disservice to the tax-

Continued on Page B-6

As far as I was concerned, I was gone. Gone. Long gone. In fact, it was a very productive period for me. Joyce and I spent a lot of time reviewing options. We had one of our rooms with butcher paper all around the room looking at options about what we would do and what our resources were and what our abilities were to connect with other things to do. It was a very satisfying period. There was a lot of relief. . . . I had calls from all over the country. I wouldn't say there were any offers, but there were lots of encouragement. [Maricopa] had a pretty bad reputation in terms of the North Central and a lot of other places. There were a lot of people that were not surprised that I would resign from here, knowing me and knowing the system, because [Maricopa] was cast among a lot of the leaders in the country as a pretty hopeless place . . .

The Second Code of Ethics

What happened in the following days is not clear. One newspaper account says Elsner did subsequently give the board members a document that listed the reasons for his resignation. The issues cited were supposedly all linked to the board's lack of compliance with the code of ethics adopted back at the meeting on November 22, 1977.

Arizona Republic, August 2, 1979.

Elsner says that board members visited him in the following days. **Grant Christensen** believes that he was one of the first to talk to Elsner after he made his initial announcement:

I told him that I knew what had upset him, and I'd get mad, too, but I said, "Hell, Paul, that's nothing to leave this district for! We need you, and you know we need you, and you've got support out there." And as I sat with him, I said, "You ought to just reconsider. You've got some different people to deal with here now. Let's just move this district along."

One way or another, some serious horse-trading appears to have gone on before the board met again two weeks later. The minutes of the August 14, 1979, meeting show that under the heading of Approval of Agenda, Elsner asked the inclusion of item II.2. "Reaffirmation of Principles of Code of Ethics."

The item in the minutes reads: "Dr. Elsner asked the governing board to reaffirm the Code of Ethics established in November, 1977, in principle with a view to having future discussion on the topic." Martinez moved that "we accept the reaffirmation of the Code of Ethics." The motion was carried 3-1 with Robertson voting no. (Barbara Hitchcock was absent from this meeting.) Newspaper stories at the time noted the irony of Robertson's vot-

April 17, 1997, video interview of Grant Christensen, Maricopa governing board member 1979-84 and 1989-1995. Transcript and audio excerpts available online.

http://www.mc.maricopa.edu/users/M3cdhistory/

ing against the same code of ethics that he had previously moved to approve in 1977.

The newspaper articles that describe this meeting say Elsner then withdrew his resignation, although the minutes contain no specific mention of the fact.

decided to come back because there was such a period of elation and clarity and peak experience while I was out. It was coming back having to rebuild all those relationships again."

At the November 14 meeting, the board formally adopted the revised code of ethics. At

Ethics that permitted me to communicate a delicate, but uncompromising issue; uncompromising because it involved a matter of principles affecting the board and the chancellor's operational philosophy. The Code saved my professional life, which I had to lay on the line.

ARIZONA REPUBLIC 8/15/79

Colleges' chief withdraws resignation

By ART GISSENDANER

Maricopa County Community College District Chancellor Paul Elsner Tuesday retracted the resignation he submitted two weeks ago.

He did so, however, only after the district's governing board reaffirmed the code of ethics it adopted in November 1977, shortly after Elsner arrived in the district.

But before the vote, board member Bob Robertson said he would vote against the code because it violated the public's right to know and the powers granted board members under Arizona law.

Robertson said after the meeting that both the American Civil Liberties Union and the attorney general should review the document.

"The document violates citizens' and board members' rights to public information," Robertson said. "It restricts board members from obtaining information from the campuses and turns the board into a rubber stamp."

The code is a list of legal powers and duties of the governing board, including ethical responsibilities. It was enacted because former board member Roger Brooks frequently visited campuses to obtain information concerning board members and district employees.

Robertson said the code allowed the administration to classify too many documents as confidential and discouraged faculty members from contacting the board without first going through administrative channels.

"I will try to get a motion passed at the next meeting that the entire document be submitted to the attorney general for review of possible statutory violations," Robertson said. "All documents must be submitted to Elsner before the board sees them."

Elsner refused to comment other than to say that the matter was between him and the board.

"We had several meetings and made tremendous progress," Elsner said. We now have the foundation for an excellent year. I want to get on with the educational agenda and forget the political one."

During the meeting, board President William Schindel said Elsner indicated in a letter to the board that he wanted to resign because of a lack of compliance with the code by the board and some district employees.

Elsner found it difficult to operate effectively, Schindel said, and he listed several violations and reasons why he was frustrated.

Schindel, who was not on the board at the time the code was adopted, said a workshop would be conducted on possible revisions in the code.

Board member Robert Martinez agreed with Schindel, but said he had reservations about some of the code's provisions.

"I feel strongly that the way to resolve the problem is to sit down and discuss it," Martinez said.

Board member Grant Christensen said that he found some problems with the code, but that some type of regulation was needed.

"I found some discrepancies and many violations on the part of the faculty and the board," Christensen said. "But if we have a code of ethics we should abide by it. If it needs changes, we should make them. The problem can be worked out."

Two weeks ago, Elsner announced that he would quit rather than face another year of potential divisiveness.

Board member Barbara Hitchcock did not attend the meeting.

Arizona Republic, August 15, 1979.

The code of ethics was, of course, merely symbolic. Elsner had finally made the board admit who was boss. Grant Christensen confirms this point of view: "I think that was a turning point in the district and in the relationship of the way the administration and the board started to function. The board recognized Paul, and Paul's authority, and weren't trying to undercut him but wanted to support him in everything and listen to him."

Even so, Elsner was not feeling particularly victorious: "There was sort of a letdown when I

the same meeting, the board announced its intentions to negotiate a new four-year contract for Elsner. The votes for both actions were 4-0; Robertson was absent because of illness, or so he claimed.

Elsner included the revised code of ethics in an article he wrote for the Winter 1979-80 issue of *Trustee Quarterly* published by Association of Community College Trustees. In that article, he explained:

I recently had an unresolvable issue with my board. I sought refuge in a Code of

Elsner then went on to list ten axioms he had developed to guide "Board-Chief Executive Officer relationships." The first one reads, "As a chief executive officer, don't surprise the board; as a board member don't surprise other board members or the president or chancellor."

A lesson well learned.

South Mountain Begins

With Elsner firmly in control of the district, South Mountain faced no further problems with the state board. The district studied three different locations and finally recommended a 104-acre site bordered by 20th and 24th Streets just north of Baseline Road. The access to 24th Street was considered an asset. The land was owned by the Heard Investment Corporation, which offered to sell the land to the district for $595,000, a price considered then to be about half the market value (*Mesa Tribune,* August 19, 1979).

"Code of Ethics and Responsibilities for Governing Board Members" *as published in* "Guidelines for Chief Executive-Board Relationships" *by Paul Elsner, published in* Trustee Quarterly, Vol. 4, No. 1, Winter 1979-80. Text available online.

http://www.mc.maricopa.edu/users/M3cdhistory/

Gazette Staff Photo by Ru:

OUT STANDING IN THE FIELD OF EDUCATION

Raul Cardenas holds silver shovel for groundbreaking today at site of South Mountain Community College, 24th Street and Vineyard. The 104-acre tract is currently a cotton field, but officials say it will be ready to open next fall Cardenas as president. (Story on Page B,1).

Phoenix Gazette for August 23, 1979. Photo by Russell Gates.

The state board gave its blessing on August 18, 1979, and groundbreaking ceremonies were held on August 22, 1979. The architect chosen for the project was Bennie Gonzales, a local architect of considerable reputation.

A clipping from the *Arizona Republic* on October 13 stated that Gonzales had presented drawings and a scale model of the new campus at the board meeting the night before. The newspaper reported that the plan was quite elaborate:

Lakes and canals, walkways lined with palm trees, and an amphitheater for weekend neighborhood gatherings are among the more distinctive features planned for South Mountain Community College, scheduled to open in 1980. . . . Facilities include a student center, library, *day-care center, classroom buildings, gymnasium, sports fields and the amphitheater. The amphitheater will be available to community groups when not being used by students.*

The one hang-up was the miserly construction budget of $8.4 million caused by the inability of the district to mount a bond election. An article from the *Phoenix Gazette* on

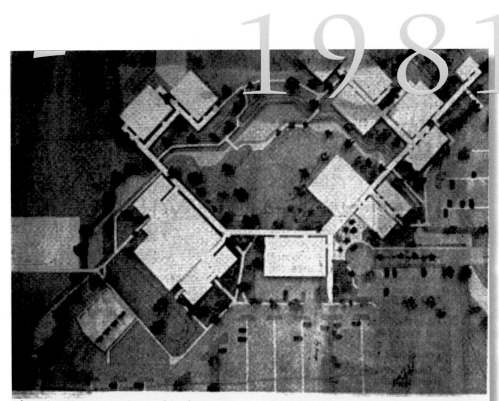

Catholic Church, the Curtis Greenfield School, and South Mountain High School. For the fall term, approximately 750 students enrolled, and that number increased to approximately 1,300 for the spring term.

A news release prepared by the South Mountain staff for May, 1981, summed up the first year of operation:

> . . . faculty, staff, and students of South Mountain Community College celebrated their second commencement ceremony on Thursday, May 13th, with fourteen graduates. Also recognized in the ceremony were 80 other students who received awards for scholarship, academic achievement, service leadership and student employment.

During this time, the community continued to influence the personality of the school. Raúl Cárdenas, South Mountain's founding president, reported that the community continued to demand that South Mountain focus on the transfer curriculum:

> There was a lot of mistrust—and rightfully so—about the educational system and how it treated its minority population. If you're a troublemaker, you end up in occupational education. If you have a problem with your language—occupational education. I was a high school principal. I had faculty members who would say, "Get him out of my class and put him in voc. ed., because he's not going to do it here." So I could sense where that was coming from. The advisory committee said, "We want to see more transfer. We want to see more of our kids go on to four-year institutions as opposed to just going to a dead-end two-year school."

As had been the case at Rio Salado College, the community was exerting its influence in

---

Scale model shows aerial view of South Mountain Community College, which is due to open in the fall of 1980. The campus is located at 24th Street and Baseline Road.

Community College Plan Blends Function, Beauty

South Mountain Community College will feature clusters of buildings strung in an oval, with an outdoor theater at its center and a scenic canal running through the campus.

That's how architect Bennie Gonzales and college President Raul Cardenas envision the campus, planned for a 104-acre site on 24th Street north of Baseline Road.

Architectural plans

Maricopa County's newest college will have several unusual features, officials said.

For example, it is the Maricopa County Community College District's first attempt to integrate a day-care center with the actual campus, they said. This will help accommodate the child-care needs of parents taking college courses, Cardenas said.

After construction of facilities and parking

be art-music, another liberal arts, another for business education and college administration, another for the library, another for the student activities center, another for the gymnasium and another for the sciences.

The clusters will be arranged in an oval and will be connected by covered walkways, Gonzales said. The campus will be an "activities-oriented college," with a grassy amphitheater in

Such a construction style, with its prefabricated components, can be completed quickly, won't be thrown off schedule by the weather, can accommodate more wall insulation and is within the $8.4 million budget set by the college district board, Gonzales said.

The first phase of construction involves facilities for music, art, liberal arts, business education and administration, Cardenas said. Gonzales hopes to have these facilities ready so classes can begin in the fall of 1980.

THE OTHER buildings, which make up the second phase of construction, will be com-

Phoenix Gazette, October 31, 1979. Bennie Gonzales's model for South Mountain Community College.

October 31 explained how Gonzales planned to keep down costs:

> Campus buildings will be of "Southwestern construction," using steel frames and stucco exterior similar to the relocatable classrooms built in recent years by public school districts, he said. Such a construction style, with its prefabricated compo-

nents, can be completed quickly, won't be thrown off schedule by the weather, can accommodate more wall insulation and is within the $8.4 million budget set by the college district board, Gonzales said.

While the construction proceeded, South Mountain began to offer classes in temporary quarters. Beginning in the fall of 1980, the new college leased space at the Holy Family

193

"I don't really
enjoy telling
people how
great I am."

Marvin Knudson

"I make no
bones about sell-
ing myself, I'm
the best person
for the job"

Linda Rosenthal

Candidates have differing view of post

By BEVERLY MEDLYN

What Linda Rosenthal proclaims, Marvin Knudson laments.

Her front yard bears a large campaign placard with "Community College Board" painted over the name of the last office she had sought.

He said he'd just as soon not have any election at all.

Their campaigns and their views of the electoral process illustrate the difference in personal style voters will have to choose from in the Nov. 6 Maricopa Community College governing board District 4 race.

Knudson is retired and retiring. A former community college president, the soft-spo-ken Sun City resident said he believes the post he is seeking should be appointed by the Maricopa County supervisors rather than determined by the voters.

That would take some of the politics out

of governing higher education, he said. And besides, "running for office is a pretty ex-pensive proposition when you consider that you don't get paid for your service."

Knudson estimates he has spent $100 tops for "gas and a few dinners," plus donated printing costs for campaign fliers.

"I can't believe he would say such a thing," the outspoken Mrs. Rosenthal said.

Of course, the board seat should be an elected office, she said, because "I believe in democracy. It is essential in this position."

In the past few years, Mrs. Rosenthal has made something of a career of being schooled in the democratic process. In 1977, her daily visits to the Capitol won respect from some lawmakers who called her "the 61st member of the Legislature."

She got to know the process and the central characters because she "always wanted to be a legislator," she has said.

Then came last year's loss in the Republi-can primary for the District 19 House seat.

Now, Mrs. Rosenthal said, she has faced the "political realities" of trying to beat an incumbent and has set her sights on a smaller governing body where she believes her vote will count more.

Her campaign is extensive, including Val-ley wide public appearances, distributing leaflets, erecting signs and direct mailing to District 4 residents.

Knudson views high-powered campaign-ing with distaste and said he is content to put his qualifications before the voters for them to take or leave.

He is a relaxed man, but is ill at ease in the role of a politician, what with all the obligatory folderal.

Election, B2

Arizona Republic, *October 29, 1979.*

ways that had never been seen before in the district. The new pattern was being rein-forced. The district was continuing to evolve.

Changes on the Board

As part of the healing process, some turnover on the board was inevitable. William Schindel elected to finish out his term at the end of 1979 and call it quits:

I fully intended to run, and when the time came, I weighed it, and I said, no, I'm not going to do it because it was very difficult traveling from here. And we were out at

June 3, 1996, audio inter-view with William Schindel, Maricopa governing board member 1978-1980. Partial transcript available online.

night most of the time, and I'd get home twelve, one o'clock. . . . I was turning seventy, and I said to hell with that. I'm not going to do it. I liked the job and I liked working with the people, and under other circumstances, I might very well have run again.

"Robertson gave the impression of being somebody who had never had a position of any authority, and when he got it, he...exploited it not wisely all the time"

The next election was scheduled for November 6, and when the September 7 fil-ing deadline was past, only two candidates declared: Marvin Knudson, the district's first director of semiprofessional education, and Linda B. Rosenthal, a former high school teacher. Rosenthal campaigned hard for the position and won.

June 12, 1996, video interview with Linda Rosenthal, Maricopa governing board member 1980 to present. Transcript available online.

http://www.mc.maricopa.edu/users/M3cdhistory/

Bob Robertson's term in office expired at the end of 1980, and in July of that year, Robertson announced that he would not be running for reelection. He cited as a reason that his employer, Western Electric (for whom he was a cable rewinder), had been giving him a lot of trouble about the time he spent on his board duties. He indicated that company officials had questioned the reason for so many absences (*Phoenix Gazette*, July 25, 1980).

In August, Dr. Roy Amrein, a Phoenix chiropractor, announced his intention to run for Robertson's seat on the board. A faculty committee had already interviewed him and approved of his candidacy. He carried the election easily in November.

Until the end, Robertson never stopped railing against Elsner. During Robertson's last months on the board, he tried hard to lead a movement to consolidate Rio, South Mountain, and Maricopa Tech into one institution, but his proposal found no supporters on the board. At his last board meeting on January 13, 1981, Robertson let rip with an angry speech about Elsner's refusal to consider his ideas. Then, his words still ringing in the air, he stormed out of the boardroom and was gone (*Scottsdale Daily Progress*, 1/14/81).

With Robertson's departure, the last traces of Roger Brooks' influence were gone. Three of the board members serving in January of 1981 (Hitchcock, Rosenthal, and Amrein), would remain on the board well into the next decade. The constant turnover that characterized the board in the '70s was over. A new era of stability was underway.

Maricopa Tech Relocates

The problem of the future of Maricopa Tech still remained. Overnight, Rio Salado had stripped away almost half of Maricopa Tech's enrollment, and Norb Breummer, Tech's president, had been deeply wounded by the theft. From an enrollment peak of 7,500 students in 1974, enrollment had declined to around 3,500 in 1978. According to Breummer,

November 16, 1996, interview with Roy Amrein, Maricopa governing board member 1981-96. Transcript and audio excerpts available online.

http://www.mc.maricopa.edu/users/M3cdhistory/

Roy Amrein, a native of St. Charles, Missouri, brought a rich and varied educational background to his term of service on the governing board.

I did my undergraduate work at several places: Logan College of Chiropractic in Washington University in St. Louis, and then Los Angeles College of Chiropractic, in the Chiropractic/Orthopedic Department. Then, after I studied all the sciences, when I came out here and I was in practice a few years, I went to Phoenix College, to do a lot of the liberal arts work. I went there for about seven years on a part-time basis while I was in practice. Also, I studied philosophy in England and philosophy in Spain. That was in 1968. I've been a perpetual student. And still am. I believe that multifaceted approach is healthy. Of course, you can see how that naturally leads into my love of the community college system.

Amrein's connections with Phoenix College led directly to his being approached to run for the board in 1979. Over the years, Amrein has provided chiropractic assistance to many other district employees as well:

I've had many patients from Phoenix College, as I was a student there, and I would say I have had fifteen to twenty teachers. . . . A number of the community college presidents have been patients here, and deans and lots of faculty members.

One of the computer labs in the front windows of the old Korrick's building. Bus benches are visible through the window.

approximately 40% of Rio's courses had formerly been Maricopa Tech's. However, Rio was not responsible for all of Maricopa Tech's problems. The downtown area had seriously declined, and the area around the old Korrick's building had become a haven for drunks, homeless people, and prostitutes. Many people simply refused to go anywhere near the old building for night classes.

Bill Berkshire, who was a faculty member at Maricopa Tech in those days, paints a vivid picture of the problem:

> On the bottom floor, which is where we held our computer classes, we had the big eight-, ten-foot windows. The students sat in the windows at the keypunch machines, and the flashers were right outside the window. . . . Of course, they were sleeping out on the benches. The bus company, when they built across the street, put in bus benches, which was terrible, because then they all laid there and slept. So they'd get up and the first thing they'd do is they'd come over and flash. It was hilarious! The

security guards said, "Don't get excited. He'll be somewhere else tomorrow, or he'll be down in the drunk tank or whatever." You'd see the fights across the street at the bar. I'm sure it had an effect on the students that came, particularly the younger students. They used to have to get the security guards to meet them at the parking garage, and they'd all come in one group.

In December of 1979, the board decided to vacate the deteriorating downtown area and move Maricopa Tech to the building at 3910 East Washington Street, where the district had already set up offices and a training facility called the Industry Education Center.

The decision to move the college was too much for Bruemmer. In the fall of 1980, he took a year's sabbatical and then joined the faculty at Scottsdale. After a national search, the board selected Dr. Charles A. Green, who would become Arizona's first African-American college president. He came to Maricopa Tech from Inver Hills Community College in Minnesota, where he was the dean of continuing education. He took office July 1, 1981.

Maricopa Tech To Leave Downtown Site Due To Declining Enrollment

Maricopa County Technical College, gearing to pull out of the Phoenix downtown area, went from an enrollment of 7,504 in the fall of 1981 to 2,969 for the current spring semester.

The decline in evening classes has been more dramatic.

In 1974, 4,817 students signed up for evening school — 64 percent of the enrollment. But last fall, there were only 666 students in evening school — 40 percent of the enrollment.

OFFICIALS cite various factors for the turnabout, and prominently mention "the neighborhood."

As Fred Gaudet, director of research and development observes, "For some of our program areas, students will not come downtown in the evening."

Gaudet cited dental assistant and other programs which traditionally attract "young girls."

Although relocation of Maricopa Tech from the old Korrick's department store building at 106 E. Washington to the Maricopa County Community College Districts' administrative complex at 40th Street and Washington was known to be under study, Gaudet said the "concept" already has been approved and removal is being "implemented."

SQUARE-FOOTAGE studies are under way and the resiting is expected to be well in progress by next fall and possibly completed by the "fall of 1982."

One problem with the present address of the technical college is that it rents 500 parking spaces in the Phoenix Civic Plaza four blocks away.

While mugging and other incidences have been low, officials think the distance between classes and the parking lot can present a "menacing" aspect of winos, derelicts and others who frequent downtown after dark.

The decline in popularity of Maricopa Tech also is tied to a new emphasis on vocational and career education and expansion of such curricula in the other six community colleges of the district.

A major loss of students was experienced when the Rio Salado college was launched several years ago. Although Maricopa Tech has some unique curricula, Rio Salado took over some areas of study.

GAUDET ALSO noted that the district's industry education center, offering drafting, electronics, refrigeration and solar technology studies, is doing business at the 40th Street and East Washington location.

There has been a dropoff in the adult population within a three-mile radius of Maricopa Tech and the new South Mountain campus is luring students to temporary sites south of the Salt River.

Phoenix Gazette, January 23, 1981.

The board allocated $1.75 million to renovate and modernize the building on East Washington, and the first classes moved over for the beginning of the spring term of 1982. An article in the *Phoenix Gazette* for March 8, 1982, reported that enrollment immediately jumped from 3,032 for the fall term to 3,891 for the spring term. The increase was attributed almost entirely to growth in the evening program; students who stopped signing up for night classes in downtown Phoenix apparently felt much safer in the new location.

Green's approach was initially quite successful, and enrollment climbed nearly another thousand students during the fall of 1982 (*Phoenix Gazette*, November 9, 1982). Partly as a result, the district decided to buy an adjacent property, the Aloha Inn Resort at 3901 E. Van Buren, for approximately $1.8 million.

This property eventually gave the district additional office space and more classroom space.

Scottsdale Cools Down

The other district college still suffering from unresolved conflicts was Scottsdale. Here, the wounds were deeper and the damage was more widespread than at Maricopa Tech.

As a result, Art DeCabooter, Scottsdale's president as of January, 1978, had faced a tall order to set things right. He reports that the tension was so great during his first two years that people would just burst into his office and start yelling:

Three people came in one time all in an uproar. I mean, this was the first year I was here, in September of '78. They really were just almost livid. I thought, "What in the world's wrong?" They said, "You can't transfer us to PC!" I said, "What . . ? I don't even . . . ! I hadn't even thought of that. What are you talking about?" "Well, we heard you were going to transfer us!" Someone told them, dropped something on them. . . . I didn't experience any personal hostility. But it's like, "Here's another one. How long will he stay?" I mean, there were seventeen administrators here before I came!

DeCabooter said he decided that the best medicine for Scottsdale's ailments was to open the lines of communication and keep them open:

It took us really almost two full-years to get people to trust us as administrators. There had been just so many slips for whatever reason over the years. We used to marvel because we were coming from

Charles Green, president of Maricopa Tech 1981-96 and Rio Salado 1986-90.

1979

Main entrance to Maricopa Tech in its new location, ca. 1983.

areas where the people would believe [us administrators]—not necessarily like [us], but at least they'd believe [us].

In addition to opening up the lines of communication, DeCabooter promoted healing by providing the first stable administration that the school had known. When two years had passed and he was still on the job, people seemed to relax. Tom Dugan, a counselor at Scottsdale Community College, agrees: "For the first time, over an extended period, we didn't have all these administrative changes. That gives you a degree of stability, and you can

know who's doing what and who you report to and who's supporting you and who isn't and all this stuff. Art definitely contributed to that."

To DeCabooter, the most important symbol of the turnaround at Scottsdale has been the acceptance of the Artichoke as the school's mascot:

> *It's really phenomenal, how the whole Artichoke thing has been turned around and become a positive thing. It was still the animosity when I came, but all the teams have turned around to the "Fighting Artichokes." The baseball people put this little Artichoke on their emblem. We have*

Artichoke hats, Artichoke shirts. When the Fiesta Bowl was here, a bunch of them on the Nebraska team wanted Artichoke shirts and stuff, so we got them Artichoke memorabilia. The hats and everything—not to mention the Lady Artichokes. They've really turned it around. We say we're one of the few schools that can eat its mascot.

Thus, most of the district's internal wounds had begun to heal. The district's fiscal problems, however, were intensifying, and the district could not become completely whole again until those wounds would begin to heal as well.

1981

"Arty" the Artichoke in 1973 and 1998.

1982

The Real Problem:

*As Arizona's community colleges need more and more money,
the state's share decreases proportionally.*

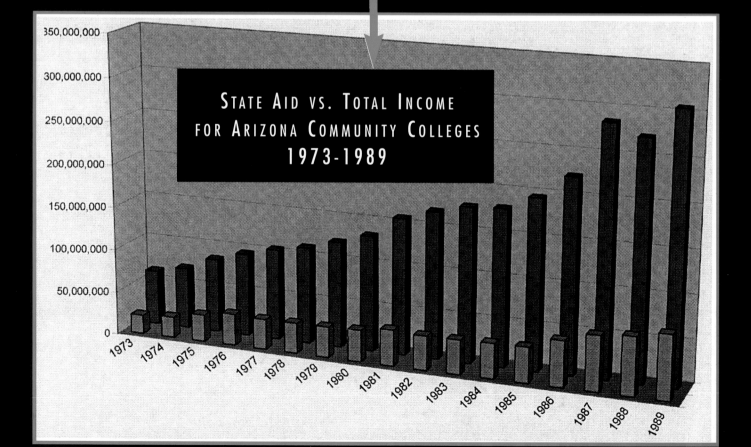

STATE AID VS. TOTAL INCOME
FOR ARIZONA COMMUNITY COLLEGES
1973-1989

Chapter Nineteen

1988
A **Rock** and a **Hard Place**

In January of 1979, Elsner's plan to freeze Maricopa's operating budget had seemed ridiculous and unnecessary, but in the fall of 1979, everything that Elsner had feared most began to come true.

For the past several years, inflation and demands for property tax relief had been causing serious budget problems for the state of Arizona. Faced with declining revenues, legislators had been reducing the state's annual education appropriation. Everywhere but Maricopa, those reductions had disastrous consequences. The newspapers were full of stories about massive layoffs in the Scottsdale and Tempe school districts. The Phoenix Union High School District was agonizing over having to close three existing high schools without the funds to build new ones in areas where new high schools were needed.

The Maricopa district had remained more or less immune to these problems because steady population growth in Maricopa County had guaranteed a virtually unending supply of new students (and, therefore, increasing FTSE). In other words, the state's education pie may have been shrinking, but the size of Maricopa's slice kept increasing.

Maricopa had been extraordinarily fortunate in this respect because community college enrollment was declining nationally, and in some areas of the country, massive staff layoffs had occurred. The Metropolitan Community Colleges in Kansas City, Missouri, saw their enrollment drop 40% between 1975 and 1980. The result was major staff cuts, including the firing of thirty tenured faculty (*Chronicle of Higher Education*, March 10, 1980). In 1980, a study by the Carnegie Council on Policy Studies in Higher Education forecast declining enrollments nationally for the remainder of the decade.

Although Maricopa had been spared that problem to date, other community college districts in Arizona had not been so lucky. To combat the effects of declining enrollments and decreasing state education appropriations coupled with increasing inflation, other districts had been forced to jack up their property tax rates to make up the difference. Increasing property tax rates in Arizona were fueling the demand for property tax relief, the very problem that Elsner had been trying to stave off with his much-despised budget freeze.

Nevertheless, something had to give. Arizona's community colleges needed to do something to compensate for the state's dwindling support. Other than raising the property tax assessment, only one other source of funding remained. All over the state, community college administrators began to whisper the dreaded "t" word: *tuition*.

From the beginning, Arizona's community colleges had been tuition-free for in-county residents who attended during the day. Ironically, most community college systems created in the '60s and '70s charged tuition right from the beginning, but not in Arizona. When the Arizona enabling legislation had been written in 1958, both of the state's then existing junior colleges were not charging tuition to daytime students. The framers of that legislation assumed that junior college students would continue to be mostly full-time, day students. Thus, the legislators

retained tuition-free education for day students at the junior colleges. Evening students had to pay, but soon, even the tuition for evening students was lifted. Mildred Bulpitt, the director of Phoenix College's evening program for many years, recalls why:

> *Cochise College and Arizona Western were in trouble. They didn't have enough money to operate, and they had to refigure how you give them money. [They decided] to count in the evening people [in their FTSE] in order to give them enough money to get by that first year—and you can't do it for them and not for us.*

But in the fall of 1979, those days appeared to be over. The system of funding created by the 1960 enabling legislation was not working, and taxpayers were threatening a Proposition 13-style initiative.

To try to head off such an initiative, the state legislators were preparing for a special legislative session for the fall of 1979. The purpose was to overhaul the state's method of funding public education and to provide some kind of property tax relief. To prepare for this session, the joint House and Senate Education Committees began to meet in late August. Addressing that group, Tom Saad, the director of administrative services for the state community college board, used the dreaded "t" word for the first time when he reluctantly recommended that community college students be required to pay tuition equivalent to about 8% of the actual cost of their education (*Arizona Republic*, August 30, 1979).

However, according to the same article, Saad qualified that recommendation by pointing out that even if all full-time community college students in Arizona paid tuition of $100 per year, the funds generated would only amount to about $5 million. Since the annual expenditures for all the community colleges in the state were already in excess of $100 million, that additional $5 million would do little to reduce the amount that the community colleges would still have to raise by increasing property taxes. Therefore, he concluded, charging tuition was not really going to solve the taxpayers' problems.

The legislators' response to Saad was mixed: *"Well, $5 million is $5 million," said Jim Cooper R-Mesa. "That would be five cents on the state property tax rate." That would mean a $3 annual tax saving on a $40,000 home. Senator Morris Farr, D-Tucson, said he has 4,000 to 5,000 Pima Community college students in his district. "If I saved them a nickel on the tax rate, then handed them a $100 tuition bill, I don't think they'd thank me," he said. Nevertheless, many members of the two panels said they favor a tuition charge and believe it is inevitable.*

This exchange is highly revealing. Jim Cooper's answer to Saad suggests that charging tuition was more important for its political or symbolic value than for its revenue-producing value. But symbolic of what? The answer appears toward the end of the same article, where other legislators' comments suggest that tuition-free education was being abused by lazy or directionless students. One legislator concluded that forcing students to pay tuition would make them more responsible. Senator Jeffrey Hill, R-Tucson, vice chairman of the Senate Education Committee, was quoted as saying: "Community colleges have become a haven for veterans who can't find jobs. They major in GI benefits."

Hill's insensitive remark may not reflect hostility toward veterans so much as the coming Reagan-era hostility toward anyone receiving public assistance. If so, then the concept of charging tuition appears to have been more important than any additional revenue that might be realized.

Eventually, the joint committees decided to accept the state board's recommendation for tuition in the neighborhood of 8% of the estimated actual cost of educating one student. Senator Hill commented: "This would result in tuition fees ranging from $100 to $170 a semester." (*Chandler-Arizona*, October 12, 1978).

Within Maricopa, students started organizing to oppose tuition, and the district faculty executive committee also began a letter-writing campaign. For the next few weeks, the newspapers were filled with reports of various groups protesting tuition.

On the evening of the special legislative session, an article in the *Arizona Republic* for November 11 forecasted a "tax-slashing movement that will crescendo in the special session." The crescendo never happened. Articles published over the next several weeks indicated that progress was slow. The *Arizona Republic* on December 21 revealed some details of the emerging SB 1001, including a provision to limit local spending for schools according to a complicated formula based on population growth and inflation, with provisions allowed for budget override elections. The key element of the plan was to be property tax relief:

Homeowners would be allowed to exempt 28 percent of the taxable value of their homes for property tax purposes, so that the average homeowner in the state would be taxed at 0.75 percent of full-cash value. The state would reimburse local governments for the amount of revenue lost because of the exemption.

Unexpectedly, the debate continued well past Christmas and into the new year. Every week, the details of the anticipated legislation seemed to change. The *Arizona Republic* on January 23 announced that the bill would actually restore the 50-50 mix of state funds and local funds for the community colleges. The next day, the same paper announced a major feature of the new bill would be that the budgets for the community colleges were to be capped, and the bill would put a double whammy on future bond elections. If the voters were to defeat a bond, the sponsoring district would not be permitted to find other money to fund the projects that the defeated bonds were to have financed. (Apparently, that provision was in response to a similar maneuver by the Pima Community College District after it had lost a bond election.) This provision was truly bad news, intended to make districts think carefully before initiating bond elections.

The one odd detail is that no one was saying anything about tuition anymore.

On March 21, 1980, the *Scottsdale Daily Progress* revealed that the nearly final form of the funding bill reneged on the state's promise to meet half the community colleges' costs. Elsner was furious. In the same article, he complained that the Maricopa district had been figuring its '80-'81 budget based on that 50% contribution from the state. Elsner then used the occasion to point out the Maricopa district's fiscal economies:

> Elsner said the Legislature is penalizing the district for its fiscal austerity. The district froze its $49.1 million budget this year, has the lowest per-student costs of any community college district in the state, and its property tax rate of 94 cents per $100 assessed valuation is among the lowest junior college rates, he said.

A few days later, the legislature passed the final form of the education funding act. In the March 26 *Phoenix Gazette*, reporter Richard DeUriarte gave the grim news: The plan removed a preexisting 4% state sales tax on food but allowed cities to levy their own 1% tax. The bill also imposed strict budget limits on all schools, including the community colleges, but spending could rise to keep up with inflation and population growth.

Homeowners' tax bills to be limited to 1% of full cash value—the same amount as California's notorious Proposition 13 but without the rollback to earlier levels of assessment.

Even so, the bill contained no mention of tuition whatsoever. The legislature simply reduced the amount of money the state would spend on education and left to the state community college board the odious task of imposing tuition to make up for the shortfall.

Elsner and the Maricopa governing board were not pleased, but budget crunch or no budget crunch, faculty salaries had to be raised to combat the killer inflation rate. At the board meeting on April 8, 1980, the board approved a 22% pay hike—spread out over two years—for the district's 1,600 employees. Nothing was said at the time about how those salary increases were going to be underwritten.

But everyone knew.

On April 17, the *Phoenix Gazette* reported how students from Scottsdale rushed to take their case to the press before the state board was scheduled to meet:

> Maricopa County Community College District officials should slash administrative costs—instead of charging tuition—to offset cuts in state aid. So say Scottsdale Community College student leaders, who are circulating petitions in support of their stance. In flyers distributed on campus, student government states, "The time has come to cut back on a bloated and oversized educational bureaucracy, and we believe serious spending cuts will alleviate the need for the charging of further tuition

> to Maricopa Community Colleges' 60,000 students."

No one listened. About a week later, the state board officially authorized all of Arizona's community college districts to charge tuition as of the fall, 1980, term.

And then—perhaps hoping that fiscal hard times for the community colleges had softened voters' hearts—Elsner went to the board with a proposal for a $45 million bond to acquire the land and to build the three campuses specified in the Tadlock report. The bonds would underwrite the district's capital construction program from 1982 through 1986. On May 7, 1980, the board approved the bond proposal for the November ballot.

While waiting to gauge the public's response, Elsner confronted the tuition issue. At the governing board meeting on May 20, 1980, Elsner regretfully announced he favored a tuition charge of five dollars per credit hour, but not all of the campus presidents agreed. Some wanted tuition held to three dollars. An editorial in the May 21 *Phoenix Gazette*, expressed concern that many students would not be able to pay, but Elsner pointed out that more than 7,600 Maricopa students were already receiving aid of one sort or another, primarily federal Basic Educational Opportunity Grants. His feeling was that aid programs would help students in need with their tuition charges.

In June, Elsner and Al Flowers presented the board with a $56.7 million budget for the '80-'81 year. This amount represented a 15.4% increase over the previous year, but Flowers pointed out—as only an accountant can—that since no budget increase had been made in the current year's budget over the previous year, the annual average increase was only 7.7%. This budget was also based on Elsner's recommended five dollars per credit tuition charge. At the same time, Flowers announced that the district would drop the tax rate from $.94 per $100 assessed valuation to somewhere between $.75 and $.79 (*Phoenix Gazette*, June 3, 1980).

At the meeting on June 3, the board accepted the budget but not the tuition, which was set at three dollars per credit hour. At the board meeting on June 10, $500,000 was sliced from student activities to make up the difference. Student representatives in attendance howled with pain, but the budget was passed 4-1, Barbara Hitchcock opposing.

Then, the suspense really began. What effect would the tuition have on enrollment at the district colleges? What effect would the tuition have on voter attitudes toward the bond election scheduled for November?

Proposition 106

The education funding act of 1980 had not been good news for Arizona's community colleges, but its purpose was to try to head off a Proposition 13-style initiative and, presumably, more draconian measures. In that respect, the bill failed.

A statewide group calling itself Citizens for Tax Relief wasn't satisfied. The group had gathered enough signatures to put a California-style property tax reform bill on the November ballot. Proposition 106 (also known as the Heuisler initiative in honor of the group's chair, William Heuisler) would further limit property taxes and roll back most assessments to 1975 levels. Future increases would be limited to 2% per year. Opponents of the Heuisler initiative threatened that Maricopa County would lose somewhere between $20 million to $25 million in revenue.

Unwilling to risk the district's bond election on the same ballot with Proposition 106, Elsner decided to call off the bond again. He wrote the board a memo citing various legal

complications, not the least of which was the fact that under the terms of the 1980 education funding act, the district would not be allowed to fund the same projects by some other means if the bond were to fail. He recommended another "pay-as-you-go" approach to fund $19 million in new construction and to purchase land for the three campuses proposed in Tadlock (*Phoenix Gazette*, 7/25/80).

As the fall semester began, the district received the first piece of good news in several months. The $3 per credit tuition fee apparently had no adverse effect on registration. In August, enrollment exceeded 60,292, a 5.7% increase over the previous fall (*Phoenix Gazette*, September 5, 1980).

As the November election approached, the district then received more good news. All the signs pointed to growing opposition to Proposition 106. Opponents were claiming that the cut in property taxes would actually raise other taxes because the shortfall would have to be made up somewhere else.

On November 5, Arizona voters went to the polls. They decided that gutting the community colleges and the rest of the state's educational institutions was a poor idea. Proposition 106 was defeated. Heuisler cried foul: "The politicians . . . spread the idea that Proposition 106 would raise taxes. That's a lie; goddamn it, we didn't work for 2 1/2 years to raise people's taxes." (*Arizona Republic,* November 5, 1980).

The collective sigh of relief could be heard all the way to California.

To Bond or Not to Bond?

The defeat of the Heuisler initiative meant a return to the status quo. Worse, the district was projecting a potential $2 million shortfall for the '80-'81 school year, and the much-needed bond election seemed more distant than ever.

Also, inflation was eating up all the benefits of the new $3 per credit tuition. Once again, Maricopa faced the equally unattractive alternatives of raising tuition and/or the property tax rate again. The first alternative could easily backfire by turning away students, but the other could just as easily backfire by angering county taxpayers, who would then be even less likely to approve the bond whenever the district finally decided to risk one.

In March of 1981, the Senate Education Committee played a cruel joke by announcing a new formula for computing state aid to community colleges. The bill (SB 1006) would have restored the long-promised 50% funding by the 1985-86 fiscal year, instead of the estimated 31% for the '80-'81 fiscal year. The bill was then sent to the Senate Appropriations Committee, where the chairman, John Pritzlaff, was quoted as favoring those funding formulas as long as the state could do so without increasing taxes, a caveat that sounded like trouble (*Arizona Republic*, March 5, 1981).

Encouraged by the committee's announcement, Elsner announced that the Chandler-Gilbert area would be the first to receive a new college when the state's funding problems were finally resolved. In doing so, he noted that Mesa Community College had already turned away 1,000 students that year for lack of space (*Phoenix Gazette*, March 24, 1981).

Everyone kept their fingers crossed, but on April 2, the *Arizona Republic* reported that SB 1006 had become stalled in the Senate. Fearing the worst, the governing board tested the waters with a proposed two-dollar increase in tuition. William Berry, president of Phoenix College, warned of the dangers of turning to tuition to pay the freight. He pointed out that Pima College had suffered a 10% drop in enrollment because it charged students tuition of seven dollars per credit for the current school year (*Phoenix Gazette*, April 17, 1981).

At the end of April, SB 1006 died. Yet, a provision added to another bill, SB 1187, limited increases to the annual state appropriations for community colleges to the 7% budget increases previously authorized for public schools. Tom Saad, of the State Community Colleges Board, claimed that this amount represented an increase of about $2 million for 1981-82 fiscal year. He added, "But that's just half the $4 million they gave us for the current year to help the schools ride out the cuts in community college funding as a result of last year's special tax session." (*Scottsdale Daily Progress*, April 28, 1981).

The groans of frustration echoed forth from all of the state's community colleges.

The death of SB 1006 meant that the state's contribution to all of Arizona's community

colleges was expected to fall to a low of 25.3%. To respond, the district took a calculated risk. It increased tuition for the fall of 1981 to five dollars per credit hour but reduced the property tax rate again in hopes that Maricopa's phenomenal growth rate would increase tax revenues anyway (*Phoenix Gazette*, May 12, 1981).

This gamble did not pay off. Enrollment for the fall of 1981 dropped to 59,231, down from 60,798 during fall of the previous year. That was the good news. The bad news was that FTSE had dropped even more because the students were taking fewer classes: a sick-

ly 26,008 FTSE, down from the previous fall's robust 33,223 FTSE. The five dollar tuition was widely blamed for the decreased enrollment (*Phoenix Gazette*, September 25, 1981).

All over the state, community college districts despaired of the state's increasing its share any-

time soon. As the Maricopa board began planning for the '82-'83 school year, board members felt they had to raise tuition yet again. At the board meeting on March 2, 1982, tuition for the following school year was increased an additional $6 to a total of $11 per credit hour with a cap of $132 for twelve or more hours per semester. The property tax rate, however, was slightly decreased again.

The district's stubbornness in putting the entire burden on the students' shoulders may seem very unfair. A report in the *Arizona Republic* for June 9, 1982, however, suggests otherwise:

The announced [Maricopa district] budget for '82-'83 would top $72 million, roughly $9 million more than the previous year. A big part of that increase would provide faculty with an 8% salary increase. Of that total, $39.3 million would come from property taxes, $16.7 million would come from the state, $6.4 million would come

from tuition, $5.8 million would come from a cash balance from the previous school year, and $3.8 million would come from miscellaneous other sources.

In other words, nearly 55% of the district's annual budget was already coming from the property tax rate, but only 9% was coming from tuition. If the district were ever going to sell a bond election to the voters, the percentage of the budget from tuition clearly had to be increased.

From Bad to Worse

In the fall of 1982, high inflation and high

statewide unemployment were strangling the state's finances. In October, the chair of the Senate Education Committee, Republican Senator Anne Lindeman from Phoenix, predicted that the state was going to have to rethink the 7% annual budget growth cap for school districts for the 1982-83 year already underway. She noted that funding for education already accounted for about 60% of the state's total spending. If the state's revenues continued to decline, the schools could see even more cutbacks (*Phoenix Gazette*, October 22, 1982).

When the legislature convened in January of 1983, Lindeman announced that she was drafting legislation to cut the current year's state aid to education by $50 million to balance the current year's budget (*Arizona Republic*, January 12, 1983). Howls of protest filled the newspapers for the next two days, but legislators claimed their hands were tied by a projected deficit of $251 million.

On February 4, House and Senate negotiators lopped off $82.9 million from the current year's state budget. They canceled $1.99 million that had already been promised to community college districts for new construction and reclaimed $1.79 million in unexpended basic state aid to local school districts (*Phoenix Gazette*, February 4, 1983).

And yet, a ray of light then pierced the gloom. The *Mesa Tribune* on February 25 reported that the education funding bill for the '83-'84 school year had at last passed the House, and—miraculously—funding would actually be increased by a modest 4%. The reason was that the economic clouds were beginning to lift a little. Local economic indicators were up slightly for the first time in several years. A Valley National Bank econo-

---

THE RICHARDSON STUDY

As the economy began to show signs of improving, the state's community colleges received help from another source. Dick Richardson and Donald Doucette, of ASU's Department of Higher and Adult Education, released the results of a report that confirmed that "community college graduates earn degrees from ASU at nearly the same rate as those who enter as freshmen. In addition, their grade point averages declined less than half a point in their first semester at a four-year institution, then rebounded to a level equal to other students. . . ."

They also concluded:

"Community colleges include in their freshman classes many students who were not admissible to a university . . . What is surprising is how well the transfer student with two years at a community college, does perform in relation to the native student. . . . When such differences as rank in high school graduating classes are controlled, the dif-ferences disappear for practical purposes. . . .

Students who attend community colleges directly after high schools differ from the university students in several ways. They are more likely to attend part-time, are more often responsible for all or part of student costs, did less well in their high school work and scored lower on national academic aptitude tests." (Phoenix Gazette, February 28, 1983).

THE EMERGING SERVICE ECONOMY

During this period, many articles favorable to the district's capital plan and '84-'85 budget appear. One, in particular, from the *Arizona Republic* for June 24, 1984, seemed especially well timed. The facts and figures included provide an effective snapshot of the changing demographics that were fueling the district's expansion in the mid-'80s:

> Education certainly has taken its lumps lately. Everybody from President Reagan on down says our education system isn't what it used to be. That may be so, but more people are consuming more of it than ever before. In 1960, when education was supposed to be so much better, less than 8 percent of all people 25 years and older had completed four or more years of college, and only about 40 percent had completed high school. By 1980, nearly 70 percent had completed high school, and the proportion of college graduates had more than doubled to 17 percent. . . .
>
> Unemployment rates for college-trained workers range from one-third to one-fourth of those not college trained. However, if manufacturing work had continued to dominate our economy, there would be plenty of unemployed college graduates. The rise of the service sector of our economy is what keeps providing them work. Four of every five college-educated workers are employed in service industries.
>
> Because of the expanding job opportunities in health care, financial services and information processing, it has been estimated that between 12 million and 13 million more college graduates will be needed in this decade. But the shrinking crowd of 18- to 24-year-olds is expected to cause the number of college students to decline for the next 10 years. However, this projected supply-and-demand problem probably will be resolved before it occurs by the increasing number of adults going back to school. The business of adult education is booming. There are more than 3 million people between the ages of 25 and 34 enrolled in school, double the number 10 years ago.

was improving. For the first five months of 1983, the annual inflation rate had declined to approximately 3%.

In the fall of 1983, more good news came. In spite of the $14 per hour tuition, fall enrollment was up significantly. The head count had

mist predicted that the recession was finally beginning to turn around (*Arizona Republic*, February 11, 1983).

In early May of 1983, the Maricopa board voted to push up tuition to $14 per credit hour for the fall. (Remember that no tuition whatsoever had been charged to in-county students only five years before!) Even so, the district reduced the tax rate again, from $.80 per $100 of assessed valuation to $.75. Al Flowers explained that the drop came about because the valuation of the county was expected to increase 18%. The board also adopted an '83-'84 budget of $82.2 million, up almost $10.7

million from the previous year, an increase of about 14%. This budget included a carryover of $2.3 million caused by "curtailing current fiscal-year spending" and included a 7% raise for employees. Total expenditures, including capital outlay, would top $100 million (*Phoenix Gazette*, May 11, 1983). Trying to be conciliatory, governing board president Grant Christensen observed that students were still being asked to pay less than 10% of the cost of their education (*Mesa Tribune*, June 15, 1983).

He needn't have worried. By then, everyone was beginning to notice that the economy

swollen almost 6% to a grand total of 66,791 warm bodies. And that was the bad news. The good news was that FTSE had jumped up from the previous year's 29,637 to a strong 31,860 (*Arizona Republic*, September 21, 1983). In other words, not only had more students enrolled, but they were also taking more classes.

At last, the crisis seemed to be over.

The 1984 Bond

The district then decided to try to cash in on its long-term gamble of raising tuition while lowering the property tax rate. In the fall of 1983, the district began to try to soften the voters by circulating reports of severe crowding at Mesa and Glendale. In an article in the *Phoenix Gazette* on September 20, Paul Elsner commented: "Mesa is in the worst shape because Glendale has a fairly large site and additions can be moved on it more readily . . . . The Mesa campus is saturated. Traffic is a problem and is even backing up onto the freeway." Norman B. Johansen, the acting president at MCC, added that 10,000 students who preregistered filled up all the basic English and Math courses. "We have 16,045 students and that pretty well saturates us." Similar articles about crowded conditions and needs for new programs appeared throughout the fall.

In the spring of 1984, the district then announced plans for an ambitious capital construction program, which would include the three new colleges Tadlock recommended. The price tag was to be $150 million, which would require a bond issue of $75 million. The rest of the money would come from other sources (*Phoenix Gazette*, March 13, 1984).

The *Phoenix Gazette* on March 14, 1984,

pointed out that the bond issue would add between 10.5 to 20 cents per $100 assessed valuation to county tax rates. This increase, however, would follow almost five years of property tax reductions, from just under $.84 (per $100 valuation) in 1978-79, to $.77 for the '83-'84 school year.

Now, who could argue with that kind of fiscal responsibility in hard times?

May 3, 1996, video interview with Phil Randolph, president of GateWay Community College 1999 to present. Transcript and audio excerpts available online.

http://www.mc.maricopa.edu/users/M3cdhistory/

In June of 1984, the district budget for the following school year was announced. The bottom line was $122.6 million, which included about $20 million for the first year of the ten-year capital improvements program. This budget was up $30.5 million from the district's previous budget, but this time, no increase in tuition was planned (or were any cuts in tuition mentioned, either).

In September of 1984, the district's gamble with high tuition and low property taxes finally paid off: Voters approved the long-delayed and desperately needed bond election by a margin of nearly 3-to-1 (although only around 5% of the eligible voters went to the polls) (*Arizona Republic*, September 28, 1984).

The district's $75 million bond was the largest ever approved for any community college district to that date. The time had come to start making Tadlock's recommendations a reality.

Maricopa Tech Becomes GateWay

Unfortunately, the district's good fortune was not shared equally at all of the campuses. At Maricopa Tech, Charles Green's predictions for increased enrollment between 1983 and 1985 did not materialize. As the economy began to turn around, Maricopa Tech's enrollment declined significantly. According to an article in the *Arizona Republic* for January 16, 1985, "Enrollment at Maricopa Tech . . . declined 18.1 percent from 1983 to 1984, compared with 1.3 percent districtwide."

In light of the Richardson study and other trends within the district, many people began to wonder if the district really needed a technical school anymore.

Eleven months later, Maricopa Tech's transformation began. Paul Elsner engineered a switch of college presidents. In December, Charles Green became the new president of Rio Salado, and Rio Salado's president, Myrna Harrison, became the new president of Maricopa Tech. An article in the *Phoenix Gazette* for December 6, 1985, explained why Elsner seemed to think this switch would help Maricopa Tech.

"We're going to be looking at expanding the role of Maricopa Tech," district Chancellor Paul Elsner said . . . "Adult literacy, general education and liberal arts programs will be

added to Maricopa Tech's technical curriculum," Elsner said, citing Harrison's expertise in running those types of programs.

Harrison felt the new direction for Maricopa Tech should be signaled by a new name. Phil Randolph, who succeeded Harrison as president of GateWay in 1988, recalls:

The theory behind it, as I understand, was that "Maricopa Tech" and then "Maricopa Technical Community College" had a tech-school stigma, and she wanted to make it more comprehensive. Her background was liberal arts and science. The college in its old days was about eighty percent occupational, about twenty percent math and English and liberal arts. It was changing to about sixty/forty, maybe fifty/fifty.

Harrison requested suggestions for the new name, and staff members submitted around seventy-five. The name Sky Harbor Community College was eventually selected. According to Randolph, "It made some sense because all of our Maricopa colleges have a name that gives a geographical identity. They went so far as to get the board resolution to name it Sky Harbor Community College because of the [proximity to] the airport."

The board sanctioned the new name in August, 1986, but the school was to remain Maricopa Tech through the following May. In the interim, though, fate intervened. Randolph recalls that the City of Phoenix began talking about renaming Sky Harbor "Barry Goldwater Airport." Randolph explained the ensuing dilemma:

Now we would be a name that meant nothing! So somewhere in those eleventh-hour gyrations, they came up with the name GateWay, and spelled with a capital W, because there are two more GateWay Community Colleges. . . . As I understand it, it was named after this area on Forty-Fourth and Van Buren, the GateWay Commerce Park.

The board sanctioned this name in February, and the change took effect as scheduled in May, 1987.

Apparently, the initial public response to the name change was not good. An article in the *Scottsdale Daily Progress* for August 21, reported that enrollment was down again:

A name change from Maricopa Tech to GateWay Community College may be responsible for an enrollment decline because students think that the college has abandoned its technical classes, said President Myrna Harrison. . . . GateWay has not dropped any of its technical or trade classes, she said, but college officials are worried that some potential students might be under that impression.

Phil Randolph would have preferred that the old name had been retained:

I would have never have done that. Maricopa Tech enjoyed in this county a fine, fine reputation. It was very clear what it was. In fact, as I understand it, a proprietary school picked up our name and used it after we walked away from it. So I spent my first three years building name recognition for GateWay. We used television advertising for a lot of our marketing, mainly for name recognition, not that it was always the most effective way to get students in. But it's okay now. Most people now here, in the tremendous growth of our Valley, know GateWay as it is.

Subsequently, Myrna Harrison switched jobs again and became the president of Phoenix College in 1988. Phil Randolph, who had been the Dean of Occupational Education at Glendale, was then appointed as Myrna Harrison's successor.

1988

A *New Model* Evolves

As the district prepared to implement Tadlock's blueprint for growth, a great truth was revealed. During all the upset and furor that had started at Scottsdale and blossomed into a full-scale insurrection over Rio Salado and South Mountain, the district's image of itself had been evolving. The district's own sense of its mission had changed. In the '60s, the district's self-image had been very clear. Maricopa was a junior college district, and everyone knew what a junior college should look like. Phoenix College was the shining example, and Glendale, Mesa, and Scottsdale were all conceived as clones of Phoenix College. But then, something started to go wrong at Scottsdale. The old model didn't seem to fit the new student demographics. And before anyone could figure out what was going on, all the turbulence started, at the climax of which Rio and South Mountain were conceived in utter chaos. Neither of those colleges corresponded to the old Phoenix College mold, and the process by which they had been created contained a new element: community involvement.

Of course, the community had been involved when Maricopa Tech had been created, but

Maricopa's seven college presidents in 1986. Seated from left to right are Chuck Green (Rio Salado), Art DeCabooter (Scottsdale), Raúl Cárdenas (South Mountain). Standing from left to right are Wally Simpson (Mesa), Bill Berry (Phoenix), Myrna Harrison (GateWay), and John Waltrip. (Glendale).

that involvement resulted more from necessity than from any deliberate innovation. No one in the district at that time knew how to start a technical college, and Maricopa Tech's founding fathers welcomed suggestions from the community that the technical college was being designed to serve. Nevertheless, the district should have been paying attention. A major factor in Maricopa Tech's success was the fact that the community had been involved in the design of the curriculum. That sort of thing would never have been allowed at Phoenix Junior College!

By the middle of the '80s, the turbulence was largely over. Planning for three new colleges was ready to begin in an orderly way. The old model was gone, but what was to be the new model?

No one could say. The district's two most recent creations, Rio and South Mountain, were too different from each other to provide any sense of future direction. The only thing that was certain was that the community would be involved in the process. This time, the district would put the community into the college before putting the college into the community.

Linda Rosenthal, who joined the governing board in 1980, agrees that the district's self-image changed in this way:

> *The whole attitude I see as the major change in the years that I'm on the board [is the change] from "We're educators. We know best. We're the proscriptors," to "Community, you own the college. You own everything that's a part of it. This is yours."*

And one community in particular wasted no time in making its presence felt.

The Squeaky Wheel

In the late fall of 1985, the board authorized $35.9 million in projects for the first phase of its $150 capital improvement plan and set the completion deadline for March, 1987. A large part of the first-phase money was for construction work at the existing colleges: Mesa Community College—which was still using all of its original portable classrooms—would receive several new buildings, including a bookstore, a security and social sciences building, a child care center, a math and business building, a ceramics lab, and a physical plant housing heating and cooling systems. Glendale Community College would receive two new buildings [$3 million], and Phoenix College would receive some desperately needed remodeling [$1.75 million]. Three buildings and a parking lot were budgeted for Scottsdale Community College [$4.75 million], and three new buildings and remodeling were budgeted for South Mountain Community College [$2.4 million] (*Mesa Tribune*, November 7, 1985).

But, then came a surprise. Money was announced for two new colleges, but not the two colleges that everyone had been expecting. The east valley site (Chandler-Gilbert) and the north valley site (Paradise Valley) were to be constructed first. Furthermore, the Chandler-Gilbert facility was to be only 70,000 square feet and to cost $5.6 million while the new Paradise Valley facility was to be 170,000 square feet, at a cost of $14.5 million—nearly three times what the Chandler-Gilbert site was to cost!

Tadlock had recommended the north valley site not be built for another fifteen years. How had Paradise Valley suddenly gone from third to first on the district's priority list?

The answer to that question may be summed up in two words: Beth Koehnemann (pronounced KAYN-uh-min). Although she resists the credit, many of the people interviewed for this book named her as the single most important force in the movement that led to the establishment of Paradise Valley Community College.

Beth Koehnemann and her husband moved to Paradise Valley, a northern suburb of Phoenix, in 1965. At that time, she found that, "The Dreamy Draw[1] was a two-lane road at the end of Phoenix, and we felt like we were just not being heard at the city council and a lot of other places. We needed a lot of amenities that we didn't have as a community. So we formed the Paradise Valley Community Council."

The PVCC soon evolved into a close-knit organization of community activists who pressured the Phoenix City Council for whatever the Paradise Valley community needed, from roads to a new fire station to a library.

Phoenix College began offering courses at Paradise Valley high schools in the early '70s, and later Rio Salado took over those courses. According to Koehnemann, "There was a great demand there at that point. That's why they had college classes at all those schools. Then we [also] had students driving to Scottsdale and Phoenix and everything."

May 8, 1997, video interview with Beth Koehnemann, Paradise Valley civic leader. Transcript and audio excerpts available online.

http://www.mc.maricopa.edu/users/M3cdhistory/

Thus, the PVCC took a great interest in the Tadlock study when it was released in 1978. They were very pleased that Paradise Valley would be one of the three sites for the next three community colleges to be built in Maricopa County, but they were not pleased with Tadlock's timetable.

They watched with displeasure as the district acquired land at Dysart and Thomas Roads in the west valley and a parcel on Pecos Road, between Gilbert and Cooper Roads in the east valley. But, the district did not buy land in their area. The Paradise Valley Community Council felt their community was being overlooked. They felt that Tadlock's population projections were entirely too conservative, and council members drafted a letter to the district to urge the next community college be constructed in their area. This letter was reported in a newspaper story that appeared in the *Phoenix Gazette* for March 11, 1981. Approximately two weeks later, Paul Elsner announced that the first new campus would be built in

Chandler to take some of the pressure off of Mesa, which was then the fastest-growing school in the system.

That announcement was a gauntlet flung down at the feet of Paradise Valley's community activists. According to Koehnemann, "We knew that we had something cut out for us to do. Of course, we had surmounted many obstacles out there before—fire stations and this type of thing—so one more challenge was just right down our alley."

First, the PVCC called a public meeting to discuss the situation. District planning officials Mike Svaco and Cliff Smith and board member Linda Rosenthal attended. Rosenthal claimed that the governing board was actively seeking a suitable parcel of land for a north valley college, but even so, a college for Paradise Valley was still years away.

Undaunted, the community continued to press the point. At the end of 1981, the PVCC formed a task force to pursue a community college for Paradise Valley in the immediate future. Reb Prophet, the chair of the PVCC, asked Beth Koehnemann to chair the new group. The tornado was thus unleashed. Her first task was clear: "In the best interests of the whole community and to

[1] The "Dreamy Draw" is the local name for the road that had been the main connection between Phoenix proper and Paradise Valley.

get the best input, we asked the president of every service organization and every educational organization to serve on our committee. And not one person refused. Even the educators—there was NFT and the NEA—they both served. Even the ministers' association was represented!"

The new group was officially known as the Community College Task Force of the Greater Paradise Valley Community Council. This task force convened another public meeting in March of 1982. Mike Svaco reiterated Tadlock's formula that a community had to show population in excess of 170,000 before a college should be established there. Demo-graphic studies estimated the population in Paradise Valley at 115,000 at the most. Koehnemann says the task force disagreed strongly. "When we encompassed all the areas that [the new college] would serve—Carefree, Cave Creek, and everything . . . it far exceeded what we needed. And we already had students in the area that were going to a community college that exceeded the FTSE that was needed" (*Phoenix Gazette,* March 31, 1982).

In November of 1982 the task force assembled representatives of the Paradise Valley Community Council, Chamber of Commerce, United School District, the planning committee, and representatives from the Arizona state legislature to produce a report for the Maricopa governing board. The report requested the immediate creation of a community college in Paradise Valley.

Still, the board resisted. John Córdova, the provost and later the founding president of Paradise Valley, explains what happened next:

> The board in essence said, "There is no substantiation for a community college. Show us the data." They went back—Beth Koehnemann and her folks—they generated data, they went back to the board and defied the Board. Defied them! They gave them not only present statistics but also the projections according to the Metropolitan Area Growth reports, according to all the other reports. They did their homework.

In March, 1983, the governing board began to yield. It officially created the Northeast Valley Community College Task Force chaired by governing board member Roy Amrein. At the same time, the board also authorized the creation of a similar task force for the east valley. Grant Christensen was appointed to chair that committee, but by then, the north Phoenix group was way ahead of the east valley group. Christensen recalls:

> In Paradise Valley, you had money and you had some influence. And what did you have in Chandler-Gilbert? You had a few farmers. And you didn't have much money. You didn't have the surrounding

homes and all with the quality in this area that you had up there. . . . Frankly, we were lucky to get what we got for Chandler-Gilbert. We just didn't have the influences that we had in Paradise Valley.

Thus, the Paradise Valley group had a head start, and at the board work session on February 28, 1984, they made a complete presentation, and when the breakdown of the first-phase construction money was finally announced in November of 1985, Paradise Valley had hit the jackpot. Chandler-Gilbert, which was to have been the district's first priority, had come in a distant second.

Paradise Valley Community College Begins

Even before the breakdown of the phase-one construction money was announced, the district had announced John Córdova would be the provost of the Paradise Valley Community College Center. [2] A familiar face in the district, he began his undergraduate studies at Phoenix College in 1965 and went

[2] For accreditation purposes, Paradise Valley operated initially as an extension of Scottsdale Community College. During that phase Córdova served as the college provost. When the school was accredited separately in 1990, Córdova became the president.

May 7, 1996 video interview with John Córdova, president of Paradise Valley Community College 1985-1992 and South Mountain Community College 1992 to present. Transcript and audio excerpts available online.

http://www.mc.maricopa.edu/users/M3cdhistory/

John Córdova, president of Paradise Valley Community College 1985-1992 and Paradise Valley Community College 1992 to present.

on to earn his BA, MA, and Ph.D. from ASU. There, he became active with counselor training through Chicanos per la Causa. Later, Lionel Martinez suggested that Córdova apply for an associate deanship at Scottsdale Community College. Córdova was accepted for that position and began work there as the associate dean of continuing education on July 1, 1976. Two and a half years later, Córdova returned to Phoenix College as dean of instruction, the position he was holding when he was tapped to helm Paradise Valley in January of 1985.

Instead of locating the new college out in the middle of nowhere, the district favored using a portion of Paradise Valley Park, 340 acres of land already bordered by established housing developments. About a month after Córdova's appointment was announced, the Greater Paradise Valley Community Council held a public meeting to gauge community reaction to this proposed location. To the council's surprise, residents in the immediate neighborhood reacted very negatively. Many objected strenuously to surrendering ninety acres of neighboring parkland to the new college. Some residents raised issues of traffic, parking, and flooding, a problem that frequently plagued that area. John Córdova remembers things nearly got out of control:

All hell broke loose when one maniac, ex-Vietnam veteran, decked out in his fatigues, basically said, in so many words and profanity, "If those college students ever peek into my bedroom, I will shoot the—" whatever-whatever-whatever. He was asked to settle down and to quit the profanities, and he said, "Well, you can go—" He just went on and on and on, and he stormed out and he slammed the door and he shook the entire building. A small building. I was standing back there, and I

WHAT'S IN A NAME?

As the founding president of the new college, John Córdova thought perhaps the time had come to break the pattern of naming each college after its geographical service area. He thoroughly underestimated the intensity of the community's identification with its new college.

I thought perhaps we could break the mold and be nontraditional and be visionary, and maybe could call it Anasazi Community College to reflect the history of our land. My vision was that each building would reflect a certain element of the Anasazi culture, and that we would bring it together maybe in a student center to celebrate our ancestry and our spirituality and whatnot.

So, I was at a community meeting giving an update at the community council. I was giving a progress report. Then, one person said, "Excuse me. When are we going to name this college 'Paradise Valley'?" I turned around and said, "Well, my sense is that we ought to look at some options." Then, I heard this murmur, and it was almost like an earthquake. In the back of my mind, I thought, "You're not going to win this one." A lady said, "Phoenix has Phoenix College. Mesa has Mesa College. Scottsdale has Scottsdale Community College. We're going to have Paradise Valley Community College." That's as far as that discussion went. I never had the opportunity to put that on the table. I drove home, and I said, "Get me a beer. There goes my dream!"

said to myself, "This is my assignment? I'm supposed to deal with this? This is supposed to be an upper-middle-class, white community, and I'm dealing with these issues? They'll kill me!"

However, the district realigned the proposed parcel of land so that it was not immediately adjacent to any existing homes. Córdova also met with city engineers to address the flood control issues, but then, he uncovered some misinformation that was being deliberately circulated to stir up the neighborhood:

They were being sold a bill of goods that their . . . housing values were going to depreciate because the college was coming in there. I said, "Folks, look at the data. Who told you that?" As I started driving around, I said, "Holy smoke! Some real estate agent is making big bucks." There were FOR SALE signs coming up all over the place. People were buying property, and you know what they were going to do with that. I said, "Time-out, folks. Check your data. Somebody's taking you to the cleaners. Once this college goes up, your appraisal is going to shoot up. . . . Every time a university or college has been built, the community profits from it.". . . I think they started believing it. But it took a lot of salesmanship.

During the summer of 1985, the new school prepared to begin offering classes at—surprise!—the local Jewish Community Center and the Paradise Valley High School. However, Córdova was not enthusiastic about this phase of the school's development:

We purposely did it very slowly. . . . Folks were saying, "I don't know how long you're going to last in this job. Because the name of the game is FTSE, and you just haven't gotten the message, have

1994

new facilities owed nothing to the old Phoenix College model. Mary Lou Mosley, who was involved in the planning for the new facility, explains:

> They wanted an open-type-feeling campus, and [they had] an idea that there were many different ways people could communicate. You would set up physical ways people could communicate, so that there were plazas, or the courtyard between the instructional buildings, so that as the students went from one building to another, as faculty went from one building to another, they'd run into each other.

For the groundbreaking ceremonies for the Northeast Valley Education Center, as it was known initially, a hot air balloon was used to show how hopes for the new school were rising.

you?" I said, "Believe me. The enrollment will come. I'm not going to be wrong on this one."

May 8, 1997, video interview with Mary Lou Mosley, Paradise Valley Community College administrator. Transcript available online.

http://www.mc.maricopa.edu/users/M3cdhistory/

Barry Wukasch, who transferred from Scottsdale as one of the early faculty at Paradise Valley, recalls that Córdova was right:

> The last semester before the campus, we had a thousand students. I remember everybody was kind of half laughing and half regretting because John said he'd been at a board meeting, and Elsner asked him unexpectedly, "What are your enrollment projections for next fall?" and just off-the-cuff, he said "Four thousand" And from then on, we were obligated to make four thousand. It turned out we did, by about a hundred people, about forty-one hundred, which astounded even ourselves.

The district chose the old Phoenix firm of Lescher and Mahoney to design the new campus—the same firm that had also designed the 1939 Phoenix College campus on Thomas Avenue. However, the plan for the

The main entrance to the Paradise Valley Community College campus.

In designing the programs for the new college, Córdova emphasized two areas primarily: technology and student development. In the first area, the architects designed a full-computer lab for the new college. The emphasis in the second area turned out to be more controversial. According to Mosley, Córdova had the idea that:

> Every employee who had contact with students had an opportunity to teach students, to help them to learn. Whether it was learn through the registration process, learn how to use a library, learn how to pay their tuition, learn how to read a schedule, learn how to figure out their classes—those simple steps all the way up.

Controversy developed because faculty maintained that instruction should be the sole province of the faculty and that learning only went on in the classroom. Some even advanced the idea that PV should become a Little Harvard of the West, an echo of the same idea that had troubled Scottsdale in its formative years.

For several years, the faculty who favored the student-development philosophy and the faculty who favored a more elitist philosophy duked it out, but by 1992, the two sides had declared an uneasy truce. At about that time, Paul Elsner moved Córdova to South Mountain and moved Raúl Cárdenas, the president of South Mountain, to PV. Whether the switch was in any way related to the tension at PV is unclear.

The Pink Palace

For the provost of the new Chandler-Gilbert Community College Center, Elsner again tapped a district insider, Arnette Ward. [3] A native of Florida, she began her undergraduate studies at Everwaters Junior College in Jacksonville, Florida. From there, she transferred to Florida A. and M. University. There, she earned her bachelor's in health and physical education in 1962. She and her husband later moved to Arizona, where she completed her master's degree in counseling education at ASU in 1971. The new degree in hand, she accepted John Riggs' invitation to become a counselor at MCC. In 1979, she became Mesa's dean of students.

As noted previously, the Southeast Valley Task Force was not formed until 1983, but once in motion, the community made its preferences known. Ward recalls:

June 11, 1996, video interview (the first of two) with Arnette Ward, president of Chandler-Gilbert Community College 1985 to present. Transcript and audio and video excerpts available online.

http://www.mc.maricopa.edu/users/M3cdhistory/

> [The community] wanted an occupational-tech institution because of their vision for growth and the type of industry that would be coming here. They felt they needed an occupational-technical training institution to respond to greater training needs for Chandler, and in Gilbert. . . . They went so far as to visit other occupational-tech schools across the country, two or three of them.

The architectural firm of Lendrum Sasaki did preliminary designs that laid out a complete campus fronting on Pecos Road and spreading back north on the 80-acre parcel. Initially, though, the $4 million construction budget would fund only one building. While that building was under construction, classes began at temporary sites. The district acquired Seton Hall, a building that had formerly been a Catholic high school, and renovated the classrooms and offices to start classes in the fall of 1985.

Three full-time faculty were hired initially, and one of the three was Mary Alcon, who had begun her teaching career in the district at Maricopa Tech in 1970. She recalls:

> We opened five classrooms at the old Seton High School. There was some office space for the provost and those people, and a sort of library/resource center. We had offices in a little house that they had rented down the street from us, and this house was very old and smelled terrible. It had been locked up for a long time. It wasn't a very pleasant odor. All of us, the first time they took us through there, weren't quite sure we could stand it, but at the same time, we knew we had no choice. We bought a lot of spray and burned a lot of candles and that type of thing. . . . Actually, our offices were the trunks of our cars. That's where we carried most of our stuff.

As would be true at Paradise Valley, the design of the new campus would break away from traditional campus models. Arnette Ward really drove the team in this area:

---

3 For purposes of accreditation, Chandler-Gilbert was begun as an extension of Mesa Community College. As was the case with John Córdova, Ward was initially appointed provost of the Chandler-Gilbert Community College Center. Ward became president when the school won its own accreditation in 1992.

1994

ARNETTE WARD BECOMES CHANDLER-GILBERT'S FOUNDING PRESIDENT

Dr. Charles Green was the first black president in the district, but Arnette Ward was the first black woman to become a district college president. When Chandler-Gilbert was begun, the population was overwhelmingly white (about 15% Hispanic, less than 2% black, and less than 1% American Indian). At the time she applied to be the provost, she had little hope of winning the job.

I figured it's a man's world, so they would choose a man. I didn't feel any pain, and I didn't have any anxiety, or stress, because I figured I wasn't going to get it anyway.

So I did all these wonderful things. I set up meetings with the leadership of all of the areas [in Chandler and Gilbert] and told them that it was more than a possibility that we were going to start this college. . . . I came out and talked to the chamber executive directors, and said, "Hi. I'm Arnette Ward, and I may be provost of your community college, your new college extension."

. . . . They were a little bit surprised, and each individual said, "Oh. Well, now! Have a seat!" I didn't look at their expressions at all, and with my bubbly self at times, I said, "Here's what I want to know. I want to make sure that we're going to give you the best. What would be the best in reference to services provided for you and your community? What kind of special programming? How would you want this provost to work with your needs?" So they told me.

After being selected as Chandler-Gilbert's provost, Ward was invited to attend a breakfast at which various civic leaders were present.

And the mayor was there and the school superintendent and one or two others, and they had

a breakfast for me. Everyone did really well with me, and I did well with them, except the mayor, bless his heart. He sat near the window in the restaurant, and he would look out the window all the time, and I was trying to talk and say what I thought we were going to be doing.

Finally, I looked over and I said, "Mayor Brooks, I know this is a bit difficult, but let me assure you of a couple of things. . . . You're going to get the state of the art in a community college, bar nothing. . . . I plan to be here for a while. I'm going to do everything I can to impress you that it's okay." It caught him so off-guard, bless his heart. He said, All right. We'll see."

He became my champion after about six months.

Arnette Ward, president of Candler-Gilbert Community College 1985 to present.

Our master plan said that we saw ourselves as a mall. It's really like a mall. When you go into a mall—the hustle and bustle that goes on in a mall, where people actually go and stay all day, do nothing, buy nothing. The kids, the youngsters have fun looking all around and don't want to go home because there's so much in the mall. It's a community within itself.

The main façade of the building was designed as a solid wall, devoid of windows, with one large opening directly in the middle—the main entrance to the mall. The only remaining question was what color to paint that wall.

When the architects got all of that information, they went out to find out what would be the most attractive type of facility. Would there be color? Would we need the Army barrack-looking building color that we get sometimes? The institutional-looking color? No. They . . . studied the history of Chandler; found that the San Marcos Hotel, years ago, when it was started, was painted blush pink.

That color became the inspiration, and the front façade was painted screaming pink. No one could possibly miss it. But, according to Ward, that effect was deliberate. "I said, 'How can we be found?' Because I never could find the damn place. So I said, 'We have to be found because it will be awhile before we have development in the area.' The pink, the rosy front, is really for that reason and no other."

The color on the outside of the building did its job too well. Plenty of students found the campus when it opened in the fall of 1987, but, as Mary Alcon recalls, the facility was inadequate from the first day:

217

1988

it offered everything a library should. It featured seating for forty students, four terminals to access the online catalog, and three terminals to access a LAN with CD-ROM references. Standard reference books were available on the shelves, and anything else the students wanted was provided via interlibrary loan. Nevertheless, the idea of an electronic library was received with some skepticism. Larry Miller, Chandler-Gilbert librarian, particularly recalls the scorn of the other faculty:

> They had trouble with the idea of a
> library being electronic to start with.
> "You mean to tell me everything's going to
> be in the computer?" "Well," I said, "it's
> not now. We're hoping it will be, but just

The atrium inside the original Chandler-Gilbert building.

Chandler-Gilbert's original home, Seton Hall. From the left, Margaret Hogan and Chuck Bedal. In the middle, Arnette Ward. On the right, Andy Bernal, Cathy Urbanski, and Mary Alcon.

April 21, 1997, video interview with Mary Alcon, Mesa Community College and Chandler-Gilbert faculty member and administrator. Transcript available online.

http://www.mc.maricopa.edu/users/M3cdhistory/

> *We had enough students enrolled in that*
> *campus from day one. Not enough office*
> *space for all the faculty; not enough office*
> *space to even offer our part-time faculty*
> *a place where they could set their books.*
> *We had no such area as a cafeteria. This*
> *conference room is bigger than where we*
> *could eat our lunch. We had to eat out in*
> *the courtyard. The bookstore was very*
> *small. You would get four or five bodies*
> *in there and it would be crowded. [shakes*
> *head] Everything was too small from the*
> *day we opened the doors.*

The lack of space was responsible for an early high-tech innovation. The lack of room for even a small library led consultants to recommend that the college pioneer the idea of a paperless library, where all resources would be accessible electronically. The strange little room may not have looked like a library, but

tell me the one book that you'd want to have, and we'll make sure we have it." One of the faculty here, Gordon Jesse, for years would say, "Well, is the one book in the library checked out, and the place have to be closed?"

Ultimately, the concept was ahead of its time. With money from the 1994 construction bond, Chandler-Gilbert subsequently constructed a more conventional library facility for itself. However, the experiment did begin a serious rethinking of the role of technology in the library, a rethinking that would lead to a major innovation at the district's tenth college, Estrella Mountain.

THE COLLEGE IN THE DELL

Contrary to popular belief, Scottsdale is not the only-college in the district to have an unusual mascot. Although Chandler-Gilbert did not begin with a team mascot, the college was nevertheless identified with a certain animal. Because the college is directly across the street from a dairy feed lot, the unoffical school mascot quickly became the Jersey cow.

The downside of being across the street from a feed lot—especially when the summer breezes blow—can easily be imagined. Even so, Chandler-Gilbert librarian Larry Miller points out that the olfactory objection is not the only problem.

Especially this time of the year as you get into the summer. The heat gets to the cows—like the rest of us, right?—even though they put huge fans out there, and some of the farmers even have misting systems. They will die from the heat, or old age, or whatever—some of the calves don't make it, either. . . . On a Monday morning, they drag them all out on the side of the road and then you'll see the four legs just standing up as the dead animals are there waiting for the county animal control people to take them away.

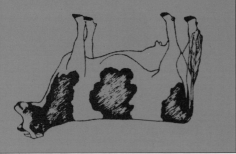

June 11, 1996, video interview of Larry Miller, Chandler-Gilbert librarian. Transcript available online.

http://www.mc.maricopa.edu/users/M3cdhistory/

Another Facet of the New Model

Paradise Valley and Chandler-Gilbert did not resemble each other in the way that Mesa and Glendale resembled Phoenix College, but certain similarities did exist from the start, and these similarities begin to illuminate the new institutional model that had replaced the old junior college model. For example, both schools opened with child care facilities, but neither opened with fine arts facilities. Both schools also opened with fitness centers—rooms full of treadmills, exercise bicycles, Cybex strength-training machines, and other similar equipment—but without conventional

athletics facilities. The omission of the latter seems particularly significant because early in the planning for both schools, complete athletics facilities had been on the drawing boards.

At Chandler-Gilbert, Lendrum Sasaki's preliminary designs for the campus included a football stadium and baseball diamonds on the north end of the property. Arnette Ward confirmed that´ the community asked for sports, but she claims that the meager start-up budget for the college did not allow for the necessary facilities to be constructed.

An article from the *Phoenix Gazette* for February 27, 1985, included a map of the proposed Paradise Valley campus. Again, a football and track field is depicted alongside softball and baseball diamonds. John Córdova maintains the decision to scuttle them was similarly financial:

> I said, "Folks, the Paradise Valley community schools are very proud about their academic achievement, scholastic honors garnered by their high school graduates. Tremendous track record as they've gone on to the universities. We ought to continue that tradition, that we put in place a very strong academic foundation. At an appropriate time, we will visit the issue of athletics, but let's get started with academics. That's the message, that's the image—Isn't that what you want?" Of course, folks said, "Of course. That's the only way to go!"

But was the omission purely for financial reasons? The new fitness centers were hardly free. The equipment required considerable

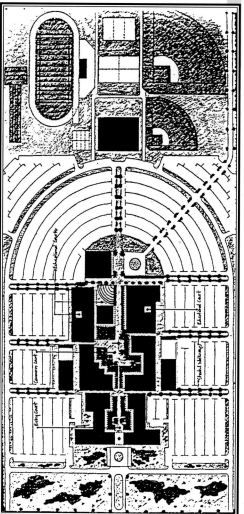

Lendrum Sasaki's original design for the Chandler-Gilbert campus. The original building appears at the bottom (south side) of the design. Note the football stadium and baseball diamonds appear at the top (north side).

capital investment, and once opened, the centers had to be staffed and the equipment maintained.

So, if lack of money was not the reason why fitness centers replaced the football fields, then what was?

Several people have speculated that the district wanted to avoid problems such as Scottsdale experienced with athletics. Barry Wukasch, a founding member of the Paradise Valley faculty, concurs:

I think Córdova had recollections from Scottsdale where he'd been an associate

dean there, and one thing he wanted to avoid was athletics because it had been such an issue there. So, he made a point early on that his philosophy was we were not going to have athletics, and he stuck to that all the time he was there.

Mary Lou Mosley disagrees. She maintains that the fitness center was preferred over conventional athletics favored because it fit better into the Paradise Valley's overall philosophy:

The philosophy here was to deal with the whole student, and student development is intellectual, spiritual, moral, physical, emotional. All aspects. The fitness center provided that kind of option for lifelong learning. . . . At the time the campus was designed, there was not enough money to do a gymnasium and classrooms and a library. So, looking at the community and the direction the college needed to go, a gymnasium was left to a later date. It's still waiting.

But waiting for what? Following the district's 1994 bond, capital funds for new construc-

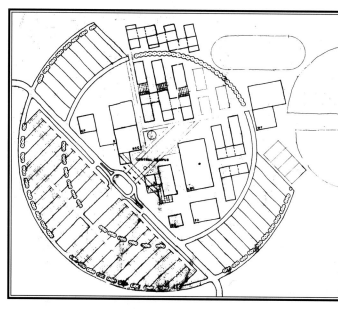

Lescher and Mahoney's original design for Paradise Valley Community College. Barely visible in the upper right corner is an outline of a football stadium. Below are outlines of baseball and softball diamonds.

tion were allocated to both Chandler-Gilbert and Paradise Valley. No gymnasium was included in the plans for either campus.

The real truth is that conventional athletics facilities (in other words, team sports) serve the needs of more conventionally aged students. The greater percentage of older students today prefers Stairmasters to stadiums. Even so, athletics seem to be making something of a comeback in the district. As of the writing of this book, Paradise Valley has initiated men's and women's tennis, cross-country, and golf. Baseball has been discussed as a possibility for the distant future. A soccer field is being discussed for the area where a football stadium was originally penciled in. In 1995, Chandler-Gilbert's dean of students Lois Bartholomew organized a committee from the community to work up a plan for athletics. According to Jeff Mason, Chandler-Gilbert's first athletics director:

We received valuable information from our committee members, ran a survey in the local high schools to find exactly what sports they would go out for if offered by CGCC, and received valuable feedback from area college and high school coaches. We decided to jump right in and compete with four highly visible sports with high participation numbers: volleyball, men's and women's soccer, men's and women's basketball, and softball.

Approximately 100 student athletes participated in the fall of 1998. The teams were known as the Coyotes.[4]

CHANGES ON THE BOARD

Bob Martinez's term of service ended in 1982, and he chose not to run for reelection. In January of 1983, his place on the board was taken by Dr. Don Campbell.

Campbell came to Phoenix originally in 1945 and was a student at Phoenix College from 1954 to 1956. Two years later he was graduated from ASU, where he majored in political science and minored in speech and Spanish. He then attended law school at the U of A for one year before joining the National Guard in 1961. (He was in Berlin during the time the Berlin wall was being erected.) Following that experience, he elected not to return to law school and went into the real estate business. From 1965 to 1969, he was employed by the City of Phoenix, for whom he served as a Housing, Health, and Welfare Specialist working with low-income families. For the Urban League, he also ran a manpower training center called CEP, the Concentrated Employment Program, an offshoot of the War on Poverty.

In 1969, Campbell went to work for ASU as director of the community services center, which was a part of the Summer Sessions and Extension area, and he also began work on his doctorate, which he received in June of 1980. In 1984, he was transferred to work at ASU West, where he became the vice provost in charge of community relations. He retired from there in 1990.

The second change on the governing board occurred in 1984. Grant Christensen was up for re-election, but a three-way race developed, and he was defeated by Phyllis Muir. Linda Rosenthal recalls:

> Phyllis was a wonderful board member.
> Phyllis was a single mother, a single parent.
> I roomed with Phyllis at a couple of meetings.

The Maricopa governing board in 1985. From left to right, Don Campbell, Linda Rosenthal, Phyllis Muir, Barbara Hitchcock, and Roy Amrein.

> She really knew about community colleges. She was a reentry woman. Her problem was she was a schoolteacher, and she taught art in the Alhambra elementary school district, and she couldn't get enough time off to really do her job well. . . . Her not to run again was a personal decision. She couldn't give the time, between the job not allowing her the time off and the time she needed to spend with her children.

Grant Christensen ran unopposed for Muir's seat and returned to the board again in 1988. However, he suffered a stroke in 1990, and decided that another term on the board was out of the question. In 1994, Ed Contreras ran for and won his seat.

Thus, athletics programs remain firmly a part of the community college system, but the evolution of the district has clearly pointed the emphasis in different directions.

Where, then, was the new emphasis being directed? The answer to that question was being revealed at Glendale Community College, where new forces were at work and the evolution of the community college model was continuing.

[4] Although CGCC does not yet have a gym, suitable facilities are available at the Williams campus. Arnette Ward says that a gymnasium is also in CGCC's future.

September 9, 1996, video interview with Don Campbell, district governing board member 1983 to present. Transcript excerpts available online.

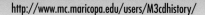

http://www.mc.maricopa.edu/users/M3cdhistory/

1994

U ntil the 1980s, changing student demographics had been the dominant force in the district's evolution, but during the 1980s, two new forces began to have an impact on the district's changing self-image. The first was the personal computer revolution. The second was the advent of innovative partnerships with business and industry that forever changed the face of occupational education in the district.

Ironically, these new forces had their greatest impact initially at one of the district's older colleges, Glendale. During the 1980s, this school was such a hotbed of innovation that Glendale insiders nicknamed the place "Camelot."

As the district moved forward into the '90s, the innovations at Glendale helped to define the district's evolving self-image.

The Personal Computer Revolution

Personal computers first began to attract attention as consumer devices in the early '80s, but computers had been in use in the district long before then.

In the mid-'50s, Al Flowers first introduced computers into the Phoenix Union High

Groundbreaking ceremony at Glendale Community College for High Tech I, 1986.

School District, then still the parent of Phoenix College. Flowers first saw the need in the registrar's office, where secretaries worked all summer to schedule every teacher and every student manually. The system was inefficient, and scheduling conflicts proliferated.

So, Flowers—never one to throw money around—went shopping for a free computer. IBM wasn't interested, but Flowers found Remington Rand's UNIVAC division was just entering the market in Phoenix, and they were willing to deal:

> *So I weaseled a keypunch for their ninety-column card, and I paid for one piece of equipment about fifty bucks a month. We had to have an interpreter because I couldn't read the holes and didn't want to learn how. So we had a keypunch interpreter and a mechanical sorter. That was our equipment.*

Technically, this first electronic marvel wasn't even called a computer. It was simply called an accounting machine, a machine that read punch cards and then printed out a report on

paper. Jim DeVere, GateWay Community College's director of computer operations, was a student at Phoenix College in the early '60s and took his first course in computers there on such a machine. In 1967, he went to work for the district as a student assistant.

DeVere explained the drawbacks of punch-cards. First, they could easily be shuffled incorrectly. "Every student would take a card and that was how they'd register. They would feed the cards in behind the student's control card and, if that student's class card got behind the wrong student, the wrong student got in the class." Second, using cards to manage data was laborious and time-intensive:

> *It would take like twenty, thirty, forty hours to punch the cards, and so it was always a slow process. The cards would never have the right room and location because by the time they punched them and got them out, the schedule would have changed, and we were always concerned about one of the card readers not functioning, not having rosters out for Monday morning.*

January 29, 1996, video interview with Jim DeVere, district computer guru. Transcript available online.

http://www.mc.maricopa.edu/users/M3cdhistory/

```
000000000000000000000000000000  0000000000000001  00000000000001  00000000
3 4 5 6 7 8 9 10 11 12 13 14 15 16 17 18 19 20 21 22 23 24 25 26 27 28 29 30 31 32 33   36 37 38 39 40 41 42 43 44 45   47 48 49 50 51 52 !   5 56 57 58 59 60 61  7 63 64 65 66 67 68   71 72 73 74 75 76 77 78
1111111111111111111111111111111  11111111 51111111 .1111111 111111  .11111111
2222222222222222222222222222222222222222222222  222222222222 .....22222222222 .....22222222222
3333333333333333333333333333333333333333333333333333333333333333333333333333333
4444444444444444444444444444444444444444444444444444444444444444444444444444444
5555555555555555555555555555555555555555555555555555555555555555555555555555555
6666666666666666666666666666666666666666666666666666666666666666666666666666666
7777777777777777777777777777777777777777777777777777777777777777777777777777777
8888888888888888888888888888888888888888888888888888888888888888888888888888888
9999999999999999999999999999999999999999999
4 5 6 7 8 9 10 11 12 13 14 15 16 17 18 19 20 21 22 23 24 25 26 27 28 29 30 31 32 33 34 35 36 37 38 39 40 4
        DD-508I
```

An eighty-column punchcard. Data was entered by punching holes in the card.

A punchcard reader. Data would be input into the computer by scanning the holes in the cards.

In 1969, the district acquired its first real computer, an IBM 360/30, and placed it in the basement of the old Korrick's building, then the site of Maricopa Tech.

In 1971, the process of moving around huge boxes of registration cards from the computer center to the campuses finally ended. Each campus was given its own IBM 1004, a small computer with a card reader on it. An acoustic coupler would then be used to make the connection to the district's UNIVAC 1100.

This system was an improvement, but the acoustic couplers had their own special problems. Jan Baltzer remembers these well. She began coordinating all the registration for the district's television courses in 1976. She had to deliver all the registration cards to the various district colleges and collect them again after the students had registered. Then, she would bring the cards back to the Korrick's building (where her office was located) and load the cards into one of the card readers connected by acoustic couplers to the district's UNIVAC. Unfortunately, the couplers worked at a top speed of 9600 baud. Baltzer remembers:

The goal was to get down there as early as you could in the morning, because after

about 8:30, a line built up behind those terminals because there were only four or five of them for the whole building. You wanted to get there early, and when you made the phone connection— because it was all dialup—you didn't ever want to unhook

An acoustic coupler. To connect with the district's UNIVAC, users would have to use a conventional telephone to dial a number. To make the connection, the telephone receiver would then be set down on the coupler.

that because of the person behind you—the contention for the lines! It was just a scream.

In 1978, the District began experimenting with video terminals connected to the UNIVAC so that the people in admissions and records could look up information online and read it on a screen instead of having to rely on a printout. In fact, Rio Salado College advertised (a little prematurely) that it would be the first college with "online" registration. Baltzer remembers the debut of this system:

There was a small conference room, and we still had all the card boxes in the room, and we had poster paper up all the way around the room. The student would call, and the person on the phone would take their registration and say, "Let me verify this in the computer." It would come, a runner

Maricopa Tech's IBM computer, ca. 1970.

would bring it in, we would run around the table, pick up all the cards, make the hash marks on the poster paper so that you could see, and run it back out and verify the student's enrollments. [laughs] That was our first semester of online telephone registration.

Eventually, the system did work, but it was still not fully interactive. Information could be accessed remotely through acoustic coupler dialins, but punch cards were still required to input data.

Elsner Decentralizes Computing

After Paul Elsner's arrival, his administrative philosophy of decentralization was soon applied to the district's computer operations, and the man charged with implementing that philosophy was Ron Bleed, whose association with the district began in 1980.

Bleed, a native of Chicago, did his undergraduate work at University of Illinois and Northern Illinois University. While still working on his MBA, he took a full-time job as a programmer for a manufacturing company in Rockford, Illinois. There, he worked on one of the first IBM 360 computers in the midwest. Next, he became the director of the computer center at Highland Community College in Freeport, Illinois. After two years

of being a self-described "one-man band" there, he moved on to Joliet Junior College in the northern Illinois area. [1]

In January of 1981, Bleed started work in the district, which had just purchased a large

IBM mainframe and was still renting the UNIVAC mainframe. At the various campuses, approximately 150 dialup-couplers connected users to the district computers, but due to limitations within the system, only eighty-four people could be online at one time. Bleed remembers how this system caused serious frustration for students:

There's the old story about how worn-out students' fingers got dialing and redialing—there was no automatic redial back then—so they could try and make the connection. You had students coming in real early in the morning, calling and making the connection, and they had a system among the students how not to hang up so that they could maintain the connection all daylong for the other students at that particular campus.

Bleed recommended that the district needed to sever its dependence on centralized mainframe computers and acoustic couplers and move instead to a distributed network of minicomputers, one box per college.

After a thorough and competitive bidding process, the district chose to acquire Digital's

VAX minicomputers for each campus. The installation began in the summer of 1982. These computers also brought the possibility of electronic mail to the district, and to enhance this function, a piece of integrated software now called All-in-One was imple-

mented. This program, which was considered very advanced in 1982, offered word processing and electronic mail and other features all wrapped up together. A1 soon became the primary tool of communication running on District computers. [2] Bleed emphasizes that the use of electronic mail within the district quickly caught on:

We started with the chancellor and presidents and vice chancellors. It was a top-down approach, on purpose, and that began to buy a lot of compliance. Soon thereafter we put the board on, also. The minute Paul Elsner started using it, and the minute that a few people got left out on a message or a meeting, compliance became automatic.

On each campus, WYSE terminals and DECmate word processors were hard-wired to a VAX computer. Thus, copper cable replaced the despised acoustic couplers. Dedicated telephone lines were then installed to link all of the campus computers to a central VAX at the district.

[1] The same school generally credited with being the first junior college.

[2] A1 was phased out at the end of 1999.

Paul Elsner learns BASIC programming at classes set up for district employees in the spring of 1982. The original caption reads, "Dr. Paul Elsner has loosened his tie as he begins to work on one of the programming assignments via a CRT." From the district computer center newsletter for April, 1982.

July 3, 1996, video interview with Ron Bleed, district vice chancellor of information technologies. Transcript and audio excerpts available online.

http://www.mc.maricopa.edu/users/M3cdhistory/

The last phase of the district's technological overhaul began in 1986. At that time, the telephone system was completely replaced. The district purchased NEC computers that handled the switching at each college, and—for the first time—the district put telephones on the desks of all employees. To link the systems at each campus, the district invested in a microwave transmission system to eliminate the telephone lines. In effect, the district became an internal telephone company.

Furthermore, the microwave system enabled a video conferencing network (the VCN) among the campuses. Although this system has never been utilized to its full potential, the district still offers somewhere around twenty courses annually via VCN. Students at several different campuses can thus interact with each other and their instructors simultaneously.

The Faculty Computer Literacy Project

Alfredo De Los Santos recalls that Elsner became very enthusiastic about increasing computer access throughout the district.

> Paul announced at a big meeting that it was his vision that all our faculty and all our employees should have access to the computer. So I thought to myself, "If the computing

VAX ARRIVES AT DISTRICT

...HEY GUYS, THE VAX IS HERE!

...let's see now, if we move the CPU over there and put the power unit on the left, no that won't work, how about setting the disks on the left and...

...Aw come on! let's quit talking and lay some cable...

...I'm glad that's done...

From the district's computing center newsletter for September, 1982.

Between 1981 and 1991, many district employees relied on Digital's VT102 to communicate with the VAX computers. The display was in green and black.

PROFILE: ALFREDO DE LOS SANTOS

De Los Santos is a native of Laredo, Texas. After earning an associate's degree at Laredo Junior College in 1955, he transferred to the University of Texas, where he completed his bachelor's in English.

I wanted to be an English teacher, an English faculty member, and I came to talk to the president at the community college, and I'll never forget what he told me. He said, "English teachers are a dime a dozen. Librarians are a dollar each. If you want to work here, get a degree in library science." He knew that when I had been a student I worked as a student assistant in the library. That's one of the things I did to earn money.

In May of 1957, he entered graduate school to earn a master's in library science. Six months of active duty in the Army Reserves followed, and then three and a half years on the faculty at Laredo Junior College before entering the Community College Leadership Program at U of T, Austin. This program was a Kellogg program similar to the one that Elsner attended at Stanford. De Los Santos comments, "A lot of us who went to school during that era were cornflake kids."

His doctorate earned, De Los Santos' next assignment was at Florida Keys Community College, in Key West. However, he did not start initially as a dean.

I was the founding librarian. I had no administrative experience, and the president then needed a librarian. What happened was that within nine months I was made a dean. So I went from being

a librarian . . . nine months later, I was a dean. I learned everything that I thought the situation and the people there could teach me in two years, so I went from there to Bethlehem, Pennsylvania, to help found another community college, Northampton County Area Community College. I was there from the late spring of 1967 to July of '71, and it was there that I got interested in computing.

The process of ordering new books for the library involved a lot of repetitive paperwork. "The man who directed the computer center and I were beer-drinking buddies, and I told him how boring [the book ordering process] was and how much time it took. So we began talking about how we could manage that."

In 1971, De Los Santos became the founding president of El Paso Community College, but in March of 1976, he and the governing board agreed to disagree. "To quote Clark Kerr, 'I left the same way that I arrived: fired with enthusiasm.'" Then, in 1978, he applied for and became one of the finalists for chancellor of Maricopa.

Elsner got the chancellor's job, but Elsner then hired De Los Santos as the district's vice chancellor for academic affairs. A major part of his work has been in the area of standardizing the curriculum throughout the district and depoliticizing the process of creating new courses. He retired from the district in 1999.

capacity that we now have cannot support our instructional program, how in the hell are we going to do what this man wants us to do?"

De Los Santos then began to look around at what other colleges were doing, and he saw that microcomputers were being widely adopted at Carnegie-Mellon, Stanford, and other top schools:

I went to a League for Innovation conference in Miami, and Ron Bleed was my roommate. I had read all kinds of stuff. I told him about the idea that I had, to recommend to the chancellor that we use another technology, not the central processing unit—the big mother computer in the sky with phone—but a microprocessor. Ron thought about it, and he said, "I can support that. I'll help you with it."

A faculty advisory committee convened to decide what kind of computers to buy, and 1984 bond money was used to buy seventy-five Apple IIe computers. But instead of secluding the machines in a few labs, Bleed and De Los Santos decided to loan the computers to preselected faculty. While the screening process was going on, De Los Santos required members of his staff—which included Billie Hughes, Mary Lou Mosley, and Jim Walters—to learn to use the machines first so that they could provide training and support. Then, De Los Santos announced the Faculty Computer Literacy Project (FCLP) to the faculty:

Have we got a deal for you! We're going to let you borrow a computer. You can take it to your office, to your home, to your significant other's home. You can keep it anywhere you want to. You have to agree to do three or four things. One is you have to come to an eight-hour training session.

December 9, 1996, video interview with Alfredo De Los Santos, district vice chancellor for student and educational development. Transcript and audio excerpts available online.

http://www.mc.maricopa.edu/users/M3cdhistory/

We're going to teach you how to operate it. And you have to agree to come once a week where we'll teach you applications. You have to find an instructional purpose. Then, at the end, you have to return it. Okay?

Over two hundred faculty responded to the initial summons. De Los Santos recalls that

his popularity declined sharply as a result. "For about two years, I was the most unpopular son of a bitch in the district because I got to select the people—and everybody wanted in!"

Over a period of about three years, approximately four hundred and fifty faculty partici-

pated in the FCLP. Then, the remaining machines were turned over to the individual colleges, and the responsibility for running the FCLP was given to the various deans of instruction.

Glendale's High Tech Centers

The FCLP also sparked a revolution in instruction in the Maricopa district, and one of the people most responsible for leading that revolution is former Glendale Community College faculty member Mark Montanus. He earned both his bachelor's and master's at Northern Illinois University in DeKalb, Illinois. He began teaching at Glendale in the spring of 1964.

Montanus is generally credited with being the first faculty member in the district to develop what has become known as the Open Entry/Open Exit mode of course delivery. In this mode, students use computers to work independently at their own pace. Ironically, his initial inspiration for this mode had nothing to do with computers whatsoever. As an undergraduate, Montanus had a double major: business and music:

> *My first job was to teach in both areas. I could handle seventy kids in a band. I could handle fifty, sixty in a choir. I've got these kids all working at different levels, and I was working with them individually because everything was individualized. . . . I looked at all that, and I thought, "I can work with these kids on an individualized basis and make it work in music. Why can't I apply some of the same techniques to the academic ideas?"*

He first began to try this approach when he started working at Glendale:

> *When I first started teaching, in the '60s, here, I had a number of students that had*

Maricopa's four vice chancellors in 1999. From left to right, Alfredo De Los Santos (vice chancellor of student and educational development), Bill Waechter (vice chancellor for human resources), Rufus Glasper (vice chancellor for financial affairs), and Ron Bleed (vice chancellor for information technologies).

a lot of difficulty. I would work with them, and I prepared a lot of self-paced materials so they could work at home on their own. I tried to get a support base for them in the tutoring center. Then I would say to them, "Okay. We've come to the

We had about $70,000 available, and there were about $800,000 worth of requests. . . .Eighty percent of all those requests were for the same equipment, the same software, and the same support. I began to think about a library and putting

attended North Iowa Area Community College in Mason City, Iowa, where he earned his associate's degree. He then completed his bachelor's degree at the University of Northern Iowa, Cedar Falls, where he majored in marketing and distributive education. After graduation, he became a high school teacher in Perry, Iowa, while he finished a master's in educational administration at Drake University in Des Moines.

April 18, 1997, video interview of Mark Montanus, Glendale faculty member. Transcript and audio excerpts available online.

http://www.mc.maricopa.edu/users/M3cdhistory/

end of the semester. It looks to me like you can make it, but I'm going to give you an incomplete. You come back the second semester and you need to attend these lectures." So those students would come back, and then, when they were successful, I would [give them their final grades] That was a lot of work for me to do. But I was able to extend the end of the semester for those students who needed it, who needed more time.

Mark Montanus, Glendale faculty member, in Glendale's computer lab known as High Tech II.

Montanus not only wrote his own text materials, but he also produced a series of fifteen-minute video clips to illustrate accounting problems. "If a student was having trouble with this, they'd check out that, and in fifteen minutes, they could review it, and review it, and review it." Using this approach, Montanus claims he was able to build up his course completion rates as high as 90%.

At about this time, he was also working as the budget director for John Waltrip, then the president of Glendale, and Montanus began to notice a pattern in the faculty's requests for personal computers.

a technology center into a library-like setting that would be open a maximum number of hours with a full-support base, letting that eighty percent of the faculty who needed it use and share the same facility. It was a sharing approach more than open entry/open exit at that time.

At this time, Montanus found an important ally in Larry Christiansen, who had come to Glendale to serve as Waltrip's occupational dean in 1982. Previously, Christiansen had

While working on his doctorate at Drake in 1974, he was offered the chair of the business division at the University of Minnesota Coordinate Campus, a two-year coordinate campus at Crookston. There, he participated in the implementation of the first IBM mainframe instructional computers in the University of Minnesota system.

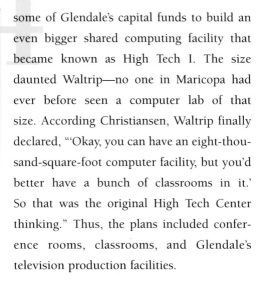

1994

May 8, 1996, video interview with Larry Christiansen, Glendale dean 1982-88 and president of Mesa Community College 1988 to present. Transcript and audio excerpts available online.

http://www.mc.maricopa.edu/users/M3cdhistory/

In 1982, Christiansen applied to become Glendale's occupational dean. John Waltrip was immediately interested because of Christiansen's computer experience, and when the school's first VAX computer arrived shortly thereafter, Waltrip told Christiansen that he was also to supervise Glendale's academic computing program. He recalls, "All I inherited when I got that was a VAX that needed twenty-four-hour care, with one person whose major experience was collecting punch cards."

Montanus could see right away that Christiansen would be the right person to talk to about his idea for a shared computer facility using personal computers:

> When I presented that idea to [Christiansen], he just sucked it up like a blotter . . . and he said, "Can you give me a complete idea of what you want?" So I laid out a grandiose scheme to open a laboratory and do this. . . . to teach computer applications, but also to invite in English, Agriculture, Art, Music, and the have-nots.

Chuck Milliner, the business department chair, and Christiansen collaborated on an internal grant proposal to fund the scheme. When the funding was approved, thirty Apple IIe's were placed in a room for the teaching of the first two OE/OE courses designed by Montanus:

> The students rolled through there by the hundreds. I ran it. I taught my full-load

and ran the lab from eight 'til ten, six days a week. . . . There were six hundred students who went through that program the first semester. Waltrip saw the figures, and he couldn't believe how you could do this. We talked about it awhile, and he and Larry and others talked John into funding another classroom next door. So we knocked down a wall, bought thirty more, and then we had sixty.

> . . . I wrote a couple more courses for the Open Entry/Open Exit classes, and other faculty began to write some, also, and English came in and did some things. We went from 600 students to 2,000 enrolled in courses specifically in open entry/open exit, and we only doubled the capacity. We quadrupled the output by doubling the capacity. We already had the staff in place. We could take the additional people [students] without spending a lot more money.

> Before it was over, in the next several years, we had knocked down all the walls in four rooms and had captured all those. As a matter of fact, we captured two rooms upstairs in the Business Department and we had two hundred and fifty computers rolling, all working open entry/open exit.

By this time, the 1984 bond had been passed, and Christiansen and Waltrip decided to use

some of Glendale's capital funds to build an even bigger shared computing facility that became known as High Tech I. The size daunted Waltrip—no one in Maricopa had ever before seen a computer lab of that size. According Christiansen, Waltrip finally declared, "'Okay, you can have an eight-thousand-square-foot computer facility, but you'd better have a bunch of classrooms in it.' So that was the original High Tech Center thinking." Thus, the plans included conference rooms, classrooms, and Glendale's television production facilities.

As High Tech I prepared to open its doors in the fall of 1987, many people wondered out loud if anyone would ever use all those computers. Christiansen recalls:

> We maxed the High Tech Center in three weeks in terms of the three hundred and thirty-six stations in the pit and in the classrooms simply because there wasn't anything that went on there that we hadn't already been running and piloting and doing.

that plans were soon put in motion for High Tech II, a slightly smaller facility that opened next door to High Tech I in 1992.

The only flaw, according to Christiansen, was that at one point, the suggestion had been made to combine the computer facility and the library into a single information resource. At the time, that idea was received with derision and hostility. "The major mistake we made was giving in to a reluctant library. We built it right behind the library, but there's still a sidewalk there [between them]."

That problem would eventually be corrected at Estrella Mountain.

1996

Glendale's High Tech I, the area known as the "pit."

Expanding Partnerships

At the same time, Glendale was becoming the site of a major innovation in the area of occupational education, and the person who is most often credited with enabling this innovation is Bertha Landrum. She is a graduate of the University of Minnesota, where she majored in psychology and minored in history. After graduation in 1960, she went to work for the Minnesota Department of Corrections as a parole agent working with juvenile girls and women. In 1963, she moved to Phoenix and began working part-time as a caseworker in the Deuce[3] for the Salvation Army. At the same time, she enrolled at ASU, where she earned a master's in educational psychology with a specialty in counseling.

In the fall of 1965, she was hired for a semester as a counselor at Phoenix College, and in the summer of 1966, John Riggs hired her at Mesa. In 1975, she was appointed dean of instruction at Glendale, and in 1980, she became the district's director of occupational education.

Shortly after this last appointment, she received a delegation from General Motors, which already had a community college partnership in Michigan. GM wanted to explore the possibility of another such partnership with Glendale. Landrum showed them the automotive facilities at Glendale, and the reaction was positive. Landrum takes up the story from there:

Their enrollments were down [at Glendale], so they had faculty availability, and we worked out a deal where the folks out at GM bought some of their time to train in their training center. . . . We started then the ASEP (Automotive Service Excellence Program) program out there with General Motors. Students that are sponsored by local dealers would go to school nine weeks, go to work for the dealer for nine weeks, go to school for nine weeks, and they got scholarships through donations the dealers put in.

[3] The slang term for what was once Phoenix's tenderloin, erased by urban redevelopment in the '70s.

September 20, 1996, audio Interview with Bertha Landrum, director of the district Office of Business and Workforce Development. Transcript available online.

"That project with General Motors gave a whole new light to what occupational programs could become."

http://www.mc.maricopa.edu/users/M3cdhistory/

231

Dealers bought them a set of tools, a uniform, and they went to school and then went to work. This worked really, really well.

Then, Landrum made another proposal. She knew that GM's training facilities in Tempe were small and very costly to maintain for the size of their training program. "I tried to convince the general manager that he might like to move out there and run it from the campus. He tried the idea out on the folks back in Detroit, and they thought, 'Not bad! Kill two birds with one stone!'"

The automotive facilities at Glendale were then remodeled to GM's specifications. Larry Christiansen recalls that no detail was too small: "The storeroom had to be to GM specifications. The way the inventory tags were put on had to be to GM specifications." But in the end, all the changes paid off. The partnership was highly successful and began to spawn other similar partnerships, such as Glendale's partnership with John Deere. Landrum recalls how this partnership began:

> It was a very short-term kind of thing, to provide the college with some equipment and some seed and fertilizer to grow some grass and for the folks from John Deere to do some training with the International Group in mowing the grass. It was very limited. It was about $6,000 or so, and we worked it out with the grounds folks to make it work. . . . Now they've got buildings out there and specialized classrooms

Bertha Landrum, director of the district Office of Business and Workforce Development. Photo copyright 1992, Arizona Business Gazette, J. Topping. Used with permission of Phoenix Newspapers, Inc.

and the green machines show up every spring, and John Deere brings in all its people from around the world and they do an annual global activity for marketing and technical people who come in for specialized training. The college has got all these buildings, and when John Deere isn't there, the college uses them.

The Knights of Camelot Go Forth

As the '80s were ending, several administrative vacancies occurred in the district all at

once. Thus, many of the innovations being tried at Glendale were then exported to other colleges as Glendale administrators were chosen to fill the vacancies.

The first vacancy was at the Maricopa Skill Center, which was preparing to move into new quarters financed by the 1984 bond. Glendale administrator Stan Grossman applied for the job, and Myrna Harrison, approaching the end of her tenure at GateWay, appointed him. Grossman is an Air Force veteran who put in twenty-six months in Vietnam. After his return to civilian life, he was injured in an automobile accident and spent a year in a body cast. Then, he floated around among several different jobs until the Veterans' office offered to pay his way through Glendale Community College. Upon arriving at the VA office at Glendale, he was quickly hired to work in the veterans' office. That was the beginning of a long association with Glendale, where he became heavily involved in occupational education until he left to run the Skill Center in October of 1987.

In 1988, three district college presidencies became available at about the same time. The first was at Mesa, where Wally Simpson had followed Theo Heap as president of Mesa in January of 1984. Simpson left MCC in 1988 to become president of Olympic College on Olympic Peninsula in Washington. Bill Berry, who had served as president of Phoenix College since 1971, announced his intention to retire at the end of 1988. Myrna Harrison, then the president of GateWay, became the president of Phoenix College. Therefore, the presidency of GateWay became the third vacancy. Glendale deans were then selected to fill the two remaining vacancies. Phil Randolph, who had been Glendale's occupational dean, was appointed the president of GateWay, and

valley—operated Estrella Mountain initially as an extension campus until the new college could qualify for accreditation on its own.

Beginning work on the creation of the district's tenth college, Lopez, followed the new institutional model by the numbers. He assembled a

skeleton support staff and set up offices near the location of the new campus. At public forums, they began working earnestly to put the community into the new college. They asked, "What are the issues that your community faces? How can a community college help resolve some of those issues? What do you want this community college to be?"

The answers to those questions quickly defined the role that the new college was to play. According to Lopez:

> One of the things that came out of dealing with all these communities was a desire to work in partnership so that we could deal with all the issues that a student might bring from a community, realizing that we're better at doing some things, but when we work in partnership, we can bring along the other agencies, the other efforts that are working on the same student or working on that person's family.

To design the new campus, the district selected the architectural firm of Daniel, Mann, Johnson, and Mendenhall, and they evolved a plan for a full-campus that would

Stan Grossman in front of the Maricopa Skill Center under construction. Arizona Republic, June 6, 1989. Photo by Christine Keith. Used by permission of Phoenix Newspapers, Inc.

Larry Christiansen, who had been Glendale's dean of administrative services, was appointed president of Mesa.

Estrella Mountain Begins

The last knight of Camelot to go forth from Glendale at this time was the dean of instruction, Homero Lopez. He was chosen to be the provost of the third and last community college that the Tadlock study had recommended. The choice was appropriate because Glendale Community College—the nearest sister institution in the west

Phil Randolph, president of GateWay Community College 1988 to present.

Larry Christiansen, president of Mesa Community College, 1988 to present.

233

1994

July 2, 1996, video interview with Homero Lopez, Glendale dean and president of Estrella Mountian Community College 1988 to present. Transcript and audio excerpts available online.

http://www.mc.maricopa.edu/users/M3cdhistory/

called High Tech III because it represented the completion of the concept that had started at Glendale. Lopez explains:

We took what would have been three different delivery areas at a typical college campus—the computing center, the library, and learning resources, learning enhancement, whatever you want to call it, where people provide supplementary support to students and faculty—and we started to see the connections. Some of the connections had to do with information, with multimedia, with computing, but it was all connected.

As an added feature of the new campus, New Mexico artists Juan and Patricia Navarette were involved in the buildings' design to create public art projects to enhance the

Homero Lopez, provost and founding president of Estrella Mountain Community College, 1988 to present.

eventually accommodate as many as 15,000 students. Beginning in the fall of 1990, Estrella offered classes in the Agua Fria, Tolleson, and Westview high schools, and the first phase of construction began in February of 1991. The $11.7 million required to build the new campus included money that had been carefully husbanded from the '84 bond.

The initial phase called for three academic buildings surrounding a sculptured green space called Ceremonial Plaza. The largest building of the three is a classroom building

called Montezuma Hall, which houses twenty classrooms and science labs plus the obligatory Fitness center. Opposite this building is Komatke Hall, the student services building that brings together advising, registration, the bookstore, financial aid office, and the food services.

The middle building, Estrella Hall, is the campus centerpiece. In addition to classrooms and the college's administrative offices, the building houses the information commons, an integrated library and computing lab that contains approximately two hundred computers among the stacks. The information commons probably should have been

PROFILE: HOMERO LOPEZ

Lopez is a native of Laredo, Texas (as is Vice Chancellor Alfredo De Los Santos), and he began his undergraduate studies at Laredo Junior College. He then completed his bachelor's degree at the University of Texas at Austin. His major was psychology and history (1971). From there, he went to the University of Michigan, where he earned a master's in education and psychology. He then returned to the University of Texas to earn his doctorate in educational psychology in 1984.

In 1975, Lopez moved to Arizona, where he was hired as Glendale's director of research, reporting to Bertha Landrum, who was then the dean of instruction. In 1978, he strayed to Phoenix College to serve as the associate dean of continuing education for a year, but he promptly returned to Glendale to become the dean of admissions. Eventually, Waltrip reorganized his administration, and Lopez became the operational dean in charge of all the general education courses.

CONRAD BAYLEY'S PERSPECTIVE

Conrad Bayley, who was Estrella's first division chair for liberal arts, had a unique perspective on the founding of Estrella Mountain. A transplanted New Englander who moved to Phoenix in 1961, he began teaching in the evening division at Phoenix College in the fall of 1963. Two years later, J. Lee Thompson—the original dean of the Maryland and Camelback extension campuses—hired him to teach English at Glendale. Eventually, he became the chair of the English/Reading/Journalism Department at Glendale before he answered the call to transfer to Estrella.

Thus, Bayley was in at the beginning of Glendale, and he was also in at the beginning of Estrella Mountain. The contrast between the two vividly illustrates the difference between the junior college model and the community college model.

> Things were done differently [at Estrella]. We're in a community that's not heavily populated, but from the very beginning there's been an interest in making the community aware of the fact that we're here, that we really want to serve them. . . . For a long time at Glendale, there was no such person. There was no such person that handled public relations or publicity or marketing or anything like that. . . . I know for myself, I'm out in the community as much as I am here in the college. At Glendale you went into the ivory tower and you waited for people to come, and you maybe dropped the drawbridge over the moat and they came in.

June 13, 1996, video interview of Conrad Bayley, Glendale and Estrella Mountain faculty. Transcript and audio excerpts available online.

http://www.mc.maricopa.edu/users/M3cdhistory/

environment. Their Native American petroglyphs in bas-relief are most prominent on the "sky bridge" in the Information Commons and on the front of the information desk in the visitors' center.

As is the case at Paradise Valley and Chandler-Gilbert, the district's tenth college has no athletic facilities, but unlike the other schools, Estrella never even had such plans on the drawing board. The fitness center, on the other hand, is considerably larger than the ones at the other two schools; it occupies a whole suite of rooms on the ground floor of Montezuma Hall.

The design of the Paradise Valley and Chandler-Gilbert campuses are hard to characterize, but Estrella Mountain strongly resembles a small business park. The landscaping, the public art, and the thoroughly functional design of all the buildings exude an undeniably corporate ambience. Estrella Hall does not have a student union, but it does contain a large community room, where the Rotary Club and the Kiwanis hold their meetings.

This corporate ambience seems to have evolved out of the trends that first emerged at Glendale: the emphasis on providing computer access to students and the emphasis on providing specialized training for business and industry. Estrella wasted no time in

Aerial view of Estrella Mountain Community College in its original form. The three main buildings, from left to right, are Komatke Hall, Estrella Hall, and Montezuma Hall. Facilities designed by DMJM Arizona, Inc., Architects and Engineers.

The skybridge over the information commons at Estrella Mountain.

establishing several such partnerships. The first big catch was a contract with the Wigwam Resort and Country Club to provide Total Quality Management to nearly a hundred middle- and upper-level managers. Another major partnership is with Power Packaging, Inc., of Tolleson, to provide various types of training to new employees.

And clearly, Estrella's constitutent communites wanted their community college to be that kind of a school because more than 2,000 students enrolled the first year, and by 1997, all the classrooms were being scheduled and space was at a premium.

The Most Remarkable College

On one hand, the origin of Estrella Mountain is the dullest story in the whole history of Maricopa. No strike. No student upheveals. No risky innovations. No rival communities slugging it out to get a bigger piece of the pie. Just a lovely, exquisitely manicured, well behaved little college that seems to be serving its service area perfectly.

On the other hand, the origin of Estrella Mountain is the most remarkable story in the whole history of Maricopa because the story is so completely unremarkable—even predictable. Since the time that Mesa and Glendale were created, none of the district's

colleges had been even the slightest bit predictable. For this reason, Estrella validates the trends observed at Glendale, Paradise Valley, and Chandler-Gilbert during the '80s. Thus, Estrella Mountain is a perfect example of what the community college in the '90s has become.

1996

Ceremonial Plaza and Estrella Hall.

COMMUNITY COLLEGE Bowl

Excerpt from the *Saturday Night Live* sketch "Community College Bowl" as broadcast originally on October 5, 1991. Transcribed with permission of NBC. In this sketch, guest-host Jeff Daniels performed as the quizmaster, Eugene Fedoric. Teams from "Jasper County Community College" and "Belt Parkway Community College" competed. After the teams fail to answer the first two questions, the quizmaster decides to pause the game to allow the team from Belt Parkway to introduce its school.

EUGENE FEDORIC (Jeff Daniels): Tell you what, last week we met our champions from Jasper County, why don't we say hello to our challengers from Belt Parkway? First, our captain, Chandra Waring, I understand you're going to tell us a little something about Belt Parkway Community College.

WARING (Ellen Cleghorne): (exaggerated New York accent) Mr. Fedoric, it would be my pleasure.

(Views of the exterior of a dilapidated building, a library with partially empty shelves, a single exercise machine in a room, an auto mechanic under a car, and students standing around video games.)

(voiceover) The campus of Belt Parkway Community College is located at 1289 Jamaica Boulevard., Queens, New York. Our library, located on the third floor, contains books by many famous authors and will reopen next fall after being closed three years for asbestos removal. The athletic facility, located on the sixth floor, includes a weight room boasting a Stairmaster. Our auto body shop is the second largest training facility of its kind in Queens. And with the recent acquisition of a Pac Man, our student lounge provides a place for students to be themselves in a relaxing and comfortable environment. Belt Parkway Community College is NSRA approved and AICS accredited. Federal and State grants and loans available. Veteran approved. Mastercard and Visa.

FEDORIC: Thank you, Chandra. Now, your major is...?

WARING: My major is Travel Agent Technology.

FEDORIC: Oh, a travel agent! That's a good way to see the world.

WARING: Yes, but mostly I just like writing out the tickets.

FEDORIC: Okay, okay. Let's move on down to Andre Jefferson. Andre, you're majoring in...?

JEFFERSON (Chris Rock): My major is dry cleaning with a minor in pressing.

FEDORIC: And Joey Fusco...?

FUSCO (Adam Sandler): Scalp Care.

FEDORIC: (not sure how to respond) Scalp care. (shuffling the game cards) All right. Let's get back to our game and Geography for 100. (reading the question) William Shakespeare referred to this island as, "this blessed plot, this earth, this realm, this...?" This what?

(Pause; no one answers. WARING chews gum and blows a large bubble.)

(prompting) Shakespeare's home island? Jolly old...?

(The BUZZER finally sounds.)

England! This realm, this England. (Sighs, his frustration beginning to show.) Okay, let's try U.S. Presidents for 100. Our third President, he authored the Declaration of Independence and was responsible for the Louisiana Purchase. Our third President...

(Pause as no one responds.)

(prompting) Washington, Adams ...?

(JEFFERSON suddenly hits his buzzer.)

(excited) Belt Parkway, Jefferson!

JEFFERSON: (asking) Jefferson?

FEDORIC: (delighted) Jefferson! Yes, yes! That's right! All right! You're on the board. Okay, Belt Parkway, you've won the toss-up on U.S. Presidents. Now, you get to confer on the following question. You'll have 20 seconds. Now, (reading from a card) the only President to serve more than two terms, he was the father of the New Deal.

(The SOUND of a clock ticking. JEFFERSON whispers something to FUSCO.)

(prompting again) The father of the New Deal ...

(FUSCO hands JEFFERSON a piece of gum. WARING glares at them.) (Time runs out, and the BUZZER sounds.)

I'm sorry, Belt Parkway. Jasper, can you take it? (not waiting) Aw, forget it. Never mind.

Chapter Twenty-Two

2000
What is a **Community College?**

The trouble with evolution is that it seldom halts at a convenient place and holds up a sign saying, "I'm all through. You can take a picture now."

In the case of a constantly evolving institution such as the American community college, that problem has created another problem—a public relations problem. The institution has been evolving faster than its public image. Four-year colleges and universities don't have this problem because they have evolved much more slowly. Parents can still take their children back to their alma mater and point out the dorms and the classroom buildings that were there when Mom and Dad were undergrads.

Following World War II, most junior colleges in America began to evolve into community colleges. A few resisted the trend, but most endured the stresses of institutional evolution, as did Maricopa. From institutions that bore more than a passing resemblance to their four-year counterparts, community colleges became chameleons, changing themselves into whatever their respective service areas needed them to be. And as the needs of those service areas changed, the colleges changed, too. The result is an institutional diversity in the community college world unlike anything in the four-year college and university world.

In the absence of a clear understanding of what the community college has become, many people cling to a pernicious stereotype. As the "Community College Bowl" sketch from NBC's "Saturday Night Live" indicates, the most common stereotype is that community colleges are primarily for "kids" who aren't bright enough to go to a "real" college.

Feeding that stereotype is the unexamined assumption that two-year schools must necessarily be inferior to four-year schools. True, community colleges don't conduct research or confer graduate degrees, but community colleges are supposed to be teaching institutions. In this area, they often outshine their university counterparts. Even university faculty acknowledge that community colleges generally do a better job of teaching freshman- and sophomore-level students. The widespread university practice of dumping first- and second-year students into large, impersonal lecture classes chaperoned by disinterested graduate students has become a national concern in recent years. The small class size and lack of teaching assistants at community colleges guarantee that students receive more personal attention from tenured faculty.

Adding further to the public relations problem is the fact that so much of what community colleges do is not on the campus. Community college programs are often dispersed among off-campus locations in high schools and shopping malls and factories. Graduation rates are also deceptive. The Maricopa colleges enroll 230,000 students annually, but in the spring of 1998, the combined colleges awarded only 4,000 associate degrees and 3,500 certificates of completion in occupational programs. The reason is that many students attend courses as needed or transfer to four-year schools but do not bother to attain a two-year degree.

The Community College Defined

The community college is an institution that resists generalization, but when the stereotypes are discarded and the institution is examined from a historical perspective, a defining characteristic emerges. With an average student age of thirty, the Maricopa County Community College District has evolved into a comprehensive provider of educational services for adults. Whatever adult students need, the Maricopa community colleges provide.

In the "Community College Bowl" sketch, Saturday Night Live regular players performed as members of teams from fictional community colleges. The team from "Jasper County Community College" includes (left to right) Mike Myers, Melanie Hutsell, and Chris Farley. Below, the team from "Belt Parkway Community College" includes (left to right) Ellen Cleghorne, Chris Rock, and Adam Sandler. The guest host, Jeff Daniels, played the gamemaster. Used by permission, NBC.

Dialogue transcribed from the "College Bowl" sketch. Used by permission, NBC.

This is a college kid.

She's typical of many homemakers today.

Faced with major changes in their lives, these women often need supplemental income to support their families or enough income to make it on their own.

For others, the need is simply to develop new interests outside the home.

The adult re-entry program at the Maricopa Community Colleges is designed for women seeking a fresh start and new opportunities. With more than 2800 occupational courses, career guidance and counseling, and hundreds of other classes, the Maricopa Community Colleges are committed to helping all students achieve their full potential.

Quality teaching. Small classes. Diverse courses. Accessible. Affordable. Responsive.

MARICOPA COMMUNITY COLLEGES

Sharing the gift of knowledge for 25 years.

Two magazine ads for the MCCCD.

prominent at the older colleges, the ones that were built in the junior college mold. The district hasn't added a football team since 1974.

At the district's newest college, Estrella Mountain, the emphasis on adult students dominates the whole design of the campus. No messy kiosks with hand-drawn posters for heavy metal concerts stand guard at the campus entrances. No pool tables or video games occupy the student union—a good thing, too, because the school doesn't even have a student union. Students pass through Ceremonial Plaza on their way from the parking lot to their classes; they don't sunbathe on the grass or play hacky-sack. A few wrought iron tables and chairs cling to the fringes of the plaza, but those are occupied by students earnestly studying between classes. Those students are adults, and they don't come to Estrella to hang out or to socialize. They come to fulfill certain very specific needs.

And what are those needs? Priorities change, but as this book is being written, the breakdown seems to be as follows: First, adults need access to academic credentials. Second, adults need access to jobs and careers. Third, adults who are already employed need access to training in the use of computers.

At the same time, the district also serves the needs of the community at large: the community needs an educated workforce to attract new business and industry, the community needs a ready supply of workers in the health care professions and certain other specific professions, the community needs a resource for many people with special needs, and the community needs a multipurpose cultural resource.

Of course, the essential functions of the old junior college model still remain because many adults still need those functions. The primary emphasis is still on the transfer curriculum with a secondary emphasis on occupational and vocational training. (Throughout the district, the majority of Maricopa's one-thousand-plus full-time faculty are still in traditional academic areas, not in occupational training.) Nor has the district turned its back on students of tradi- tional college age. Football teams, a capella choirs, college newspaper staffs, pool tables, and video games can still be found at most of the district's colleges—but those features are more

1. Adults Need Credentials

Many people wrongly believe the community colleges only offer access to associate degrees and certificate programs, but other types of credentials are available as well.

One of the most popular credentials that the Maricopa community colleges provide is the GED (General Education Development) diploma program. Rio Salado College has received funding from the Arizona Department of Education since 1979 for the purpose of providing Adult Basic Education (GED Preparation, basic skills remediation, and English for Speakers of Other Languages) classes throughout Maricopa County. Growing from 749 enrollments in the first year of the program to somewhere over 23,000 adults today, the Rio Salado program is one of the largest—if not the largest—in the country.

One reason why GED students are important to the district is that more than a third go on to enroll in college-level courses. Research shows that the majority of GED students actually dropped out of high school because they became ill or because they had to go to work. Only six percent say the reason is because their high school grades were poor.

Adults also need bachelor's degrees and master's degrees, and many community colleges are looking into providing access to these degrees as well. Estrella Mountain partnered briefly with both Northern Arizona University and the University of Phoenix to allow students to work on four-year degrees and do graduate level work at the Estrella campus. Although those programs are no longer in effect, NAU continues a similar partnership with Paradise Valley, where graduate-level courses are being offered in PVCC's facilities. Ron Bleed, the district's

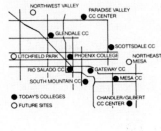
vice chancellor of information technologies, feels that this trend will continue throughout the district. "Maricopa will be a four-year degree-granting institution within ten years. We will be doing it by combining the resources of NAU, of other people, and we could even have the stamp of the four-year degree on it. It's inevitable, I believe."

Indeed, a movement is building again to empower Arizona community colleges to offer their own bachelor's degrees. A bill was introduced into the 1997 Arizona state legislature to allow community colleges in Arizona to grant applied baccalaureate degrees within certain guidelines. Rio Salado's president Linda Thor explained,

241

"We do not want to become another university, offering baccalaureate degrees in English or history. Rather, the benefits of this legislation would be most obvious in applied programs, or practitioner degrees." For example, Rio cited their Law Enforcement Technology program, designed in partnership with local law enforcement agencies. The program is now a two-year associate of arts degree program. Rio wanted to make an applied baccalaureate degree available in this program, something that the state's universities have been reluctant to provide.

The state legislature eventually approved the bill, but Governor Fife Symington vetoed it. However—as was the case with Senator Giss' 1958 bill to create junior colleges—the failed bill has led to further study of the idea.

Cover of Rio's brochure for the Adult Basic Education program.

RIO SALADO
COMMUNITY COLLEGE
640 North First Avenue
Phoenix, Arizona 85003

Adult Basic Education
GED Preparation
and
English as a Second Lang
Student Handbook

The staff of Rio Salado Commu
congratulate you on your d
to continue your educat

Complete your B.A. degree at a distance with

Governors State University — Governors State University

in partnership with

RIO SALADO COLLEGE

The Board of Governors Bachelor of Arts Degree Program
A DISTANCE LEARNING DEGREE PROGRAM

• Open to students with at least 30 semester hours of academic credit
• An individualized curriculum that meets your professional goals and interests
• Television, correspondence and Internet courses available through GSU
• Earn a degree at your place, at your own pace and at times convenient to you
• Low tuition and fees (about $100 per credit hour)
• Personalized academic advising
• Transfer up to 80 lower division semester credit hours from RSC to your B.A. degree
• Gain academic credit for learning based on your experience

Flexibility is the key.
The Board of Governors B.A. is for adults with work and family commitments who seek to advance their careers by earning a bachelor's degree.
GSU, located just south of Chicago, is a regionally accredited state university with nationally recognized academic programs designed for adults.

Enroll in YOUR Future

...ALADO College
...formation call
...ent Services
.2/517-8540

Governors State University
University Park, IL 60466

An example of another four-year degree program being piloted in the Maricopa district, Rio Salado's partnership with Governors State University provides a convenient way for distance learning students with at least 30-semester hours from Rio Salado to complete their bachelor's degree while still studying at home.

September 16, 1996, video interview with Linda Thor, president Rio Salado College 1990 to present. Transcript and audio excerpts available online.

http://www.mc.maricopa.edu/users/M3cdhistory/

2. Adults Need Jobs

Next to providing adults with access to academic credentials, the district's greatest service is providing adults with access to jobs, and one of the district's greatest success stories in this area is the thirty-six-year-old Maricopa Skill Center. This facility is located in an area of south central Phoenix once known as Nuestro Barrio. The 75,000-square-foot building was constructed in 1989 and was designed to be a model training facility.

One very striking visual detail of the Skill Center is the lack of graffiti on the outside of this building. According to Stanley Grossman, the Skill Center's executive director, the neighborhood community seems to value ownership of the Skill Center:

> I could probably take you around and introduce you to gang members from five different gangs, but all that stays outside. This is neutral territory. . . . The community watches because this place belongs to

> them. I remember when we put up the new sign on the street, people said, "Oh, you're going to have graffiti." We don't have graffiti, and we don't have security. That's just the philosophy.

At the Skill Center, training for approximately 250 job training certificates is grouped into twelve programs. Among them is the meat-cutting program, one of only two in the state. Inside the Skill Center is a classroom

that has been turned into a meat sales room where the students' homework is sold. Stan Grossman adds, "We also process deer, elk, and javelina for the hunters as well. We do party trays for people, and we accept food stamps for our students or any of the community that would like to come in and stretch their dollar a little further by utilizing what we have to offer." The center also operates a full-service travel agency and a print shop that does much of the printing for the Maricopa district.

For the students, the Skill Center is almost a guaranteed pipeline to a job, and Grossman is not shy about this fact:

> We place 80% of our students. Of those who are placed, 89% are with that company a year later. Not necessarily in the same job, but with the same company. They've probably been promoted and moved up and done those things. So those are real good selling points to business and industry when they go out there.

The Skill Center has been so successful in leading students to good jobs that in 1996, the district approved $4 million for the creation of a second skill center on land adjoining the campus of Estrella Mountain. Plans eventually call for two more skill centers to be constructed in the Glendale area and the Chandler area.

Beyond the programs offered at the Skill Center, traditional occupational programs (auto mechanics, nursing, office management, etc.) exist at the various colleges, but in recent years, these programs have been joined by specialized occupational programs that individual Maricopa colleges have developed in response to specific community needs. For example, Phoenix College has initiated its Golf Course Operations Program, which offers certificates in Pro Shop Technology, Horticulture Technology, Turf Equipment Technology, Pesticide Technology, and Turf & Irrigation Technology. Phoenix College president Marie Pepicello explains, "The golf people in the pro shops and golf courses these days, the managers, tell us that they are bringing student interns in from Kansas and Ohio and the east coast to work in pro shops and in management because there is not a program in the state."

In 1996, Mesa Community College initiated its Mortuary Science Program, the only one of its kind in Arizona. According to Dr. Tom Taggert, the program's director, 500 people requested applications or information about the program when it was announced. (The pro-

gram could initially accommodate only 45 students.) The program is housed in renovated facilities at the newly acquired Williams Education Center.

Perhaps leading the district in community-related occupational programs, Scottsdale Community College has developed twenty-three different career programs that mirror the special needs of Scottsdale and the other communities within its service area. One of the best known of these is the culinary arts program. Scottsdale's president Art DeCabooter likes to point out, "We have over three hundred applicants for that program. Many of those students are sponsored by the various resorts and restaurants in the area." Another signature program for Scottsdale is its equine program. "Our equine program reflects the horse industry in

Brochure for the Meat-Cutting Program at the Skill Center.

Brochure for Phoenix College's Golf Course Operations Program.

243

Scottsdale. Much of the program is off-site, at rented facilities for the riding, etc., but we have over four hundred students active in that program."

A new employment opportunity in the community is supplying workers for the developing casino industry on nearby reservations. DeCabooter explains, "When you're open seven days a week, twenty-four hours a day, the number of people you need is phenomenal. We already have classes going at several casinos, down at Ak-Chin and up at Fort McDowell, but it's going to just explode."

Chandler-Gilbert's unique occupational program is its aviation maintenance technology

training lab built in cooperation with Johnson Controls and other industry partners. This laboratory aids in training technicians on systems found in the semiconductor industry buildings and central plants. The Johnson Controls Institute also uses this lab to train its own employees (as well as customers) from all over the world. Students placed

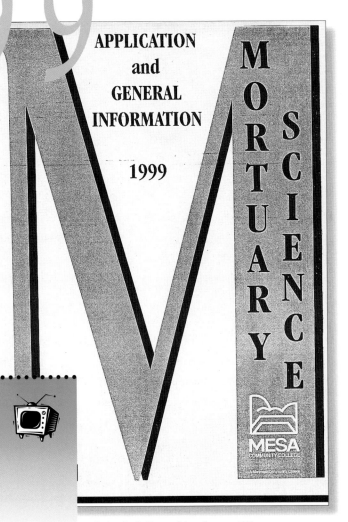

APPLICATION and GENERAL INFORMATION

1999

MORTUARY SCIENCE

MESA
COMMUNITY COLLEGE
A Maricopa Community College

June 12, 1996, video interview with Marie Pepicello, president Phoenix College 1993 to present. Transcript available online.

http://www.mc.maricopa.edu/users/M3cdhistory/

Brochure for the Mortuary Science Program at MCC.

program. Chandler-Gilbert president Arnette Ward likes to brag:

> *We started it, and it's going really well at Williams. We have about two hundred and fifteen in those different components. For the last four years, our students have won the gold, silver, and bronze medals in the state skills competition, and they've gone on and won the national best for three years. America West worked with us in the initial development of the program, provided a lot of services for us and a lot of advice. We're known in the industry.*

The Facility Systems Technology program taught at GateWay Community College utilizes a specially equipped environmental

from these programs can expect to find entry-level positions from $25,000 to $30,000 a year with growth potential to over $50,000 a year.

Paradise Valley Community College has pioneered an Environmental Health and Safety Technology (EHST) program to meet employers' demands for trained environmental professionals. The program consists of the Environmental Health and Safety Certificate program and an Associate of Applied Sciences (AAS) degree program. The goal is to produce graduates who can manage hazardous materials and wastes in compliance with government regulations, but also who can demonstrate the oral and

written communication and numerical skills employers demand.

To date, the district's biggest specialized program is the Semiconductor Industry/Education Partnership developed to increase the number of skilled technicians available to the industry. In cooperation with Intel, SGS Thompson, Motorola, Microchip Technologies, and other companies, four district colleges have developed a special program which has enrolled about 2,300 students as of the spring, 1998. The need for the workers in this industry is so great that many are being hired when they are only halfway through the two-year program.

3. Adults Need Computer Training

In the last ten years, access to computers has become one of the most important services that the Maricopa community colleges offer. The fact that Estrella's Information Commons was developed as the centerpiece of the campus was no accident. Computers are so expensive and the technology changes so rapidly that few people can stay current for long. When people need computer training, the community colleges are prepared to fulfill that need.

At Mesa Community College, a new integrated library/high tech center now dominates the campus. The three-story facility will eventually contain hundreds of computers and every other imaginable information resource. Mesa

Above: South Mountain Community College offers an associate of applied science in supermarket management and two certificate programs in its Supermarket Management Program, developed in partnership with the Arizona Food Marketing Alliance.

Chandler-Gilbert's Aviation Center at the Williams campus offers certificate programs in Aircraft Maintenance Technology, Aircraft Flight Technology, Aviation Electronics Maintenance Technology, and Aviation Construction Technology.

Brochure for the semiconductor program.

Left: "The dog ate my homework," is a credible excuse for students in Scottsdale's Culinary Arts Program, but that excuse would be a tragedy. The students' work is highlighted weekly in the program's dining room, where 150 diners each week may enjoy such delights as stuffed trout with three-pepper sauce, osso bucco Milanaise, candied roast duck with berries, and warm shrimp salad with basil butter. Photo by Michael Isaac from Ed Cetera Winter, 1993.

![1999]

president Larry Christiansen explains why:

It's a commitment to information access for students. Knowledge is power. Information is part of that knowledge and accessing that information is what that will do. If you're wealthy and have three thousand dollars to have your own computer system and can access all those libraries, great. Most of our people, most of our students, do not have that. They don't have the ability, the technical support. They don't have the equipment. They don't have the log-in codes. They don't have all of the kinds of fees paid to be able to access the areas. That facility will do that. I think we're a forerunner in terms of looking at that information access through that facility.

4. The Community Needs an Educated Workforce

The need of many adults for academic credentials runs parallel to the community's need for an educated workforce. In particular, the community needs people to complete

at least a high school degree. The district's GED initiatives have already been discussed, but Maricopa is surprisingly active in other areas of secondary education as well, and the programs are as varied as the community's needs.

Estrella Mountain has created the Genesis West program in cooperation with several local high schools. Estrella president Homero Lopez explains: "We took very bright, talented high school dropouts who were gone from the system and set up a program on campus where the students are mainstreamed into our regular classes, into a combination of some developmental classes and other classes." Ironically, the college functions as a kind of branch campus of the high school; students are registered at their high school but take all of their work at the college. "Then the high school takes the college work, whether it's developmental or regular, and it's like a reverse transfer." In the fall of 1998, ninety students were enrolled in this program.

Architectural rendering of MCC's Integrated Library/High Technology Center.

The ACE ("Achieving a College Education") program is an unusual high school program at South Mountain Community College. According to South Mountain's president

Logo for the ACE program and the logo for South Mountain Community College.

John Córdova, "The ACE program is a different model, not just another high school program where students take college courses." The college actively recruits Tempe and Phoenix Union High Schools to take college classes during the summer months and on Saturdays during the school year. Typically, ACE students earn up to 24-credit hours by the time they complete high school. Tuition is underwritten through a grant, so students pay no tuition. The goal is to increase high school graduation rates by giving students a head start on their college education. In this way, the program forms a unique partnership among high schools, parents, and Arizona State University, with South Mountain as

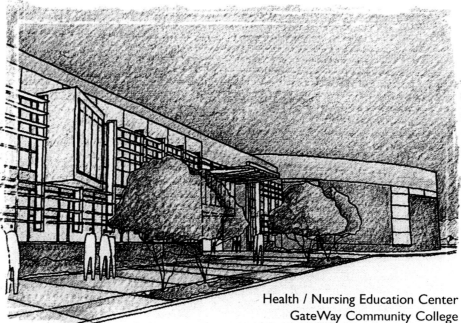

the link.

The most unusual high school program in the district is GateWay Community High School, the only charter high school in Arizona that is part of a community college campus. Phil Randolph, GateWay's president, came up with this idea:

Being an old high school teacher, I saw people who failed to finish high school for many reasons. It could be finances, it could have been pregnancy, it could have been family moved, and sometimes it was because they just got to be a little hotheaded. . . . They left sort of "The hell with you!" and "I'll show you guys!" and, two years later, they know they've made the world's greatest mistake. And the system did not allow them a noble way back.

. . . When these kids try to go back— and they may be adults at that time— to school, it's kind of like us going into a

kindergarten class and sitting in the little chairs, how uncomfortable we feel. I'm saying we've got to have some way where people who, for whatever the reason, didn't get their high school diploma can come back with a lot of anonymity and a lot of focus in a situation and succeed.

This high school program is also unusual because it does not use the community college faculty to teach the courses. Randolph hired six full-time teachers who have secondary school certificates. When interviewed for this book, he also said that the program currently had three hundred students enrolled and a waiting list to get in.

5. The Community Needs Specialized Training

The community also needs a steady supply of workers in certain specific areas, the most important being workers in the health care professions. Not surprisingly, Maricopa is the state's largest provider with more than fifty different health occupation programs enrolling approximately

2,500 students annually at all the district colleges. For example, GateWay Community College has the state's largest nursing program. In the fall of 1998, a grand total of 883 students were enrolled in GateWay's nursing and health sciences programs; which include respiratory therapy, nuclear medicine, medical radiography and diagnostic medical ultrasound. These programs attract many people who already have other academic credentials, and some of the programs have extensive waiting lists for admission. Using money from the 1994 bond, GateWay has constructed a new state-of-the-art Center for Health Careers Education, which opened in the fall of 1999, to offer students a chance to apply their skills in simulated hospital settings before entering the workforce.

The need for trained workers in these areas is so great that partnerships are the rule and not the exception. For example, in March of 1998 the Rio Salado School of Dental Hygiene opened, representing a unique alliance between the college and Arizona's

Architectural Rendering of GateWay's new Health/Nursing Education Center.

Brochure for GateWay Community High

Health / Nursing Education Center
GateWay Community College
Rendering by: GOULD EVANS ASSOCIATES L.C.

247

dentists. In order to ease a serious shortage of trained dental hygienists, Rio Salado College partnered with the Arizona Dental Association and Delta Dental Insurance, who together contributed $1.2 million to renovate an 8,200 square-foot-building in downtown Phoenix. After completing the 15-month program, students become candidates for the Associate of Applied Science degree from Rio. Upon passing the appropriate state exams, graduates then become registered dental hygienists. According to Rio president Linda Thor, "This program exemplifies Rio Salado's approach to meeting the needs of the community by partnering with employers. The result is a triple win—for students, for the dental community, and for the college."

In addition to training new workers for specific areas of need, the community colleges also provide specialized training directly for various individual businesses and industries. The Maricopa system is also the state's largest provider in this area as well. The district offers customized training to thousands of employees of both local and relocating businesses in the metropolitan Phoenix area. For example, Homero Lopez describes one of Estrella Mountain's most prestigious training programs:

> One of our earliest partners was the Wigwam Resort. Most people don't realize, but the Wigwam Resort is a major employer. They have around seven hundred employees. . . . We're involved in a customer service quality training program. . . . The CEO of the Wigwam, Cecil Ravenwood, also completed the program, as I did, too. I took it along with my own employees. He received his certificate this past May at the ceremonies, and I received my certificate last year. If you don't believe in your own product, it's pretty

hard to sell it to others.

Scottsdale Community College's partnerships are as varied as are the people in its service area. SCC partners with the Mayo Clinic to provide an in-service training program leading to an Associate of Applied Science degree; the Phoenix Opportunities Industrialization Center to provide a summer institute for inner city youth; and the City of Scottsdale and the Scottsdale Chamber of Commerce to sponsor Scottsdale Leadership (a program that fosters leadership skills and prepares citizens for leadership positions). Choice Hotels has entered into a partnership with SCC's Hospitality Program, and the City of Scottsdale and SCC partner to offer personal development classes at the Paiute Neighborhood Center targeted at the residents in the immediate community.

Rio Salado has developed a number of customized degree programs for specific corporate customers. Linda Thor describes Rio's program for America West Airlines:

> A new employee to America West Airlines completes a training program that results in a certificate in airline operations from Rio Salado. Regardless of where that employee may be ultimately assigned—whether it's Las Vegas or Los Angeles or Phoenix—they are able to complete their general education through distance delivery or through a more traditional approach if they want, resulting in an Associate of Applied Science in airline operations. We do the same kinds of programs with the Arizona Law Enforcement Academy, with the Department of Economic Security, with American Express, and so on.

Training partnerships within the district are coordinated through the district's Office of

Business and Workforce Development. According to Bertha Landrum, who heads this office, these partnerships represent big money to the district. Between 1994 and 1996, contracts to provide specialized training for various Maricopa businesses and industries brought over $5.5 million in additional revenue to the district. In return, the district trained nearly 12,000 people for Fox Animation, TRW, Safeway, Sumitomo, Super Shuttle, and other corporate clients. Landrum likes to point out that Super Shuttle moved its headquarters to Phoenix, and the district helped them to set up a franchise system to establish additional Super Shuttle operations at other airports around the United States. The district also designed their training program.

The district's contracts often go beyond merely providing training. Many small companies use Landrum's office as a kind of surrogate personnel office. Landrum gives the following example:

> A little company, a French bakery in downtown Phoenix—this one's called a labor of love. They've been hiring people who have been homeless, and they're located down there right off Van Buren, right off the capital. They turn out croissants and various French pastries, and it got started by these two people from Argentina, who became citizens. They love the United States, and they're hiring all these people out of this downtrodden area of Phoenix and putting them to work. It's fantastic! . . . We're helping them with hiring processes and establishing systems for people management; now that they're getting so many people, they have to be able to manage them. And then the training program—we've set up an on-the-job but very well monitored and laid-out on-the-job training program for

MOTOROLA UNIVERSITY:

One of the largest and most successful business partnerships in the district is the contract that Mesa Community College has with Motorola. Bertha Landrum and Larry Christiansen describe how this partnership developed over the years.

Landrum: We've worked with [Motorola] ever since 1968. Bob Galvin [Motorola's CEO] had said all employees will get a minimum of sixteen hours of training per year on company time, and that was revolutionary for a corporation to come up with that. This would be paid, on company time—two whole days out of the production! That's a big commitment. You've got 20,000 people in town and you're going to give away 40,000 days of training each year.

We were offering classes from the electronics program and English classes and math classes and whatever they wanted—Spanish classes. We'd send a teacher out there, and Motorola would publish a schedule of classes, and they were our classes.

And so, they were struggling with how to get that up. They had temporary help workers plunking away on little baby Macs and they were trying to register people, and then they had another worker who was running around

The campus of Motorola University at the Arizona State University Research Park in Chandler. Photo by Kelley Kirkpatrick.

trying to find rooms to put classes in. People would call in, and say they wanted to take such and such a class, and they'd register them, and then they'd change their mind, and they'd reregister, and they'd change their mind, they'd register . . . and they were getting nowhere! All they could handle was 3,000 person days of training per year.

Out at Glendale, I had been managing the scheduling for 12,000 a year, so I said, "This is not what you do best." So we set about to see how we could do it. They sort of distrusted what a community college could do for them a bit. So, I volunteered to run a pilot project in the summer of '88, about forty-five sections of their brand new course called "Understanding Six Sigma."[1] We brought on a group of faculty, trained the faculty, got Motorolans all enrolled. Boy, it went really great, and they said, "That's a wrap! Let's do it! Let's cut that contract!" And so we penned out a contract, and the contract is still the contract we basically have today.

We needed a place to hold it, and Mesa had a building with plenty of room, and the majority of Motorola employees are in the Mesa area, so that was a good spot to locate because it cut down on the travel time. And January 1, 1989, Motorola U opened.

Christiansen: We did that. We took three classrooms. Then the chair of the math department, Jack Twitchell called me a variety of names and talked about some fly-by-night program that had little or no place in the institution and it would never last. $75,000 worth of contract.

Landrum: They wanted us to hit around 6,000 person days of training in the first year, and we hit 7,000. And the next year, we hit 12,000 person days of training.

Christiansen: It grew; we took it off-site . . . . They worked a deal with the City of Mesa and Joe Woods for the downtown Motorola University, forty thousand square feet of premier instructional space. We leased back twenty-nine percent for our own business and industry operation, which was colocated with them. Our contract grew to in excess of $7 million in terms of delivery instruction.

Landrum: And then we outgrew that one when we hit 65,000 person days of training there, and so we moved to the ASU Research Park. So that's been going on for the last seven years. . . . It's achieved a lot of national reputation and acclaim, nationally and internationally.

[1] A design process intended to save money by reducing manufacturing defects.

each person who comes in and a cross-training program, so that if somebody leaves, somebody can fill and manage the process on a high production basis. Real economic development!

In the early '90s, the Maricopa district became an active partner with the Greater Phoenix Economic Council. Landrum felt that the group then was on the wrong track. They were trying to promote Phoenix as a source of cheap land and available unskilled workers. "They were selling low-cost dirt, low wages, low—you know, a place to come and do business on the cheap. And that doesn't [create economic growth]—that does not build and add wealth to a region." She began to preach the gospel that an educated workforce would attract businesses and industries to the area more effectively. Today, the district has become a major force in the economic development of the Phoenix area. Boosters trying to attract new employers to Maricopa County actively tout the district's ability to recruit and train workers and—when needed—retrain workers to adapt to new technology.

6. The Community Needs Help for Adults with Special Needs

This category includes many different groups. For example, Art DeCabooter describes some of the special needs programs at Scottsdale:

One class is a very captive class. They come to class in handcuffs and shackles. We have a program with the prison, with the jail, with the community, where their prisoners come over to the computer center. And they're in shackles, the whole bit. Now, it's off-campus; it's at their computer center, but we offer all that. We also have a program worked out with Motorola so people on dialysis—and there's a fair number on

dialysis from the Indian community— while they're on dialysis, they'll be able to take a self-paced computer course.

Phoenix College serves a very different group of students with special needs. According to Marie Pepicello:

We have a significant number of refugees from Eastern Europe, as well as, certainly, South and Central America. We also have students from Romania and Bulgaria and the Ukraine, and numbers of students who are Spanish-speaking and students who still need work to become proficient in English. Some Asian students. Students from Africa, students from Arabia. Central Phoenix is a site for refugees and immigrants from all over the world.

Pepicello takes justifiable pride in the success that many of these students find at Phoenix College. "We had nine students who graduated in 1996 with 4.0s, and from those students we selected a speaker to represent all the valedictorians. Our student speaker came to this country four years ago from Peru, speaking no English; went to school full-time, worked full-time as an accountant for the Motor Vehicle Division of ADOT; and graduated with a 4.0 in business—and is dyslexic."

But the people with special needs are not always found on the campus, and a recent trend at all the Maricopa colleges has been an integration of community service into the academic programs. Arnette Ward explains how Chandler-Gilbert emphasizes cooperative learning and service learning:

We liked the notion that President Clinton advanced when he was elected, the idea of national service. We thought that if the students leave here feeling a part of the community, then wherever they go, they will actively seek to become a part of that community and help resolve the community problems. It started with one or two faculty. It caught on not only with the faculty but also with the students. It has become a part of the curriculum for many of our faculty.

Addressing the American Council on Education in February of 1998, Paul Elsner emphasized the connection between service and learning:

Faculty claim that students see disciplines come alive after choosing to volunteer in one of some 87 different agencies. Writing a perfect topic sentence holds no comparison with the requirement to write from a passionate and personal revelation of working in a crisis nursery center.

7. The Community Needs a Multi-Purpose Cultural Resource

All of the district colleges provide plays, concerts, exhibitions, and lectures of various kinds. A particularly interesting trend in this

Brochure for Chandler-Gilbert's service learning program.

Service Learning
at Chandler-Gilbert Community College

"A good college affirms that service to others is a central part of education."
The Carnegie Foundation

Chandler-Gilbert Community College • 2626 E. Pecos Road, Chandler, Arizona 85225 • (602) 732-7000

area in recent years has been the popularity of community bands at Scottsdale, Glendale, Mesa, and Phoenix. Chandler-Gilbert's jazz band, which includes senior adults and twenty-somethings reading "charts" off the same music stands, has become extremely popular.

The district campuses also reflect various public art projects, too. South Mountain recently completed a major face-lift that included renovated stucco walls with Hohokam-style motifs designed by artist Marilyn Zwak. She also designed the arresting three-dimensional campus map near the front entrance, plus adobe seating structures, "gateway" signs, and thematic "medallions" that now identify each building. Also, Glendale Community College commissioned architect/sculptor Paolo Soleri to design the school's new amphitheatre.

But the district serves as a cultural resource

Workers putting the finishing touches on an adobe wall at the main entrance to the campus, part of South Mountain's public art face-lift in 1997. Photo by Louise Gacioch.

in more unusual ways, too. For example, the long hallways of the Skill Center are filled with original framed prints. The art was paid for by money realized from vending machine sales. According to Stan Grossman, more than $25,000 of this money has been used to buy the works of art on the walls:

> *That was an idea that I brought in. Those were awfully long, empty-looking halls down there, and I thought, "Well, this is something that our students might not necessarily have in their homes, but would be nice." It's unique. You hear students walking around and saying, "Hey, you need to go over in that other hallway and see this picture." They appreciate it. When I first started doing this, the thing was, "Oh, well, how are you going to attach it to the wall? People will steal it." We have— knock on wood—been here seven years and I have not lost one piece of art, and you could pick any of them off the wall. You see students going around straightening the art and appreciating it, and it's*

theirs. That makes this Center theirs.

Another major cultural resource for the community is international education, and Raúl Cárdenas explains how Paradise Valley has

Brochure for international education at PVCC.

PASSPORT TO THE WORLD

CENTER FOR INTERNATIONAL STUDIES

International Business Degree and Certificate Programs

PARADISE VALLEY COMMUNITY COLLEGE

and

WORLD TRADE CENTER ARIZONA

PARADISE VALLEY COMMUNITY COLLEGE   WORLD TRADE CENTER ARIZONA

deliberately taken the lead in this area:

We are the flagship college, in my opinion, in international ed. First, we became a regional center for the East-West Center. The East-West Center is out of University of Hawaii, and it's in Asian studies. The other thing is we applied for a Federal grant for international ed. Very few community colleges get international ed. grants; we received one. We were able, then, not only to support our East-West center, but also to develop another area of interest, which is Mexico.

Station manager Carl Matthusen dressed up as J. S. Bach for the inaugural of KBAQ, the district's classical music Public Radio station in 1994.

In 1998, the Paradise Valley Community College Center for International Studies received the International Intercultural Achievement Award from the American Council on International Intercultural Education of Des Plaines, Illinois The college was cited for its "comprehensive efforts in international development for faculty, establishment of an international resource center, and publicity for international activities."

By far, Rio Salado supports the district's most

wide-reaching cultural resources. These include the district's two Public Radio stations—KJZZ and KBAQ (which offer jazz and classical music respectively)—and Sun Sounds, a radio reading service for the visually impaired. Dating back to 1979, this station broadcasts a closed-circuit signal on a subcarrier of KJZZ, and a special radio is required to receive the signal. The signal is also relayed throughout most of the state of Arizona. Bill Pasco, the director of Sun Sounds, explains how the station operates:

What Arizona has done, which is quite innovative, is we have Sun Sounds, the central station, where we're sitting now, which handles most of the material. We do all of the national material from here and then we do, of course, all the material for this Valley from here. But we have a small subsidiary station in Tucson that takes care of all the Tucson information but carries us like a network for the rest of the time. Flagstaff does the same thing, and we plan to do it in Yuma and Kingman also.

In addition, Sun Sounds has also embraced Internet delivery of its 24-hour broadcast.

Through Sun Sounds' RealAudio broadcast (hosted by Rio), printed information is currently accessible anywhere in Arizona or the world. According to Pasco, "We don't ever want to hear that a person couldn't read something just because they couldn't see."

The real backbone of the service is the corps of volunteers who read daily newspapers and other publications:

We get people who say they want to give back to society for some reason. We get people who just like to read and say this gives them an excuse. They don't have to feel guilty; they can come in here and read. Some people are frustrated professional broadcasters or frustrated actors and use this as a vehicle to keep their hand in. We get a handful of people that are professionally in the broadcast field and consider this kind of fun, something a little different than the usual. We get men and women of all ages, down to about age eighteen and up to . . . they won't tell.

One other cultural resource available in the district is the classical studies program, which is now in its tenth year at Phoenix College. Marie Pepicello describes the program:

It is a learning community, very competitive, of twenty-five freshmen and twenty-five sophomores. They take their classes together, and they do the Great Books curriculum. They're all honors students, and those students transfer anywhere they want to. . . . They take Latin, some Greek, the Great Books, biology, calculus. It's a very stringent academic program.

Pepicello is correct about the transfer rate. Graduates from this program have been accepted at such schools as UC Berkeley, Whitman, Lewis and Clark, Hillsdale,

1999

252

SUN SOUNDS

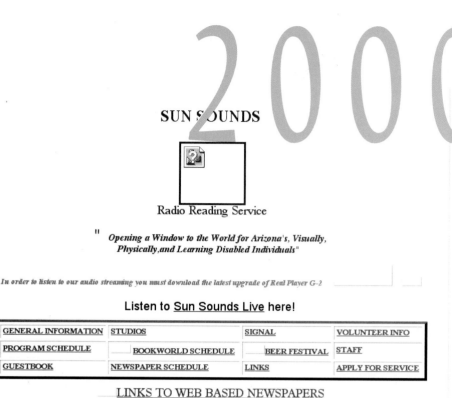

Radio Reading Service

" *Opening a Window to the World for Arizona's, Visually, Physically, and Learning Disabled Individuals*"

In order to listen to our audio streaming you must download the latest upgrade of Real Player G–2

Listen to Sun Sounds Live here!

GENERAL INFORMATION	STUDIOS	SIGNAL	VOLUNTEER INFO
PROGRAM SCHEDULE	BOOKWORLD SCHEDULE	BEER FESTIVAL	STAFF
GUESTBOOK	NEWSPAPER SCHEDULE	LINKS	APPLY FOR SERVICE

LINKS TO WEB BASED NEWSPAPERS

Sun Sounds Radio is a member of the National Association of Radio Reading Services(NARRS). Sun Sounds Radio is an outreach project of Rio Salado College in Tempe, Arizona.

Home page for Sun Sounds. [http://sunsounds.rio.maricopa.edu/]

CLASSICAL STUDIES PROGRAM

Phoenix College

Brochure for Phoenix College's Classical Studies Program.

Mishaela Duran, transferred to Yale.

Wheaton, UC Santa Barbara, Tulane, and Claremont McKenna. Mishaela Duran, who was graduated from the Classical Studies Program in June, 1998, transferred to Yale.

So much for the idea that community colleges are only for "kids" who aren't bright enough for a "real" college.

No More New Colleges?

Of course, all of the above only describes what the Maricopa district is at the moment this book is being completed. As was observed at the beginning of this chapter, evolution tends to keep on going. Whether or not this moment was the right time to take a picture or not remains to be seen. In fact, the Maricopa district's self-image as a multi-college district already seems to be obsolete.

The district went to the well again in 1994 and asked the voters to approve another record-setting bond.[2] The voters assented, and the result was nearly $400 million for capital improvements at all ten district colleges. But for the first time in Maricopa's history, none of the bond money has been budgeted to start new colleges.

A new trend seems to be underway. Most of the district's colleges are using their bond money to create neighborhood franchises. South Mountain now operates its Guadalupe Learning Center in the heart of one of Maricopa county's poorest areas; nearly 300 students are enrolled there each semester. Rio Salado operates its Sun Cities Learning Center in the heart of one of Arizona's largest retirement communities. Chandler-Gilbert is operating the Sun Lakes Education Center. In 1997, a consortium formed by Phoenix College, GateWay, Rio Salado, and South Mountain transformed Rio's former headquarters into the City Colleges Center. A 22,000-square-foot center with seven classrooms and computer labs provides more than 250 students access to general education classes, computer courses, GED programs,

[2] The district first went to the voters in 1992, and that bond was rejected. Insufficient public information and a decision to hold the election in June were widely blamed. Two years later, the voters approved virtually the same bond proposal they had rejected in 1992.

English as a Second Language, and citizen preparation classes. Bond money also went into improving facilities at the former Williams Air Force Base, where several district colleges operate a variety of programs. These new facilities joined the center that Mesa was already operating in downtown Mesa and Motorola University.

The most significant expression of this trend is in east Mesa at Power and McKellips Roads. At one time, an eleventh college was under discussion for that site, which the district acquired in 1985. Rio Salado promptly began offering classes there in portable classrooms, and many expected money from the 1994 bond would be used to build Red

Mountain Community College there. Following the same pattern as Chandler-Gilbert, the new college would have begun life as an extension of Mesa Community College, but Mesa's president, Larry Christiansen, proposed a different institutional growth model:

The issue that I have raised with the chancellor is we now have ten colleges in Maricopa County and we have a district office. As we look to future growth, how many more full-blown comprehensive colleges can we afford in terms of operational dollars? Our last three have been operational-dollar intense because of our desire to have full-blown comprehensive institutions. You must lay in place your administrative, your student services, and your instructional services components, then overlay your instructional program, using NCA accreditation as a benchmark.

Instead, Christiansen recommended that the new facility become a branch campus of Mesa. "It's another way of saying [that] we're going to build another great big campus, but we're going to use the same administrative team and select collaborative use of services." Paul Elsner agreed with this suggestion: "I think we have a better opportunity to have ten colleges with

maybe hundreds of locations or a different program thrust, than thirteen colleges with fewer of those thrusts."

Paralleling the franchise trend is the district's increasing experimentation with computer-based distance learning courses. Faculty at all ten district colleges are beginning to offer online versions of their courses, and as of the spring, 1999 semester, Rio Salado offered 250 distance learning courses, including 125 over the Internet. Other formats include CD-ROM, audio and /or video cassette, audio and/or video conferencing, print-based, online, and mixed media. Current students include working adults in Maricopa County as well as military officers deployed overseas.

Ron Bleed sees this development as a logical continuation of the process of decentralization that Chancellor Paul Elsner initiated. "If you really look at what's happening now, the access points are beyond the colleges. They're in the homes of the students, at their offices, etc. We've gone from central office to college, but centralized at the college, then to offices and labs at the college. Now we're going to the homes of the learners, students."

In sum, Maricopa has begun to evolve into a multi-college and a multi-campus system—and some of those campuses are as small as a single computer screen on a single student's desk.

The End of an Era

But how long will even that trend continue? A major sea change for Maricopa occured on June 30, 1999. Paul Elsner retired—this time for real—and Raul Cardeyas became the district's acting chancellor while the search continued to find Elsner's successor. Considering all the commotion stirred up the last time the

254

Maricopa governing board member Linda Rosenthal and district chancellor Paul Elsner celebrate the success of the district's 1994 record-setting bond election.

district inaugurated a chancellor, Maricopans have every reason to expect the district's turbulent evolution to continue.

Even so, the turbulence has not been all bad for the district. The source (as this book has tried to demonstrate) is Maricopa's junior college heritage, which is now only a memory—a shimmering dream of an idyllic little school that *Look* magazine once placed at the head of the list of America's finest junior colleges.

Today, that vision is no mere nostalgia. It exerts a force that challenges each district innovation to demonstrate its worth and serves as a standard against which each new method is evaluated. And Maricopa is nothing if not innovative. The district keeps evolving and reinventing itself frantically to fulfill its current self-image as a ubiquitous provider of postsecondary education for adults. These two self-images are not incompatible, but they do form a volatile mix.

Thus, the tension between Maricopa's heritage and its destiny should continue to shake the ground for many years. Nobody really likes academic earthquakes—especially academics —but even William Rainey Harper would have to admit that all the shaking has produced some amazing results. Out of all the turbulence has emerged America's largest communi-ty college district with the highest rate of public participation of any similar institution, a spectacular success rate for transfer students, and a phenomenal record for job-training programs that have significantly enriched the whole economy of Maricopa county. If *Look* magazine were around today, Maricopa would still be at the head of the list.

And Benjamin McFall would have been damn proud!

Index

About the Author

Since 1990, Richard Felnagle has been a faculty member at Mesa Community College where he teaches courses in English and humanities. Previously, he also taught at the Community College of Allegheny County, South Campus (Pittsburgh, PA), and Centre College (Danville, KY). He earned a BA in English (emphasis in creative writing) from Pomona College and an MFA in directing from Carnegie-Mellon University. His other publications include a textbook, *Beginning Acting: The Illusion of Natural Behavior*, published by Prentice-Hall, and two plays: *Another Tortoise, Another Hare* published by Samuel French and *A Canticle for Leibowitz* (adapted from the novel of the same name) published by the Dramatic Publishing Company. Among other projects, he also wrote several scripts for short, industrial films produced by GTE, including one nominated for a local Emmy in the Boston area. He is married and has two children. His wife teaches fifth grade.